The Garde Nationale 1789–1815

France's Forgotten Armed Forces

Pierre-Baptiste Guillemot

Helion & Company

Helion & Company Limited
Unit 8 Amherst Business Centre
Budbrooke Road
Warwick
CV34 5WE
England
Tel. 01926 499619
Email: info@helion.co.uk
Website: www.helion.co.uk
Twitter: @helionbooks
Visit our blog at http://blog.helion.co.uk/

Published by Helion & Company 2022
Designed and typeset by Mach 3 Solutions Ltd (www.mach3solutions.co.uk)
Cover designed by Paul Hewitt, Battlefield Design (www.battlefield-design.co.uk)

Text © Pierre-Baptiste Guillemot 2022
Cover: Standard bearer of Puteaux Garde Nationale, 1790–1791 (Patrice Courcelle © Helion & Company 2022). *Attaque de la Convention Nationale, journée mémorable du 13 Vendémiaire An 4e de la République française*, engraving by Berthault after Abraham Girardet (Library of Congress).
Illustrations © as individually credited.
Maps © Jean-Claude Colrat 2022

Every reasonable effort has been made to trace copyright holders and to obtain their permission for the use of copyright material. The author and publisher apologise for any errors or omissions in this work, and would be grateful if notified of any corrections that should be incorporated in future reprints or editions of this book.

ISBN 978-1-915113-88-7

British Library Cataloguing-in-Publication Data.
A catalogue record for this book is available from the British Library.

All rights reserved. No part of this publication may be reproduced, stored in a retrieval system, or transmitted, in any form, or by any means, electronic, mechanical, photocopying, recording or otherwise, without the express written consent of Helion & Company Limited.

For details of other military history titles published by Helion & Company Limited, contact the above address, or visit our website: http://www.helion.co.uk

We always welcome receiving book proposals from prospective authors.

Contents

Acknowledgements		iv
Foreword		vi
Preface		viii
Chronologies		xiv
1	The Garde's Ancestors	19
2	The Beginnings of the Garde Nationale Parisienne	32
3	The Provinces Followed: Local Gardes Nationales	74
4	From Gardes Nationaux to Volontaires Nationaux	126
5	The Federations Movement and the Garde Nationale Flags	153
6	The Pivotal Years	182
7	The Garde in the Republican Era	219
8	The Decline of the Garde?	263
9	Of Purple Cloak and Battlefields	280
10	Conclusion	347
Bibliography		355

Acknowledgements

I would like to extend my gratitude to all the people who have contributed to this book. It owes a great deal to my friend Thibaut de Barros Conti, a Frenchman living in the United States for many years. Passionate about history and a formidable connoisseur, Thibaut was one of the first to encourage me to write a book on the Garde Nationale. He gave me his unfailing support throughout this adventure, questioning me each and every day on the progress of the project. Finally, he was my faithful proof-reader, providing valuable linguistic help for the French-speaking author that I am. Many thanks to him.

This book would not have been possible without the prolific contribution of Yves Martin. As a passionate historian, he inspired me from my youth. As early as 2017, he provided me with a wealth of excellent material relating to the Garde. In the summer of 2020, we discussed at length the feasibility of a study on the subject. His unparalleled knowledge of iconography, which is legendary in the field, made it possible to gather high-level documentation in record time. Even on the most complex subjects, Yves always finds the perfect nugget, sometimes the only one available. I am also proud that he was willing to write the foreword to my book.

My thanks also go to Patrice Courcelle, whom I admire and have known since I was a teenager. He has illustrated all my published articles on the subject in French and I am naturally very happy that he has accompanied me across the Channel for this project. His remarkable artistry has, I think, captured the best of these Guardsmen, from the most famous of them, La Fayette, to the most humble of them. With his paintbrush, Louis-Sébastien Rosaz, Armand Gentil, Joseph Leplat and Jean Moisson have thus come to life.

I am also grateful to Jean-Claude Colrat, president of the historical association Le Briquet, based in Orléans, France. Jean-Claude was mainly responsible for a series of flags, most of them unknown, which you will find in the first plate section. His well-known concern for exacting standards made it possible to reproduce as faithfully as possible emblems never seen before in print. Jean-Claude has also drawn all the maps in this book with brio, and has carried out a multitude of meticulous tasks for the iconography.

This book would not have been the same without the passion of many collectors. In this respect, François Vinot-Préfontaine allowed me to present

ACKNOWLEDGEMENTS

numerous miniature portraits and physiognotraces from his extensive collection. I would like to thank him for his availability and the quality of the works he has entrusted to me. Among these, a portrait of an officer by Duvaucel de Marsoeuvre caught my attention: indeed, this painter was himself a Garde Nationale officer in Bordeaux. Stéphane Broyard has an ability to scour the internet and unearth the most tenuous information. I owe him many of the examples in this book. My colleague Fabien Pacaud gave me the benefit of his extensive knowledge in the field of armaments. Several pieces from his collection, pikes and sabres, are included in the book. Some of Boisselier's works come from the collection of Guillaume Bretegnier. Finally, special thanks to the expert Arnaud de Gouvion Saint-Cyr. In an article for a French magazine, we highlighted his ancestor Jean-Baptiste Gouvion, La Fayette's right-hand man, who was killed at the fight at La Glisuelle, near Maubeuge, on 11 June 1792.

I also wish to congratulate the titanic work of the Carnavalet Museum and Anne S.K. Brown Military Collection, which have digitised tens of thousands of documents from the Revolution and the First Empire.

Thanks to my publishers, Helion and Company, for their confidence and to their series editor Andrew Bamford for his enthusiasm, availability, and patience. Thanks to my parents, my lifelong supporters.

Before concluding these thanks, I cannot forget Bernard Coppens, Belgian author and illustrator, and Didier Davin, doctor and passionate researcher, both of whom passed away in 2020. Reading Bernard's book, *L'Empire de Napoléon*, was my first experience with the exciting period of the French Revolution and the First Empire. I was then nine years old. Bernard was very familiar with the Garde Nationale, having studied it on several occasions, both in his *Patience* and on his website. Didier, for his part, contributed greatly to my interest in the strangest and most misunderstood military units of the era. The Garde Nationale is undoubtedly one of them. My deepest thoughts go out to these two so cultured and yet so humble people.

Pierre-Baptiste Guillemot
Landas, 10 August 2022

Foreword

On 13 October 2016, in the wake of the 2015 terrorist attacks, then President of France François Hollande grouped all military and civilian security forces under the name of 'Garde Nationale'.

After more than 150 years of absence, the term 'Garde Nationale' was once again used for a defensive force which is both civilian and military. For most French people, the only Garde Nationale they have heard of, is, at best the United States National Guard state units. Some may even have thought that this was, yet again, a proof that France was increasingly bent on copying American institutions.

It is actually exactly the opposite which is historically correct.

The United States National Guard can claim to have its roots in the very first militia organized by colonists in the early seventeenth century. However, the term 'National Guard' was only used for the first time when the Marquis de La Fayette came back to the United States. The 2nd Battalion, 11th New York Artillery adopted the name in his honour as he had been the creator of the 'Garde Nationale' and commander of the 'Garde Nationale de Paris'.

The 'Garde Nationale' was indeed La Fayette's brainchild. He was most probably inspired by his own experiences of American units composed of armed citizens, highly motivated and willing to fight to the death for their liberty and rights. But La Fayette's units did not materialize out of thin air. Pre-1789 French towns boasted myriads of 'bourgeois' militia, 'shooting societies'. Revolutionary fervour was to bring new life… and blood to these. The 'citizen-soldier' was born.

For close to a century, the 'Garde Nationale' was part of the French institutional landscape. Born during the Revolution, composed of armed civilians, it was always to have a political flair to it. It had its ups and downs. Understandably, Napoleon, who had 'terminated the Revolution' was no big fan… yet when some of its units proved their mettle in 1809, he created a Garde Nationale regiment in his Garde Imperiale as a token of his gratitude.

During the nineteenth century, the Garde Nationale balanced between being a docile governmental force repressing insurrections or being quite the opposite, a fire-breathing revolutionary force which would topple regimes.

In July 1871, the Garde Nationale was finally disbanded. This came after the Paris Commune bloody civil war. Garde Nationale units had provided the bulk of the rebellious fighting forces. The new government had no wish to maintain an institution which had proven so volatile and dangerous. The new 'citizen soldier' would be a young conscript 'called under the flags' trained as part of the regular army. This model would hold until 1996 when conscription was stopped, and the French army turned into a strictly professional military force.

Lately, this scheme which seemed adequate for the post-cold war new world order has been challenged. The 2016 decision was proof of that. At the time of writing (summer 2022), events have shown, yet again, how a people when called to arms and motivated could resist and push back an enemy. Therefore, the reader should in no way look down on this study as the telling of 200-year-old events. It holds lessons for the present day, as is often the case with military history.

Pierre-Baptiste Guillemot belongs to the new generation of French historians. For several decades, military history was frowned upon in academic circles. Social and political aspects were considered prime, if not the only factors in the understanding of the past. Yet, gradually, new generations of historians have understood that History is all-encompassing.

For Pierre-Baptiste, narrating the history of the Garde Nationale is considering it in a global approach: organisation, men and even uniforms, an often neglected aspect but of prime importance for those men of the 1790s–1810s which saw the emergence of national symbols and of such characters as 'Beau Brummell'.

This is most probably the first in-depth study on this topic in the English language. It provides the reader with a spotlight on units which were largely the cradle of Napoleon's Grande Armée, and which, in time adapted to the Bourbon restoration.

Reader, read on! Citizens, to arms!

Paris, 16th Thermidor, the Year 230
Yves Martin

Preface

The Garde Nationale is currently one of the most misunderstood and forgotten revolutionary and imperial institutions. This lack of interest is surprising when one realises the major historical importance of this institution. A re-examination of the history and role of the Garde allows us to re-evaluate certain key episodes of the Revolution and then the First Empire, in which it was involved from the revolutionary dawn in the summer of 1789 to the fall of the Napoleonic Empire in the summer of 1815. The Garde Nationale was also at the heart of debates concerning citizenship and the maintenance of public order. Consequently, this book is the result of the contrast between the importance of the Garde 200 years ago and the relative silence of historians that has since surrounded it.

In the nineteenth century, much was certainly written about the Garde Nationale. But these were often hagiographic chronicles by authors who themselves were members of the Garde and wished to recount its deeds. They were therefore marked by their authors' illusions and preoccupations more than historic reality. This applies of course to Paris and the country's main cities, but also to much smaller towns.

In the twentieth century, the Garde Nationale was generally side-lined by French revolutionary historiography. Its place was very limited, including amongst studies published on the occasion of the Bicentenary. Not a single one of the 549 colloquia listed during this event dealt, in one way or another, with the Garde. The same silence is obvious when one checks the summaries of the *Annales Historiques de la Révolution Française*, though over a longer time span. Similarly, François Furet and Mona Ozouf's *Dictionnaire critique de la Révolution Française*[1] did not even include a specific article to the Garde. Jacques Godechot, by contrast, devoted a few pages to it in his study of French Revolutionary and Imperial institutions. In fact, only two relatively recent French-language works cover the 1789–1815 period. The first is by Georges Carrot,[2] a former police commissioner specialising in policing matters. His book covers the entire history of the institution, both in Paris

---

1   François Furet and Mona Ozouf (eds), *Dictionnaire critique de la Révolution française* (Paris: Flammarion, 1988).
2   Georges Carrot, *La Garde nationale (1789-1871): Une force publique ambiguë* (Paris: L'Harmattan, 2001).

PREFACE

This oil on canvas was long attributed to renowned painter David. In any case, it was painted in 1791, after it became clear that the Festival of the Federation was not the perfect culmination of the ongoing Revolution. Nevertheless, the artist wanted to give the onlooker the illusion that the union of the Nation, the Law and the King was embodied in the person of La Fayette on 14 July 1790. (Musée Carnavalet)

and in the departments. In addition, the author takes stock of all existing local monographs and complements them with his own academic research on Grasse's Garde Nationale. However, his approach suffers from a narrow, institutional view of the topic and from an emphasis on the issue of law and order, which he regards as the essential vocation of the Garde Nationale. The second study is by Roger Dupuy.[3] According to him, the Garde Nationale was a major collective actor that had fallen into oblivion at the end of the nineteenth century. Consequently, he sets out to reassess its role. This ambitious 600-page study is almost exclusively political. However, it is unbalanced towards the revolutionary decade and Parisian space. Finally, some historians have studied the Garde in specific territories. Thus, Pierre Arches has focused on its action in Rouergue and Quercy, while Roger Dupuy, in his doctoral thesis, studied the gardes in Ille-et-Vilaine. Finally, an important symposium on the subject, the first of its kind, was organised in 2003.[4] This fine volume, which brings together contributions from 28 authors and is edited by Serge Bianchi and Roger Dupuy, aims to cover the full existence of the Garde Nationale, from its creation in 1789, in the wake of the nascent revolutionary impetus, to the dissolution of the patriotic militia in 1872, in the aftermath of the Paris Commune. Although the firmly local and social approach adopted provides the necessary nuances, the First Empire is almost completely forgotten and is only discussed in a single paper. The same general observation applies to Anglo-Saxon historiography. It is true that several works have been devoted to La Fayette. Similarly, Micah Alpaugh has examined the formation of the Garde Nationale Parisienne in the summer of 1789. Dale L. Clifford has devoted a series of articles to this institution, with a focus on the 1789–1791 period. The federations were studied by Micah Alpaugh, and David Andress wrote about the Champ de Mars massacre. The history of the Garde under the First Republic and the First Empire has obviously been largely neglected.

This fairly widespread historiographical denial seems to be explained by several concomitant factors. A complex institution with controversial origins, diverse existence and intermittent action, the Garde was so intimately interwoven into the history of the Revolution and the First Empire that it did not seem necessary to leading historians of the period to write its history. Probably these very same historians did not feel they had to consider the Garde as a determining phenomenon in order to account for the dynamics of the 1789–1815 period. Other considerations undoubtedly also played a part. Being identified, from the outset, with the emblematic personality of La Fayette, the Garde Nationale suffered from many historians' judgement that the 'hero of two worlds' was a figure of limited stature. In the same way, the Garde Nationale undoubtedly suffered from the discredit which, from the 1930s onwards, struck military history in France. Moreover, the special booklet that the venerable Société de la Sabretache devoted to the Garde stated that although it represented 'an original element in France's military

---

3   Roger Dupuy, *La Garde Nationale 1789-1872* (Paris: Gallimard, 2010).
4   Serge Bianchi and Roger Dupuy (eds), *La Garde nationale entre nation et peuple en armes: Mythes et réalités 1789-1871* (Rennes: Presses Universitaires de Rennes, 2006).

history, it does not appear to be the ideal subject for a publication: few shiny uniforms, few heroic feats of arms'.[5] A serious study of the Garde comes up against the problem of sources. Massive archives lie dormant in confidential boxes and are scattered all over France, in departmental and often municipal archives. The documents concerning the Garde Nationale of Paris were undoubtedly numerous, but they disappeared in the flames in 1871, during the Paris Commune. The collections of the Service Historique de la Défense remain underused. In particular, it is possible to consult numerous sets of documents relating to the active Garde Nationale, whether under the Revolution or the First Empire. Legislation concerning the Garde is certainly easily consultable, although many texts from the revolutionary and then imperial periods were not published. It is nevertheless possible to consult *The Moniteur Universel*, the minutes of the various revolutionary assemblies, but also the *Bulletin des lois*, not forgetting, for the imperial period, the *Correspondance de Napoléon*, an updated and enriched version of which has just been published in France. The combination of all these elements explains why we have long had an intermittent, fragmentary and fragmented history of the Garde. Our study aims to provide the first synthesis on the subject in English.

It is organised into nine chapters. The first one focuses on the Milices Bourgeoises of the late eighteenth century, their missions and their relationship with the other security forces at the end of the Ancien Régime. They played a significant role in the outbreak of the French Revolution in a number of cities. From the beginning of 1789, armed formations were indeed organised to deal with both popular revolts and aristocratic plots. The second chapter unfolds the eventful framework in which the Garde Nationale Parisienne, soon to be led by the Marquis de La Fayette, emerged in the turmoil of July 1789. The improvisation of its formation led to a slow stabilisation lasting until the early summer of 1790. Following the storming of the Bastille, the provinces followed and armed themselves: this is the starting point of the third chapter. In the context of the 'municipal revolution' and the troubles of the Great Fear, the Milices Bourgeoises provided a favourable framework for the development of the Garde Nationale, even if the latter was not always a reactivation of the urban Milices. Indeed, rural communes equally raised Gardes Nationales. This chapter also discusses the organisation of these armed forces, their social composition and their missions, as well as the sometimes conflicting relations with the municipalities and even among the gardes nationaux themselves. Chapter 4 examines the complex relationship between the gardes nationaux and the line army, both of which were essential for maintaining internal order and external security. Louis XVI and his family's failed flight at the end of June 1791 led to the raising of the first Volontaires battalions from the Garde Nationale. Over the next two years, hundreds of new battalions were raised and added to the strength of the French armies. In this war context, the Garde Nationale, through its Volontaires, certainly fostered the transition from a professional army

---

5   François Buttner, 'Introduction', *Gardes Nationales 1789-1871, Carnets de la Sabretache*, 50 (1979), p.133.

to a genuine national army. The fifth chapter returns to the chronological framework and looks at the federative movement which concerned the whole of France between the summer of 1789 and the summer of 1790. The first federations born in an unstable context in the summer of 1789 were soon followed by ever larger gatherings intended to demonstrate the patriotic unanimity of the entire country. The Parisian Federation, organised on 14 July 1790, was the apotheosis: it celebrated the glory of the Garde Nationale, the incarnation of the triumphant and appeased Revolution, but also that of La Fayette. The next chapter covers the time span from the summer of 1790 to the summer of 1792. During this period, the Garde Nationale was involved, both in Paris and in the departments, in a series of crucial events, such as the Nancy mutinies, the implementation of the *Civil Constitution of the Clergy*, King Louis XVI's flight and the Champ de Mars massacre. The year 1791 was also marked by the organic law of 14 October, then by La Fayette's withdrawal from his duties as Commander General of Paris' Garde Nationale. In early 1792, the events culminating in the overthrow of the monarchy on 10 August revealed deep divisions within the Garde. Chapters 7 and 8 deal with the Republican era. The Garde Nationale became more democratic, particularly in Paris, where it became the armed wing of the sections. However, in the summer of 1793, it backed the federalist movement in several departments. Elsewhere, it faced competition from the armées révolutionnaires from September 1793 to spring 1794. Originally a municipal institution, it adapted rather badly to a centralised organisation. After Robespierre's fall, the Garde was taken over by property owners and openly shifted towards royalism on 13 Vendémiaire. From then on, the Garde withered away, whilst the army became increasingly powerful: the latter was the driving force behind the *coup d'état* of Fructidor Year V, then ensured the success of that of Brumaire Year VIII. The Consulate and the First Empire form the temporal background to chapter 9. The Garde was frequently confined to symbolic functions. However, the levies carried out from 1805 onwards made it an army auxiliary. This evolution, a consequence of Napoleon's needs, but also of his uncertainties and mistrust, led to the formation of genuine gardes nationaux armies at the twilight of the Empire.

I have been fascinated by the French Revolution and the First Empire for some 20 years. As far as I can remember, I first encountered the subject through *L'Empire de Napoléon* by the late Belgian historian and illustrator Bernard Coppens. I was very early interested in military history and its lesser-known aspects. I studied the legions of the Revolution, the Corps Francs of the late First Empire and, more recently, the royalist *émigré* troops. The common feature of these units is to have been raised in difficult circumstances and returned to obscurity as soon as they were disbanded. In October 2016, under François Hollande's presidency, the Garde Nationale was recreated in France after an eclipse of almost 145 years. It was a coincidence that at this very time I began my research on this subject which I felt had unjustly fallen into oblivion. I published a series of articles in historical journals in France. They were illustrated by Belgian painter Patrice Courcelle, who also produced several plates for this book. These first works made me aware of the ever-changing character of the subject. It is indeed possible to combine political, social and military history. The investigations for the present book allowed me, among other things, to take a more nuanced look at the major figure of La Fayette and to shed light on lesser-known personalities, such as Santerre and Hanriot. My interest in contemporary iconography was sharpened by the abundance of little-known sources on the subject. Numerous examples are reproduced in this book, although it was necessary to sort and prune beforehand to retain only the best. I hope you will enjoy reading this volume as much as I enjoyed writing it.

Pierre-Baptiste Guillemot
2022

Chronologies

Political Chronology 1789–1815

1789
28–29 April. Reveillon riots in Paris.
17–20 June. French Constituent Assembly formed. Tennis Court Oath.
14 July. Storming of the Bastille in Paris.
Late July–early August. 'Great Fear' in the French countryside.
4–5 October. *'Journées'*: demonstrations ending with the King and the Constituent Assembly returning to Paris.

1790
12 July. Civil Constitution of the Clergy.
14 July. Festival of the Federation in Paris.

1791
21–22 June. Louis XVI's failed flight to Varennes.
17 July. Champ de Mars massacre.
14 September. The Constitution of 1791 is proclaimed.
1 October. The Legislative Assembly first meets.

1792
10 August. Storming of the Tuileries Palace. Fall of the monarchy.
21 September. Abolition of monarchy, France declared a Republic.

1793
21 January. Louis XVI guillotined.
29 May–2 June. Revolutionary *'Journées'*: Montagnards and Paris Commune versus the Girondins.

1794
28 July. Fall of Robespierre and his supporters.
April–May. Popular uprisings in Paris.

1795
5 October. Royalist uprising in Paris.
2 November. Five-man executive 'Directorate' government formed.

CHRONOLOGIES

Life drawing by Girardin of gardes nationaux from Narbonne in 1790. That year, most companies wore a red uniform with white buttons, celestial blue collar piped white, and white lapels, cuffs and turnbacks. Other companies were dressed in blue with yellow buttons and scarlet collar, lapels and cuffs piped in white. (Anne S.K. Brown Military Collection)

1797
4 September. *Coup d'état* of 18 Fructidor Year V against the royalists.

1799
9 November. *Coup d'état* of 18 Brumaire Year VIII. Beginning of the Consulate.
24 December. Constitution of Year VIII. Napoleon is First Consul.

1802
4 August. Constitution of Year X. Napoleon First Consul for life.

1804
18 May. Constitution of Year XII. Napoleon proclaimed Emperor.

1814
6 April. Napoleon I abdicates. First Restoration of Louis XVIII.

1815
20 March. Napoleon I arrives in Paris. Start of the Hundred Days.
22 June. Second abdication of Napoleon I.
8 July. Second Restauration of Louis XVIII.

THE GARDE NATIONALE 1789–1815

Military Chronology 1789–1815

1792–1797. Wars of the First Coalition.
1792, 21 September. Battle of Valmy.
1792, 6 November. Battle of Jemmapes.
1793, 18 March. Battle of Neerwinden.
1794, 26 June. Battle of Fleurus.
1798–1802. Wars of the Second Coalition.
1803–1806. Wars of the Third Coalition.
1806–1807. Wars of the Fourth Coalition.
1807–1814. Peninsular War.
1809. War of the Fifth Coalition.
1809, July–December. Walcheren Expedition.
1812. Russian Campaign.
1813–1814. War of the Sixth Coalition.
1815. War of the Seventh Coalition. Waterloo Campaign.

The Garde Nationale, 1789-1815 Chronology

Date (Gregorian)	Date (Republican)	Event or Law
National Constituent Assembly		
1789, 13 July		Creation of a Milice Bourgeoise in Paris
1789, 15 July		La Fayette, general commander of the Parisian Milice Bourgeoise
1789, 16 July		The Parisian Milice Bourgeoise is renamed Garde Nationale de Paris
1789, 10 August		Gardes Nationales' subordination to municipalities
1789, 21 October		Institution of martial law
1790, 7 January		Civic oath sworn by the gardes nationaux
1790, 12 June		Compulsory service in the Garde Nationale to keep active citizenship rights Censal recruitment of the Garde Nationale Suppression of military games companies, Milices Bourgeoises and armed brotherhoods
1790, 19 July		Regulation of the Garde Nationale uniform
1790, 5 September		Regulation of the Garde Nationale button
1790, 6 December		Passive citizens who have served in the National Guard since its formation are allowed to continue their service
1790, 23 December		Modification of the Garde Nationale button
1791, 21 June		Activation of the gardes nationaux of the kingdom
1791, 13 July		'Final' regulation of the Garde Nationale uniform
1791, 5 August		Suppression and recreation of certain units of the paid Garde Nationale Parisienne
1791, 12 August		Each Volontaires Nationaux battalion is set at 568 men

CHRONOLOGIES

Date (Gregorian)	Date (Republican)	Event or Law
Legislative Assembly		
1791, 12 September		Organisation of the Garde Nationale Parisienne
1791, 14 October		Law for the Garde Nationale
1792, 13 March		Organisation of the Garde Nationale's artillery companies
1792, 6 May		Raising of 31 new Volontaires Nationaux battalions. Each Volontaires Nationaux battalion is set at 800 men
1792, July 22		33,600 gardes nationaux raised to create 42 Volontaires battalions
1792, July 24		Army generals are allowed to request part of the Garde Nationale's grenadiers and chasseurs
1792, 1 August		The Garde Nationale is open to passive citizens
1792, 19 August		Organisation of Paris' armed sections. Reduction of the Parisian Garde Nationale battalions from 60 to 48
National Convention		
1793, 21 February		Creation of 196 line infantry demi-brigades
1793, 24 February		300,000-men levy
1793, 25 July		Mounted gardes nationaux are requisitioned
1793, 23 August		Levée en masse
1793, 5 September		Creation of the Armée Révolutionnaire Parisienne
1793, 20 September		Suppression of the Garde Nationale's grenadier and chasseur companies
1794, 8 January	Year II, 19 Nivôse	Effective implementation of the infantry demi-brigades
1794, 16 April	Year II, 27 Germinal	Dissolution of the Armée Révolutionnaire Parisienne
1794, 6 August	Year II, 19 Thermidor	Organisation of the Garde Nationale Parisienne
1795, 17 March	Year III, 28 Ventôse	Organisation of the Garde Nationale Parisienne service
1795, 17 April	Year III, 28 Germinal	Reorganisation of Paris Garde Nationale
1795, 28 May	Year III, 10 Prairial	Less fortunate citizens are exempted from service in the Garde Nationale
1795, 16 June	Year III, 28 Prairial	Reorganisation of the Garde Nationale of the departments
1795, 8 October	Year IV, 16 Vendémiaire	The Parisian Garde Nationale's staff, cavalry and elite companies are suppressed
Directory		
1796, 6 May	Year IV, 17 Floréal	Creation of mobile columns within the sedentary Garde Nationale
1797, 12 August	Year V, 25 Thermidor	Reorganisation of the Garde Nationale
1797, 30 August	Year V, 13 Fructidor	Organisation of the Garde Nationale service
1797, 5 September	Year V, 19 Fructidor	The measures of 25 Thermidor Year V and 13 Fructidor Year V are cancelled

THE GARDE NATIONALE 1789–1815

Date (Gregorian)	Date (Republican)	Event or Law
1797, 25 September	Year VI, 4 Vendémiaire	No valid citizen can be refused service in the sedentary Garde Nationale
1798, 5 September	Year VI, 19 Fructidor	Compulsory conscription for all French people aged 20 to 25 (compulsory military service)
First Empire		
1805, 24 September		Reorganisation of the Garde Nationale
1805, 30 September		Organisation of the sedentary Garde Nationale
1806, 12 November		Organisation of the Gardes Nationales of Northern France
1809, 6 August		Activation of 30,000 gardes nationaux in eight military divisions of the northern part of the Empire
1810, 15 September		Expenditures made by various departments on the occasion of the Garde Nationale's raising
1812, 13 March		Division of the Garde Nationale into three bans. Call for 100 cohortes of the first ban
1812, 14 March		Organisation of the Garde Nationale of the first ban into 88 cohortes
1813, 12 January		Conversion of the 88 Garde Nationale cohortes of the first ban into 22 Line Infantry regiments. Transfer of the 88 cohortes artillery companies into the army's artillery regiments
1813, 3 April		Call to arms of 80,000 men from the Garde Nationale's first ban (24,000 transferred into the Garde Imperiale)
1813, 5 April		New organisation of the Garde Nationale. Creation of departmental legions with Garde Nationale grenadier and chasseur companies
1813, 17 December		Organisation of Garde Nationale cohortes for service in fortresses
1814, 6 January		Formation of gardes nationaux reserve armies to protect Paris, Lyon and the fortresses. Creation of 121 battalions organized in 18 military divisions
1814, 8 January		Activation of the Garde Nationale in Paris
First Restoration		
1814, 13 May		The Comte d'Artois, Colonel General of all the Gardes Nationales of France
1814, 16 July		All the Gardes Nationales in the Kingdom of France are sedentary. Division into urban and rural Gardes
First Empire (Hundred Days)		
1815, 10 April		New organisation of the Garde Nationale

1

The Garde's Ancestors

Pre-1789

The Milices Bourgeoises at the End of the Ancien Regime

Prior to the French Revolution, the Kingdom of France had a professional army, the bulk of which consisted of regulated troops made up of foreign soldiers and lower-class recruits. In the Middle Ages and in the Early Modern era, a number of towns in the kingdom were allowed to muster burghers into defence corps. These Milices Bourgeoises, which were promptly asked by the municipal authorities to contribute to the maintenance of public order, were not always efficient and exemplary. In the second half of the eighteenth century, accounts and harsh judgements against them abounded. In 1758, the colonel of the Milice Bourgeoise of Rennes – who was also the mayor of the town – acknowledged that 'in its present state, the Milice can only be useless and the privileges of the officers are a burden on society'.[1] Nearly 40 years later, in 1789, the author of a memorandum calling for the creation of a citizen's troop in Tours was just as harsh on the city's Milice. According to him, the latter was only intended to 'serve the grandeur of public celebrations'.[2] Pointing out the military inadequacy of these troops, which were somewhat archaic in many respects, and their decrepitude, most historians have paid little attention to them. French historian Georges Carrot stated that 'the Garde Bourgeoise was most often nothing more than a ceremonial troop with gleaming uniforms, bright scarves and coloured plumes, which were taken out on feast days or for public ceremonies'.[3] In fact, no overall study has been undertaken on the form, existence and functions of the Milices Bourgeoises in modern France.

---

1 Archives Départementales d'Ille-et-Vilaine (ADIV): C1143, mémoire, 1758.
2 Béatrice Baumier, 'De la milice bourgeoise à la Garde nationale: L'exemple de Tours des années 1760 à 1792', in Serge Bianchi and Roger Dupuy (eds), *La Garde nationale entre nation et peuple en armes: Mythes et réalités 1789-1871* (Rennes: Presses Universitaires de Rennes, 2006), p.113.
3 Carrot, *La Garde nationale*, p.26.

THE GARDE NATIONALE 1789–1815

Private and officer of Sens Milice Bourgeoise, circa 1780–1789. Henri Boisselier relied on the municipal archives and a period portrait to draw these figures. In 1789, the Marquis de Chambonas commanded the Milice Bourgeoise in Sens, a city 100 kilometres southeast of Paris. (Yves Martin)

In the eighteenth century, the military role of the Milices tended to fade. Thus, the dispatch of detachments to the coastal areas mainly took place during the reign of Louis XIV. This type of mobilisation then became exceptional. The authorities were more likely to call on the seaside towns or those fairly close to the Atlantic Ocean, but they did not forget those inland and the contingents requested were in proportion to the population of the town. In Brittany, the last notable mobilisation of detachments took place in 1746 during the British landing in Lorient. The Milices of Vannes, Rennes, Nantes and Morlaix, in particular, were mobilised and marched to the shore. During the Seven Years' War, as the British threat to the Channel coast became clearer, some Milices Bourgeoises were then given the task of guarding, or even escorting, prisoners of war. In small localities, guarding the British meant mobilising the entire Milice and setting up regular sentries and patrols. Surveillance was easier in towns with a fortress. Rare mobilisations, which were much smaller or occasional, took place later, particularly in the early 1780s.

Each of these mobilisations highlighted a serious lack of weaponry and led to the acquisition of muskets. However, the maintenance of these weapons was generally deficient, so much so that after a few years, they were hardly operational. The purchase of these firearms was therefore a waste of money. The lack of weapons and ammunition, as well as the absence of officers, considerably limited exercises and training. The mayor of Rennes, for example, deplored in 1758 that 'the ignorance of the inhabitants making up the milice bourgeoise has reached the point of not knowing how to load their muskets'.[4] Five years later, Rue, *aide-major* of the Landerneau Milice, made an observation that was at least as disillusioned: 'The Milices Bourgeoises are considered useless. They are abandoned to themselves and are barely assembled every ten years. The overwhelming majority of their men do not know right from left'.[5] Indeed, during the Seven Years' War, there were calls for drills to be held on Sundays and public holidays and for all militiamen to be regularly trained in shooting. In this context, the revival of the *papegaai* (or bird shooting) was at one time envisaged. However, although it had been used as a shooting exercise in the past, this was no longer its role, as it mainly brought together the upper classes. Each new member had to be co-opted and pay a membership fee. Therefore, despite all the wishes expressed, the *papegaai* could at best provide shooting practice for officers.

---

4   ADIV: C 1143.
5   Service Historique de la Défense (SHD): 1M 1770, mémoire du 25 juillet 1763.

THE GARDE'S ANCESTORS

Left: Soissons and Nancy Compagnies de l'Arc, circa 1775–1780, by Henri Boisselier. Milices Bourgeoises and bourgeois Guets were born of the freedoms granted to towns in the medieval period and the obligation for towns to defend themselves by their own means. Based on volunteering and co-optation, the military sports companies (bow, crossbow and arquebus) supported them by training some of the bourgeois in the use of modern weapons. (Yves Martin)

Below: Chambéry Compagnie de l'Arc, circa 1780 and St Menehould Compagnie de l'Arquebuse, 1776, by Henri Boisselier. Eighteenth-century men had a passion for uniforms. Changes were very frequent, especially in the second half of the eighteenth century. It was the same with the military sports companies, which very closely followed the evolution of military fashions. Their costumes were more and more gleaming and neat during the century. (Yves Martin)

Not all the 'military' functions of the Milice had disappeared, however, and these units served as auxiliary forces in maintaining order. The bourgeois theoretically ensured the security of the towns. They guarded the gates, patrolled the ramparts and occupied one or more guard posts. In addition, they carried out night patrols, regardless of whether it was windy or rainy, although these were not necessarily sufficient to stop disorder and ensure real public safety in the town. One of the main limitations of such patrols was the geographical area they covered. They were often smaller than the area of the city itself, so that the faubourgs (suburbs) were generally left out. The reactive capacity of the Milices Bourgeoises was therefore of varying success. Such units certainly played a rather modest role in the fight against common urban crime, but they did not give free rein to the cut-throats. Moreover, the psychological aspect of the patrols – which watched over the sleep of the bourgeoisie – cannot be underestimated.

Law enforcement was not limited to the fight against crime and ordinary delinquency. It was sometimes necessary to disperse and repress gatherings. This was indeed one of the missions of the Milice Bourgeoise, but interventions of this type remained very rare. This was the case in Vannes in 1765 and in Tours in 1770 and again in 1774. Embedded in the urban social environment, these bourgeois were understandably reluctant to take up arms against their neighbours, whose feelings they potentially shared. Moreover, since these revolts usually targeted the state and its representatives, the bourgeois generally did not feel threatened, hence their passivity on such occasions. On the other hand, the threat to the social order by sections of the urban proletariat was much more mobilising. Property owners, who had an obvious interest in combating disorder and potential looting in their communities, generally acted as a last line of defence against popular agitators. For the well-to-do and affluent, the Milice Bourgeoise was in some ways the surest guarantor of their tranquillity, a safeguard and security against the unpredictable outbursts or demands of the 'rabble'. It defended property and individual liberty and had to be able to oppose the looting of shops, warehouses and factories, and to stifle any aggressive desire on the part of the poorer people.

The Milice also played a key role in firefighting. It was not so much a question of fighting fires as of keeping out onlookers, preventing disorder and guarding the burnt-out areas to prevent theft. They also periodically carried out a number of 'police' missions, visiting the granaries and the homes of the inhabitants who had to house the troops.

The Milices Bourgeoises were an integral part of the municipalities, and the eighteenth century saw the town councils strengthen their collaboration with the officers of these units. The latter, who knew their neighbourhood well, carried out various administrative tasks: preparing the list of young men destined to be drawn for the provincial Milice, identifying the inhabitants who were suitable for housing the soldiers, establishing and checking the capitation rolls. Such a connection was not surprising: the mayor was usually the colonel of the Milice and many of the officers were themselves aldermen or former aldermen. All belonged to the notables, the urban elites. More generally, the members of the Milice constituted a useful intelligence network which could inform the municipality about the state of opinion or specific threats.

The gathering of all or part of a town's Milice Bourgeoise also took place during festivals or the visits of illustrious figures. The ceremonial, which was strictly regulated by etiquette, showed the power of the host city and the Milice were naturally obliged to comply with it. By nature unpredictable and irregular, the gatherings during the *Te Deum* celebrating royal victories were other highlights for the Milice. Ordered by the king on the occasion of the capture of a city or a victorious battle, the *Te Deum* took place in all the cities of the kingdom. The celebration was divided into two phases: first the religious ceremony punctuated by the singing of the *Te Deum*, then the public rejoicing. These gatherings showed the Milice Bourgeoise as military troops. However, in towns where units of the royal army were staying, the close proximity of the two troops during the celebrations did not fail to cause problems of precedence. The soldiers benefited from their professional status, but the bourgeoisie could oppose them on the grounds of tradition and permanent residence in the town. The royal power never confirmed the Milice Bourgeoise's claim to a certain priority over the regular troops and some regiments did not hesitate to challenge the established practices.

Security Forces at the End of the Ancien Regime

The 'insignificance of the security forces' was a feature of eighteenth-century France, both in the cities and in the countryside, where the Maréchaussée operated. For the most worrying situations, the authorities relied on the line army, whose concentration in garrisons, the slowness of its movements, not to mention its lack of adaptation to the missions of maintaining order, made its use a delicate matter.

The case of Paris, the most populous city in the kingdom of France in the years 1770–1780, testified to the inadequacy of the means called upon to ensure order as well as to their anarchic superposition. Comprising barely 400 men, the majority of whom were scattered throughout the Ile de France and the generality of Paris, the Maréchaussée ensured the security of communications. Dating back to December 1254, a Compagnie du Guet was more specifically responsible for the service of prisons. It was abolished by an edict of 5 September 1771, but a new one was instituted by royal decree on the 16th of the same month and its 70 men were subjected to the military discipline of the Garde de Paris created by Sartine. In 1776, the latter was reorganised into nine divisions: two cavalry divisions, a commanding division comprising the élite of the infantry – and intended to supplement the cavalry when vacancies arose – four infantry divisions and two port divisions. From 800 infantrymen and 245 cavalrymen at its creation, its strength was increased to 1,190 infantrymen and 265 cavalrymen at the outset of the summer of 1789. At night, it was the duty of the Garde to ensure that drinking establishments and the gates were closed. In the city and its faubourgs, it also had to put an end to disturbances and brawls, pursue thieves, and 'collect' prostitutes, beggars and drunkards. During the day, the Garde also had to clear the

THE GARDE NATIONALE 1789–1815

roads clogged with cars and merchants' stalls, watch over the mont-de-piété, and check that the shops were closed on Sundays and public holidays. In addition, it assisted the guild leaders against rebellious journeymen and arrested soldiers who recruited without permission, as well as young men who refused to follow recruiters after they signed their engagement. Lastly, the Garde was largely responsible for maintaining order at celebrations. In short, it was responsible for everything in urban policing that was deemed unworthy of regular troops. A half-bourgeois, half-military troop, largely composed of provincials, the Garde de Paris was truly a corps apart and therefore complex to define. With no barracks and no contract of enlistment, its soldiers were mixed with the little people of Paris. Often disowned by the upper echelons of the administration as well as by the judiciary, they were very poorly perceived by the population, which gave them a whole series of nicknames: the infantrymen were thus called 'sad-legged' (tristes-à-pattes') or 'grippe-Jesus' (a slang expression meaning 'gendarme') while the cavalrymen were known as 'shod rabbits' ('lapins ferrés'). They were reproached for their sometimes indiscriminate brutality, as well as for their strict application of the regulations on stalls from 1776 onwards: the Gardes ruthlessly dispersed all merchants with mobile stalls.

Garde Française, coloured engraving by Nicolas Hoffmann, 1780s. The Gardes Françaises, French nationals with a minimum height of 1.73 metres, enlisted for an eight-year period. They were dressed, like this grenadier pictured by Hoffmann, in the distinctive royal blue coat with red cuffs first introduced in 1685. (Yves Martin)

An elite unit of the royal infantry numbering 3,600 men and stationed continuously in Paris since 1763, the Gardes Françaises provided honour and guard duty. In 1788, on the eve of the Revolution, they occupied 16 different barracks in Paris, located in both working-class and affluent areas of western Paris. The route of the regiment's patrols broadly followed the geography of working-class Paris. The companies located in the well-to-do suburbs such as the faubourg Saint-Germain headed primarily eastwards and therefore towards the working-class areas. The companies located in the working-class districts carefully patrolled the faubourg Saint-Marcel and the Halles district.[6] Stationed in Versailles, the Regiment des Gardes-Suisses was usually employed in Paris, as were the Gardes Françaises. In case of serious events, it was always possible to employ different corps of the King's Garde stationed in Versailles, as well as troops from the provinces, the closest of which were garrisoned on the northern frontier of the kingdom, a vast area encompassing Lille, Arras, Reims and Amiens.

---

6 Clément Monseigne, 'Maintien de l'ordre et maintien des ordres: Les logiques spatiales du régiment des Gardes-Françaises à Paris à la veille de la Révolution', *Carnets de géographes*, 15 (2021).

Despite shortcomings and structural defects, in particular an undeniable diffusion of command, this organisation was nonetheless an important asset in the hands of the royal power.

The First Revolutionary Milices: Select Case Studies

The monarchy was in great need of such means, for in the years 1770–1780, France was in a profoundly paradoxical situation. It was both confined to old structures and teeming with novelties, initiatives and challenges. In other words, the structures of eighteenth-century society no longer corresponded to the economic and social realities of the time. The resulting imbalance caused latent discontent, which was amplified by the writings of the philosophical movement. The high political personnel certainly perceived the need for a profound reform of social relations and administrative simplification, but the royalty proved incapable of imposing the necessary arbitration between the divergent interests. Moreover, the economic situation was unfavourable: the liberal policy of the state aggravated the tensions, since after Turgot's attempts, a free trade agreement was signed with Britain in 1786. This decision was accused of having unwisely opened the borders to British manufactured goods, causing competition that the domestic iron and textile industries were unable to withstand. The decline in domestic demand was said to have combined with the lowering of living standards to lead to increased unemployment. Unemployment sent vagrants to the streets and dangerously increased the number of destitute people in the cities. The discontent of the middle and upper classes was echoed by the anxiety of the most working-class sections of French society. Hunger risked undermining their age-old resignation: this was bound to be the result of the serious agricultural crisis, the beginnings of which dated back to 1787–1788.

For political opponents of all kinds, it was a tempting option to use the pressure of these worried and hungry crowds against the royal authority. In 1787, the monarchy's attempts at reform, embodied by the successive Controllers of the Finances, Calonne and later Loménie de Brienne, came up against resolute opposition first from the notables and then from the members of the parlements. Louis XVI had engaged in a showdown with the aristocratic opposition without being assured of any popular support. On the contrary, the members of the parlements, supported by the patriot party and its network of correspondents, were skilful in linking their cause to that of the little people. Thus, riots broke out in most towns where a parlement was located. While in Paris strong preventive measures succeeded in maintaining calm, this was not the case in the provinces. In May and June 1788, in Toulouse, Pau, Aix-en-Provence, Dijon and Besançon, the royal troops were besieged and the parliamentarians reinstalled by the crowd. In Grenoble, on 7 June 1788, in response to the decree of exile against its parlement, the population mobilised and prevented the departure of the parliamentarians. The rioters climbed onto roofs and rained bricks and tiles on the soldiers of the Regiments d'Austrasie and Royal-Marine, who eventually withdrew. The reaction of the authorities to the unrest was generally characterised by sluggishness, lack of resolve and, above all, by the absence of precise directives. The army was more or less alone in intervening. As for the Milices Bourgeoises, they only took up arms belatedly and only to prevent houses and goods from being pillaged. In Rennes, but also in Toulouse and Aix, the officers of the Milice Bourgeoise even made a pact with the insurgents. On 25 August 1788, Loménie de Brienne, disowned by Louis XVI, withdrew to make way for Necker. The popular enthusiasm was translated into noisy street demonstrations. From the first bursts of firecrackers and rockets in the Place Dauphine, the Garde de Paris was charged with dispersing the crowds, so that on the 29th the crowd rushed to the guard posts. At the Pont-Neuf, *Sergent* Thouret faced the riot, but his seven soldiers abandoned him. If the *sergent* of the Marché-Neuf post had not gathered several squads, all the posts would have suffered the same fate. The guards were scattered and could not offer any resistance. Grouped together, they fired on the mutineers in the Place de Grève. In any case, Paris was shaken until the end of September by violence, looting and fires. In the autumn, the members of the parlements opposed the principle of dual representation of the Third Estate in the future Estates-General and discredited themselves in the eyes of public opinion. Rejected in the aristocratic camp, they no longer enjoyed the support of the common people, whose role had proved so decisive in bending the King's will. Nevertheless, the fact that they had encouraged the popular masses to storm official buildings was not without consequences at a time of looming famine.

From the end of 1788 onwards, there was unrest in the cities and in the countryside. Fearing a shortage of grain, the inhabitants stopped and looted wheat convoys. There were also riots at the markets and attacks on granaries. However, riots against bakeries were rare. When they did occur, they were directed at shops in large cities. The crisis worsened in the first months of 1789 and riots of varying degrees of severity broke out, sometimes degenerating into anti-fiscal movements. Until then, the authorities had dealt with the usual means at their disposal, namely the Maréchaussée and detachments of the royal army. However, the military could not be everywhere and their action sometimes lacked vigour. Using the popular uprisings as a pretext, groups recruited from the youth of the bourgeoisie organised and armed themselves in a number of towns and cities in the kingdom. They also wished to impose themselves on more conservative local oligarchies and aimed to protect themselves from aristocratic plots. This process appeared in places as diverse as Brittany and Provence from the beginning of 1789.

In January 1789, political turmoil was at its peak in Rennes, the main city of Brittany. Libels and pamphlets mushroomed, as did clashes between gentlemen and law students. Moreover, the nobility took advantage of the rise in the price of bread to set the 'lower Third', that is to say all the servants and lowly earners, against the 'upper Third', represented by the bourgeoisie. On the morning of 26 January, a large number of servants and chair-bearers, raised covertly by the nobles, gathered at the champs de Montmorin, south of the city. Historians generally estimate their number at between 600 and 1,500 servants, but a careful examination of the testimonies leads to a lower

THE GARDE'S ANCESTORS

Incendie du corps de garde sur le Pont Neuf, le 29 août 1788, drawing by Abraham Girardet, 1788. On 25 August 1788, Minister Loménie de Brienne's dismissal and Minister Necker's return to office caused unrest on the Pont-Neuf. Brienne's effigy was symbolically condemned to the stake. On the Place Dauphine, the Garde de Paris ruthlessly dispersed the crowds that had greeted the announcement of Necker's recall to power. The mob took revenge by burning the Garde's posts on the Pont-Neuf. (Musée Carnavalet)

estimate of between 200 and 600 individuals.[7] On this 'journée des Bricoles', the servants' motivations appear to be diverse and sometimes cumulative. They demanded lower prices for bread, exemption from housing for soldiers, the abolition of the patrol and the corvée, a fairer distribution of taxes and a reduction in the capitation tax for the lower classes. The assembly decided to take these complaints to parlement, which agreed to lower the price of bread to 24 *sols*. The servants and porters then spread out in the surrounding streets. The first clashes broke out between the demonstrators, some of whom were drunk and armed with cudgels, stones and sticks. Youths gathered in front of the Café de l'Union, their meeting place. The clashes quickly spread to the whole city centre. Overwhelmed, the students and youths retreated and, that same evening, called upon the patriotic youth of neighbouring towns for help. As the historian Roger Dupuy explains, the agitation of 26 January was initially directed against the 'upper Third', before suddenly turning against the youths. Following this first skirmish, the nobles again attacked the young men, who were accused of besieging them in the hall of the provincial states, and the confrontations became even more violent. Caught off guard the day before and consequently largely unarmed; the students had this time taken the necessary measures. Testimonies describe them as carrying pistols, sabres and above all swords, in flagrant contradiction

---

7   Julien Le Lec, 'Tuez la noblesse et qu'il n'en reste point! Culture de la violence et culture politique lors des journées des Bricoles à Rennes les 26 et 27 janvier 1789', *Société d'Histoire et d'Archéologie de Bretagne* (2017), p.42.

with the numerous prohibitions promulgated by the municipality as well as by parlement. Such weapons corresponded to the typical armament of students, as found throughout the Ancien Régime in towns with colleges or universities. Between 4:30 p.m. and 6:30 p.m., the Place du Palais was the scene of a real battle which spread to the west and south of the town. On this occasion, the Milice Royale depot was looted and young men sounded the *tocsin* after breaking down the door of the clock tower. Parliamentarians and the Maréchaussée roamed the streets to appease the rioters, but they were unable to restore calm. On the evening of the clashes, nearly 60 people had been injured and three killed: Joseph Bellavoine, a butcher's boy, and two young aristocrats. The nobility withdrew to their chateaux, vowing to avenge them with the help of their peasants. Such a threat provoked the mobilisation of all the young patriots of the province and even of Anjou and Poitou, who sent detachments and deputations to Rennes. On 3 February, realising the advantages they had at their disposal and probably encouraged by the highly reserved attitude adopted by the military command towards them, they organised themselves into a true armed federation of young patriots. They pledged immediate mutual assistance against all attempts at revenge by the nobility. The associates were to wear 'a ribbon bearing an emblem of the Third Estate, and the motto "win or die"'.[8] The young Breton patriots' first stand against the aristocratic threat was thus accompanied by the organisation of a league extending far beyond the province's borders.

In March 1789, Marseilles, a large southern city of over 100,000 inhabitants, was on the verge of an uprising. The dreaded explosion took place on 23 March. In the afternoon, the crowd gathered and tried to force their way into the house of Rebuffel, the director of the city's tax farms. The rioters then went to the Hôtel de Ville whose windows were broken. The municipal authorities announced a reduction in the price of bread and meat, but this was hardly enough to appease the popular anger. After relative appeasement on the night of the 23rd and 24th, a new outbreak of violence occurred on the morning of the 24th. This time the mob looted the house of the farmer-general Rebuffel, then threatened to attack the cod and wheat warehouses on the quai de Rive-Neuve. The riot had immediate results, since on the morning of 24 March, even before the end of the troubles, the aldermen convened the town council, reinforced by the deputies elected to the assembly of the Third Estate for the Estates General. This assembly ratified the price reduction of bread and meat announced the evening before. It also abolished the taxes levied by the community on foodstuffs and appointed 12 commissioners to 'look into ways of relieving the people'.[9] More than that, one of the immediate consequences of the unrest was the formation of a Garde Citoyenne, which appears to have been largely spontaneous. On 23 March, according to artillery officer Mézières, several volunteers went to the rescue of the looted houses and in fact helped to limit the damage. In the afternoon of the 24th, on the initiative of Jean-François Lieutaud, these same volunteers

---

8   Dupuy, *La Garde nationale*, p.56.
9   Monique Cubells, 'Marseille au printemps 1789: Une ville en dissidence', *Annales du Midi*, 173 (1986), p.69.

encouraged a large number of young people to meet at the Arquier tavern in the Allées de Meilhan. They decided to organise themselves into a Garde Citoyenne and formed companies. On the same day, the porters, under the leadership of Jean-Joseph Arnaud, went to work for the town council, which they escorted to the end of its meeting. As the council, accompanied by the porters, was about to proclaim its decisions, it met Lieutaud, who gave it the minutes of the meeting in the Allées de Meilhan. These were read out publicly and the young men joined the porters. The Garde Citoyenne, whose estimated strength was close to 6,000, was born.[10] Its members were dressed in civilian clothes and wore a scarlet plume on their hat. They were soon divided into four companies and distinguished by a cockade and a pompom (black and white, blue and white, yellow and blue, red and blue). The majority of the staff was made up of notables. The commander of the Garde was the Chevalier de Libertat, a former soldier and knight of Saint-Louis. Jean-François Lieutaud, its initiator and also *capitaine* of a company, was the son of a merchant. Fabre, a former gendarme, and the lawyer Brémond-Jullien were also present. According to Mézières, the participation of the bourgeoisie and the members of the guilds seems to have been proven: 'The bourgeois youth formed a very considerable body under the title of Marseilles Volontaires. They had invited the young nobles to join them and had received the most satisfactory response. All the guilds provided their contingent to swell the army'. Thus, if the Garde Citoyenne was rather diversely composed, it was nonetheless made up of young people from well-to-do families, ranging from bourgeois or noble to artisan. In addition, it undoubtedly included a certain number of porters, this guild having been one of its basic elements from the beginning. It was also traditional to employ these individuals to reinforce the municipal police. It does not seem that this first recruitment made room for the working class, whom it was on the contrary to contain. After having justly contained the Marseilles lower classes and curbed an insurrection against the collection of local consumption taxes, the Garde Citoyenne turned against the local administrators. It demanded a reform of the municipal administration, the abolition of the tax farm and the introduction of a much fairer tax system. It then engaged in operations outside Marseilles which prompted the Comte de Caraman, the military governor of the province who had a tendency towards firmness, to intervene. Once he had received reinforcements, he entered the city on 20 May. One of his very first decisions was to abolish the 'young men' Garde, which was replaced by a new paid Garde. It consisted of 60 companies, each commanded by a *capitaine* and 14 *lieutenants*. The officers were appointed by the town council from among the nobles, lawyers and merchants. Age conditions were required: at least 36 years for *capitaines*, 30 years for *lieutenants*, 25 years for *sous-lieutenants* and 20 years for ordinary soldiers. In addition, officers had to swear an oath of loyalty to the King, obedience to the municipal administrators and to officers of a higher rank. Only they had sufficient financial means to afford a blue uniform with a blue collar, white lapels, cuffs and turnbacks, with extensive

---

10   Mézières, *Précis historique des principaux événements qui se sont passés à Marseille depuis le 23 mars 1789 jusqu'en septembre 1790* (Marseille: F. Brebion, 1790), p.38.

gold embroidery on the collar and cuffs. As for the weapons, they were always to remain in the guardhouses. The precautions were certainly taken to surround the Marseillais with a corps recruited from the ruling classes and to avoid entrusting the maintenance of order to too young individuals. On the evening of 25 May, officers had been appointed, but very few ordinary soldiers had turned up. In fact, recruiting companies proved to be very complicated, with guilds showing little enthusiasm for service. The Garde never reached its full strength and could only field 51 incomplete companies.

This solution, which the King's representative imposed on Marseilles, was implemented in other towns in western Provence, which had been shaken by a serious popular uprising since the beginning of March. On the 25th, in Aix-en-Provence, which was hit by a food crisis, clashes broke out between the demonstrators and the troops, who were chased out of the Grand Cours. The following night, the looting of grain continued. Three thousand landowners belonging to the nobility and the bourgeoisie met the next morning to form a Milice intended 'for the defence of their properties'.[11] That same evening, the Milice, with the help of the army, re-established order. Shortly afterwards, it received flags blessed by the archbishop and bearing allegories celebrating the reunion of the three orders. In Toulon, calm was restored by means of Milices organised on the 29th on a corporate basis and allowed to participate in the service alongside the garrison. After the attack on a women's convent, a corps of about 30 companies was created in Barjols, bringing together 'honest bourgeois craftsmen and peasants'.[12] On 18 April, 30 or so companies were formed in Montpellier with a total of 2,636 men and intended to 'ensure freedom, protect the collection of taxes, defend property and people'.[13] Etampes, Caen, Orleans or Limoux equipped themselves with similar organisations between the beginning of April and the beginning of May 1789. It was the same in Pézenas. In April, fearing a popular riot, the consuls wished to reinforce the Milice there. 'Patrouillotism', more than enthusiasm, guided them. In a letter of the 18th of the same month, the Comte de Périgord, Governor of Montpellier, suggested that they 'form a Garde Bourgeoise composed of reliable citizens to maintain tranquillity'. He also advised them 'to exclude the lower classes, because of the lack of confidence that could be placed in them in such a circumstance'.[14] On the 21st, he added that

> when the bourgeois patrols are mounted and their service is regulated, arrest and put in prison those who would allow themselves to make seditious remarks or seek by other means to disturb public order and tranquillity. I gave the order that all nomadic people as well as suspect foreigners, especially Italians and Provençals, be arrested in Montpellier. It is partly to this precaution that we owe

---

11   Carrot, *La Garde nationale*, p.35.
12   Archives Municipales de Barjols (AMB): Délibérations municipales 1786–1789.
13   Joseph Duval-Jouve, *Montpellier pendant la Révolution* (Montpellier: C. Coulet, 1879), p.51.
14   Claude Achard, 'Les fastes de la gloire: Milice bourgeoise et garde nationale de Pézenas (1770–1871)', *Etudes Héraultaises*, 2 (1973), p.29.

THE GARDE'S ANCESTORS

the tranquillity we enjoy there. You would do well to use the same means.[15]

Many authors, focusing only on the military or law enforcement aspect, perceived the Milices Bourgeoises of the eighteenth century as moribund. However, the ruling elites remained mostly attached to this institution and had not forgotten its military roots. The municipalities sought to renovate it. At the end of the 1780s, minds were still open to the military mobilisation of the bourgeoisie in case of urgent necessity. Thus, from the end of 1788 and even before the meeting of the Estates-General, citizens had taken up arms in many cities of the kingdom. In Rennes, as in Marseilles, there was an obvious, albeit thwarted, desire to use this bourgeois armament in the political struggle against the traditional local powers and the monarchy. The demands of the nascent Revolution made these forces useful. The Milices Bourgeoises of the Ancien Régime provided a framework for the development of the Garde Nationale, even if the latter did not always result from a reactivation of the urban Milices. However, the Milices lacked an ideal, or even a *raison d'être*. The patriotic ferment of 1789 was to give them one.

Soldier and officer of the Regiment Royal-Niort, circa 1780–1789, by Henri Boisselier. Niort had a Milice Bourgeoise since 1572. In 1621, King Louis XIII decided to reward its excellent behaviour at the siege of La Rochelle by giving it the title of Regiment Royal-Niort. Thereafter, this unit had only a police and coastal guard role to prevent troops landing. (Yves Martin)

---

15   Achard, 'Les fastes de la gloire', p.29.

2

The Beginnings of the Garde Nationale Parisienne

1789–June 1790

In the spring of 1789, Paris, a vast agglomeration of 600,000 inhabitants, showed all the signs of a city under stress. Its problems were, of course, quite similar to those of other large cities in the Kingdom of France. The wealthy classes (the nobility and the clergy, but also the bourgeoisie) were particularly concerned about the imminent convening of the Estates General in Versailles. The representation of the Third Estate in the future assembly was the subject of much heated debate and dispute, as was the way in which the opinion of the elected representatives would be collected during the forthcoming debates; vote by order or individual vote of each deputy? This was in fact a reflection of the emergence of national sovereignty. When King Louis XVI and his popular finance minister Jacques Necker claimed to speak in the name of the nation, the nobility claimed to be its natural emanation. For its part, the bourgeoisie asserted that the nation was identified with the interests of a Third Estate representing more than 90 percent of the French population. The reference to the primacy of the nation undeniably benefited the bourgeois claims. But first, the Third Estate had to be unanimous or – at worst – to appear so, which was not a given. The working Parisian people were not fooled by the attitude of the bourgeois towards them. The content of the Parisian *cahiers de doléances* was above all a response to the concerns of the notables, whether they were lawyers or merchants. In fact, *doléances* of the 'fourth order' were published, as well as virulent pamphlets denouncing the contempt of these bourgeois with regard to the daily anxieties of the people of Paris. The selfishness of the wealthy was particularly condemned, especially since the bourgeois needed the arms and legs of the people to impose the demands of the Third Estate. In truth, misery, which was increased by the polar cold of the winter of 1788–1789, was at the heart of the preoccupations of the labourers, the day labourers and the unemployed. However, the supply of wheat was relatively regular, in contrast to the provinces. It was even a real state affair. All wheat not used for local consumption within a radius of

THE BEGINNINGS OF THE GARDE NATIONALE PARISIENNE

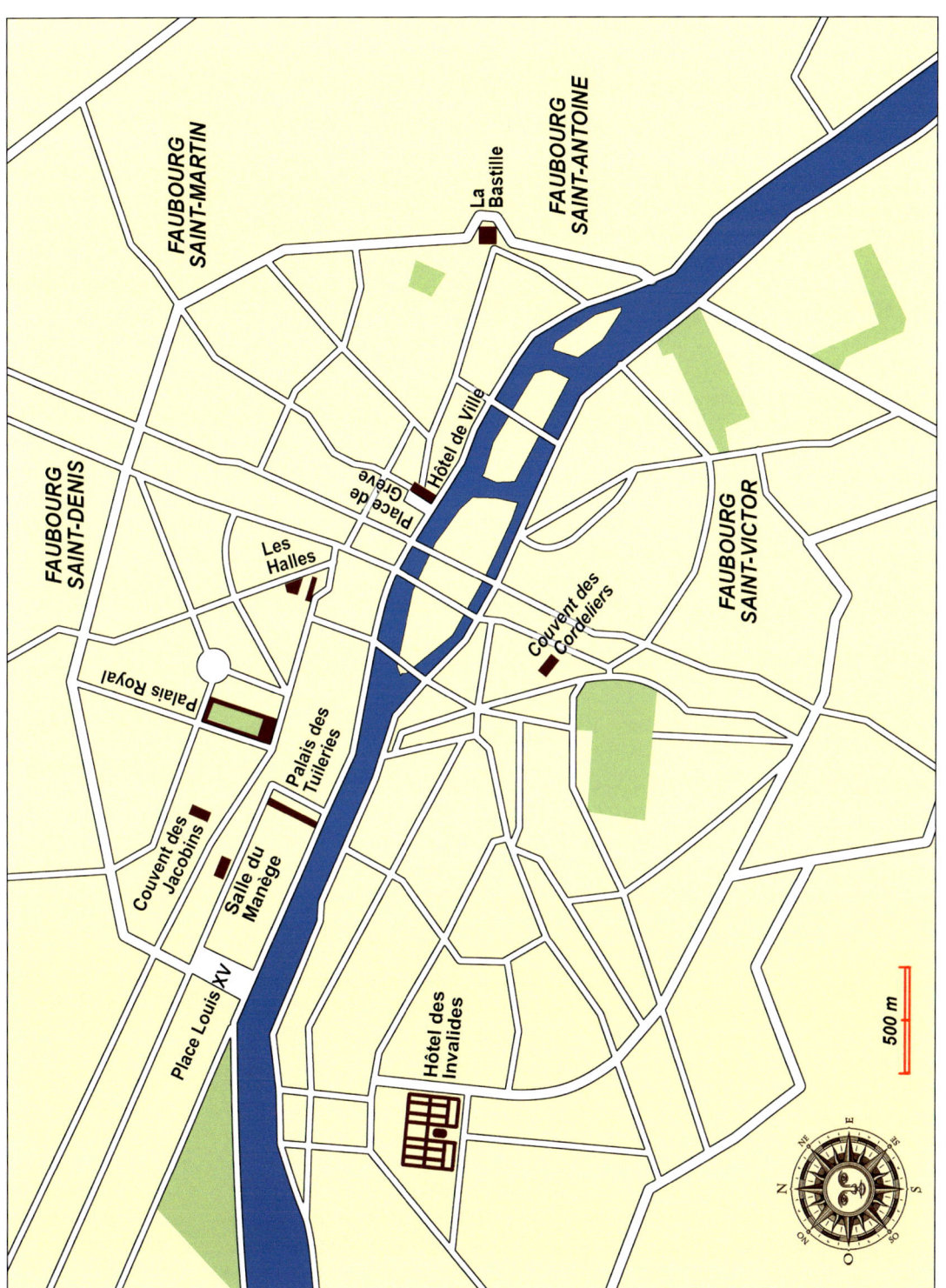

Map 1. Main Parisian locations mentioned.

30 miles of Paris was transported to the city. Specialised private companies also bought large quantities of grain from abroad, which was then sold at highly fluctuating market prices. The difficulty was therefore not so much with supplies but rather with the limited financial possibilities of underpaid or unemployed people and the quality of the products offered. Thus, the detestable quality of certain flours distributed to Parisian bakers to calm popular anger contributed above all to persuading the population that they were being poisoned.

The Réveillon Affair and its Aftermath

In this electric context, Parisians were sensitive to the words of Jean-Baptiste Réveillon, a wealthy wallpaper manufacturer in the working-class faubourg Saint-Antoine. At an electoral assembly held on 23 April 1789, this rather philanthropic businessman, who had a reputation for paying his workers well, had said he was in favour of abolishing the subsidies on flour. This demand also corresponded to that of the workers of the faubourg, who hoped for a reduction in the price of bread. Réveillon was aiming for a chain reaction: the fall in the price of bread was to lead to a reduction in wages associated with a lowering of the cost price of manufactured goods. Such a mechanism ensured that he would be able to compete effectively with foreign products, the massive arrival of which had been facilitated by a free trade treaty concluded with the British in 1786. Scalded by having been excluded from the election of the deputies of the Third Estate to the Estates General, the working class retained from the manufacturer's words the vague and conditional intention to reduce wages. The proposal was widely reported and amplified by rumours spread in the workshops and cabarets, and immediately gave rise to protest rallies in front of the Réveillon factory. On the 24th and 25th, the agitation seemed to subside, only to pick up again on Sunday the 26th. This time it concerned the faubourg Saint-Marcel, whose tanners, installed along the river Bièvre, were hard hit by unemployment. The next afternoon, a motley column of several thousand demonstrators (unemployed workers, craftsmen and small businessmen) gathered in the vicinity of the Bastille fortress. After crossing the Seine, it swept through the faubourg Saint-Antoine and the Hôtel de Ville, chanting slogans as varied as 'Death to the rich! Death to the aristocrats! Death to the hoarders! Bread for two cents! Down with the bloody priests!'[1] An effigy of Réveillon was symbolically hung in the Place de Grève. Moreover, as a detachment of about 50 Gardes Françaises protected the private mansion of the wallpaper manufacturer, the crowd unleashed itself instead on that of the saltpetre manufacturer Henriot, who had unwisely supported Réveillon's motion. On 28 April, thousands of demonstrators from the faubourg Saint-Marcel swelled the crowds surrounding Réveillon's hotel and factory, so that 350 additional Gardes Françaises were dispatched. During the afternoon, rioters

---

1   Georges Carrot, *Révolution et maintien de l'ordre, 1789–1799* (Paris: S.P.M.-Kronos, 1995), p.39.

THE BEGINNINGS OF THE GARDE NATIONALE PARISIENNE

Attroupement au faubourg Saint-Antoine, le 28 avril 1789, engraving by L'Epine. On 28 April 1789, a strong security force was deployed around the Réveillon factory. The engraving depicts a charge led by a detachment of the Regiment de Cavalerie Royal-Cravates in the street leading to the faubourg Saint-Antoine. On the right, Gardes Françaises have positioned themselves in front of the factory's entrance. (Musée Carnavalet)

stopped the Duc and Duchesse d'Orléans, who were on their way to the races at Vincennes. Proclaimed to be the 'only true friend of the people',[2] the Duc harangued the crowd and distributed the contents of his purse, suggesting that he understood popular demands. On her return from the races, the Duchesse obtained permission to pass through the rue de Montreuil which ran alongside Reveillon's factory. The soldiers on duty did not dare to block her passage and opened the barriers. The crowd then took advantage of the situation to push aside the police, rush into the breach and invade the factory. The entire building was ransacked and all the equipment and furniture burnt. Galvanised by their success, the rioters attacked the reinforcements of the Gardes Françaises and Gardes-Suisses which had been slowly dispatched by the *Lieutenant General de Police*. The rioters bombarded them with roof tiles and some of the furniture. The jostled and exasperated soldiers retaliated, firing live ammunition. In the evening, the Rue de Montreuil and the whole of the faubourg Saint-Antoine were cleared by charges from the Regiment de Cavalerie Royal-Cravates. Order was restored, but at what cost? Equivalent to that of the bloodiest revolutionary *journées*, the human toll was particularly heavy: several hundred demonstrators – from 300 to 900, according to the historians – had been massacred.[3]

During most of May and June, several fears affected the different strata of the Parisian Third Estate. Bread prices rose steadily during May, a rise that

---

2 Dupuy, *La Garde nationale*, p.15.
3 Jacques Godechot, *14 Juillet 1789: La prise de la Bastille* (Paris: Gallimard, 1965), p.191.

35

the working class attributed to a plot by ministers and aristocrats to starve them. While the fear of famine and an aristocratic plot agitated the working classes, the bourgeoisie was worried about a new popular explosion. The arrival of 10,000 unemployed people from the outskirts of Paris, gathered in charity workshops on the heights of Montmartre, crystallised their concerns. To the fear of an outburst of popular violence was added the possibility of an aristocratic plot. In the eyes of many bourgeois, for whom the two threats were closely linked, the massacre that had just been perpetrated on the rioters could also have been carried out against the patriots of the Third Estate by aristocrats determined to preserve their privileges at all costs.

On 17 June, after two months of fruitless negotiations with representatives of the clergy and nobility, the deputies of the Third Estate decided not only to reject definitively the division of French society into three orders – and thus the very notion of a privileged order – but also to proclaim themselves the National Assembly. The court was outraged, as were most of the aristocrats. Six days later on the occasion of a royal session, Louis XVI tried to regain the initiative by imposing the preservation of the three orders and – through Dreux-Brézé, his master of ceremonies – instructed the deputies of the Third Estate to evacuate the Salle des Menus Plaisirs. However, some of the Gardes-Suisses and two companies of the Gardes Françaises categorically refused to disperse the Third Estate deputies, and a crowd massed in front of the gates of the Château de Versailles. In truth, the attitude of the Gardes Françaises was hardly surprising. Mostly stationed in Paris and therefore living among the population, they had deplored their repressive role following the Réveillon riots. Celebrated as citizen soldiers protecting the deputies, they were in unison with the Third Estate whose demands and hopes they shared.

The insubordination of the Regiment des Gardes Françaises did not fail to worry the monarch, who, after having had their actual loyalty verified, called upon the royal army regiments stationed in the garrisons of the north and east of his kingdom. From 26 June to 1 July, the Minister of War sent movement orders concerning no less than 30,000 soldiers. Their arrival in the capital on 7 July was supposed to allow Louis XVI to carry out the authoritarian measures he planned against the National Assembly. It only fuelled the revolutionary process.

The royal session of 23 June had made the bourgeois feel the urgency of opposing a *coup de force* which had become obvious. As for the forthcoming arrival of regiments – often foreign – at the gates of Versailles and Paris, it made the hypothesis of an aristocratic plot credible. It was claimed that Necker was going to be chased out, the Estates General dissolved, and the patriots assassinated. The fear of a plot had become general and obsessive. In this context, the support of the Gardes Françaises alone was no longer sufficient. It was necessary to arm the Third Estate, and in particular the bourgeoisie. If, in the past, Paris had had a Garde Bourgeoise, it had become a 'fossil institution'.[4] The majority of Parisians had retained only a vague memory of it and the *cahiers de doléances* had hardly proposed its reestablishment.

---

4 Jean Chagniot, *Paris et l'armée au XVIIIe siècle: Étude politique et sociale* (Paris: Editions Economica, 1985), p.84.

Following continued contentious gatherings during the Jeu de Paume Oath crisis, on 26 June, journalist Nicolas de Bonneville, a Third Estate elector from the Carmes-Déchaussés district, called for the force's reestablishment in the Assembly of Electors at the Hotel de Ville. A debate was opened, but the option of reestablishing it did not seem to be an immediate necessity. The very next day, in Versailles, the ministers learned from an informant that the Paris bourgeois were planning to 'form a troop and guard themselves'.[5] On the 29th, the same informant added that this bourgeois troop would be used to contain the rabble and that its establishment would make it possible to abolish the *Lieutenant General de Police*, the all-powerful representative of the King and the only person responsible for order in Paris. On 1 July, the electors of Paris asked the King to withdraw the troops massed in the western districts of the city and, in order to curb the growing disorder, to re-establish the Garde Bourgeoise. On the 7th, the arrival of the 'foreign' regiments on the immediate outskirts of Paris worried public opinion. The next day, Comte de Mirabeau, in a moderate speech, denounced these concentrations of troops and respectfully asked Louis XVI to remove them. The representative for Provence suggested Gardes Bourgeoises being raised in Paris and Versailles to keep order instead. On the 9th, incidents multiplied throughout Paris, in the alleys of the Palais-Royal as well as in the working-class suburbs. In fact, on 10 July, electors put the urgent creation of a Garde Bourgeoise to defend the districts back on the agenda regardless of the King's response. In all, five proposals were made. They advocated guarding against government undertakings that might threaten public liberty, but also, because of the 'too frequent popular riots', ensuring the safety of the capital and 'maintaining social order'.[6] Although the atmosphere became tenser by the hour, no immediate decision was taken.

First Riots and the Creation of a Milice Bourgeoise

On 11 July, pressured by his most conservative councillors, Louis XVI sacked his reformist ministers, including Jacques Necker, the finance minister. The news, which reached Paris on the morning of Sunday the 12th, alarmed the bourgeoisie, stirred up the most liberal individuals and agitated the mass of the people. In other words, the dismissal of Necker temporarily abolished the divide between rich and poor which had until then undermined the solidarity of the Third Estate. At the same time, the Parisians learned of the formation of a ministry composed of declared opponents of the policy that had just led to the transformation of the Estates General into the National Assembly. A wind of panic swept over

---

[5] Micah Alpaugh, 'A Self-Defining Bourgeoisie in the Early French Revolution: The Milice Bourgeoise, the Bastille Days of 1789, and Their Aftermath', *Journal of Social History*, 47:3 (2014), p.6.

[6] Jean-Sylvain Bailly and Honoré-Nicolas-Marie Duveyrier (eds), *Procès-verbal des séances et délibérations de l'assemblée générale des Électeurs de Paris réunis à l'Hôtel-de-Ville le 14 juillet 1789, rédigé depuis le 26 avril jusqu'au 21 mai 1789, par M. Bailly depuis le 22 mai jusqu'au 30 juillet 1790, par M. Duveyrier* (Paris: Beaudouin Imprimeur, 1790), vol.I, p.131.

the strollers on the Champs-Elysées and in the Tuileries Gardens, with the most diverse rumours spreading at a frantic pace. The immediate dissolution of the National Assembly, famine, the bankruptcy of the kingdom, not to mention a 'Saint Bartholomew of the Patriots' fomented by the court of Versailles, were all feared. In the Palais-Royal, speakers, including journalist Camille Desmoulins, urged armed resistance, but guns were sorely lacking. In the afternoon, several thousands of bourgeois improvised parades which came up against detachments of the royal army here and there. This was notably the case at Place Vendôme, where the mob tried to disarm a dragoon squadron. The latter were rescued by the Regiment de Cavalerie Royal-Allemand commanded by the Prince de Lambesc, which had been stationed in Place Louis XV. The crowd ran for refuge into the Tuileries Gardens while pelting the cavalrymen with stones. The troopers were ordered to clear the gardens by charging at a slow trot. Because of their small numbers, they were forced to move back as quickly as possible. Few of the demonstrators were injured, but the rumour that the Regiment Royal-Allemand had perpetrated a massacre was immediately confirmed and Paris was stirred. As the *tocsin* sounded and cries of 'To arms!' rang out, the Gardes Françaises left their barracks on the Chaussée d'Antin of their own accord to take up the cause of the Third Estate. Some of them spilled out onto the boulevards leading to the Tuileries and fired on detachments of the Regiment Royal-Allemand. For their part, the protesters sought to obtain weapons: they approached individuals likely to possess them and looted armouries. Dismayed by the sedition of the Gardes Françaises as much as by the determination of the Parisian crowds, the leaders of the royal army reacted timidly and slowly. Late on the night of 12–13 July, and despite the reinforcements that had reached them in the meantime, they finally chose to abandon the Place Louis XV and retreat to the Champ de Mars. At around 11:00 p.m., a large number of electors met at the Hôtel de Ville and decided to form patrols of trusted people in order to avoid the looting of shops, particularly bakeries. Left to its own devices, the city of Paris was, throughout the night, criss-crossed by bands of several hundred demonstrators. Taking advantage of the retreat of the royal troops, they looted and burned down some 40 custom barriers built in 1785 to tax goods entering the city, which in their eyes symbolised the high cost of living. They also attacked convents, convinced that the grain harvested on the property of churchmen or obtained through tithes was hidden there.

At the end of a night of anarchy punctuated by the smoke of the fires, the sound of the *tocsin*, and the discharges of the alarm cannon which some districts used to mobilise the citizens promptly, a part of the Parisian electors met at 8:00 a.m. on 13 July at the Hôtel de Ville. They took, in urgency, two major decisions. Firstly, it was unanimously decided to form a Permanent Committee chaired by Jacques de Flesselles, the *Prévôt des Marchands de Paris*. In correspondence with the 60 districts of Paris, this Committee was intended to ensure the direction of the city's affairs. Moreover, as the royal army had not intervened to put an end to the disorders, the electors perceived the need to replace it with a force capable of imposing itself on

THE BEGINNINGS OF THE GARDE NATIONALE PARISIENNE

Paris gardée par le peuple, nuit du 12 au 13 juillet 1789, engraving by Pierre-Gabriel Berthault after a drawing by Jean-Louis Prieur. This picture captures the feverish atmosphere in Paris on the night of 12 to 13 July 1789. Prieur depicted a popular patrol made up of small craftsmen, shopkeepers, workers and a woman. Pikes and muskets, inclined parallel to each other, suggest a certain discipline. (Musée Carnavalet)

the rioters, which could only be done in the name of the Third Estate. The constitution of a Milice Bourgeoise was thus decided, which only amplified the mobilisation of the day before. At the end of the morning, a decree fixed the manpower at 12,000 men, that is 200 men in each of the 60 districts of Paris. Unfortunately, this solution proved almost immediately insufficient. Indeed, the royal troops present on the outskirts of the capital remained a threat. Moreover, the riot turned into an insurrection. Spontaneously forming, gangs had ransacked and pillaged the convent of Saint-Lazare, before attacking several Parisian prisons. At the beginning of the afternoon, the Permanent Committee consequently issued a new decree. This rather elaborate text – which showed that the Committee was organising itself for the long term – brought the number of Milice to 48,000 men enrolled in the 60 districts, 200 men on the first day and so on for the three next days. The 60 districts would form 16 legions: 12 would be composed of four battalions and four would be composed of three battalions. Each battalion, composed of 800 men, would be divided into four companies. To take on what many perceived as a formless, lower-class crowd, the districts based their alternative model on regimented order. In the absence of a uniform and in order to be recognised, the wearing of a two-coloured blue and red cockade was adopted. Very restrictive, the decree specified in this respect that 'any man found wearing this cockade without having been registered in one of the

THE GARDE NATIONALE 1789–1815

Cortège hétéroclite après le pillage des armes du garde-meuble royal vers la Place de Grève, engraving, 1789. On 13 July 1789, the crowd rushed to the Garde-Meuble, which was full of a variety of much-needed weapons, many of them old. This scene depicts a crowd wearing outdated armour and helmets and brandishing all types of bladed weapons. (Musée Carnavalet)

districts will be handed over to the justice of the Permanent Committee'.[7] In fact, the districts had been invited to draw up roll-sheets on which would appear 'known men', in other words electors. But in the dramatic atmosphere of the moment, they responded enthusiastically. Several of them took special initiatives and were prepared to accept all citizens without exception. Others showed themselves ready to welcome all the soldiers who had joined the insurrection, especially the Gardes Françaises. On the evening of 13 July, the Assembly of Electors consulted with them to take the necessary measures for their reunion with the Parisian Milice. Nearly 3,000 Gardes Françaises were then distributed in the districts and provided the framework of the battalions. Other corps simultaneously made offers of service. This was particularly the case for the clerks of the two Bazoches, that of the Palais and that of the Châtelet, the clerks of the notaries, the students in surgery, as well as the Guet de Paris. On the night of the 13th to the 14th, the Compagnie de l'Arquebuse followed suit. The Permanent Committee also validated spontaneous initiatives, such as that of a certain De Soulès, who wished to raise a cavalry company. For their part, the inhabitants of the Saint-Jean-de-Latran parish formed a special corps called 'Legion'.

However, the supply of arms to the Milice remained a crucial problem. On this occasion, Flesselles, the *Prévôt des Marchands de Paris*, sought to gain time. He claimed not to know where to find them, before reluctantly distributing 360 muskets stored at the Hôtel de Ville and indicating that others were kept at the Hotel des Invalides. But Governor Sombreuil replied that before delivering the coveted muskets, he had to take his orders from the King and that consequently he would not be able to respond to the requests of the Parisians until the following morning. In the meantime, the bourgeois and the common people threw themselves on the official buildings in the hope of finding weapons. The results of their investigations, particularly at the Garde-Meuble royal depot, were on the whole disappointing. The Permanent Committee responded to the most urgent need by having pikes and halberds made; 50,000 pikes were reportedly made in less than 36 hours by Parisian craftsmen. In the evening, 35 barrels of gunpowder were seized from a barge

---

7   François-Emmanuel Toulongeon, *Histoire de France depuis la Révolution de 1789* (Paris: Treuttel et Würtz Libraires, 1801), vol.I, p.57.

in the port Saint-Nicolas, so that the new Milice was able to begin patrolling immediately with all those who had firearms. As a result, the night of 13–14 July was much less turbulent than the previous one.

The Bastille Insurrection

By 6:00 a.m. on 14 July, several thousand Parisians, still looking for weapons, converged on the Hôtel des Invalides. The governor tried in vain to parley before the crowd invaded the buildings. In fact, the invalid soldiers did not oppose the insurgents, who got their hands on nearly 32,000 muskets and 12 artillery pieces. The only thing left for them to do was to obtain powder and ammunition, and the invalids indicated that a large quantity had been transported to the Bastille prison. During the whole of the morning, royal troops hardly reacted despite being stationed nearby. They did not react either in the afternoon when armed bands marched on the Bastille. Abandoned in an insurgent city at the head of a tiny garrison of 82 invalid soldiers reinforced by 32 grenadiers of a Swiss regiment and anxious to avoid unnecessary bloodshed, Governor De Launay preferred to capitulate four hours after the attack began. The capture of the Bastille was only the confirmation of the new balance of power which had allowed the popular victory. The crowd, armed with scythes, pikes, axes and muskets, had shown its firm will to seize the Bastille. The Gardes Françaises and a few defectors from other royal army units had provided them with a good framework. The royal army, on the other hand, had proved incapable of sending any reinforcements to the besieged garrison. Finally, the cannons were used effectively and played a decisive role in the surrender of the fortress.

The fighting and subsequent seizure of the Bastille destabilised the fragile social order that the Milice Bourgeoise had tried to cultivate. The fall of the fortress was followed by a massive demonstration back towards the Place de Grève, with a crowd of 'Bastille victors' – militiamen, people and Gardes Françaises – dragging both cannons and prisoners. The event seemed festive: crowds lined the streets and celebrated the victorious forces. Even the death of Launay and some Bastille guards en route did not dampen the festivities. Nor did the growing disorder cease afterwards. Paris was plunged into further confusion by rumours of a royal counter-attack. On the night of the 14th and 15th, mobilisation efforts got underway as fears of an imminent invasion grew. 'All the streets were barricaded and entrenched', described one witness.[8] The Milice Bourgeoise temporarily extended beyond the active citizens of the city, and even beyond the limits of gender and age. 'All the citizens, women, old men and children, expected an attack by the enemy and gathered a great number of stones and other instruments to throw at the soldiers if they entered the city'.[9] Rumours spread that the invasion

---
8   Alpaugh, 'A Self-Defining Bourgeoisie', p.12.
9   Louis-Abel Beffroy de Reigny, *Précis exact de la prise de la Bastille* (Paris: Baudouin Imprimeur, 1789), p.96.

THE GARDE NATIONALE 1789–1815

The foreground of this oil on canvas by Jean-Baptiste Lallemand (1716–1803) shows a group of ragged-looking fighters. One of them is even dressed in armour. Also of note are the tricolour ribbons arranged to look like a cockade. (Musée Carnavalet)

had already begun, with cannon fire at around 1:00 a.m. alarming several districts. The inhabitants were told not to sleep, for fear that everything would be needed to stop the enemy forces.

The Birth of the Garde Nationale Parisienne

However, when fears subsided on 15 July, the Milice Bourgeoise reasserted control. 'The number of bourgeois troops had increased prodigiously and the whole city was full of armed men, all having leaders and all marching in order', noted one observer.[10] A thousand men armed with cannon guarded every gate of the city and the bridges over the Seine. Cannon sufficient for the whole force had been collected and gunpowder (after pillaging the Bastille) was now held in large quantities. The Milice kept the city in a state of virtual lockdown. In Versailles, the Parisian events of 14 July were not known until early evening. The National Assembly was the great beneficiary of the popular insurrection without having orchestrated it. On 16 July, the 88

---

10   Alpaugh, 'A Self-Defining Bourgeoisie', p.13.

delegates of the National Assembly arrived in Paris, 'filled with shock and fear and armed against all foreigners'.[11] They immediately realised that measures would have to be taken without delay. It was imperative that they regularise this taking up of arms to put an end to the disorder. This was precisely one of the delegation's main tasks.

The events of early July 1789 had caused the collapse of all the Parisian institutions inherited from the Ancien Régime. There was no longer an *Intendant*, and the *Lieutenant General de Police* had disappeared. The *Prévôt des Marchands* and the four *échevins* forming the Bureau de Ville had given way to a Commune composed of a mayor and an Assembly of Representatives from the 60 districts responsible for regulating municipal administration. Incidentally, Flesselles, the *Prévôt des Marchands*, had been murdered by a pistol shot just after the storming of the Bastille. His head was then carried on a pike through the streets of the capital. The next day, his successor, Jean-Sylvain Bailly, a scientist and member of the National Assembly, was elected mayor of Paris by acclamation.

As early as the evening of 13 July, the Permanent Committee had thought of giving the Paris Milice Bourgeoise a regular command. To do this, it had appointed the Duc d'Aumont – a close associate of the Duc d'Orléans – as commander-in-chief. The Marquis de La Salle, who was in favour of reforms for the Third Estate, was appointed second in command. The next day, however, the former asked for 24 hours' reflection, so the Committee appointed the latter as commander-in-chief. On 15 July, King Louis XVI, for his part, sought to neutralise the movement by appointing two general officers to head the Parisian Garde Bourgeoise, which he thus de facto recognised. His attempt immediately failed. On the same day, the electors were concerned that the general command had not been formally entrusted to the Marquis de La Salle. One of them, a certain Moreau de Saint-Méry, conveniently pointed to the bust of the Marquis de La Fayette that the State of Virginia had donated to the Hotel de Ville, and the electors chose the 'hero of two worlds'. In the afternoon, the crowd confirmed this choice with a general acclamation. Emboldened by his American military past, the Marquis, who was a representative of the Auvergne nobility to the Estates General and then vice-president of the National Assembly, was given the title and powers of *Colonel General* of the Milice Bourgeoise. On 16 July, he had a new title accepted which was far more appropriate for a citizen troop, that of 'Garde Nationale'. Meanwhile, Louis XVI consecrated the *fait accompli* and confirmed his position the next day during his historic visit to Paris. On the 18th, however, La Fayette informed the Assembly of Electors that, 'if the King had deigned to confirm his election, made by acclamation', the latter was not 'proof of a universal suffrage'. 'He could not consider himself truly endowed with the necessary authority' without 'knowing the wish of the people'[12]. The districts were quick to ratify his appointment.

---

11   Albert Denis, 'La Révolution à Toul en 1789', *Annales de l'Est*, 5 (1891), p.548.
12   Bailly and Duveyrier (eds), *Procès-verbal des séances et délibérations de l'assemblée générale des Électeurs de Paris*, pp.116–117.

Considering themselves to be the embodiment of the sovereign people, many districts refused to relinquish effective control over their gardes nationaux, convinced that they were their rightful owners. If, from the moment he took office, La Fayette was sometimes fiercely contested, his popularity was undoubtedly an undeniable asset in carrying out a simple but difficult plan. In fact, there was no shortage of questions. How to bring together several tens of thousands of citizens? How to choose between all those who would come forward? Moreover, what position should be taken with regard to the soldiers who had placed themselves at the service of the Commune? The Marquis wanted to have a disciplined and barracked troop, receiving a salary. It should be able to maintain security in the city on a regular basis and be strong enough to influence events. Finally, La Fayette wanted to disarm the popular masses, but was aware that doing so by authority was not psychologically desirable.

Organising the Garde

The daily political news was constantly in demand, which obliged La Fayette to delegate to his collaborators the details of the organisation of the Garde Nationale Parisienne. As early as 16 July, the Permanent Committee invited the districts to designate one deputy each to form a Military Committee responsible for preparing regulations for the new institution. It was not until 20 July that all the deputies of the Military Committee were finally brought together and working sessions were then organised for three days, from morning to evening. Organised at La Fayette's house, they brought together the Military Committee as well as some of the prominent members of the National Assembly, among whom were Lameth, Barnave and Duport. Mathieu Dumas, La Fayette's main collaborator, was charged with synthesising their views. On 31 July, the Military Committee made the Assembly of Representatives of the Commune adopt the first three chapters of a *Règlement pour la formation, organisation, solde, police et administration de la Garde Nationale Parisienne*. Three other chapters were then presented from 3 to 5 August. On the 8th, after having noted that 43 districts had adhered to the regulation, the Assembly of the Representatives adopted it and ordered its execution. Each of the 60 districts must form a battalion with five companies of 100 men. One of these companies would be paid and active. It would bring together the soldiers who had joined the insurrection and in particular the former Gardes-Françaises. The 60 districts were further grouped into six divisions of 10 battalions. A grenadier company was attached to the first battalion of each division. The number of men thus reached 30,000, instead of the 48,000 initially planned, including 24,000 citizen gardes and 6,000 paid gardes. The whole force was under the command of a general commander – in other words, La Fayette – elected by the Assembly of Representatives of the Commune, which acted as a provisional municipality. All the 1,058 officers were, for their part, appointed by the districts, which desired to control their battalion closely.

THE BEGINNINGS OF THE GARDE NATIONALE PARISIENNE

Divers personnages révolutionnaires, gouache by Lesueur, circa 1790–1792. Alongside key personalities of the Revolution, Jean-Baptiste Lesueur gouaches also depict a number of forgotten figures. Thus, alongside the mayor of Paris, Jean-Sylvain Bailly, appears the Garde Nationale *Commissaire Général* Charles-Joseph Viguier de Curny. He was assassinated during the prison massacres on 3 September 1792. (Musée Carnavalet)

THE GARDE NATIONALE 1789–1815

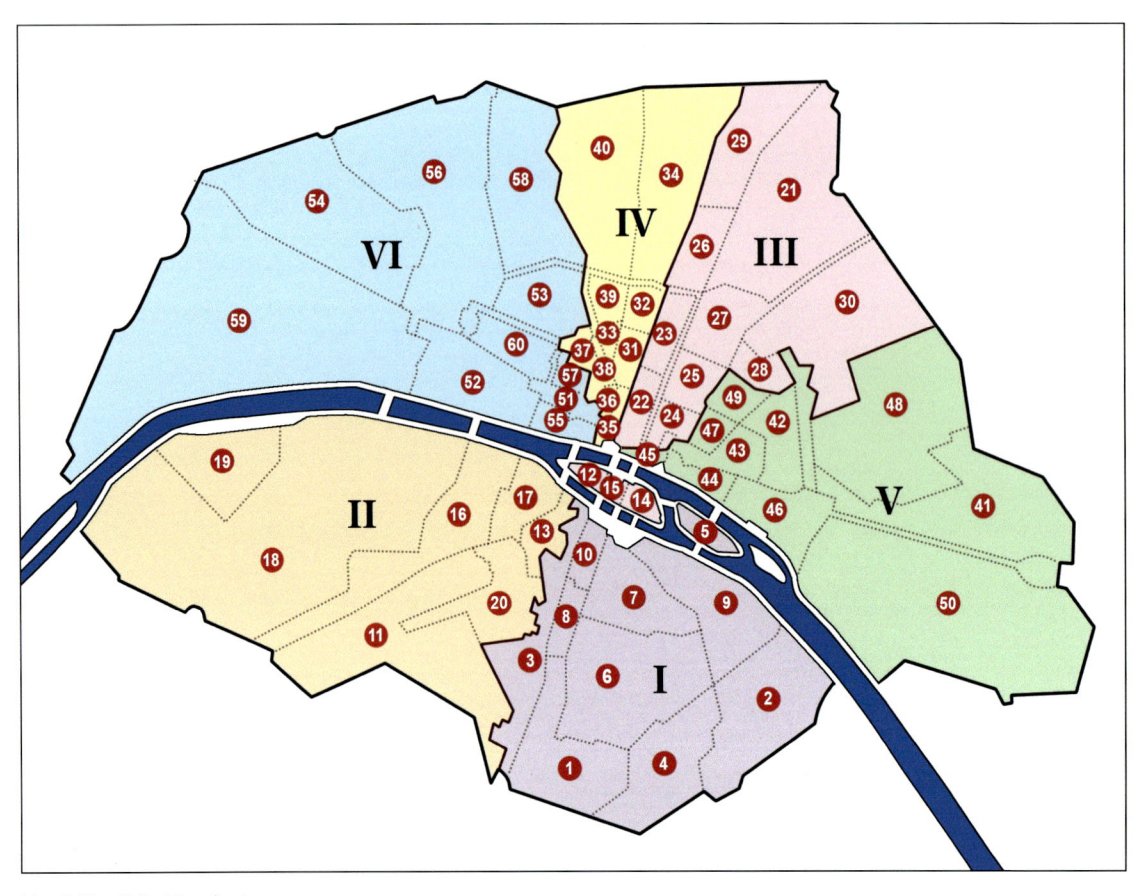

Map 2. The 60 Parisian districts organised into six military divisions, 1789.

Table 1. The 60 Parisian districts organised into six military divisions, 1789.
Under the Ancien Regime, Paris was divided into 21 neighbourhoods ('quartiers', in French). In early 1789, with a view to elections to the Estates-General, the city was instead provisionally divided into 60 districts.

1st Division		**2nd Division**		**3rd Division**	
1	St Jacques du Haut Pas	11	Les Prémontrés	21	Les Récollets
2	St Victor	12	Les Barnabites	22	St Nicolas des Champs
3	St André des Arcs	13	Les Cordeliers	23	Ste Elisabeth
4	St Marcel	14	Notre Dame	24	St Médéric
5	St Louis en l'Isle	15	St Séverin	25	Les Carmélites
6	Le Val de Grâce	16	Petits Augustins	26	Les Filles Dieu
7	St Etienne du Mont	17	L'Abbaye St Germain	27	St Martin des Champs
8	La Sorbonne	18	Les Jacobins St Dominique	28	Les Enfants Rouges
9	St Nicolas du Chardonneret	19	Les Théatins	29	St Laurent
10	Les Mathurins	20	Les Carmes Déchaussés	30	Les Pères Nazareth
4th Division		**5th Division**		**6th Division**	
31	St Jacques l'Hôpital	41	Ste Marguerite	51	L'Oratoire
32	Bonne Nouvelle	42	Les Minimes, Place Royale	52	Les Feuillants
33	St Leu	43	Petit St Antoine	53	Les Filles St Thomas

34	St Lazare	44	St Gervais	54	St Philippe du Roule
35	Ste Opportune	45	St Jean en Grève	55	St Germain l'Auxerrois
36	St Jacques de le Boucherie	46	St Louis de la Culture	56	Les Jacobins St Honoré
37	Les Petits Pères, Place des Victoires	47	Les Blancs Manteaux	57	St Honoré
38	St Eustache	48	Trainel, Faubourg St Antoine	58	Les Capucins, Chaussée d'Antin
39	St Magloire	49	Les Capucins du Marais	59	Les Capucins St Honoré
40	St Joseph	50	Enf. Trouvés, Faubourg St Antoine	60	St Roch

Table 2. Organisation of Paris Garde Nationale, summer 1789

	Unpaid Officers	Salaried Officers	Unpaid troops	Salaried Troops
General Staff	1	13		
Divisional Staff	66	72		6
The Six Infantry Divisions	720	180	24,000	6,000
	787	265	24,000	6,006
Of which ;				
Officers	1,052			
Troops	30,006			
General Total	31,058			

Application of the regulations was not without some difficulties. The constitution of the paid Garde – which formed the 'centre company' of each district – seemed to be the simplest and therefore the fastest. The former Gardes Françaises represented almost half of the planned strength. On 21 July, Louis XVI had agreed to the entry of these men into the Garde Nationale, on condition that they were granted a *congé absolu* (an absolute leave). So, on 22 August, La Fayette was able to announce that their distribution among the various companies had been completed. The 'centre companies' were complemented with royal army deserters who had joined the Parisian patriots. In this particular case, the difficulty lay in the excess of candidates. On 14 August, Louis XVI had amnestied all soldiers who had left their units without permission since 1 June. He allowed them to rejoin their regiments with the assurance that their mistakes would be forgiven. Despite these generous measures, new soldiers kept coming in, which worried the Assembly of Representatives. The problem seemed to be resolved in the first few days of September, as La Fayette's correspondence suggests.[13] The fact remains that these paid gardes, housed in *chambrées*, received a pay 50 percent higher than that of the line infantry and had opportunities for promotion. It was at the cost of such measures that La Fayette secured the loyalty of these men. By bringing together these paid companies, he and his staff had a permanent force capable of acting everywhere as quickly as possible; in short an effective tool for ensuring a gradual return to order in the streets of Paris.

---

13 Sigismond Lacroix, *Actes de la Commune de Paris pendant la Révolution* (Paris: L. Cerf, 1895), vol.I, p.507.

Table 3. Composition of Paris Garde Nationale infantry companies, summer 1789

	Paid Company	Unpaid Company
Capitaine	1	1
Lieutenant	1	1
Sous-Lieutenant	1	1
Sergent-Major	1	1
Sergent	4	4
Caporal	8	8
Appointé	8	–
Tambour	2	1
Grenadier / Fusilier	77	86
Total	103	103

Setting up the companies of the unpaid Garde was not without problems either. In theory, 'any domiciled citizen, married or unmarried, from the age of 20 until 50' could join the ranks of the Garde Nationale.[14] But as the Garde remained eminently bourgeois and was dedicated to defending the interests of this social group, article 4 of the regulations decreed that 'all workers, artisans, non-domiciled persons, having to be kept for their work, will consequently be exempt from this service. All people in a state of domesticity will be excluded'.[15] Although workers and artisans were not formally banned from armed service, several measures aimed to ensure that the Garde had a homogeneous bourgeois character. Inspired by the district of Saint-Germain-des-Prés, the Assembly of Electors endeavoured to disarm the workers by promising nine *livres* to all those who would deposit their weapons with the authorities of their district. It was a kind of cash-for-arms program. Similarly, all officers and unpaid gardes nationaux (except drummers) were required to dress and equip themselves at their own expense. In other words, the uniform became a major part of the strategy to keep low-income citizens out of the Garde. In some districts, the high cost of equipment and weaponry became a significant barrier to the registration of volunteers. La Fayette was so alarmed that, on 23 August, the Assembly of Representatives decided that the equipment and armament of the unpaid Garde would be paid for by the Commune. It was a tangible sign of Paris Mayor Bailly's willingness to consolidate his relationship with La Fayette in order to achieve a return to a more peaceful daily life as quickly as possible. As a member of the Military Committee noted, the citizens would 'no longer have any other concern than to procure clothing which could no longer be an extra burden for any of them'.[16]

Nevertheless, the formation of the companies was slow. The delays also stemmed from the desire of certain professions to form specific units rather than to merge into the Garde Nationale. This was notably the case for the clerks of the Châtelet. The attitude of the districts towards them was

---

14 Anon., *Règlement pour la formation, organisation, solde, police et administration de l'infanterie nationale parisienne, titres I, II, III et IV* (Paris: Lottin, 1789), p.2.
15 Anon., *Règlement pour la formation*, p.2.
16 Lacroix, *Actes de la Commune de Paris*, vol.I, p.87–90.

nuanced. While some categorically refused to admit them, others more subtly asserted that 'any distinction would be contrary to the harmony' that should reign within the Garde. The Bazoche du Palais was much more recalcitrant. It remained so until June 1790, after the National Assembly had adopted a decree stating that 'all particular corps of Milice, arquebusiers or others, under any name whatsoever, would be required to be incorporated into the Garde Nationale'. Finally, the patriotic enthusiasm of the unpaid gardes gradually waned month after month. The daily service, which was apparently not very demanding, was usually carried out by 2,000 men, 1,500 of whom were paid. Each company had to provide one or two men in turn, with at least 48 days between each tour of duty. However, increasing absenteeism caused this interval to be reduced to once a month, not counting the parades and other reviews imposed by the Commander-in-Chief. This relative heaviness of the service explained why La Fayette had been able to impose the existence of paid companies despite the districts' reluctance. By providing a permanent service, these companies relieved the non-professional gardes nationaux who only provided additional manpower and therefore saw their service lightened.

A pupil of the well-known painter David, Jean-Louis Laneuville joined the Garde Nationale Parisienne as a 'citizen soldier' in late July 1789. Shortly afterwards, he dedicated to La Fayette a project for a gilded copper standard 'in imitation of that of the Romans', which remained unfinished. (Musée Carnavalet)

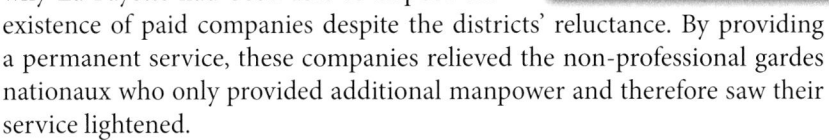

However, things were moving forward. On 12 August, La Fayette definitively constituted his staff, which included Jean-Baptiste Gouvion and Louis de la Colombe, two companions from his American adventures. On 24 August, the forces of an entire district, that of Saint-André-des-Arts, appeared in the uniform of the Garde Nationale. On 29 August, the Assembly of Representatives authorised La Fayette to convene all the officers of the paid Garde and the former Gardes Françaises the following day to swear an oath of loyalty 'to the Nation, the King and the Paris Commune' within the walls of the Hôtel de Ville.[17] Although this ceremony marked the first consecration of the Garde Nationale Parisienne, La Fayette was accused of asking his officers to swear personal allegiance. Moreover, these same officers were said to have been pressured to select companies from among the unpaid gardes nationaux whose availability and obedience they could ensure. French historian Roger Dupuy asserts that La Fayette would first have formed a core of paid Garde before setting up elite companies carefully recruited by the officers of most battalions.[18] Relying on these troops of proven fidelity, he would then have sought to obtain the enthusiastic rallying of the entire

---

17 Lacroix, *Actes de la Commune de Paris*, vol.II, p.89.
18 Dupuy, *La Garde nationale*, p.30.

THE GARDE NATIONALE 1789–1815

King Louis XVI is shown wearing the first uniform of the Parisian Garde Nationale. However, this engraving is completely fictitious: the king never wore it. In 1791, he claimed that he did not know whether it was in accordance with the Constitution. *On the other hand, the Dauphin wore it on several occasions. (Musée Carnavalet)*

Garde. Regularly organised reviews glorified it. Parisians admired the beauty of its uniforms but also its ability to manoeuvre and handle the weapons at its disposal. La Fayette was above all a soldier and he knew the recipe for *esprit de corps* that gradually separated the Garde Nationale from the rest of the population. The multiplication of oaths and flag blessings were part of the same logic.

Despite the districts' growing reluctance, the organisation adopted at the end of July undoubtedly responded to the situation and stabilised the situation in the capital. On 30 August, 1,500 citizens sought to carry a motion to Versailles calling on the royal couple to come and settle in Paris. However, no delegation made it to the château, as the gardes nationaux of the western Parisian districts promptly intervened and blocked the path of the protesters, whose leaders were arrested the next day. For good measure, La Fayette had the sentries at the city gates doubled and the bridge guards reinforced.

By proving itself capable of slowing down the revolutionary movement, the Garde became, throughout September, the target of orators and newspapers. It was accused, in particular, of forming an aristocracy of 30,000 men in arms within a disarmed population that was once again rumbling. Moreover, the flour arrived in Paris irregularly in insufficient quantities to reassure the masses who, consequently, blamed Mayor Bailly, the National Assembly and the court of Versailles. The Versailles municipality was aware that its Garde Nationale was too weak to protect the King and the National Assembly from a potential *coup de force* by the Parisian mob. Also, on 23 September, the municipality obtained the reinforcement of its military means by the arrival of 1,000 men of the Regiment d'Infanterie de Flandre. This displacement of troops excited the Parisians who were reminded of the events of July. On the evening of 1 October, the Gardes du Corps of Louis XVI offered a banquet to the officers of the Regiment d'Infanterie de Flandre. On this occasion, the tricolour cockades were torn from the headdresses, trampled on and replaced by black cockades in honour of Queen Marie-Antoinette, who was cheered. The event was known in Paris on 3 October, and, on the 4th, Paris was in an uproar.

Strengthening the Garde

On the morning of Monday the 5th, in the pouring rain, a gathering of women asking for bread took place on the Place de Grève, in front of the Hôtel de Ville. Between 11:00 a.m. and noon, the Place emptied, only to fill up again with the battalions of gardes nationaux urgently summoned

THE BEGINNINGS OF THE GARDE NATIONALE PARISIENNE

3e événement du 5 octobre 1789, coloured print by Janinet. The artist shows La Fayette leaving the Hôtel de Ville in the early evening of 5 October 1789. He is flanked by an aide-de-camp – perhaps Romeuf – and, presumably, by Paris Mayor Bailly. He is greeted by his troops. The flag of the Enfants Rouges district can also be spotted, although its design is somewhat approximate. (Yves Martin)

by most of the districts and soon mingled with new demonstrators, mainly men. At about 1:00 p.m., a crowd of 5,000 to 7,000 people, mostly women, set off for Versailles without any serious measures being taken to stop it. In fact, La Fayette was deliberating on the situation with Bailly. He eventually went to the Place de Grève where almost all the Parisian gardes nationaux were gathered. They were certainly divided on what to do. Half of them had decided to march on Versailles as well. Their motives differed, however: they wanted to force the King to endorse the decrees abolishing privileges and to accept the *Declaration des Droits de l'Homme et du Citoyen*, but also to distance himself from the influence of his court, which was considered harmful and pernicious. The other half – in particular the battalions of the Minimes, Blancs-Manteaux, Filles-Saint-Thomas, Saint-Roch and Capucins districts – were reluctant to follow the processions of demonstrators. In this tense atmosphere, La Fayette, who took the opportunity to remind the gardes of their oaths, held firm until 5:00 p.m. After displaying the Commune's order to march on Versailles, he then put himself at the head of his troops. It is likely that he believed that the Versailles authorities had done what was necessary to disperse the processions, which he expected to see flowing back into Paris. But as nothing happened, it became preferable to limit the now foreseeable disorder. Towards midnight, Versailles was in sight. La Fayette then had his troops stop and renew their oath 'To the Nation, the Law and the King', before going to the National Assembly and the Château to reassure both the deputies and King Louis XVI. He also had to take care of his men for the night, including setting up patrols. At dawn on 6 October, demonstrators climbed over the gates of the Château and broke into the royal couple's private apartments, but were evicted by the gardes nationaux who had arrived promptly. Taking the situation in hand, their general then encouraged Marie-Antoinette to appear on a balcony, with her children in her hands, to the cheering crowd. As for Louis XVI, he not only signed the pending decrees, but entrusted the security of the Château to La Fayette and let him know that he agreed to reside in Paris, at the Tuileries Palace. The deputies of the National Assembly declared that they too would place themselves under the protection of the Garde Nationale.

Had La Fayette hoped for this outcome? The debate continues to rage among historians. On the evening of 6 October, as the royal family's carriage made its way to Paris, the *Commandant General* certainly appeared to be the real and only beneficiary of the events. Indeed, the royal army and the behaviour of its officers were discredited among the patriots. As a counterpoint, the Garde Nationale Parisienne appeared to embody the fundamental interests of the Nation. Moreover, by forcing the King and Queen to settle in Paris, it apparently made all future counter-revolutionary ventures impossible. Finally, it seemed to be the only organised force capable of imposing its will on the rioters and, by the same token, of containing popular violence.

From 13 October, La Fayette set about strengthening his position and guarding against a new popular revolt. Thus, he received from Louis XVI the command of all the troops located in Paris and its surroundings. Then, skilfully arguing that service to the Tuileries and the National Assembly

THE BEGINNINGS OF THE GARDE NATIONALE PARISIENNE

required large numbers of troops, he managed to get the Commune to accept various projects, all of which led to a strengthening of his military resources. Six new paid companies were created and distributed in the districts so as to release a permanent reserve of grenadiers. In addition, the Guet de Paris and the former Garde de Paris were officially integrated into the Garde Nationale Parisienne. De Rulhière, their chief, had 600 infantrymen and 800 cavalrymen assigned to the surveillance of ports and quays. Besides, a unit of Chasseurs Nationaux Parisiens – better known as Chasseurs aux Barrières – and a unit of Gardes of the Hôtel de Ville were formed, putting an additional 900 men under the command of La Fayette. With some 100 staff officers and aides-de-camp at his disposal, he could now count on a permanent and homogeneous force of about 10,000 properly paid, well-equipped and accurately commanded men to maintain order in the Paris area. The staff of the Garde Nationale Parisienne could moreover rely on the politically moderate battalions of the unpaid garde. Two elite companies of grenadiers and chasseurs were created within the 60 battalions, which made it possible to attract the services of 6,000 young bourgeois. Suitably equipped and ready to undergo military training, they shared the political convictions of the general staff and could provide valuable reinforcement in case of popular riots. To make this series of measures even more effective, a regulation on discipline was issued for the very first time on 12 October. A military breviary taking up the essence of the 1776 regulation for the infantry of the royal army was simultaneously published to perfect the military instruction of the unpaid gardes nationaux.

In October 1789, La Fayette certainly had a solid instrument for maintaining order, but he still had to be able to use it lawfully. The events of the end of that month provided him with just such an opportunity. At around 10:00 a.m. on 21 October, Denis François, a 28-year-old baker, saw his shop in the Notre-Dame district invaded by a crowd. During a thorough search, 10 dozen fresh bread rolls were discovered. They were intended for the consumption of the Constituent Assembly, which, since the forced return of the King to Paris, had set up home not far from Notre-Dame Cathedral. In only a few minutes, François took on the appearance of a hoarder in the eyes of the crowd. While the subsistence crisis was in full swing and the famine was raging, he was the ideal scapegoat. As an ever more threatening crowd surrounded him, the baker asked to be questioned at his district office. The district officers had him taken to the Hôtel de Ville, but the crowd was furious and managed to seize François, only to bring him to the Place de Grève where he was hung from a lantern and then decapitated with a sword. According to a well-established ritual, the bloody head was then stuck on the end of a pike and carried into town by a few men. The Garde Nationale arrived on the scene too late and could not prevent anything.

Miniature portrait of a Garde Nationale Parisienne chasseur, circa 1789–1790. He is wearing the first uniform of the Garde: blue coat with red collar, white cuffs and green epaulettes. (Nathalie Lemoine-Bouchard)

THE GARDE NATIONALE 1789–1815

Printmaker Janinet depicts the lynching of baker Denis François (1761–1789), a victim of slanderous rumours in a context of food crisis. His gruesome murder led the deputies of the National Assembly to promulgate martial law. (Yves Martin)

THE BEGINNINGS OF THE GARDE NATIONALE PARISIENNE

A spontaneous isolated and therefore unforeseeable event which occurred in a context of famine, the murder of baker François highlighted the complete gap between the concerns of a people faced with hunger and those of deputies deeply shocked by the event. That very evening, the Constituent Assembly used it as a pretext to institute martial law, an authoritarian measure that had certainly already been in the making since the women's march on Versailles of 5 and 6 October. Symptomatically, Comte de Custine and Comte de Mirabeau had both proposed, between the 10 and 14 October, to introduce a law against gatherings. La Fayette, for his part, called for martial law on the grounds that, without it, 'the tranquillity of Paris could not be guaranteed'.[19] Such a measure aimed to specify the terms for the use of public force against street disorder. The municipal officers would first have to ask the crowd the cause of their meeting and their grievances. Then they were to display a red flag – signalling that gatherings, whether armed or unarmed, were criminal and could therefore be dispersed by force – and warn the population that the public force, after three prior summons, could open fire to disperse the troublemakers.

From then on, La Fayette was seen as the embodiment of a middle way desired by a large part of public opinion and as the protector of the new regime. In agreement with Bailly, he guaranteed the Constituent Assembly the possibility of deliberating freely. He also allowed Louis XVI to try an experiment in constitutional monarchy based on the devotion and loyalty of the Garde Nationale, combining the exaltation of the Nation with the traditional devotion to the person of the King. At the beginning of 1790, La Fayette had managed, despite some setbacks, to maintain a high level of popularity. The latter was undoubtedly enhanced, in the eyes of the supporters of order, by curbing the pamphleteers, who were now closely monitored, prevented from publishing – their works being destroyed – and deprived of the support of their sponsors. On 22 January, the most famous of them, Marat, protected by Danton and the gardes nationaux of the Cordeliers district, thus resisted the guardsmen of the Barnabites district who had come to apprehend him. He was nevertheless temporarily forced to leave France to take refuge across the Channel and several copies of his newspaper, *The Ami du Peuple*, were seized. In any case, La Fayette had set up a complex and

The Marquis de La Fayette at the height of his power in 1790. He is wearing the first uniform of the Garde Nationale Parisienne and watching a parade of gardes nationaux at the Champ de Mars. (Musée Carnavalet)

---

19   Charles-Elie de Ferrières Berville and François Barrière (eds), *Mémoires du Marquis de Ferrières, avec une notice sur sa vie, des notes et des explications historiques* (Paris: Baudouin Frères Imprimeurs-Libraires, 1822), p.342.

effective system of intelligence and intervention. Several newspapers – *Le Moniteur*, Brissot's *Le Patriote français* and Condorcet's *Chronique de Paris* – were sympathetic to him, while in the Assembly, individuals were paid to applaud each of his interventions. The Garde Nationale controlled the streets of Paris: it policed the populous city, guarded the gates and ensured the arrival of supplies. The correspondence between La Fayette and his subordinates, but also with the Parisian municipality, provides an insight into the daily reality of such missions. To achieve his aims, La Fayette made the centre companies omnipresent. In most districts, these were reinforced by elite companies of grenadiers or chasseurs, made up of young bourgeois who were devoted to him and supervised by battalion chiefs carefully selected. In addition, the *Commandant General* had a solid network of informers which enabled him to prevent or disperse popular movements before they got out of hand. Finally, his repeated resignations, which he always ended up reversing, appeared to be a way of perpetuating his position by bringing into play the sense of responsibility by battalion commanders who were mostly in favour of his cause. The resignation thus became a plebiscite invigorating his legitimacy.

Dealing with the Districts' Opposition

Opposition to La Fayette had not yet developed within the Garde Nationale Parisienne. It came mainly from the districts' civil authorities, at the same time jealous of maintaining their autonomy, worried about the centralising policy of the *Commandant General*, and wishing to limit spending on the Garde, which was deemed to be costly to the public finances. On 3 March 1790, the districts succeeded in having a new expansion of the corps of chasseurs rejected. In addition, the artillery remained the weak point of the Garde Nationale Parisienne, most of its pieces having been distributed within the battalions. However, even though it was provided for in the initial regulations, the formation of a real artillery corps always came up against the firm opposition of the districts. In order to spare them, Gouvion proposed, rather than 'concentrating all the artillery in one point', 'to establish a park in each division' and to make 'all the citizens compete in the guarding of these parks', while leaving each of the grenadier companies of the six divisions with two artillery pieces.[20] This artillery corps would be formed of two companies of paid gunners and, in each division, of a volunteer artillery company. Such a project however raised new objections on the part of the districts. According to them, not only would it involve an excessive expenditure, but would also be dangerous for public freedom, because the six parks thus created would be like 'six fortresses more fearsome than Bastilles'.[21] On 8 March, the districts finally got their way; the planned creation would be postponed indefinitely.

---

20   Lacroix, *Actes de la Commune de Paris*, vol.III, pp.322–323.
21   Maurice Genty, 'Les débuts de la Garde nationale parisienne', in Serge Bianchi and Roger Dupuy (eds), *La Garde nationale entre nation et peuple en armes: Mythes et réalités 1789-1871* (Rennes: Presses Universitaires de Rennes, 2006), p.162.

In the spring of 1790, La Fayette thus had at his disposal, for all artillery, only the 240 deserters of the Regiment de Toul-Artillerie serving the cannon confiscated from the Regiment d'Infanterie de Flandre in October 1789. On 27 June, in order to regularise the fate of the gunners, the Bureau de Ville nevertheless adopted a new provisional regulation, stipulating that 'each of the six companies of volunteer grenadiers' would continue to have two guns. On 13 March, the municipality refused this time to comply with La Fayette's request to establish 'a band for each division of the Garde Nationale Parisienne'.[22] In fact, the 45 musicians from the Gardes Françaises continued their service without being attached to a company. On the other hand, the districts supported with some enthusiasm the creation of a battalion of veterans, whose existence had been envisaged as early as 24 November 1789 by the Cordeliers district. Open to all citizens over 60, this unit was to be composed of 540 members, or nine per district. Supported by nearly three-quarters of the districts, the project was adopted on 29 March 1790 by the Assembly of Representatives, but on 10 April the National Assembly did not consider it necessary to address this point. The existence of this veterans' unit therefore remained deferred until September 1791.

Bernard Sarrette, portrait by miniaturist Jean-Baptiste Isabey. Following 14 July 1789, Sarrette (1765–1868), from Bordeaux, brought together 45 musicians from the Regiment des Gardes Françaises depot. In May 1790, the Parisian municipality took charge of this band, which now totalled 70 members. Among them were several musicians affected by the disorganization of Parisian musical life. They all took part in numerous civic and patriotic events. (Musée Carnavalet)

Stabilising the Garde

The Garde Nationale Parisienne was now more or less stabilised. However, on 21 May 1790, after several days of debate on the need to reform the administrative organisation of Paris, the law on the municipality of the city replaced the 60 districts inherited from the election of the Estates General by 48 sections with new topographical limits. However, the Garde Nationale retained its 60 battalions and their previous recruitment areas. The correspondence between the civilian and military frameworks thus ceased, a discrepancy that the Assembly was suspected of having favoured in order to break the harmony between them. The deputies apparently wished to dissociate the political and administrative instances from the militarised structures of the Garde Nationale in order to prevent armed citizens from deliberating on the political issues of the moment and ending up imposing their point of view through arms.

---

22   Lacroix, *Actes de la Commune de Paris*, vol.V, p.235.

THE GARDE NATIONALE 1789–1815

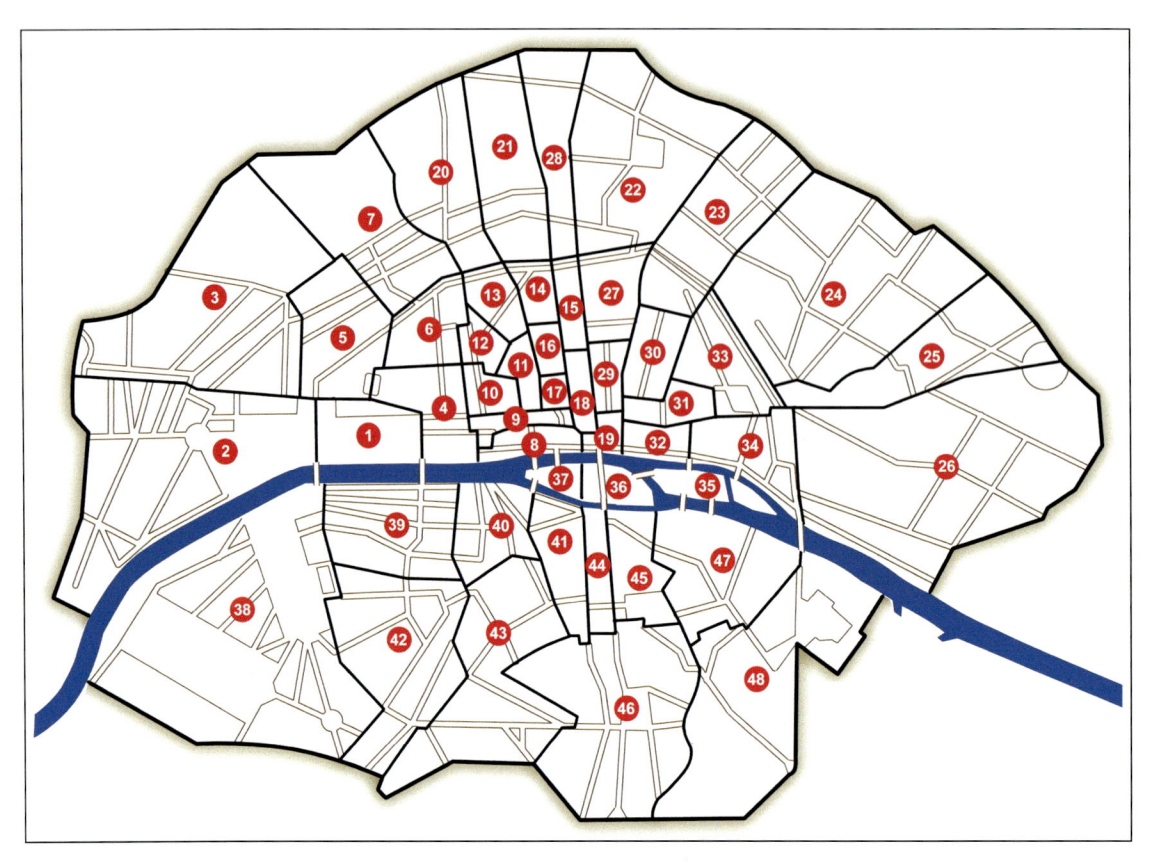

Map 3. The 48 Parisian sections, 1790.

Table 4. The 48 Parisian sections, 1790.
By a decree of 21 May 1790, the Constituent Assembly created 48 sections (meaning a territorial and administrative division) to replace the 60 districts. Each section was made up of a civil committee, a revolutionary committee and an armed force. These sections were often named in honour of martyrs (such as Marat and Lepeletier) or revolutionary principles (Unity, Fraternity).

Section Number	Original Name (1790)	Other Names (1792-1794)
1	Section des Tuileries	-
2	Section des Champs-Élysées	-
3	Section du Roule	Section de la République (October 1792)
4	Section du Palais-Royal	Section de la Butte-des-Moulins (August 1792) Section de la Montagne (July 1794)
5	Section de la Place Vendôme	Section des Piques
6	Section de la Bibliothèque	Section Quatre-Vingt-Douze (September 1792) Section Lepeletier (October 1793)
7	Section de la Grange-Batelière	Section de Mirabeau (August 1792) Section du Mont-Blanc (December 1792)
8	Section du Louvre	Section du Muséum (May 1792)
9	Section de l'Oratoire	Section des Gardes-Françaises (May 1792)
10	Section de la Halle-aux-Blés	-
11	Section des Postes	Section du Contrat-Social (August 1792)
12	Section de la Place Louis XIV	Section du Mail (December 1792) Section Guillaume-Tell (December 1793)

THE BEGINNINGS OF THE GARDE NATIONALE PARISIENNE

Section Number	Original Name (1790)	Other Names (1792-1794)
13	Section de la Fontaine-Montmorency	Section Molière et Lafontaine (October 1792) Section de Brutus (September 1793)
14	Section Bonne-Nouvelle	-
15	Section du Ponceau	Section des Amis-de-la-Patrie (September 1792)
16	Section de Mauconseil	Section de Bon-Conseil (August 1792)
17	Section du Marché-des-Innocents	Section des Halles (October 1792) Section des Marchés (May 1793)
18	Section des Lombards	-
19	Section des Arcis	-
20	Section du Faubourg-Montmartre	Section du Faubourg-Mont-Marat
21	Section de la rue Poissonnière	Section du Faubourg-Poissonnière
22	Section de Bondy	-
23	Section du Temple	-
24	Section de Popincourt	-
25	Section de la rue de Montreuil	Section de Montreuil
26	Section des Quinze-Vingts	-
27	Section des Gravilliers	-
28	Section du Faubourg-Saint-Denis	Section du Faubourg-du-Nord (January 1793)
29	Section de Beaubourg	Section de la Réunion (September 1792)
30	Section des Enfants-Rouges	Section du Marais (September 1792) Section de l'Homme-Armé (June 1795)
31	Section du Roi-de-Sicile	Section des Droits-de-l'Homme
32	Section de l'Hôtel-de-Ville	Section de la Maison-Commune (August 1792) Section de la Fidélité (July 1794)
33	Section de la Place-Royale	Section des Fédérés (August 1792) Section de l'Indivisibilité (July 1793)
34	Section de l'Arsenal	-
35	Section de l'Île-Saint-Louis	Section de la Fraternité (September 1792)
36	Section de Notre-Dame	Section de la Cité (August 1792)
37	Section Henri IV	Section du Pont-Neuf (August 1792) Section Révolutionnaire (September 1793) Section du Pont-Neuf (December 1794)
38	Section des Invalides	-
39	Section de la Fontaine-de-Grenelle	-
40	Section des Quatre-Nations	Section de l'Unité (April 1793)
41	Section du Théâtre-Français	Section de Marseille (August 1792) Section de Marseille et Marat (August 1793) Section de Marat (February 1794) Section du Théâtre-Français (February 1795)
42	Section de la Croix-Rouge	Section du Bonnet-Rouge (October 1793) Section de l'Ouest (May 1794)
43	Section du Luxembourg	Section Mutius-Scaevola (October 1793) Section du Luxembourg (May 1795)
44	Section des Thermes-de-Julien	Section de Beaurepaire (September 1792) Section de Chalier (February 1794) Section des Thermes-de-Julien (February 1795)
45	Section de Sainte-Geneviève	Section du Panthéon-Français (August 1792)
46	Section de l'Observatoire	-
47	Section du Jardin-des-Plantes	Section des Sans-Culottes (August 1792) Section du Jardin-des-Plantes (July 1794)
48	Section des Gobelins	Section du Finistère (August 1792)

THE GARDE NATIONALE 1789–1815

Philippe Mathé-Curtz, also known as Curtius, physiognotrace portrait by Gilles-Louis Chrétien, 1790. Curtius was a German artist who kept for many years cabinets of wax figures under the galleries of the Palais-Royal. On 13 July 1789, he joined the Milice Citoyenne and was elected *capitaine* of the Pères de Nazareth district. In the Spring 1790, his portrait was drawn by Jean-Baptiste Fouquet using Gilles-Louis Chrétien's physiognotrace machine. (Musée Carnavalet)

It seems undeniable that in the late spring of 1790 there was a strong desire on the part of the political elites to protect themselves from the disadvantages of direct, permanent and armed democracy. The proliferation of clubs must be understood in this context: it was a way of preserving the political decisions and the modalities of their local applications to the elites in place, while ensuring the widest possible support from the public. In early June, a month before the Festival of the Federation was to take place in Paris, some suspicious deputies insisted that the Garde Nationale – which existed in fact more than in law – be organised and that its strength be carefully limited. The decree of 12 June introduced to their specification a censal recruitment system for the Garde. From 1 July onwards, the ranks of the Garde would only be open to active citizens or sons of active citizens aged between 18 and 60 who could pay a contribution representing three days' work. Moreover, no man could claim to bear arms unless he was first entered in the register created for this purpose. Such a decision implied the exclusion of men of modest means, including those of good reputation and those who volunteered to serve. The same decree definitively dissolved all military formations, corporate Milices and shooting societies inherited from the Ancien Regime.

In this context, the case of the 'Victors of the Bastille' raises questions. These 954 individuals, nearly 70 percent of whom were craftsmen or shopkeepers working in the faubourg Saint-Antoine, had formed an association shortly after the capture of the fortress. On 8 June 1790, Bailly asked La Fayette to intervene on their behalf at the Assembly. 'They deserve honour and money', he wrote.[23] It was also necessary to care to give them an 'honourable place'

---

23 Etienne Charavay, *Le général La Fayette 1757–1834: Notice biographique* (Genève: Slatkine-Megariotis Reprints, 1977), p.569.

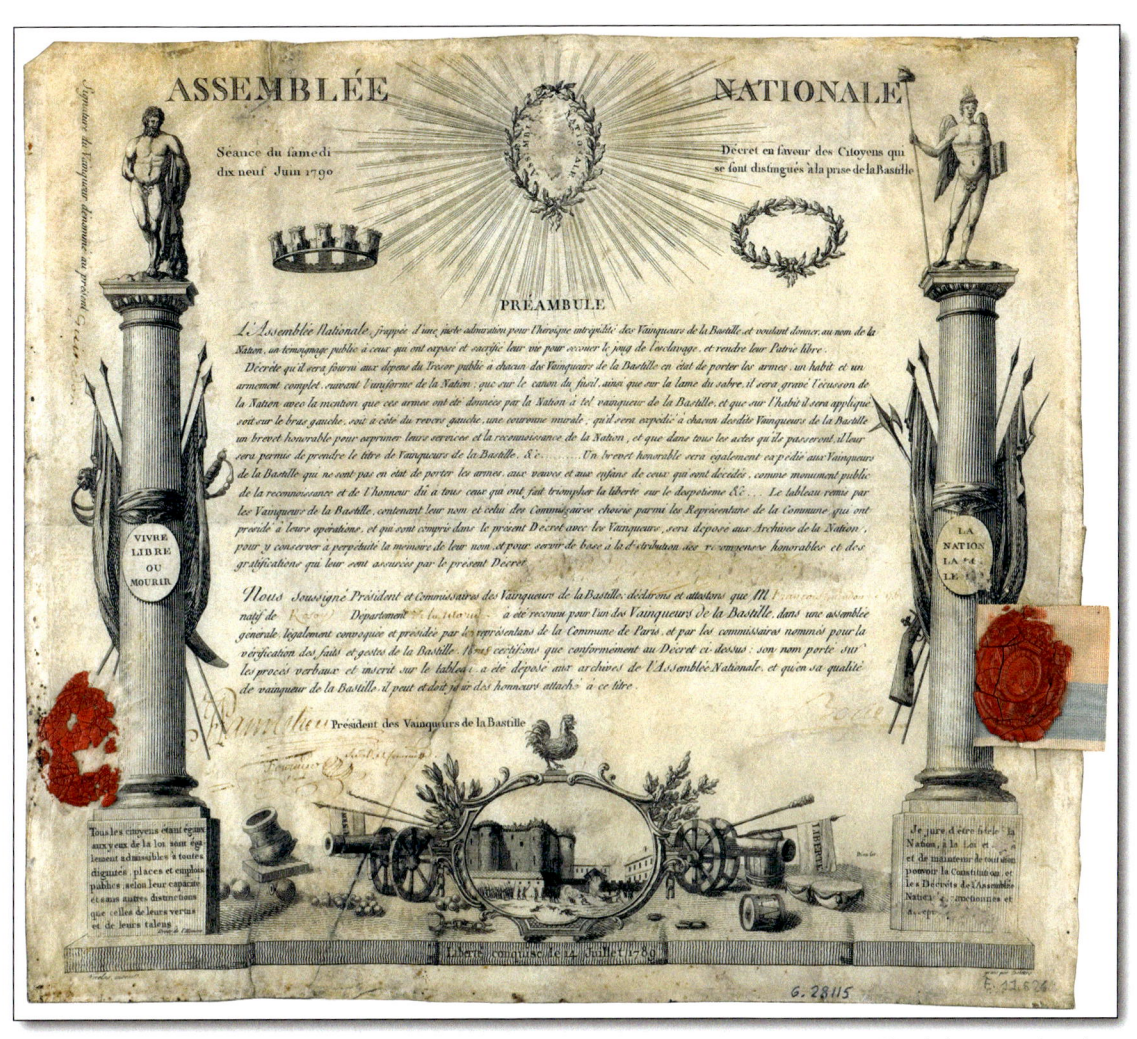

THE BEGINNINGS OF THE GARDE NATIONALE PARISIENNE

during the Festival of the Federation.[24] On 19 June, on the proposal of the deputy Camus, the Assembly granted them various rewards:

> It will be provided, at the expense of the Public Treasury, to each of the Victors of the Bastille in a state of being able to bear arms, a complete *habit* [clothing] and a set of weapons. On the barrel of the musket as well as on the blade of the sabre, the escutcheon [emblem] of the Nation will be engraved with the mention that these weapons were given by the Nation to such Victor of the Bastille. On the habit, it will be applied, either on the left arm, or beside the left lapel, a mural crown emblem. An honourable brevet will be sent to each of these Victors of the Bastille to express their service and the gratitude of the Nation.[25]

This diploma is attributed to François Guindon, born in 1760 in Rosoy, in the Marne. It is signed by the president of the 'Victors of the Bastille', Jean-Armand Pannetier, a grocer located on rue du faubourg Saint-Antoine and by two secretaries, Boris and Fournier. It is decorated on the right with the tricolour satin ribbon of the Victors and their red wax seal. (Musée Carnavalet)

---

24 Charavay, *Le général La Fayette*, p.569.
25 Charavay, *Le général La Fayette*, p.569.

61

The Victors were also given a prominent spot among the Garde Nationale in the forthcoming Federation. Nevertheless, the resentment against them ran high: both the decoration and the location caused difficulties. The Victors promptly renounced them – a fact that was acknowledged in a decree of 25 June – but they retained the habit, the full armament and the possibility of being issued a diploma. The reluctant manner in which the Victors of the Bastille were honoured showed the hesitations and concerns of the deputies. It would have been imprudent to give these men a place of honour at the Festival of the Federation, and this was avoided. It would have been better to give them a glittering diploma and a few awards.

The creation of the Garde Nationale led by the Marquis de La Fayette was the founding act of the Revolution in Paris. 'For a vast majority of Parisians, the first act of citizenship was going to a local meeting place and joining a citizen patrol, and their first electoral act was choosing Garde Nationale officers', Dale L. Clifford wrote.[26] In the early summer of 1790, as the Festival of the Federation loomed, La Fayette still appeared to be the undisputed commander of the Garde Nationale Parisienne, born in the turmoil of the events of July 1789 to regularise an insurrectionary situation. The confused conditions surrounding its creation led to uncertainty and a slow stabilisation. But what was the situation in the French provinces? Did the Garde Nationale phenomenon have the same extent of support as in the largest city of the kingdom?

Uniforms and Equipment

The Parisian Milice of 13 and 14 July was devoid of any uniform, apart from the cockades hastily adopted in some districts. On the 17th, the guard of honour which lined the main streets of the capital to welcome King Louis XVI to Paris included Gardes Françaises but also a large number of ordinary Parisians wearing the cockade. La Fayette was aware that enforcing order on his Milice was the first step in restoring calm in Paris. He understood the role that uniforms could have in this process.[27] From the outset, the Garde Nationale Parisienne was eager to mark its identity and to give itself signs of recognition. It was intended that its very first uniform should be red, following the example of the city's arquebusiers at the end of the *Ancien Régime*. Although textual sources confirm this, iconography is lacking.

Defining a Uniform
From 20 to 31 July, a Military Committee charged with devising regulations for the new armed force met daily at La Fayette's home. On the 25th, La Fayette proposed to divide the Committee into six *bureaux* in order to speed up the work. The conclusions of the 4th *Bureau* – specifically responsible for

---

26 Dale L. Clifford, 'Can the Uniform Make the Citizen? Paris, 1789–1791', *Eighteenth-Century Studies*, 34 (2001), p.378.
27 Clifford, 'Can the Uniform Make the Citizen?', p.369.

THE BEGINNINGS OF THE GARDE NATIONALE PARISIENNE

the clothing and equipment of the troops – were discussed on the evening of 27 July. The minutes reveal that

> it was agreed that the coat would be blue, with a scarlet collar. Lapels, cuffs and lining would be white with scarlet piping, the waistcoat and breeches white, the buttons gold. The same uniform for the cavalry, with the exception of the buttons and the aiguillette, which would be in white. As for the cockade, white being the national colour, it is proposed to make it of broad basin ribbon, edged in blue and red, to indicate the colours of the town.[28]

Four days later, such a regulation was published. It stated that the Parisian Garde Nationale would be composed of 6,000 paid gardes – whose uniforms would be provided at the expense of the city of Paris – and 24,000 volunteer gardes, who were expected to acquire their own uniforms. On 2 August, 120 copies were distributed to the Assembly of the Representatives of Paris, which ordered its execution on the 8th. However, on 3 August, the fourth issue of the newspaper *Les Révolutions de Paris* noted that 'we saw today the uniforms of the Garde Nationale: blue coat, red collar, white lapels, cuffs and lining'.[29] In addition to the regulations, the descriptions included in various almanacks, as well as an abundance of high-quality iconography – such as portraits, engravings by Nicolas Hoffmann and even recruitment posters – provide a very clear vision of this first 'official' uniform of the Garde Nationale Parisienne.

Headgear

The gardes wore a hat trimmed with black silk braid. The cockade was held in place by a black loop and a small uniform button. A pompom indicated the division to which each garde belonged, according to a strictly defined colour scheme: blue for the 1st Division, red for the 2nd, white for the 3rd, blue and red for the 4th, blue, white and red for the 5th and blue and white for the 6th. The bonnet de police was to be made of blue cloth. The headband would be of scarlet cloth, the front decorated with a white cloth plate on which a scarlet nave would be sewn. The hair was styled into a single curl which descended to the middle of the ear.

The Gardes' Uniform

The 'blue coat' was certainly the main feature of the Garde Nationale's uniform. In the early weeks of the Revolution, there had been calls for Garde Nationale volunteers to wear minimal uniforms, perhaps a cockade and a belt, so that as many Parisians as possible could serve. This approach made sense in times of crisis, but it was neither safe nor practical from a command perspective. La Fayette unambiguously wanted a regular Milice.

What did a full Garde Nationale uniform cost? Historians have frequently put forward the figure of four *louis*, or 48 *livres*, or a month's wages for a

---

28 Bernard Coppens, 'Garde nationale de Paris, 1789', <https://www.1789-1815.com/arfr7_gnat01.htm>, accessed 11 Sept. 2022.
29 *Les Révolutions de Paris*, 4 (1789), p.102.

THE GARDE NATIONALE 1789–1815

In 1789, the Garde Nationale was conceived as a Milice Bourgeoise created to defend property and to ensure social order. This bourgeois pride can be perceived in the portraits of guardsmen painted at the beginning of the Revolution. One such example is citizen Nau-Deville's portrait, painted in 1790 by Jean-François Berlier. Nau-Deville is depicted as a self-confident man, proud of the role he plays in a socially conservative organisation. (Musée Carnavalet)

M. Estellé, marchand de galons rue Saint-Honoré, en uniforme de capitaine des chasseurs de la garde nationale, 1790. Estellé is shown in his cluttered shop with objects related to both his professional and private life. Furthermore, he proudly displays his dual status as both a merchant and an officer of the citizen's armed force. His profession as a braid maker led him to provide his fellow officers with the marks of their rank. (Musée Carnavalet)

labourer. In reality, this is only an average, with surviving invoices indicating a cost of between 31 and 97 *livres*. The latter was relatively high and would have de facto led to the exclusion of low-income citizens. As early as 1789, a few pamphleteers and publicists had expressed their concern. The following year, Prudhomme, director of the newspaper *Les Révolutions de Paris*, wrote: 'If there are no longer liveries, the national colours seem to take their place. By this arrangement, it happens that social distinctions, whose number one seeks to decrease, in fact increase. The people, who made the revolution without being in uniform, murmur in vain about this daily violation of the rights of Man and Citizen'.[30] In truth, many of the volunteer gardes nationaux saw the uniform as one of the new marks of equality and not as a sign of inequality. The 'national habit' was seen as a symbol of civic virtue and an object of personal pride.

A man of modest means had several ways of appearing on duty in uniform without spending the famed sum of 48 *livres*. Second-hand dealers organised a lucrative trade centred on the sale of used uniform parts. Pawnbrokers also accepted and sold uniforms, often from young, cash-strapped guardsmen. Some gardes nationaux deplored the fact that it was possible to buy a uniform from a second-hand shop for 30 *livres* or less. As each garde was only called to

---

30   *Les Révolutions de Paris*, 67 (1790), p.83.

THE BEGINNINGS OF THE GARDE NATIONALE PARISIENNE

From the outset, portraits made with the physiognotrace machine were conceived as objects of professional promotion. The elites jockeyed to be among the first to be given the opportunity to get their physiognotrace. The officers of the Garde Nationale were no exception. From left to right and top to bottom: Mr De Lormes, probably a *sergent* (Musée Carnavalet), an anonymous officer (Author's collection), Mr Sonnelot (Musée Carnavalet) and Mr Domaranzac, a Paris Garde Nationale officer (Musée Carnavalet).

duty once every two or four weeks, it was possible to share a uniform. By the end of the summer of 1789, the poorer districts of Paris were calling for help in equipping potential volunteers. The financial help of the municipality did not materialise, so the districts ended up taking matters into their own hands. No fewer than seven districts provided uniforms for their gardes nationaux on a fairly large scale. The funds came from donations. Loans of uniforms were also arranged. Among the archives of the Sorbonne district are the receipts that the gardes signed on receiving their uniforms. They undertook to acquire their hats and gaiters and to return their uniforms to their battalion if they were to move to another district. Next to each signature was that of a co-signer who acknowledged that his fellow citizen was trustworthy. Other documents mentioned the loan of a uniform for 48 *livres*, on condition that the citizen-soldier paid the sum of six *livres* for eight consecutive months. Finally, some gardes borrowed money to buy only part of their uniform.[31]

Clad over a white cloth waistcoat fastened with 12 polished copper buttons, the 'blue coat' was cut from medium-fine Louviers or Sedan royal blue cloth. The collar was scarlet, the lapels and cuffs, white with red piping. Fitted with blue shoulder tabs piped in red, the coat was fastened with yellow buttons decorated with the city's coat of arms (a nave). They were also stamped with the number of the division on the upper part and the number of the battalion on the lower part. Iron grey capotes were distributed to the gardes required as sentries.

Breeches were made of white cloth. Gardes were issued two pairs of black gaiters for winter service and two pairs of white linen gaiters for summer service, with small plain copper buttons. According to the newspaper *Le Magasin des Modes* of 1 October 1789, the gardes wore buckle-less shoes when wearing gaiters. In the opposite case, they used white cotton stockings and square copper buckles with slightly rounded outer corners.

Weapons

The first armament of the Parisian Milice Bourgeoise was undoubtedly a heterogeneous collection of all the firearms and weapons that could be assembled. The royal collections of the Garde-Meuble were even put to use. Most of them were collectors' items, judging by the strange appearance of the first parades, with an armament made up of pertuisanes, halberds and spontoons brandished by city dwellers in civilian clothes. This armament probably remained in use for several weeks, at least until regular supplies arrived. In addition, soldiers from the Gardes Françaises and line infantry regiments probably kept their weapons. On 23 August, the Commune's Assembly of Representatives decreed that equipment and weapons would henceforth be provided and paid for by the municipality, in an understandable concern for uniformity. A musket with iron fittings and a red leather sling constituted from then on the gardes nationaux' main armament. On 8 September 1789, a convoy carrying 7,168 muskets intended for the Paris and Versailles Gardes Nationales left the Maubeuge weapons factory and headed for Compiègne.[32] Similar deliveries appear to have taken place again later in the month. Chasseurs, for their part, were armed with an additional brace of pistols.

As for the sabre, it was theoretically the so-called *sabre de mineur* with a blackened leather handle and a 'Montmorency' blade. If it remains complex to determine precisely when and in what proportions such sabres were really carried, there were numerous variants whose *gardes à coquille* highlighted revolutionary attributes representing the nave of Paris, the union of the three

---

31 Bibliothèque Nationale de France (BNF): NAF 2696, f.199-217.
32 Alexandre Tuetey, *Répertoire général des sources manuscrites de l'histoire de Paris pendant la Révolution française* (Paris: Imprimerie Nouvelle, 1890), vol.I, p.391.

THE BEGINNINGS OF THE GARDE NATIONALE PARISIENNE

In 1789, the 'Petit Montmorency' sabre experienced an amazing proliferation. A non-regulation sabre, it was intended to equip the troops that were developing outside the line army. The brass hilt is in this case decorated with the 'three-order' design. (Collection and photo Fabien Pacaud)

orders, fasces, or liberty caps. At the beginning of the Revolution, La Fayette was an eminently popular figure. This undeniable popularity led to the production of thousands of swords with his effigy in profile – his bust cut off at the shoulders, in the garb of commander-in-chief of the Garde Nationale Parisienne. As there were no variations, it was more or less an official model. Among all the soldiers and politicians of the French Revolution, La Fayette was the only one to see his effigy featured on the 'petits Montmorency' sabres. The weapon was suspended from a bleached buff leather belt. Embellished with an oval copper plate stamped with the city's arms, the giberne, which must have been 33 inches off the ground when on the garde's body, was supported by a *banderole* also made of bleached buff leather.

Drummers

Drummers' uniforms were distinguished by a tricolour braid bordering the collar, cuffs and lapels. Their drum cases were made of wood, in imitation of the Gardes Françaises, the only regiment to have kept such, whereas all the infantry had adopted copper drum cases following the royal order of 25 April 1767. They also allowed decoration with motifs and allegories, which perfectly suited the state of mind of the early days of the Revolution.

Grenadier and Chasseur Companies

Although texts ensured that 'the grenadier and chasseur companies will not have any post of honour assigned exclusively to them, in order to preserve the spirit of equality and fraternity which must animate citizen troops,'[33] grenadiers and chasseurs nevertheless constantly sought to mark their difference, which was achieved through a whole series of uniform features. Grenadiers wore a bearskin cap with a plume similar in colour to that of the fusiliers' pompoms and, above all, a copper plate. This was described as follows by artillery officer Vieilh de Varennes:

> It shows the arms of France and those of the city of Paris, in the middle of which is a bundle in saltire, consisting of a sabre surmounted by the cap of liberty, above which is a motto: 'Vaincre ou Mourir'. On the left is a hand of justice and on the right a sceptre, all bound with laurel branches. Underneath are barrels of gunpowder, grenades and scattered cannonballs.[34]

---

33   Lacroix, *Actes de la Commune de Paris*, vol. VII, p.103.
34   Raymond Augustin Vieilh de Varennes, *Description curieuse et intéressante des soixante drapeaux que l'amour patriotique a offerts aux soixante districts de la ville et des faubourgs*

THE GARDE NATIONALE 1789–1815

Top: A chasseur of the Garde Nationale Parisienne wearing a helmet, by Nicolas Hoffmann. He is armed with a brace of pistols held in a sash. (Anne S.K. Brown Military Collection)

Bottom: Chasseur des barrières de Paris, anonymous artist, 1790. This is one of the few images of this little-known unit. It almost perfectly matches uniform information given in officer Vieilh de Varennes' book. However, this chasseur is bearing a tricolour pompom, instead of a green one. He wears a giberne in the style of a *carchera*, on a belt, over the stomach. (Anne S.K. Brown Military Collection)

Furthermore, grenadiers had narrow red woollen epaulettes, a sign of their status. As for the chasseurs, they wore either a hat or a helmet. In fact, a deliberation of 29 March 1790 confirmed that chasseurs were authorised to wear such headgear, 'provided that each company had the same uniform'.[35] In addition, the chasseurs wore green woollen epaulettes and blue breeches with Hungarian knots, following a similar logic to the grenadiers.

Chasseurs Nationaux Parisiens

The creation of a corps of Chasseurs Nationaux Parisiens (also known as Chasseurs aux Barrières) with six companies, assigned to guard tax collection entry points, was envisaged as early as mid-September 1789. Several districts protested until the end of November, but the companies were nevertheless organised. Two new companies, intended to guard the Halle au blé and to escort grain convoys, were subsequently instituted. These men wore hats topped with green tufts. They had a royal blue coat, the turnbacks of which were adorned with hunting horns and green cloth naves. The gilded brass buttons were embossed with the city's coat of arms and displayed the company number. The pantaloons were decorated with two red Hungarian knots and a woollen braid of the same colour along the outer seam. The chasseurs aux barrières wore brodequins with a red cord and tassel. Their weaponry consisted of a musket, a pair of pistols worn on the belt and a

---

de Paris, précédée de l'état-major général de la garde nationale parisienne (Paris: Sorin, 1790), p.13.
35 Lacroix, *Actes de la Commune de Paris*, vol.VII, p.103.

dragoon sword fitted with a green sword knot. The cartridge pouch was worn on a belt over the stomach.

Veterans

On 23 December 1789, the *Journal Général de la Cour et de la Ville* hinted that the Paris Garde Nationale Veterans 'would be dressed according to the costume of the ancient Gauls'.[36] In fact, their uniform was not seriously discussed until the spring of 1790. Some members of the unit 'wished it to conform exactly' to that of the other gardes nationaux of the capital.[37] At the meeting of 20 April, it was decided that it would be similar, at least in outline. The coat would nevertheless differ from it by 'its breadth'. It would also be 'buttoned from the collar to the waist' and without lapels, referred to as 'Bavaroises' in the minutes of the meeting. As for the button, it would be 'with the city's coat of arms and without number'. In addition, the Veterans were differentiated by the use of a large batiste sash with white fringes. 'Some members wished it to be worn as a saltire. But it was decided, by a large majority, that it would be worn as a belt'.[38] The headdress identified the unit at first glance. It was a Henry IV-style hat, embellished with a white plume and 'a cockade in the colours of the nation'. A white *bourdalou*, edged in scarlet, bore the words 'Pour la Loi et le Roi' ('For the Law and the King') embroidered in scarlet wool. The armament was plethoric. Also called a pertuisane in contemporary texts, a pike 'seven feet long with its spearhead' replaced the musket.[39] In addition to this polearm, there were a sabre and a pair of pistols. Charles Thevenin's *Fête de la Federation* appears to be the only contemporary representation of this uniform.

Cavalry

The creation of a Parisian Garde Nationale cavalry was studied as early as July 1789, before it was effectively set up, without any particular difficulty, in late September. Called the 'division de cavalerie nationale parisienne', it initially comprised six paid companies before two new paid companies were added in mid-October. The unit was commanded by Chevalier Rulhière and numbered 800 men, 100 per company.[40]

In late July 1789, the cavalrymen's uniform was planned to be similar to that of the infantrymen, 'except for the buttons and the aiguillette which would be white'.[41] It turned out that the cavalrymen wore a distinctive yellow woollen aiguillette on their left shoulder. Their hats were adorned with a pompom whose colours matched those of the six infantry divisions. In the early winter of 1789, the colour of the 7th and 8th companies' pompoms had not yet been determined. The horsemen had buff-coloured gloves and wore

---

36 *Journal Général de la Cour et de la Ville*, 96 (1789).
37 Lacroix, *Actes de la Commune de Paris*, vol.IV, p.540.
38 Lacroix, *Actes de la Commune de Paris*, vol.IV, p.540.
39 Lacroix, *Actes de la Commune de Paris*, vol.IV, p.541.
40 Augustin-Julien Alletz and Bretelle, *Etrennes Aux Parisiens Patriotes, Ou Almanach Militaire National De Paris* (Paris: Guffier Jeune Libraire, 1790), p.16.
41 Bernard Coppens, 'Garde nationale de Paris, 1789', <https://www.1789-1815.com/arfr7_gnat01.htm>, accessed 11 September 2022.

riding boots. Strong boots might be used for night duty. The sword was fitted with a leather sword knot. The saddle cover and holster-covers were made of scarlet cloth with yellow braiding.

Officers and NCOs

When on duty, the officers wore a gilded copper gorget with a silver plate representing the city's coat of arms crowned with the liberty cap. Ranks were distinguished by epaulettes and the sword knot. However, on 12 August 1789, the proposal to abandon epaulettes was submitted in the Filles-Saint-Thomas district 'to maintain the most perfect equality between the citizens composing the Garde Nationale'. The officers of the unpaid companies were to wear 'epaulettes and other insignias only when they fulfilled their duties'.[42] On 2 September 1789, the Military Committee took up the issue. It affirmed 'that one could not assimilate the officers with the soldiers, as for the insignia of rank' and the epaulette affair was closed.[43] Officers carried a gilt-copper hilted sword. *Sergents* were armed with officer's muskets.

La Fayette's Uniform

The importance of La Fayette's figure can be gauged from the plethora of iconographic works devoted to him: no fewer than 160 representations are listed for the 1789–1791 time span. Portraitists were quick to seize on his image. In the spring of 1790, his portrait was commissioned by Thomas Jefferson to be included in a gallery representing the heroes of American history. Joseph Boze, who was in charge of this project, did not have the opportunity to pose La Fayette and reproduced the expression of the bust created by Houdon. Jean-Jacques Hauer portrayed him, together with his wife Adrienne, in charge of the organisation of the Festival of the Federation. Shortly after 14 July 1790, the King's painter, Jean-Baptiste Weyler, fixed his features at the express request of the gardes nationaux fédérés. The painting was completed in October 1790 and exhibited at the Paris Salon the following year. Moreover, the revolutionary events were a real boon for the producers of quality prints. Mainly composed of nobles and bourgeois conscious of living through a period of exceptional upheaval, their clientele was keen on prints depicting the great days of the Revolution and their main protagonists. Although these productions are of uneven quality, those of Levachez, Debucourt and Fiesinger stand out for their informative value. In the latter case, the engraver had enlisted the services of gifted miniaturist Jean-Urbain Guérin. Guérin, who had been commissioned to paint the portraits of the members of the Constituent Assembly, managed to obtain two 10-minute poses from La Fayette, on 28 June and 3 July 1790 respectively. Such an arrangement offered a serious guarantee of resemblance to the engraved portrait. Of inferior artistic quality, the works of Nicolas Hoffmann should not be dismissed in view of the uniform details they contain. A native of Hesse, Hoffmann was a true documentalist and produced a number of high-quality

---

42 Maurice Genty, 'Controverses autour de la Garde Nationale parisienne', *Annales Historiques de la Révolution Française*, 291 (1993), p.74.
43 Genty, 'Controverses', p.75.

THE BEGINNINGS OF THE GARDE NATIONALE PARISIENNE

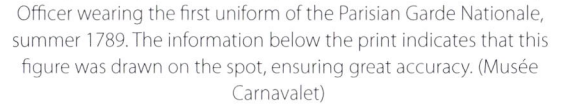

Officer wearing the first uniform of the Parisian Garde Nationale, summer 1789. The information below the print indicates that this figure was drawn on the spot, ensuring great accuracy. (Musée Carnavalet)

This watercolour by Lucien Rousselot perfectly replicates a period painting. *Capitaine* d'Audiffret is dressed in the first uniform of the Garde Nationale Parisienne. Note the unusual sabre attachment. (Anne S.K. Brown Military Collection)

military prints. Finally, the Marquis himself rushed to have his portrait taken by the physiognotracist Edmé Quenedey. Immediately recognisable in his uniform, La Fayette probably conceived of his engraved portrait as an object of professional promotion. 'The clients who came before the physiognotrace often used it as a visiting card', notes French historian Guillaume Mazeau.[44] Some of them had their current or past profession engraved next to their name. La Fayette was hardly an exception and his physiognotrace indicated his function as '*Commandant General de la Garde Nationale Parisienne*'.[45] This small portrait was considered 'very resembling' by an editor of the *Journal de Paris* on 21 August 1789.[46] It could be purchased for 18 *sous* from the author, 10, rue Croix des Petits-Champs. Numerous colour and black-and-white prints were made afterwards.

Contemporary iconography inevitably shows La Fayette wearing a powdered queue. In reality, the Marquis was strictly applying the

---

44 Guillaume Mazeau, 'Portraits de peu: Le physionotrace au début du XIXe siècle', *Revue d'Histoire du XIXe siècle*, 45 (2012), p.43.
45 Author's collection: Physionotrace du marquis de La Fayette, Commandant General de la Garde Nationale Parisienne.
46 *Journal de Paris*, 233 (1789), p.1053.

THE GARDE NATIONALE 1789–1815

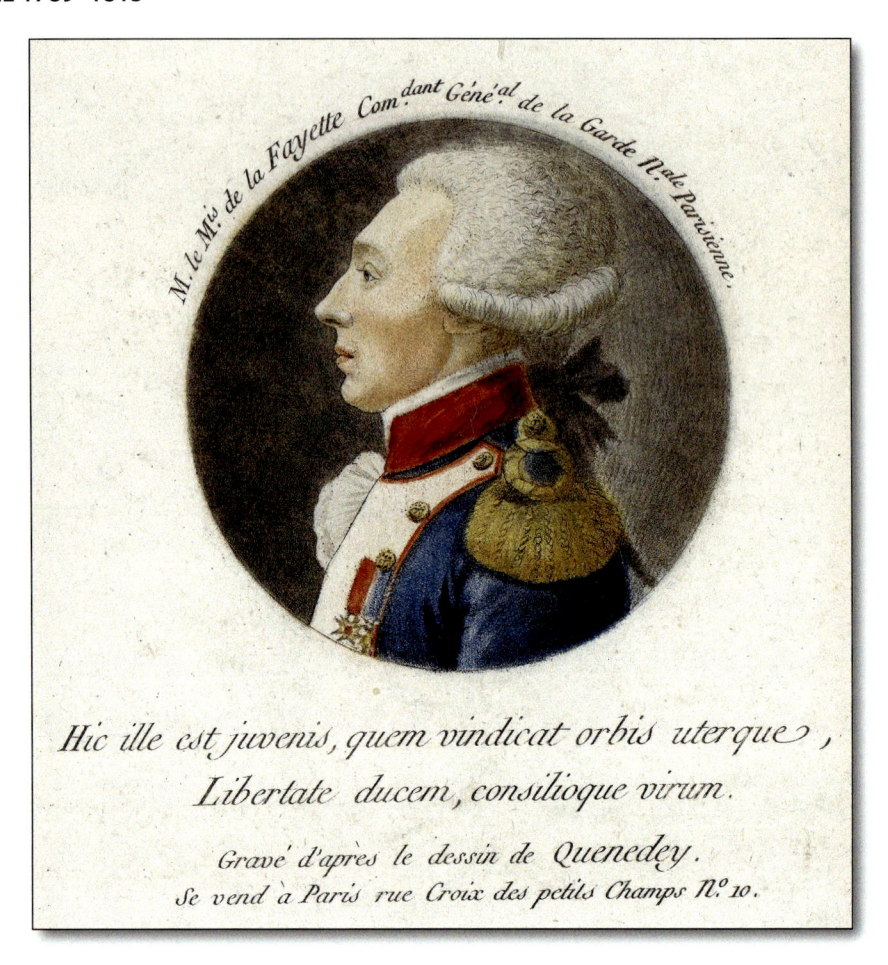

The Marquis de La Fayette, Commandant General de la Garde Nationale Parisienne, physiognotrace portrait by Edmé Quenedey, August 1789. (Musée Carnavalet)

Règlement pour la formation, organisation, solde, police et administration de la Garde Nationale Parisienne. All members of the Garde Nationale Parisienne staff wore hats and La Fayette made no exception. Thus, only a plume indicated his functions as commander-in-chief. The regulations of 31 July 1789 stipulated that 'the commander-in-chief shall wear a white feather topped by the colours red and blue'. However, both Debucourt and Hoffmann showed a white plume, whereas Hauer painted it entirely blue. In his painting of La Fayette's oath, David depicts a bicoloured model: the upper third scarlet, the lower two-thirds white. No doubt these different arrangements were successively the norm, although it is impossible to date them precisely. Like his subordinates, La Fayette wore large cockades held in place by a black loop.

La Fayette donned the Garde Nationale coat for the very first time on Sunday 9 August 1789, during a mass in the church of Saint-Nicolas-des-Champs. Made of royal blue cloth, it was undoubtedly of excellent quality. The buttons were cast in gilded copper and bore 'the arms of the city, without number'. Reproduced in Louis Fallou's *Le bouton uniforme français*, this pattern is supported by an anonymous engraving taken from Quenedey's physiognotrace. Lesueur drew a curious coat with stapled lapels and scarlet cuffs, a common arrangement on other gouaches in his series.

THE BEGINNINGS OF THE GARDE NATIONALE PARISIENNE

'Huge epaulettes, like those worn by the Americans, distinguished La Fayette from the rest of the French army', said François-Félix France d'Hézecques, then a young page at Louis XVI's court.[47] In fact, the Commander-in-Chief's epaulettes were a reminder of his American experience. Popular with the general officers of the Continental Army, this model appears in a portrait of young La Fayette by Charles Wilson Peale. Later, Quenedey and Hoffmann perfectly reproduced its massive aspect. Hauer showed a very different pattern, albeit in accordance with the above-mentioned regulations. Featuring a narrow strap, these epaulettes were to be 'lined with scarlet cloth'.[48] Hoffmann and Hauer are the only artists to show La Fayette wearing a gorget. In view of the seriousness of the former and the status of the latter as a Garde Nationale officer, such an arrangement cannot be discredited.

La Fayette commonly wore the Cross of Saint-Louis, awarded by Louis XVI for his service in America. An engraved portrait by Levachez and an oil on canvas by Joseph Boze show him decorated with the 'Bastille lozenge'. Hanging from a tricolour ribbon, this decoration was awarded to NCOs and soldiers of the Gardes-Françaises who took part in the siege of the Bastille, as well as to some officers of the Garde Nationale Parisienne. It bore in its centre a verse by the Latin poet Lucan – 'Ignorant que datos, ne quisquam serviat, enses' (Do they ignore that weapons were given against servitude?) –, chosen by La Fayette himself. Finally, as a veteran of the American War of Independence, the Commander-in-Chief was a member of the Order of Cincinnatus, the insignia of which was designed by *Major* Pierre Charles L'Enfant. The jewel consisted of a bald eagle with a blue medallion in the centre, showing Cincinnatus at his plough. The Society of the Cincinnati had a French offshoot that brought together officers who had fought for the independence of the United States of America, which Louis XVI recognised as belonging to the first foreign order. Therefore, the decoration was to be worn after the Cross of Saint-Louis, a provision that La Fayette complied with.

---

47 François-Félix France d'Hézecques, *Souvenirs d'un page de la cour de Louis XVI* (Paris: Librairie Académique Didier et Cie Libraires-Editeurs, 1873), p.328.
48 Anon., *Règlement pour la formation*, p.14.

3

The Provinces Followed: Local Gardes Nationales

1789–1790

'Municipal Revolution' and the Milices' Arming

In the provinces, the announcement of the storming of the Bastille marked the starting point of a vast armament movement, diverse in its causes and in its effects. French historian Georges Carrot laconically observed that 'as many cities, as many different situations'.[1] In reality, several factors were combined. For example, the authority of certain Ancien Régime municipalities won over by fear was, to say the least, lacking. In many towns, determined and ambitious patriots, who had been kept out of positions of authority until then – usually bourgeois who had become rich in trade, lawyers or doctors – took advantage of the general turmoil to take up arms and overthrow the administrators in place, judged to be too conservative, and thus change the composition of the municipality. They were also eager to modernise the administration of their cities by making them not only more fair but also more efficient. The absence of garrisons, the varying degrees of energy shown by the military commanders and their ability to adapt to the new local power relations were certainly other important elements. The intensity of the food crisis, the varying levels of misery and the capacity of the working classes to bear it were other factors. The distance from Paris and the challenges of obtaining reliable information in a timely manner also affected the nature of the protagonists' actions and the strength of their reactions.

In the aftermath of 14 July, the Constituent Assembly hesitated as to whether or not it was necessary to generalise the armed mobilisation of patriots throughout the national territory. Alerted by the numerous incidents brought to their attention, some liberal deputies, among them Mounier

---

1 Carrot, *La Garde nationale*, p.46.

and Lally-Tollendal, proposed during the session of 18 July to vote on a proclamation calling on the municipalities to set up Milices Bourgeoises. They urged that only 'individuals incapable of harming the Nation and capable of defending it' be admitted to them.[2] However, the monarchists opposed this measure, fearing – and rightly so – that revolutionary Milices, outside the King's authority, would be formed throughout France. In the end, Mirabeau and Barnave insisted on the need to first organise the municipalities within which the Milices Bourgeoises would evolve. This way, they thought they would remove them from the influence of the old ruling oligarchies. Nevertheless, the discussions bogged down and on 23 July the Assembly confined itself to an anodyne declaration inviting the French 'to maintain public order and tranquillity, and to respect the laws' without saying anything about the means to achieve this.[3] Implicitly, it was up to the military authorities to continue to provide this.

However, events outpaced the parliamentary debates. This meant that, despite the Constituent Assembly's caution, communities of inhabitants eager to protect themselves had formed Milices in imitation of the one set up in Paris. This was the case in Argenteuil on 16 July and in Versailles two days later. The movement then spread in a circular motion, in a sort of 'concentric contagion', as historian Roger Dupuy puts it.[4] Chartres and Dreux organised their Milice on the 20th, Saint-Germain-en-Laye the next day. This momentum soon affected regions far from the Parisian epicentre, starting with Rennes and Nantes on 17 July. Next came Angers and Bordeaux on the 19th, Brest on the 21st, Lille and Cherbourg on the 22nd, Lunéville on the 28th and Carcassonne on 3 August.

In all those towns, as in most of the main cities of the kingdom, authorities in place barely resisted. This 'municipal revolution', an event much less well known than the 14th of July or the abolition of privileges the night of 4 August 1789, was a replica of the Parisian events in the French provinces. It was widespread but was not as homogeneous as it might seem. This popular or bourgeois takeover, which led to a re-composition of local powers and the establishment of provisional mini-governments, greatly varied according to location and context. In Dunkirk, Toulouse or Aix-en-Provence, the former administrations, appreciated by the population or strong enough to cope effectively with the pressures, managed to stay in place. If the transition was relatively violent in Cherbourg and Strasbourg, in Normandy as in Poitou, the former administrators, more cautious, made room for their opponents. However, to get the municipal bodies of the Ancien Régime to accept the need to share or even relinquish power, the newcomers frequently resorted to the formation of permanent committees – or patriotic committees – quite similar to the one that administered the capital. Mainly formed by voters in the Estates-General, these parallel organisations, which were primarily concerned with public order, made the Garde Nationale, which

---

2 Jérôme Madival and Emile Laurent (eds), *Archives Parlementaires de 1787 à 1860 – Première série 1787–1799* (Paris: Librairie Administrative P. Dupont, 1884), vol.VIII, p.248.
3 Madival & Laurent (eds), *Archives Parlementaires*, vol.VIII, pp.266–267.
4 Dupuy, *La Garde nationale*, p.44.

their members had often helped to create, their armed wing. In sum, the permanent committees and the Garde Nationale were intimately linked.

The attitude of the military command, in charge of maintaining order, proved ambiguous. Sometimes accused by patriots of being violently opposed to the recent course of events, the military authorities did their utmost to slow down the process of arming the new Milices by granting, for example, only some of the muskets that they were crying out for. In Provence, the Comte de Caraman, pointing out the disadvantages of 'arming a whole province with muskets', succeeded in delaying the delivery of firearms.[5] At the same time, he sought to establish close links between the Garde Nationale and the army by forming mixed patrols in Marseilles. In Lorraine, *Maréchal* de Broglie secured the arms depots on 16 July. In Saint-Malo, Governor Chifoliau only agreed to give up custody of the forts following a threatened attack on 21 July. On the other hand, the young bourgeois of Lyon took the fortress of Pierre-Scize without a fight, and the governor, no doubt wishing to escape the sad fate of Governor De Launay, handed over the keys without the slightest resistance. In Bordeaux, the commander of Château-Trompette acted in a similar fashion. In Rennes, nearly 2,000 soldiers from the Regiments d'Artois, de Lorraine, d'Île-de-France and d'Orléans-Dragons mutinied on 16 July against the military governor, Langeron, then fraternised with the young patriots of the city and exchanged uniforms. The next day, soldiers and young people walked together through the streets of the city to reassure the inhabitants and, on the 18th, they created a 'Armée Nationale', very similar in composition to the Garde Nationale Parisienne. From then on, mixed formations carried out patrols and searches in the vicinity of Rennes to recover alleged grain hoarding. Soldiers also took advantage of the situation to denounce the unnecessary harsh discipline, such as the withholding of pay and especially the infamous punishment of sabre cuts when an officer would inflict 30 to 60 blows with the flat of a sword on the offending soldier. The municipality, aware of these complaints, asked the Comte de Langeron for a softening of all these punishments and obtained the temporary suppression of sabre cuts. On 19 July, couriers coming from Paris announced simultaneously that Necker was back as finance minister and of the formation of a corps of national Milice under the command of La Fayette. The next day, Langeron expressed the wish to wear the national cockade but all patriots, indignant, opposed it. They accused the commander of the crime of 'lèse-Nation' and did not hesitate to demand his death sentence. A less expeditious solution was finally adopted and Langeron was asked to leave the town immediately, which he did that evening under escort of the new 'Armée Nationale'.

Gardes Nationales' appearance was therefore closely linked to what historians have called the 'municipal revolution'. The simultaneity of these troop raisings, but also their ideological kinship despite the diversity of the methods employed, suggest the creation and enactment of a vast overall plan by many deputies of the Third Estate. On 15 July, Barnave, who nevertheless

---

5 Archives Départementales des Bouches-du-Rhône (ADBR): C1380: Lettre du Comte de Caraman aux Commissaires des députés des Communes, 2 août 1789.

opposed the organisation of the Milices during the debates of the Assembly, wrote to his Grenoble correspondents that 'two things were needed: multiple addresses to the National Assembly and Milices Bourgeoises ready to march. One should not lose time spreading these ideas in all parts of the province!'[6] On the 18th, Deputy Mortier announced to his Cambrian electors that 'it is decided that we will have in all the kingdom a Milice Nationale'.[7] In this case, it was misinformation probably spread on purpose. That same day, Deputy Bouche spoke in these terms to his electors in Provence: 'We think that it would be appropriate to establish in vulnerable cities and places a Milice Bourgeoise for their safety.'[8] Most of the time, it was certainly a desire for a return to calm which led to the creation of a Garde Nationale by the local authorities. Such a Garde had to impose itself on the people, which it did on several occasions. In Vitré, in July 1789, French historian Serge Bianchi notes, it suppressed workers' riots bringing together 700 to 800 people armed with axes and sticks.[9] Similarly, 200 peasants demonstrating in Bain for food provoked the intervention of royal troops acting in concert with urban militiamen. On 3 August, 50 young people from Rennes joined soldiers to keep order in Fougères. At the same time, the Garde Nationale had to dissuade soldiers from attacking patriots. In addition, it was necessary to infiltrate and then neutralise elements who, either because of their youth or their social origin, could constitute a danger of immediate and excessive radicalisation within the new Garde Nationale itself. In some provinces, fairly violent episodes of what historians have called the 'Great Fear' further evidenced this repressive tendency.

Great Fear over France

The 'Great Fear' of the summer of 1789 has become one of the key episodes in any history of the first year of the French Revolution. The panics that shook France at the end of July are now fully identified with the peasant revolution, according to the logic of the 'three revolutions' of the summer of 1789: the revolution of the jurists in mid-June, the revolution of the urban Parisian people in mid-July, and finally the revolution of the provinces with the 'Great Fear'. Since 14 July, anti-nobility movements had taken place from the Normandy bocage to much further east in southern Alsace. The movement of troops from one town to another and the spread beyond Paris after 14 July alarmed regions that had remained calm until then. The accommodation and subsistence of the soldiers were also a particularly heavy burden on the already weakened village economies. The rural population suffered from expeditions undertaken by small and large town Milices to

---

6   Carrot, *La Garde nationale*, p.48.
7   Georges Lefebvre, *La Grande Peur* (Paris: Armand Colin, 1932), p.99.
8   ADBR: C 1380.
9   Serge Bianchi, 'Les gardes nationales en Ille-et-Vilaine et dans le sud de la Seine-et-Oise: Bilans comparés', in Serge Bianchi and Roger Dupuy (eds), *La Garde nationale entre nation et peuple en armes: Mythes et réalités 1789–1871* (Rennes: Presses Universitaires de Rennes, 2006), p.376.

obtain wheat. Many contemporaries described them as real acts of piracy. On 28 July, a panic started in Limours and spread south of Paris, throughout the Hurepoix region. The raids by detachments of the Parisian Milice in search of grain were partly responsible for the general anxiety that developed as far as Chevreuse, Longjumeau, Brie-Comte-Robert and Choisy-le-Roi. At the same time, the bourgeoisie, now the masters of a large number of towns, were anxious to reduce both the number of mouths to feed and the potential triggers of disorder. The towns did not hesitate to expel from their walls the unemployed and vagrants without the slightest consideration. The latter travelled in bands, pilfering and pillaging to survive. A few incidents triggered episodes of fear at several points. From 20 July to 6 August, these panics started from six main areas – Franche-Comté, Champagne, Beauvaisis, Maine, the Nantes region and the southwest – identified as early as 1932 by French historian Georges Lefebvre in a pioneering work soberly entitled *La Grande Peur*. They then swept through a large part of the Kingdom of France in a chain reaction, but spared the Landes, the northern and north-eastern provinces protected by the numerous garrisons of the border fortresses, and Brittany, where young patriots multiplied their patrols and controls to reassure the population. In the countryside hit by famine following poor harvests, false news and strange rumours spread. A stranger passing through or an inhabitant of a neighbouring town would come to announce the imminent arrival of 'brigands' who had been seen, the day before or the same morning, ransacking everything in their path. The popular imagination transformed bands of vagabonds into armies of thousands of brigands and even soldiers from neighbouring states. There was also talk of fires, a major fear for peasants when grain could not yet be harvested. To make matters worse, disturbing news came from Paris, where there were reports of a 'St. Bartholomew's Day of the Patriots'.[10]

Alarms spread from one village to another as the throbbing sound of the *tocsin* resounded. Village Milices formed: after Paris and the most important cities, the countryside was now under arms. Peasants and local notables equipped themselves as best they could and according to their means. In Collonges, in the Limousin, the future *Colonel* Bial, then just 16 years old, recalled in his *Memoirs* that

> the inhabitants of the village and the surrounding area, warned by the *tocsin*, arrived in crowds, armed, some with old muskets, others with scythes and even simple vine stakes. This gathering of men without order or discipline presented a very curious picture. Everyone was talking and shouting without being heard. First of all, former soldiers were taken on as NCOs to show the men how to behave while on guard or on duty.[11]

---

10 Roger Dupuy, 'La Garde nationale: Du déni historiographique à la nécessité d'un nouveau questionnement', in Serge Bianchi and Roger Dupuy (eds), *La Garde nationale entre nation et peuple en armes: Mythes et réalités 1789–1871* (Rennes: Presses Universitaires de Rennes, 2006), p.20.

11 Gabriel Soulié, 'Collonges sous la Révolution', *Bulletin de la Société scientifique, historique et archéologique de la Corrèze*, 45 (1923), p.116.

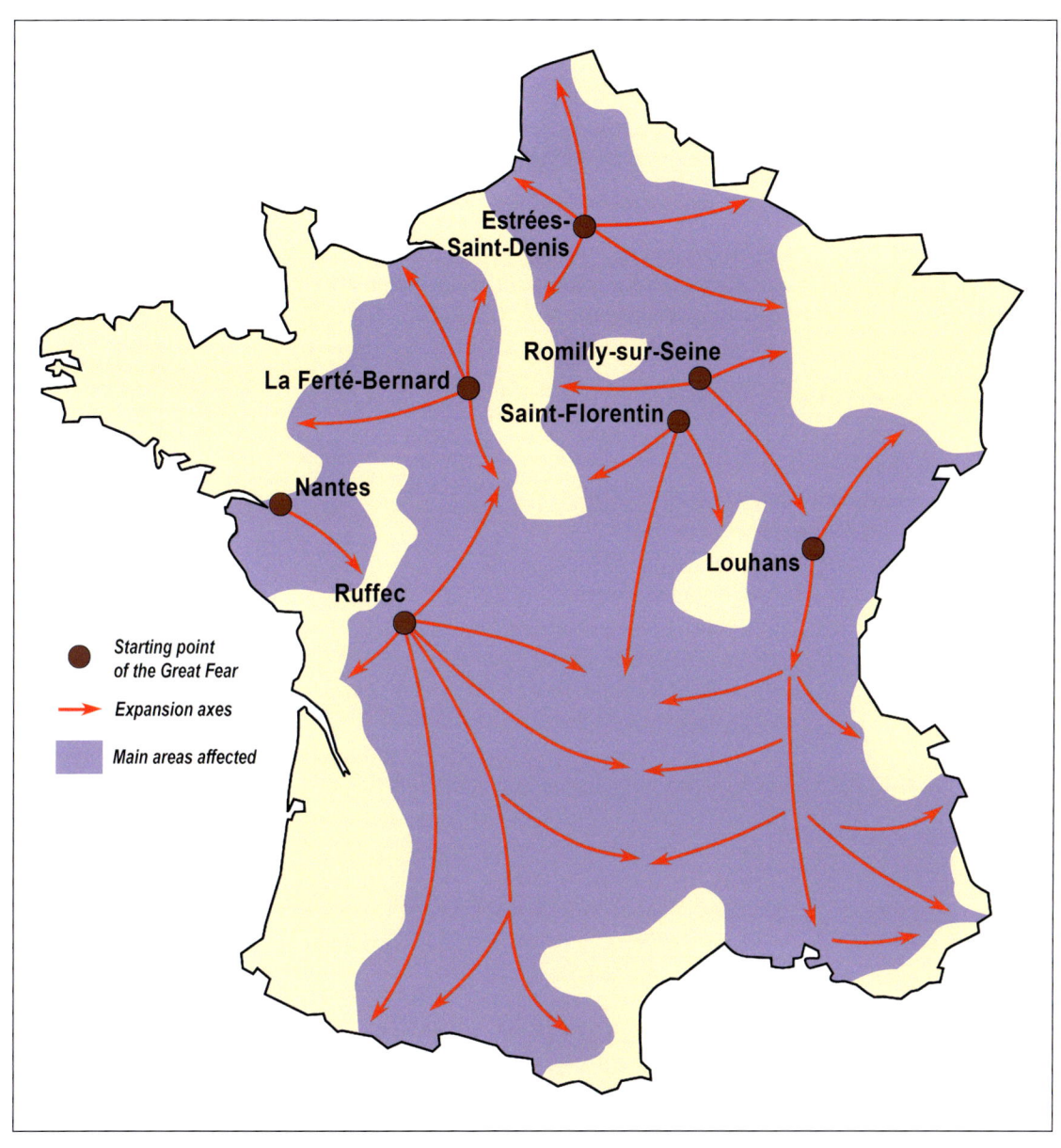

THE PROVINCES FOLLOWED: LOCAL GARDES NATIONALES

Map 4. The Great Fear of summer, 1789.

Once armed, the Milice was on the lookout for the arrival of the dreaded hordes. In Caussade, in the southwest, 'twenty-five elite men, most of them on horseback, commanded by M. Thouron, a bourgeois', were sent on patrol.[12] The rural population did not see anything coming, and for good reason. The classic stories of the 'Great Fear' evoke the transition from a defensive phase against the brigands to an offensive and punitive phase against the lords. Armed by the 'Great Fear', the peasants, learning that the 'brigands' were only the result of false news, let their anger explode against the feudal regime, all

---

12   Pierre Arches, 'La Garde nationale de Saint-Antonin et les Fédérations du Rouergue et du Bas-Quercy (juillet 1789-juillet 1790)', *Annales du Midi*, 68:36 (1956), p.376.

the more easily since the rumours insinuated that the brigands were paid by the aristocrats to punish the Third Estate for attacking the privileged. When, as historian Roger Dupuy points out, 'the disputes were particularly heavy and anti-seigneurial hatred was deep, as in the Mâconnais and the Dauphiné, dozens of châteaux were ransacked'.[13] The seigniorial archives, especially the property plans and the old charters in which feudal rights were recorded, were burnt. Sometimes, with the help of alcohol and anger, the chateau itself was burnt down.

The most recent historiography and research, however, strongly qualifies this traditional history. For example, the division of the 'Great Fear' into two phases – one defensive, the other offensive – is now disputed. Entire regions of the kingdom of France, such as the Auvergne and the Soissonnais, experienced a 'Great Fear' that did not degenerate into a war against the châteaux. Moreover, in many places, the 'Great Fear' was experienced as a moment of social harmony. Political differences and local conflicts were momentarily forgotten because of the danger, and it was not uncommon for a nobleman, a priest or a former officer to be placed at the head of the local Milice. This was the case in Ambialet, for example. On 3 August 1789, when the imminent arrival of 'brigands' was reported, the Chevalier de Bourdès was proclaimed commander of the Milice Bourgeoise by the inhabitants of this Tarn village. Moreover, the usual association between the 'Great Fear' and the peasant revolt is based on fragile foundations. The fear of the 'brigands', the main driving force behind the 'Great Fear', can hardly be reduced to the peasant mentality alone. Through their speeches, their extraordinary measures and their very understanding of popular violence, the elites, whether municipal officers, notaries, priests, lawyers or merchants, actively participated in spreading the Fear by communicating their own fear of anarchy to large sections of French society. The invocation of 'brigands' certainly enabled them to reach a very broad social spectrum and to meet the rural population's own aspirations for order and security.

Getting Things in Order

From Provisional to Institutionalisation
Faced with the chaotic situation in the kingdom, the deputies of the National Assembly had to act, or rather, to improvise. They first attacked the root causes of the disorder and, during the famous night of 4 August, sacrificed feudal rights. In an exalted context of patriotic one-upmanship, the deputies of the privileged orders (nobility and clergy) renounced the hereditary advantages of their personal status, which had become incongruous in a nation of citizens who were now legally equal. They also accepted the redemption of the seigneurial rights that constituted their source of wealth. The next day, debates on the disorders of the kingdom led to a motion stating that it was 'the duty of the municipalities and the Milices Bourgeoises' to

---

[13] Dupuy, *La Garde nationale*, p.51.

protect property and persons and to ensure the free circulation of wheat and flour.[14] The National Assembly thus refused to entrust the restoration of order to the royal army. On 10 August, the Constituent Assembly adopted, at Mounier's insistence, a decree which officially confirmed the existence of the 'Milices Nationales', soon to be renamed 'Gardes Nationales'. This legislative text henceforth recognised their leading position in the hierarchy of forces to which the internal order of the kingdom was entrusted. In fact, the Maréchaussée – which became the National Gendarmerie in 1791 – appeared to be an auxiliary force. As for the line army, it had to obey the orders of the municipalities, which did not seem very credible in the rural parishes. But these were of course general principles designed to dispel the fears of recourse to the King's regiments. To avoid any unnecessary disorder, the Milices Nationales were to keep a special watch on 'people without confession and without profession': the unemployed, beggars, migrant workers and the small urban proletariat.[15] Between the brigands of the 'Great Fear' and the populace, which was distrusted as much as it was feared, the border was so porous that measures for the former were perfectly suited to the latter. The fact remains that the denunciation of brigands undoubtedly produced a broader social consensus. Finally, all gardes had to take an oath in the hands of their commander – and not before the municipal authority – and swear to 'serve well and faithfully for the maintenance of peace, for the defence of citizens and against those who disturb public peace'.[16]

The decree of 10 August 1789 thus recognised a *fait accompli* by granting the Milices a legal existence, often dependent on the municipalities. Once the Great Fear had subsided, what it had largely helped to produce was retained: Milices Bourgeoises used as instruments of public order within the kingdom. The measures taken after the panic movements showed that both rural and urban elites sought to capitalise on these fears by producing a new legitimization of policing. Mobilisation and arming at the time of the Great Fear sometimes led to the informal constitution of a milice that did not evolve into the formation of an organised Garde. But more often than not, the need to perpetuate hitherto provisional Milices, and thus to organise them definitively, was absolutely felt. After a phase of tumultuous and anarchic creation on the occasion of the Great Fear, a phase of institutionalisation followed. At the same time, Milices Bourgeoises multiplied in cities that were little or not affected by the Fear.

Drafted from the end of July to the end of August by the Milices themselves, by the municipalities or by the permanent committees, and frequently amended over time as the need arose, the few regulations that have been preserved perfectly reflect these concerns. First of all, they varied in the form of the service required. In Bordeaux and Toulouse, two of the major cities of southwest France, volunteers were called upon only as a convenient means of eliminating certain undesirable social categories as well as political opponents. Elsewhere, service was more or less compulsory for those who

---

14   Madival & Laurent (eds), *Archives Parlementaires*, vol.VIII, p.351.
15   Dupuy, *La Garde nationale*, p.49.
16   Madival & Laurent (eds), *Archives Parlementaires*, vol.VIII, pp.378–379.

THE GARDE NATIONALE 1789–1815

Hommage des bas officiers et volontaires de la 2e Compagnie de Croncels au capitaine Boilletot, 28 June 1790. Pierre Boilletot (1748–1827) belonged to an old family of long-established merchants in Troyes. In July 1789, he was appointed *capitaine* of the 2nd Company of the 2nd Battalion of Troyes Garde Nationale, known as the Croncels Battalion. (Musée Carnavalet)

were admitted to it. Failure to attend assemblies meant a fine and, even more so, public disgrace for the offending guard. It was often possible, as in Brest, to be replaced by other citizen-soldiers, or to pay a replacement from the poorer social classes, who were not registered in the Milice registers and whom the municipality or the standing committee took charge of approving. As soon as it was won, the right to armed service became a duty that brought with it personal and financial obligations. In this way, the municipal authorities sought to balance the needs of public order while making sure the security of towns was in the hands of those they considered safe. Study of the various regulations also shows that the emphasis was placed on the discipline required of the novice soldier. In both urban centres and rural towns, Milices were organised according to a military logic, in battalions divided into companies. In the Lorraine commune of Mirecourt, the 200 men who presented themselves at the end of July 1789 were immediately divided into four companies. In Troyes, the organisation into 14 companies was modelled on the Milice of the Ancien Régime. In Tours, notes historian Béatrice Baumier, the municipal authorities adapted the new troop to the demographic realities of the city by creating no less than 22 companies.[17] In this way, they demonstrated their desire to keep a close eye on all the districts, especially those on the outskirts of the town (La Riche, Saint-Éloy and Saint-Pierre-des-Corps) where working classes attracted by the town's recent economic boom had settled. The units' staff was generally very large. On 6 August 1789, the *Règlement concernant la milice nationale de la ville de Saint-Antonin* decreed that each of the 20 companies would have 'a *capitaine*, a *lieutenant*, a *sergent*, two *caporaux* and twenty soldiers'.[18] In the gardes of the rural communes in the eastern part of the Paris basin, each company was generally led by a *capitaine*, a *lieutenant*, two *sous-lieutenants*, two *sergents* and four *caporaux*. In Tours, the companies were each composed of 15 officers, 64 soldiers and a drummer. They were grouped into four battalions placed under the orders of as many commanders.

Choosing the Officers

The appointment of the officers was of particular importance. Command varied according to time and place. Officers were sometimes appointed by the municipalities or by the permanent committees: this was particularly true of the earliest Milices. However, the new organisational principles of French society meant that citizens should not obey leaders whom they had not freely chosen. Nevertheless, the sociological constraints remained such that the hierarchy established in the provinces within the Garde Nationale matched the social hierarchy almost exactly. Nobles were very often designated to occupy the highest positions. This was no surprise, since the nobleman still embodied, in the population's mind, the man-at-arms – the one most capable of instructing and leading the armed citizens. In the provincial capitals in which popular outbursts were feared, command was devolved to general or senior officers, either on reserve or active service. In Bordeaux, the Duc

---

17   Baumier, *La Garde Nationale entre nation et peuple en armes*, p.118.
18   Arches, 'La Garde nationale de Saint-Antonin', p.377.

de Duras was proclaimed *generalissimo* of the patriotic troops. The Prince de Poix and the Comte d'Estaing succeeded each other at the head of the Versailles Milice. In Moulins, the capital of the Bourbonnais, a 'Regiment National', organised on the model of the Parisian Milice Bourgeoise, was set up on 17 August 1789. In this context, the Milice of the Ancien Régime was swept away in one fell swoop and a gathering of citizens electing their officers took its place. The leadership of the troops was entrusted to *Maréchal de Camp* Giraud des Echerolles. Alexandrine, his daughter, recounted the scene in her *Memoirs*:

> Citizens assembled, they appointed officers. Here is the Garde Nationale established. They want a leader, my father is chosen. He walked on the courts of Moulins, he was surrounded, then proclaimed colonel. He refuses, one is obstinate, one presses him and after having hesitated a while, he gives himself up and accepts.[19]

A knight of Saint-Louis, the new leader was battle-hardened. He had indeed participated in the Seven Years' War during which he had been wounded and captured at the battle of Rossbach. The three officers who followed him in the ranks – including Du Myrat, *colonel en second*, and Vialet, *lieutenant-colonel* – were also knights of Saint-Louis. Their great military experience made it possible to effectively lead the newly created Garde Nationale. In Cherbourg, as in Marseilles, command was entrusted to serving senior officers. A similar logic prevailed in Clermont-Ferrand. Until then *colonel* of the battalion of the Chasseurs d'Auvergne, Comte Jean-Pierre François de Chazot was given command of the staff of the town's Garde Nationale in view of 'his patriotic zeal and his noble and firm intention to contribute to the common good, his admirable eagerness to line up under the banner of liberty and to display the national cockade'.[20] Until the King fled, the former local lord frequently took command of the rural gardes formed in the Ile-de-France. This was the case in Épinay-sur-Orge, Crosne, Corbeil, Viry, even in communes deemed to be the most patriotic. However, the nobleman did not necessarily hold the highest rank within the citizenry. Thus, in Bergerac, in the Périgord, memorialist Edmé de la Chapelle found himself placed, as a *caporal*, under the command of a man who, before the Revolution, had served under him in the Regiment du Lyonnais. However, when the municipal authorities wished to promote him to the rank of *capitaine*, which was more in keeping with his long service in the line army, he was reluctant to do so: would accepting higher responsibilities not be tantamount to drawing attention to himself? Moreover, probably feeling isolated, since he was surrounded exclusively by commoners, he preferred, after two months' service, to ask for his replacement. He also subjugated himself to the new revolutionary demands by explaining his choice to his assembled company.

---

19   Alexandrine des Echerolles, *Une famille noble sous la Terreur* (Paris: Plon, 1907), p.10.
20   Archives Départementales du Puy-de-Dôme (ADPD): F 152: Procès-verbal de l'assemblée des officiers municipaux et citoyens de la ville de Clermont, 20 août 1789.

THE PROVINCES FOLLOWED: LOCAL GARDES NATIONALES

Garde Nationale officers of Bouchain (left) and Brienon l'Archevêque (right), gouaches by Henri Boisselier. (Yves Martin)

The nobility generally reserved for themselves the highest ranks, or at least the majority of officer positions. In this, they were imitated by the bourgeoisie from the world of finance, the professions and administration. The composition of the staff of the provincial Gardes Nationales corresponded to the realities of the first months of the French Revolution. It was intended to symbolise the continuity between the Ancien Régime and the new, but also the hoped-for concord between all the social categories of a renewed urban elite. For these men, belonging to the Garde Nationale's staff could be understood as a way of showing their patriotism. Moreover, the Garde Nationale and related positions of responsibility were a springboard to municipal office.

Removing the Unwanted

The recruitment of Milices was dependent on circumstances. Those created before 20 July and the beginning of the 'Great Fear' were raised in a revolutionary perspective and intended as instruments of pressure for the bourgeoisie to secure a monopoly. Yet it would have been imprudent to keep away all those of age and able to bear arms. This logic applied to Troyes, Toulouse and Rodez. During the very first weeks of its existence, the Garde Nationale of Amiens also presented itself as being both bourgeois and popular. Since it did not exclude any part of the city's population, it embodied the sovereignty of the entire nation.

However, once the rumours had died down and the danger of the Great Fear had passed, this universalism could seem dangerous. The paradox faced by these Milices in the months that followed often lay in the fact that they armed precisely those whose revolt was feared. What could be expected from people with precarious living conditions who were not interested in defending their property? Many authorities tried to resolve this predicament by a range of measures that revealed the aspirations of an oligarchy that was protesting politically yet was still conservative in terms of social values: either by imposing a military discipline on these new armed bodies through regulations, oaths and the establishment of a strict hierarchy, or by limiting access to the Milice through the implementation of a census threshold. In Villefranche-de-Rouergue, in southwestern France, only landlords were accepted. In Clermont-Ferrand, social segregation was openly claimed by some of the new Milice's promoters: 'Only resident citizens and owners were admitted to the town Garde. No simple day labourers or labourers', thus congratulated Lawyer Bergier.[21] In Elbeuf, in Normandy, any new candidate had to be sponsored by two gardes who had already been accepted and had to pay more than 12 *livres* in direct taxes. In Amiens, a significant fringe of the population – workers and journeymen in particular, unable to pay the contribution of 20 *sous* or the equivalent to three days' work yet required to be recognised as an active citizen and to join the ranks of the Garde – was deliberately excluded. Finally, a few rare communes, such as Millau or Saint-Antonin, carried out an authoritarian purge of the ranks. In Saint-Antonin, Article 5 of the supplement to the regulations ordered the reform of 'people without a home or property, as servants or otherwise'.[22] This decision was all the more brutal because it excluded elements which had sincerely, or not, been accepted during the July alarms. In the towns where access remained theoretically open to all citizens, discrimination against certain social classes had nevertheless been put in place. Servants were nearly always excluded by an almost general prejudice. In Pont-à-Mousson, neither ploughmen nor day labourers were admitted. In Dunkirk, only workers 'under the control of those who had factories' were accepted and care was taken to disarm them immediately after service.[23] Such mistrust was also at work in Tours, where the elites were reluctant to rely on men from modest backgrounds such as journeymen or craftsmen. The patriotic bourgeoisie expressed its distrust of social categories considered dangerous either because of their suspected loyalty to 'aristocratic' masters or for their propensity to revolt. In Limoges,

---

21   Francisque Mège, *Gaultier de Biauzat, député du tiers-état aux États généraux de 1789: Sa vie et sa correspondance* (Clermont-Ferrand: Bellet et fils, 1890), p.264.
22   Arches, 'La Garde nationale de Saint-Antonin', p.379.
23   Archives Nationales de France (ANF): AD/VI/50: Pièce imprimée.

Toul or Châteauroux, it was enough to exempt 'citizens who needed daily work for their subsistence or that of their families'.[24] Under the guise of humanity, elements perceived as dangerous were smoothly removed. They were nevertheless included on the rolls, with the indication that they would only be called up in the event of an extraordinary situation.

Special Units

This fairly general pattern varied according to various situations. It was further complicated by the fact that special units – volunteer companies, youth, veterans and elite companies – coexisted with the Garde Nationale.

Voluntaires' Companies
In the early weeks of the Revolution, young people who shared the same political convictions and enthusiasm formed separate corps. In Angers, some 'young citizens' requested authorisation to create two volontaire companies. The permanent committee referred the applicants to the Milice commissioners who gave a favourable opinion. On 14 August 1789, the 'young citizens' of the town of Angers, therefore, decided to organise a volunteer corps, an initiative that was validated by the Committee the following day. Unlike their counterparts in Rennes who after forming a short-lived 'Armée Nationale' with the soldiers garrisoned in the city almost immediately merged into the Milice organised by the municipality, the volontaires in Angers led an existence marked by hesitation between autonomy and integration into the Garde Nationale system. The young men did not seek to replace the gardes nationaux, but on the contrary wanted to 'work in concert with them to ensure public tranquillity'.[25] Consequently, they provided a double service: one within the Garde Nationale, the other grouped together in a special troop with its own distinctive uniform and hierarchy. Designated on 14 August, the three chiefs – Bodard, Choudieu and Proust – undertook obeying the orders of the Milice staff. On 18 August, it was the turn of the 'young amateurs in music' to form a corps of 'Musiciens Volontaires' attached to both the national Milice and the Anjou Volontaires.[26] Like the latter, they had their own officers, approved by the Milice staff, as well as their own distinctive uniform. The companies of volontaires nationaux were not an original creation of the city of Angers. As early as mid-July, the young people of Saumur had wanted to set up a special troop, which was quickly created, since the *Règlement de la Milice Nationale de la ville de Saumur*, drawn up on 22 August by the permanent committee, provided for the Volontaires Saumurois' company to be increased to 120 men. Unlike its counterpart in Angers, this unit was not intended to be truly integrated into the Garde Nationale. The volontaires had a special uniform

---

24 Carrot, *La Garde nationale*, p.55.
25 Claude Petitfrère, 'La jeunesse angevine et les débuts de la Révolution française', *Annales de Bretagne et des pays de l'Ouest*, 81:4 (1974), p.718.
26 Archives Municipales d'Angers (AMA): EE 6.

THE GARDE NATIONALE 1789–1815

Garde Nationale volontaires' units, 1789–1790, gouaches by Henri Boisselier. From left to right: Brigadier of Marennes Mounted Volontaires, Pont Saint-Esprit Volontaires and Lannion Chasseurs Volontaires. (Yves Martin)

which, in reality, differed from that of the Milice only in the colour of the collar and the buttons. Above all, they were exempt from serving in the Milice companies and were commanded by a *lieutenant-colonel* assisted by a special staff. According to the regulations drawn up on 16 September 1789, the admission of new members would be subject to being accepted by two-thirds of the general assembly of volontaires. Access to the companies would also be forbidden to boys under the age of 16, married men and foreigners. Finally, each volontaire would have to contribute equally to expenses. These provisions, which probably inspired the regulations adopted three months later by the volontaires in Angers, obviously had the effect of keeping out most lower social classes. There were no doubt other volontaire companies in Anjou in addition to those of the two main towns. In Cholet, a company was formed under the leadership of a certain Combault. In the rest of the kingdom, examples are undoubtedly legion. On 31 July, during the 'Great Fear', a man named de Bastard offered to create a dragoon company in Dijon, which was promptly renamed 'Volontaires Nationaux'. Tasked with assisting the surrounding villages, these cavalrymen received their regulations on 17 September and their flag on 2 October. Their example was followed by an artillery unit. In Caen, a horse volontaire company was raised and in Le Havre, a foot company. In Dunkirk, each guild was authorised to form a specific company.

Youth Units

It was certainly not uncommon for teenagers to sign up for the Garde Nationale. Thus, in Marchiennes, a small town in northern France, the future *Général de division* Jean-Baptiste Juvénal Corbineau, then just 13 years old, volunteered. In addition, companies of adolescents were formed in various parts of the kingdom. If a Compagnie de l'Espérance bringing together 35 boys aged between 12 and 17 operated in Saumur, the case of the Auvergne is certainly the best documented. Taking advantage of the civic mobilisation that animated the month of July 1789, groups of schoolchildren in Clermont-Ferrand, driven by an adolescent and spontaneous militancy, set up children's Milices that explicitly echoed the Spartan model and, above all, their school reading. On 21 July, the 10 companies of the Milice Bourgeoise marching through the city were imitated by a hundred or so schoolchildren. Armed 'with sticks as muskets' and having 'a blue paper standard', they 'chose *capitaines* by a plurality of votes' and paraded behind François Biauzat, son of a Third Estate deputy at the Estates-General.[27] A *Règlement pour la formation et l'organisation de deux compagnies de jeunes citoyens en la ville de Clermont-Ferrand* promptly institutionalised the formula. This text responded to a twofold desire: that of the local elected officials to control young people who were future voters – a desire perhaps combined in some cases with admiration for the Lacedemonian model – but also that of the adolescents themselves, who wished to become effectively involved in the revolutionary movement. It intended that each of the companies would progressively comprise 28, 36, 44 or 60 children aged eight to 18. The only conditions for enrolment were a baptismal certificate and parental authorisation. Children were then assigned either to the 'major company' or to the 'minor company', although it is not known on which basis. Age nevertheless seems to be the preferred criteria, as rank was only attained at age 14 for the 'major company' and at age 10 for the 'minor company'. Appointed to their posts by the municipal officers and Chazot, the young gardes nationaux had to stand guard in front of the town hall on Sundays and feast days. 'Bad subjects' were assigned to their parents, who were allowed to choose their own punishment.[28] The example of Clermont-Ferrand inspired a similar situation in Riom which spread to the smallest towns in the district.

Elite and Cavalry Units

Elite companies of grenadiers and chasseurs were created. They were grouped together by social affinity and wore more expensive uniforms than the ordinary companies. Following a similar logic, cavalry units were organised, preferably bringing together wealthy individuals. Such formations existed in Valenciennes – in the form of a squadron of 46 cavalrymen, not including officers – Poitiers (a company), Nîmes (a company of dragoons, recruited from the town's Protestant community) or Pézenas in the Hérault (also a company). It was not uncommon that when there were disagreements within a company, opponents ended up organising themselves separately. It also

---

27 *Feuille hebdomadaire pour la province d'Auvergne*, 27 (1789).
28 Mège, *Gaultier de Biauzat*, p.116.

THE GARDE NATIONALE 1789–1815

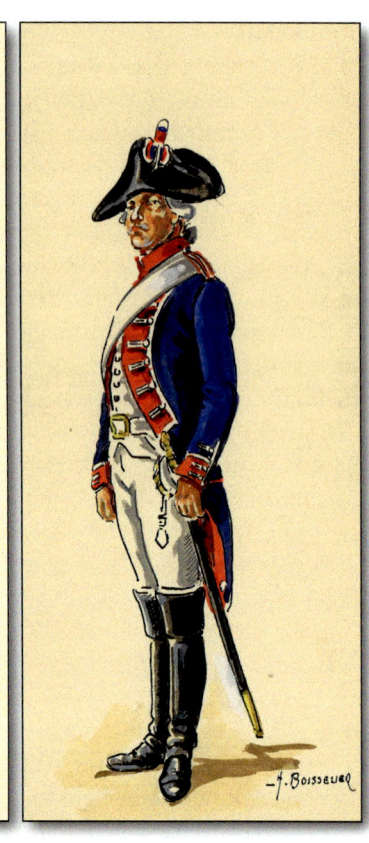

Garde Nationale cavalry units, 1789–1790, gouaches by Henri Boisselier. From left to right: Strasbourg Garde Nationale officer – Altkirch Chasseurs à Cheval – Fontenay-le-Comte Garde Nationale cavalryman. (Yves Martin)

happened that, having failed to become *capitaine*, an individual formed his own company so as to be appointed for sure.

The Survival of Military Sports Companies

In a fairly large number of towns and cities, there were still military sports companies, particularly those of the Arquebuse, the Bow and the Crossbow. After nearly a century of lethargy, the events of the summer of 1789 brought these shooting companies back to life. The Arquebuse was certainly the most modern sport and the only one still of military interest. The bourgeois practised with the musket, not only for the pleasure of shooting birds, but more commonly to target shoot. French historian Georges Carrot considers that such companies 'which did not want to join the new Milices, met among themselves and created a separate service'.[29] He, therefore, gives them little importance in his work on the Garde Nationale. The writings of French historian Christine Lamarre are far more nuanced. 'Did military sports companies provide officers for the Gardes Bourgeoises? Did they staff volunteer units until they were incorporated into the Garde Nationale on 12 June 1790?', she asks.[30] The case of Dijon allows us to shed some light

---

29 Carrot, *La Garde nationale*, p.58.
30 Christine Lamarre, 'Les jeux militaires au XVIIIe siècle: Une forme de sociabilité urbaine négligée', *Histoire Urbaine*, 5 (2002), p.103.

THE PROVINCES FOLLOWED: LOCAL GARDES NATIONALES

Military sports companies, 1789, gouache by Henri Boisselier. The first Gardes Nationales sometimes included a military sports company, like this Troyes arquebusier or this Nogent-sur-Seine arquebusier officer. These units were dissolved in accordance with a law of 12 June 1790. (Yves Martin)

on the matter. The activities of the Compagnie de l'Arc came to an abrupt halt in the days following the opening of the Estates General, well before the troubles of the summer. On 16 August 1789, the Compagnie de l'Arquebuse decreed that the service of regular activities would be carried out with other citizens, but that the knights would offer another service, free of charge and together, whenever necessary to maintain public peace. It was also decided that shooting exercises would continue. Moreover, the proportion of archers and arquebusiers among the officers of the Garde Nationale and volontaires was significant during the first months of the Revolution. However, some of the knights, probably hoping to retain their individuality, deliberately stayed away from the new institutions. At the end of 1789, concern was evident in the intense correspondence between the knights and their counterparts in Paris and neighbouring towns. The objective was to define the basis for a collaboration with the Garde Nationale, which was now firmly established. Such collaboration would make it possible to preserve, in an atmosphere of mistrust, the singularity of the military sports companies. The knights were in fact trying to keep their company alive. So, it came as a complete surprise when the National Assembly announced the abolition of the companies in June 1790.

THE GARDE NATIONALE 1789–1815

Officer of the Canonniers de Lille, 1789, watercolor by Henri Boisselier. (Yves Martin)

Artillery

Lille, one of Northern France's major cities, was certainly an exception in the field of artillery. In 1483, the Confrérie of Sainte-Barbe was established and then lived through the ages until the revolutionary upheavals. As early as April 1789, the gunners took part in the guard and patrol service instituted to curb disorders. In August, a Garde Bourgeoise was formed, in which the Confrérie was integrated. The guns were placed in storage at the town hall and training exercises, which had been somewhat neglected for several years, were intensively resumed. The granting of flags in April 1790 seemed to indicate that the Garde had been formed for a lasting period. Events decided otherwise. In fact, the festival of the Federation of the departments of the Nord, Pas-de-Calais and the Somme, in early June 1790, was the last event in which the unit participated before its dissolution. Indeed, the suppression of all armed guilds put an end to their existence and the Confrérie's members bowed to the law. However, this episode did not mark the end of Lille's artillery: the gunners soon regrouped in the form of artillery companies integrated into the Garde Nationale, as authorised by the law of 14 October 1791.

In November 1789, faced with this somewhat anarchic situation, the National Assembly, after confirming the subordination of the Gardes Nationales to municipal power, tried to limit their proliferation. It claimed that it was necessary to wait for the decree finally regulating its organisation before considering the creation of new units.

The Gardes on Duty

What were the missions of the gardes in the provinces during the first months of the Revolution? A whole series of regulations, more or less similar to those of Paris, aimed to define the framework of these missions and relations with the municipalities. The scarcity of such texts for the rural communes invites us to evoke more particularly the case of the urban gardes. Sundays and feast days were used for exercise and in particular for the handling of weapons. Regular reviews were held at the parade ground, even in small communities.

The urban gardes intervened preferentially in the countryside and carried out missions to monitor the supply of wheat, an essential factor in maintaining order. It was not only private property that a food riot could threaten, but the very success of the revolutionary movement, as it was feared that unrest could be exploited in some way by the aristocrats. It was thus vital to enforce the free movement of wheat, which the rural inhabitants repeatedly opposed. Detachments charged with visiting millers and granaries but also with escorting the transport of wheat were therefore organised and achieved uneven results. In addition to scouring the countryside for wheat, the gardes also policed the markets, patrolling the streets and setting up guardhouses at key points in the city. They had to keep order at public events: fairs, end-of-year celebrations, departures of regiments, shows or particularly important political events. They were also invited to express their enthusiasm for the Revolution by taking part in major ceremonies and civic celebrations, as in the case of the federations. Finally, they provided valuable assistance during natural disasters, fires or floods, and retained their function as parade escorts, following the example of the Ancien Régime Milices.

Everywhere, there was a desire to protect property, and the fruits of the land in rural communes, but also to maintain good order and peace. In Quimper, the gardes intervened in particular in the spring of 1790 when two fishermen violated the ban on dredging the Odet to harvest oysters. The authorities immediately sent a dozen men under the command of Bérardier, *major* of the Locmaria Milice, to stop the illegal activity. The gardes of this Breton commune also intervened to arrest citizens engaged in fraudulent sales of alcohol and tobacco. Chasing 'strangers' – wanderers and vagrants in particular – was certainly one of the guardsmen's main concerns. In Lorraine, the municipality of the small village of Chaumont-sur-Moselle claimed that its gardes played an essential role on the road to Nancy because of the brigands who infested the surrounding forests. In some towns, such as Tours, they patrolled the vicinity of the charity workshops as well as the working-class neighbourhoods, in more or less close collaboration with the garrison regiments. During troubled times, night patrols were organised but faced many problems of availability and turnover. In Troyes, they began at 9:00 p.m., had to last at least an hour and were carried out 'in the greatest silence'.[31] On this occasion, the gardes fought against disturbances in the streets, arresting drunk and rowdy youths. Finally, they were required to apply martial law whenever public order was threatened by demonstrations. Proposed by Mirabeau, this text was voted in only a few hours on 21 October 1789, following the rather horrific murder of the Parisian baker François. Establishing the boundaries of illegality and *de facto* legitimising the use of the Garde Nationale, this law was aimed at subsistence disturbances but also applied to other forms of popular movement demands. Proclaimed by municipal officers – which testified to the subordination of the gardes

Poitiers Garde Nationale firefighter, 1789, gouache by Henri Boisselier. (Yves Martin)

---

31   Anon., *Règlement pour la formation d'une garde nationale volontaire, sanctionné par les officiers municipaux le 17 octobre 1789* (Troyes: Veuve Goblet, 1789), p.10.

THE GARDE NATIONALE 1789–1815

Erection d'un arbre de la liberté, watercolour by Etienne Bericourt. Planting of liberty trees began in 1790. They multiplied at a frantic pace in the spring and summer of 1792. The ceremony of planting liberty trees took place with great solemnity. The magistrates, the judges, the clergy, the army and, of course, the Garde Nationale all took part in the ceremony with the same patriotic enthusiasm. (Musée Carnavalet)

nationaux to the municipalities – martial law granted legality for the use of the Garde Nationale.

A Disruptive Force?

However, facts belied the idea that the Garde Nationale was only a force of order executing the National Assembly's economic, military and religious policies and was subordinate to the municipalities. It frequently amplified local conflicts by being a catalyst for antagonistic groups. In December 1789, the consuls of Toulon refused to proclaim martial law against arsenal workers who were demonstrating against the fleet commander. The main leaders of the royal navy were momentarily sequestered after having unsuccessfully sought the protection of the Garde Nationale. At the same time, companies in the working-class faubourgs of Saumur demonstrated their discontent by taking up arms. On 3 January 1790, during riots at the barriers, elite companies of the Garde Nationale, volontaires from Saumur, knights of the Arquebuse and some officers of the companies from the faubourgs took up arms to maintain order. Facing them, their men found themselves on the side of the demonstrators. Such a situation was a reminder that the gardes nationaux were far from cohesive units. The strength of both sides was large. This confrontation openly opposed bourgeois circles,

THE PROVINCES FOLLOWED: LOCAL GARDES NATIONALES

defending law, property and the municipal budget, to popular circles, demanding exceptional measures to address the high cost of living. On 4 and 5 January, despite patrols, the last of the eight barriers in Saumur were broken down. The municipality found that it could not restore them. The demonstrators had prevailed. In Quercy, the Montauban Garde Nationale – mostly Protestants – showed little inclination to oppose their co-religionists who were attacking Catholic properties. From the end of January until the end of February 1790, the urban gardes nationaux had to intervene in the western countryside where peasants refused to buy back feudal rights. The threat, sometimes followed by action, of noble landowners to bring the recalcitrant before the seigneurial justice only increased the wrath of the rural population. The latter waged a 'war on chateaux' and a 'war on titles'. The urban gardes nationaux, like that of Rennes, showed little willingness to intervene, or did so reluctantly, to protect aristocratic residences burning in the surrounding countryside and to shoot at peasants. Moreover, had not the patriots courted them a few months earlier during the elections to the Estates General? 'In the countryside, it was even worse', says historian Georges Carrot.[32] The archives that have been preserved show that the village gardes nationaux often participated more or less forcibly in the revolt. They provided the protesters with both an apparatus and men. In fact, municipal officers and the village gardes nationaux were too close to the rioters to be

Le serment civique d'un village, print by Jules Rebel. The engraving shows the members of a village Garde, grouped around the mayor, as they take the oath be faithful to the Nation, the Law and the King. The men's poor appearance is noticeable. In contrast, the town council has obviously purchased a flag, which can be seen in the background. (Musée Carnavalet)

---

32 Carrot, *La Garde nationale*, p.69.

able to act brutally against them and were even often placed at the head of the processions. As such, no one could demand harsh measures. When, in spite of everything, action was taken by the troops, the scruples of the leaders deprived their subordinates of all power. Consequently, the image of a purely 'bourgeois' Garde Nationale must be qualified considering its participation in popular movements.

On 8 December 1789, the incompatibility of municipal functions with those of the Garde Nationale was decreed. A month later, another decree stipulated that the oath of obedience to the *Constitution* should henceforth be taken in the hands of the mayor and his municipal officers. This was a clear reaffirmation of the supremacy of civil power over military power. 'It was also to deny the Garde Nationale the power to deliberate politically under arms,' rightly notes French historian Roger Dupuy.[33] Finally, on 2 February 1790, the Assembly prohibited citizens organised in armed companies from 'interfering directly or indirectly in the administration of the municipalities' and committed them to 'obey the municipal officers in accordance with the decrees of the National Assembly'.[34] In addition to martial law of October 1789, such measures were clearly aimed at reinforcing the subordination and dependence of the gardes nationaux to municipal power. However, in some cities such as Douai, Troyes, Lyon or Toulouse, these legislative measures did not change anything. Opposition between the moderate municipality and part of the gardes nationaux was expressed in the form of motions, denunciations and sometimes violent incidents. Resignations were also commonplace.

The elections of February 1790 led to a considerable lessening of these tensions: either the aristocratic adversary was eliminated from the town halls or his influence was curbed. The consuls of Lyon had delayed, as long as they could, the formation of a Garde Nationale, arguing that there was a joint Milice Bourgeoise and a Volontaires corps. Public opinion nevertheless demanded the renewal of this Milice and the replacement of its cadres with officers elected by the citizens, as in the other towns of the kingdom. The attempt by the first alderman Imbert-Colomès to keep the Volontaires corps against all odds led to serious incidents. On 7 February, the arsenal was looted and the volontaires, some of whom were massacred, were routed. The Milice Bourgeoise, which had just been democratically reorganised, made hardly any attempt to protect them. The next day, this corps was officially disbanded, and its members were called up to register with the Garde Nationale. Similarly, the Marseilles Milice Bourgeoise was replaced on 11 February 1790 by a more popular Garde Nationale totalling 14,000 men, of which almost 40 percent of the *capitaines* were craftsmen.

If all those quarrels only had a limited resonance on a national scale, the situation was different in Montauban and Nîmes, two towns in the Midi

---

33   Dupuy, *La Garde nationale*, p.51.
34   Jean-Baptiste Duvergier (ed.), *Collection Complète des Lois, Décrets, Ordonnances, Règlements, Avis du Conseil d'Etat* (Paris: A. Guyot et Scribe Libraires-Editeurs, 1834), vol.I, p.97.

where the formation of Gardes Nationales had replayed the old religious confrontations between Catholics and Protestants. Both cities had a predominantly Catholic population. However, the wealthy bourgeoisie was Protestant. Enriched in the manufacture and trade of cloth and silk, they had taken the lead in the revolutionary movement and monopolised most of the officer positions in the Garde Nationale. Yet the elections of February 1790 shuffled the cards. Relying on the Catholic populace, which hated the Protestant oligarchy, the bourgeoisie of the lawmen and some nobles hostile to the Nation were legally set up in the town hall. In addition to the rivalries between the municipality and the Garde Nationale, there were religious quarrels dating from the preceding century.

Once the municipalities had been conquered, the victors created new companies of gardes nationaux recruited amongst the masses and supervised by the nobility. In Montauban, a fourth battalion, called 'lou cadis' or 'the goldfinches', and made up of supporters of the Ancien Régime, was added to the three already existing. The Catholics sought to incorporate these new formations into the real patriotic garde nationale, both to comply with the decrees of the National Assembly and to displace the majority and take control of it. The Assembly refused to recognise the new Catholic gardes, but the conservative municipalities did not care. In the absence of an impossible agreement between the parties, the antagonism created a climate of growing tension whose bloody epilogue was linked to the first measures of ecclesiastical property seizures: Protestants were accused of seeking to recover religious buildings that had been taken away from them following the revocation of the Edict of Nantes. On 10 May 1790, the people of Montauban opposed the inventories, which were a prelude to the sale of certain religious buildings. The dragoons of the Protestant Garde Nationale opened fire in an attempt to break through. They were repulsed and besieged in their barracks. Five were killed and 55 others, taken prisoner, were imprisoned by order of the mayor. The Protestant gardes nationaux of Montauban called on their counterparts in Bordeaux, Toulouse and Cahors, with whom they had federated a few weeks earlier, to help them. Bordeaux, which had strong commercial relations with Montauban Protestant merchants, was the quickest to react militarily. Immediately 1,500 gardes nationaux set off on an expedition, while those from Toulouse prepared to do the same, prompting the 'aristocrats' of Montauban to release their prisoners and claim their patriotism. A confrontation had been narrowly avoided and the Bordelais withdrew at once.

In Nimes, it was even more serious. Since March, there had been frequent brawls between the Protestant Garde Nationale and the new companies of 'cébets' or onion-eaters, as their Protestant opponents had derisively called them. To put an end to this, the Protestant minority called on their co-religionists from the Cévennes Mountains who invaded the town between 13 and 16 June. The royal army observed strict neutrality and hardly intervened. The Regiment de Guyenne thus limited itself to lining up in front of its barracks while the Protestant gardes nationaux, after having broken down the doors of the garrison's arsenal, forcibly removed cannon which were immediately used against the entrenchments of the 'cébets'. The clashes were

THE GARDE NATIONALE 1789–1815

Artist Prieur shows Catholic gardes nationaux and the mob slaughtering Protestants. To the right of the composition, a Protestant is mistreated beneath a white flag: the artist thereby emphasises the political nature of the struggle. A few weeks later, similar clashes happened in Nîmes. Protestants were in a position to defend themselves vigorously this time. It is probably for this reason that Prieur did not depict this event. (Musée Carnavalet)

particularly bloody, with 300 victims on the Catholic side and 90 among Protestant gardes nationaux. The slaughter only ended with the intervention of the Montpellier Garde Nationale between the antagonists. Following this 'Nimes brawl', the Catholic companies were dissolved. The Protestants, for their part, obtained full satisfaction and maintained their hegemony but the gap between the two communities had only widened further.

Such episodes raise two main points. First, they certainly revealed a deep split in public opinion. This coincided with the great federative movement that led to the Parisian Festival of the Federation on 14 July 1790. Historian Georges Carrot wonders whether such bloody confrontations do not contradict the unanimity that, according to some historiography, characterises spring and summer 1790.[35] Moreover, this event sequence reveals the omnipresence of the Garde Nationale, which can be considered the main and almost unique actor in all these confrontations. Indeed, it provided both the protagonists of the conflict and the actors of the final appeasement process.

---

35 Carrot, *La Garde nationale*, p.74.

THE PROVINCES FOLLOWED: LOCAL GARDES NATIONALES

In 1789–1790, the Poitiers Garde Nationale battalions had a colourful look. For example, the Compagnie Colonelle wore a white uniform with red lapels and the Volontaires Nationaux had a blue uniform with red lapels. However, several suburban companies were without uniforms, for example this guardsman of the 1st company of the 2nd battalion and this *sergent* of the 1st company of the 3rd battalion. (Yves Martin)

Early Uniforms, 1789–1790

In those early months of the French Revolution, the Garde Nationale, as historian Roger Dupuy has argued, 'was obsessed with its uniform'.[36] Putting on the uniform was certainly far from trivial. It was a sign of patriotism but also a social factor which discriminated against the most popular social categories. In Tours, officers were obliged to buy it at their own expense and to wear it when on duty. As for the fusiliers, they were only obliged to wear a cockade and a *houppette* attached to their hat. In Poitiers, the companies of the faubourgs, in civilian clothes, coexisted with others in colourful uniforms. In Lyon, it was not compulsory to wear a uniform. At the beginning of 1790, claiming that there was 'no town in your generality that was poorer and had fewer local resources than ours' and that 'the hail and bad weather had made the poverty of the people worse', the municipality of Saint-Antonin asked Montauban to hand over clothes of the former provincial troops. Such reused uniforms were intended to clothe the '67 poorest inhabitants'.[37] However, the term 'people' used by the town councillors certainly referred to

---
36 Dupuy, *La Garde nationale*, p.48.
37 Archives Départementales du Lot (ADL): C 770.

99

Clermont-Ferrand Garde Nationale, 1790, by Henri Boisselier. (Yves Martin)

the artisanal world, and not to the most popular social strata, which would have been designated by the term 'populace'. The uniform also clearly distinguished urban gardes nationaux from their rural counterparts. Thus, on 6 September 1789, during the oath of the Gardes Nationales of the Clermont-Ferrand district, only the Clermont-Ferrand delegates wore uniforms, unlike those from the neighbouring villages of Beaumont and Aubière. The uniform made the sociological differences between the Clermont gardes and those of the adjacent communes eminently visible: 22 percent farmers in the first case, 53 percent in the second; respectively 49 percent and 12 percent shopkeepers, three percent and 20 percent craftsmen, 24 percent and 10 percent liberal professions, two percent and five percent *rentiers* and ecclesiastics, not to mention a marquis and a music master.[38]

Moreover, wearing a uniform brought the young bourgeois closer to the appearance of line troop officers. These officers sneered at such pretensions, exasperated by the sudden multiplication of *colonels* and *lieutenants* wearing epaulettes, even though they had no recognised military skills. The prestige attached to being in uniform was significant. The gardes, for example, made a point of appearing uniformly dressed for the federative festivities, during which they were called upon to march. At the festival organised in Lille on 26 April 1790, a local citizen noted that 'the entire Garde Nationale was in full dress, and almost all in uniform'.[39] In Marseilles, as in Epinal, the gardes were given uniforms in anticipation of the Festival of the Federation.

Finally, the uniform made an impression on women, as an anonymous garde national from Troyes unambiguously admitted: 'As it was, with or without epaulettes, the uniform alone inflamed the hearts of the newly enrolled. It has a very nice effect and is very popular with the ladies'.[40]

Contemporary Sources for Uniform Studies

Without any claim to completeness, *L'Etat militaire de la garde nationale de France pour l'année 1790, contenant l'état nominatif des officiers et bas-officiers des troupes patriotiques de Paris, de la banlieue, de toutes les villes et bourgs*

---

38 Philippe Bourdin, 'Fonder une garde nationale: Tensions sociales, éducation au civisme et enjeux politiques (Moulins – Clermont-Ferrand, 1789-1791)' in Serge Bianchi and Roger Dupuy (eds), *La Garde nationale entre nation et peuple en armes: Mythes et réalités 1789–1871* (Rennes: Presses Universitaires de Rennes, 2006), p.186.

39 Ate Richebé (ed.), *Journal d'un bourgeois de Lille pendant la Révolution 1787–1793* (Lille: D. Prévost Imprimeur, 1898), p.15.

40 Jacques Schweitzer, 'La Garde nationale à Troyes en 1789', Troyes d'hier à aujourd'hui, <https://www.jschweitzer.fr/la-r%C3%A9volution-fran%C3%A7aise/garde-nationale/>, accessed 1 September 2022.

THE PROVINCES FOLLOWED: LOCAL GARDES NATIONALES

du royaume, la couleur de l'uniforme, l'empreinte des boutons – two volumes *duodecimo* format – describes a large number of uniforms worn in the main cities of the kingdom, as well as in the larger villages. The *Almanach National pour l'année 1790* also devoted a very long section to the so-called 'Milices Bourgeoises'. It indicated, as far as possible, the organisation of the Gardes Nationales, the names of the officers, the description of the uniforms and flags. Its editors deplored, though, that

> this part of the *Almanach* was far from complete. In spite of the precautions taken to obtain information in all the capital cities of the kingdom, we were only able to obtain very poor results. Some people were quick to respond to our wishes. Others observed that the Milices existed in a shapeless manner. Still others remained silent. It must be admitted that the Milices are not yet organised. In several places, they have no staff or officers, or these change every week. They will not be truly up and running until the Assembly has decreed their organisation.[41]

Table 5. Uniforms of a selection of Gardes Nationales, 1789–1790 (from texts and iconography)

	Coat	Collar	Cuffs	Lapels	Turnbacks	Buttons
Hennebont	Dark blue	Scarlet	Scarlet	White	White	Yellow
Marseille	Blue	Scarlet	White Scarlet piping			Unknown
Epinal	Celestial blue	Celestial blue	Scarlet	Scarlet	White	White
Trie	Blue	Scarlet White piping	White	White	Blue	Initials 'MN'
Clermont-Ferrand	Royal blue	Crimson	Crimson	Unknown	Crimson Blue fleur-de-lis	White Stamped with the town's coat of arms Motto 'Nobilissima Averna Civitas'
Narbonne (most of the companies)	Red	Celestial blue White piping	White Celestial blue piping			White
Narbonne (the other companies)	Blue	Scarlet	Scarlet	Scarlet	White	Unknown
Lille	Blue	Red White piping	Red	Red		Stamped with the city's coat of arms Motto 'Garde Nationale de Lille'
Pézenas	Royal blue	White Scarlet piping	Scarlet	Scarlet	Unknown	Unknown
Frontignan	Scarlet	Celestial blue	Celestial blue	Celestial blue	White	White

---

41 Anon., *Almanach national pour l'année 1790* (Paris: Cuchet, 1790), p.226.

THE GARDE NATIONALE 1789–1815

Valenciennes	Blue	Red Blue piping	Red Blue piping	Blue Red piping	Red Blue piping	White
Chartres	Royal blue	Red	Celestial blue Red piping	Celestial blue Red piping	White Red fleur-de-lys	Yellow Stamped with the city's coat of arms
Dax	Red	Red	White Red piping	White Red piping	Red White fleur-de-lys (fusilier companies 3, 4 and 5)	White Stamped with the city's coat of arms
Feurs	Royal blue	Scarlet	Scarlet	White	White	Yellow Stamped with the coat of arms of France Motto 'Milice Nationale de Feurs'
La Rochelle	Dark blue	Scarlet	White	White	White Scarlet piping	Yellow Stamped with the city's coat of arms
Loriol	The same as that of Paris					Yellow Stamped with a dolphin Motto 'Régiment de Loriol'
Roanne	The same as that of Paris					Yellow Stamped with the city's coat of arms Motto 'La Loi, le Roi' et 'Roanne'
Grenoble	Red	Red	Black	Black	Red	Yellow Stamped with a dolphin
Montbrison (1st Company)	Scarlet	Sky blue	Sky blue	Sky blue	Sky blue	White Stamped with the city's coat of arms
Montbrison (the five other companies)	Dragoon green	Red	Red	Red	Yellow	Unknown
Saint-Malo	Red	Blue	White	White	Red	White Stamped with both the city's and the King's coat of arms
Néronde	Royal blue coat					
Toulon	Royal blue	Royal blue	Daffodil yellow	Daffodil yellow	White	Stamped with the city's coat of arms Motto 'Telo Martius'
Tours	Blue	Red	White Red piping	White Red piping	White Red piping	Stamped with the city's coat of arms
Troyes	Celestial blue	Red White piping	Red White piping	Red White piping	White	White Stamped with the city's coat of arms

THE PROVINCES FOLLOWED: LOCAL GARDES NATIONALES

La fête de la Fédération, le 14 juillet 1790, au Champ de Mars, oil on canvas by Charles Thévenin, circa 1792. The Festival of the Federation was notably marked by the gathering of the various Gardes Nationales from all over France. Their uniforms are under-studied as most assume they were of the blue, white and red colours, which was far from universal in July 1790. (Musée Carnavalet)

Historians have argued that 'credit must be given to the legislator's imagination in detailing gleaming uniforms.'[42] However, such regulations did not always exist, and when they did – as in Lyon, where the description of the uniform is contained in an eight-page brochure – they are nowadays extremely rare. Municipal deliberations often mention the creation of a Garde. They make it possible to know its objectives, its strength and to sketch its social composition. They also provide, as is the case in Tours or Troyes, useful information about the uniform being worn. In Tours, this was 'a blue coat, white lapels and cuffs piped in red, red collar, white breeches and jacket, white gaiters in summer and black in winter'. The buttons were 'yellow and stamped with the arms of the city'. 'The contre-epaulettes were red and decorated with a gold braid in the shape of a trefoil. The turnbacks were adorned with a fleur-de-lys and a scarlet tower'. A 'hat trimmed with a white striped basin cockade, decorated with two circles of woollen cloth, one of ponceau colour and the other of bleu-de-Roi' complemented the silhouette.[43]

Iconography also provides a considerable amount of data. Alongside the inevitable portraits – miniatures or otherwise – the plates of printmaker Nicolas Hoffmann are of particular interest. This Hessian artist was undoubtedly a shrewd businessman. Depending on the means of his client,

---

42 Pierre Arches, 'La Garde nationale de Saint-Antonin et les Fédérations du Rouergue et du Bas-Quercy (juillet 1789-juillet 1790)', *Annales du Midi*, 68:36 (1956), p.380.
43 Archives Municipales de Tours (AMT): EE 14.

THE GARDE NATIONALE 1789–1815

he either opted for a basic colouring or for a thorough reworking of his prints. During the Festival of the Federation, he produced a series of plates for the attendees and even for interested *amateurs*. Several gouached engravings depicting provincial gardes nationaux, mostly from Breton cities, have been preserved. Hoffmann used his generic plates devoted to the Garde Nationale Parisienne, which he modified for the purpose. Thus, a grenadier of the Nantes Garde Nationale was curiously fitted with a bearskin plate bearing the nave of Paris.

The Colour Choice

In the provinces, many gardes nationaux wore a uniform inspired by the one issued in Paris. However, cuffs and lapels were not always made of white cloth. In other municipalities, green, celestial blue, scarlet or white cloth was used. Did the colours of the uniform have any particular significance? Almost everywhere in France, gardes adopted the colour scheme of the capital. This was the case in a number of communes in Picardy, north of Paris, but also in Marseilles. On the occasion of the Festival of the Federation, the Garde Nationale was given a blue uniform with a scarlet collar and whose lapels, cuffs and turnbacks were cut from white cloth piped in scarlet. However, the opposite happened in Lyon. It seems that the volontaires formed in July 1789 adopted a uniform quite similar to that of the Garde Nationale Parisienne, in which blue, white and red were dominant. A few weeks after its late formation, the city's Garde Nationale, wishing to avoid confusion, therefore chose a different uniform. Other Gardes Nationales were inspired by line infantry uniforms. In Sens, in 1789, the men wore a white uniform with yellow buttons and scarlet collar, cuffs and lapels. It was very much inspired by the uniform of the Regiment de la Reine as defined in the 1786 clothing regulations. In Auxerre, the uniform closely resembled the blue one but with the distinctive reddish white of the Regiment Royal-Suedois. In Saint-Antonin, the old white uniforms of the Milice Provinciale were used. Such a situation was hardly unusual. On Charles Thévenin's *Fête de la Fédération*, provincial guardsmen are dressed this way. In Brest, administrators wrote that they had adopted

In 1790, the Garde Nationale of Sainte-Ménéhould was dressed in a red coat, black waistcoat and breeches. Their uniforms used the colours of the town's former Compagnie de l'Arquebuse. On 21 June 1791, when the royal family fled, the Garde Nationale took up arms at around 11:00 a.m., just as the population of the commune was worried about the arrival of cavalrymen charged with awaiting and then escorting the King and his family. (Yves Martin)

THE PROVINCES FOLLOWED: LOCAL GARDES NATIONALES

a scarlet uniform, black cuffs and lapels. We have decided that the officers will wear gold epaulettes according to their rank, in accordance with the Paris regulations. This mark of distinction is necessary more in Brest than elsewhere, firstly to impress the aristocracy, and secondly to instil in the hearts of patriots the desire to deserve, by their services, this honourable distinction which will be the only prize for their devotion.[44]

In the past, the wearing of a uniform had been refused by the Duc de Penthièvre so that there would be no possible confusion with the military nobility present in the city. In 1789, the Garde Nationale of this major harbour on the Atlantic Ocean was wearing a uniform as a form of social revenge.

Rainbow Warriors

In 1789–1790, all kinds of fantasies seemed to have been allowed, so much so that the provincial gardes nationaux could be called 'rainbow warriors'. Some common points are nevertheless identifiable among undeniably diverse uniforms.

Headgear

The gardes were most often wearing a felt hat, trimmed with 'goat hair' in Troyes and black silk in Valenciennes and Lyon. The latter was adorned with a cockade, which alternated blue, white, blue and red on the outside in Valenciennes. In Nîmes, the Protestant gardes nationaux wore a blue and white cockade. This emblem was maintained by a small uniform button and a black loop in Orléans, yellow in Hennebont and Grenoble and white in Nîmes. In Valenciennes, the colour of the plume identified the companies, which were additionally numbered. In accordance with the clothing regulations enacted on 19 April 1790, the Lyon gardes nationaux were given a tricolour plume – blue at the base, red at the top – made of rooster feathers.[45] In Poitiers, battalions and companies were distinguished by the colours of the tuft on the hat. The same logic applied in Pézenas: the pompom was white for the 1st company, green for the 2nd, black for the 3rd, blue for the 4th, lilac for the 5th, yellow for the 6th and red for the 7th. In Nîmes, the Catholic gardes nationaux were subtly differentiated from their Protestant counterparts by wearing a red pompom on their hat.

As for the grenadier companies, they had either the hat or the characteristic bearskin cap. The body was made of a combination of sewn-together leather pieces and covered with bearskin, brushed from bottom to

It has not been possible to find out to which Garde Nationale this guardsman belonged. He is dressed in a blue uniform with pale yellow lapels, red collar, both piped with *aurore* and fitted with white buttons. His hat is adorned with a tricolour plume. (François Vinot-Préfontaine's collection)

---

44 Archives Municipales de Brest (AMB): 2D19: Lettre du 24 août 1789.
45 Anon., *Arrêté du commandant général de la garde nationale de Lyon concernant l'uniforme* (Lyon: Aimé Delaroche Imprimeur, 19 avril 1790), p.4.

THE GARDE NATIONALE 1789–1815

Grenadiers of Poitiers Garde Nationale (left) and of Dol Garde Nationale (right), watercolours by Henri Boisselier. (Yves Martin)

top. It was topped by a circular patch with two white wool braids forming a cross. The inner cap was made of calfskin and canvas. Such a headdress was frequently embellished with a cord and a plume. In Poitiers, for example, the grenadiers marked their status with an entirely white plume. Finally, the cap was fitted with a plate. Local variations existed before a 'standardisation' took place in the spring of 1790. From then on, the Garde Nationale plates were almost identical in size from one copy to another. Made of stamped brass and attached to the cap by a steel wire, they were surmounted by a crude palmette and presented an overabundant iconography. Two medallions occupied the centre. The left one featured three fleurs-de-lys, while the right medallion was usually decorated with the arms of the city to which the garde belonged, such as Lyon, Orléans or Chartres. However, some medallions bore generic inscriptions, such as 'La Nation, La Loi, Le Roi' ('the Nation, the Law, the King'). A spear or a sword surmounted by a Phrygian cap separated them. On a ribbon was inscribed the motto 'Vivre Libre ou Mourir' ('Live Free or Die'). Plates were further decorated with a trophy of flags, weapons, musical instruments, the royal sceptre and fasces, drums, an oak branch and a laurel branch, cannon and their cannonballs. A flaming grenade was placed in each of the two lower corners.

THE PROVINCES FOLLOWED: LOCAL GARDES NATIONALES

Early Gardes Nationales buttons proved to be very diverse. They were regulated shortly after the Festival of the Federation. From left to right and top to bottom: Generic model marked 'Gardes Nationales de France' – buttons of the Gardes Nationales of Riom, Clermont-Ferrand, Joinville, Beauvais and Marseille – generic models, one of which is stamped with the words 'Liberté Egalité' – button of Nantes Garde Nationale staff. (Private collection, France)

Coat

The overwhelming majority of coats had lapels, but sometimes it was cut straight across the front, as in Clermont-Ferrand. The coat and its lapels were of various colours. The buttons were even more varied. The very first ones were stamped with the fleur-de-lys or bore the words 'Milices Nationales', appearing on two lines. Sometimes, as at Trie in the Oise, the gardes abbreviated it to 'MN'. In many places, local particularities and habits prevailed. The citizens who armed themselves constituted, for example, a 'Milice Patriotique d'Angoumois', a 'Regiment National' in Beaune and Moulins, a 'Garde Bourgeoise' in Versailles or a 'Troupe Nationale' in Valenciennes and Perpignan. All wanted to display these regional names on their buttons, often accompanied by the coat of arms of the towns from which they came. The city's motto could also appear on the buttons, as in the case of the buttons of the gardes nationaux of Beauvais or those of Clermont-Ferrand, which bore the Latin motto 'Nobilissima Averna Civitas'.

Grenadier companies were frequently distinguished – in Chartres, Poitiers and Nîmes for example – by red epaulettes. In Poitiers and Troyes, scarlet grenade badges were applied to the turnbacks of the grenadiers' coats. In Nîmes, the uniforms of the chasseur company, created in 1790, were

THE GARDE NATIONALE 1789–1815

Versailles garde national, 1789. Made of fabric using a Nicolas Hoffmann's plate, this grenadier wears a uniform very similar to that of Paris, just 20 kilometres away. Note the red cuffs, rather than the white ones. (Anne S.K. Brown Military Collection)

Bearskin plate of a Versailles Garde Nationale grenadier. (Ink drawing by René Louis, coloured by Jean-Claude Colrat)

adorned with green epaulettes. In Troyes, the turnbacks of the chasseurs' coat were embroidered with hunting horns.

Breeches

Breeches were usually white. This was notably the case in Lille, Valenciennes, Epinal, Narbonne and Pézenas. In Lyon, they were made of white wool in winter and of white cotton canvas or basin in summer. By contrast, they were blue in Amiens or Montélimar and black in Grenoble. It was also black in Troyes, but only from 1 October to 1 May. Gaiters were made of black woollen fabric in winter and white canvas in summer, as in Poitiers and Lyon.

Officers

Officers' dress was broadly similar to the troops, but they had a distinctive gorget. In Valenciennes, it was suspended from a tricolour ribbon and bore a lion surmounted by two fleurs-de-lys. In Lyon, it is described as being 'gilded and having a silver plate with the King's arms'.[46] Depending on the town, the distinctive marks of the ranks were either silver or gold. When under arms or on duty, officers wore boots.

Drummers, Musicians and Musical Instruments

The appearance of Garde Nationale drummers and musicians remains poorly known. In Lyon, the drummers wore the same uniform as the troops, with the sole difference that six tricoloured woollen braids were placed across the entire length of the sleeves of their uniform. Similar braids also

---

46   Barthélémi-Régis Dervieu Du Villars, *Arrêté du commandant général de la garde nationale de Lyon concernant l'uniforme* (Lyon: Aimé Delaroche Imprimeur, 1790), p.4.

THE PROVINCES FOLLOWED: LOCAL GARDES NATIONALES

Top: *Banquet civique donné par les gardes nationales de Lille aux troupes de la garnison, le 27 et 28 juin 1790*, coloured engraving by Albane, 1790. It is a scarce representation of Lille Garde Nationale band. Two oboists, a fifer, a bass drummer and a cymbal player are clearly identifiable. (Anne S.K. Brown Military Collection)
Left: Orléans Garde Nationale drummer, 1790, original gouache by Daniel Lordey. This watercolour is based on a painting by Maurice Orange. The drum is currently displayed in the Musée de l'Empéri, Salon-de-Provence. (Le Briquet's collection)
Bottom right: Scale model of a drum of the Orleans National Garde Nationale in 1790, after an authentic example kept in the Musée de l'Empéri in Salon-de-Provence. (Jean-Claude Colrat)

THE GARDE NATIONALE 1789–1815

adorned the collar, lapels and cuffs. In Toulon, 15 young musicians made up the harmony of the city's Garde Nationale. They marched at the head of it during general reviews, but also during parades which took place at 4:00 p.m. on Thursdays and Sundays in front of the town hall and on Sunday mornings, at 11:00 a.m., in front of the cathedral. They wore a uniform of scarlet cloth with blue lapels and cuffs. The white cloth turnbacks were decorated with fleurs-de-lys and a yellow woollen aiguillette was carried on the right shoulder. Led by a drum major, the 20 drummers of the Garde had the same uniform. *L'Etat militaire de la garde nationale de France pour l'année 1790* reports that the musicians of the Rodez Garde Nationale wore a red uniform with white lapels and cuffs piped in blue. Collar and lapels were additionally embellished with gold braid.

Instruments that can be attributed to the Garde Nationale are incredibly rare. A bass drum used by Poitiers Garde Nationale is still preserved. The case, made of wood and painted blue, is decorated with three fleur-de-lys surmounted by a royal crown, as well as a bicoloured flaming grenade, red and yellow. The words 'Garde Nationale de Poitiers' appear in a scroll. Also preserved is an Orléans Garde Nationale drum, probably made for the local federation festival of 9 May 1790. The drum case is painted with blue and red flames, largely hidden by the central motif: a pale blue disc decorated with two oval medallions and topped by a crown. Around the disc is painted, in black letters, the inscription 'Garde National d'Orléans' followed by a fleur-de-lys, also in black. On each side, a bundle of flags surmounts a cannon and a pyramid of cannonballs. The rims are painted with oblique tricolour stripes. Between the blue and red stripes, the white stripes are narrower. In Lyon, the regulation of April 1790 stated that drum cases would be made of copper and that the name of the district would be engraved on them.

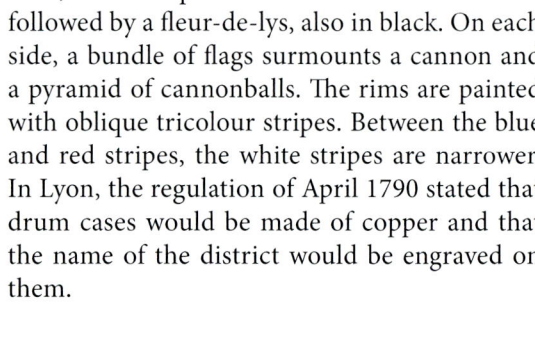

Portrait of a young – he was then 16 years old – Lorient Garde Nationale dragoon. He is dressed in a red coat with black lapels and is wearing a dragoon helmet. He is armed with a broadsword-like sword. (Yves Martin)

Cavalry

Mounted units were organised in various Gardes. In Altkirch, a corps of chasseurs à cheval was formed and given a green coat with red collar and buff breeches. On 17 July 1789, two volunteer dragoon squadrons were set up in Lorient. Over a white cloth waistcoat, each dragoon wore a scarlet coat with black velvet collar, cuffs and lapels. Breeches and gloves were yellow. The hat with a national cockade adopted in 1789 was replaced, before January 1791, by a dragoon helmet. The armament consisted of a sabre with a white thread sword knot, a musket and its bayonet, and a pair of pistols. The trumpeter had a uniform similar to that of the troop, the only difference being that silver braid adorned the collar, cuffs and lapels. In Narbonne, a corps of two squadrons of dragoons performed routine service on foot and on horseback wearing a green uniform with red lapels and copper buttons. Collar and cuffs were piped in red. The waistcoat was buff, as were the breeches. The dragoons of Narbonne wore a black hat with a two-coloured green and white plume. During the first months of the Revolution, the dragoon company of the Nîmes Garde Nationale had a green coat with pink collar, lapels and cuffs. Made of white metal, the buttons were embossed with the town's arms and the words 'Légion Nîmoise'.

Medical Services

A regulation enacted in Lyon was the only one to mention the presence of *chirurgiens-majors* of the districts. They were dressed in a uniform 'conforming to that of the troops', but cut from grey Conti cloth. Gold brandebourgs were embroidered on lapels and cuffs.

The Arms Puzzle

The armament of the provincial gardes nationaux proved to be diverse. In the cities, officers usually carried a sword. The latter had a gilded hilt in Valenciennes and Lyon. In Amiens, the sabre was favoured. As for the NCOs – *sergents* and *caporaux* – they were equipped with a musket, its bayonet and a sabre, while the ordinary fusiliers had a musket and its bayonet. In early August 1789, the Epinal Garde Nationale was solely armed with a hundred or so pikes decorated with tassels. In Auxerre, the veterans' company, made up of men over 55 years old, was equipped with a sabre and a halberd. The towns made varying efforts to adequately arm their Gardes Citoyennes. The permanent committee of Tours made a rather mediocre effort. Either because of a shortage of finances or because the situation was not as perilous as feared, the city limited itself to using the sabres and cannons stored in the city's arsenal and only a handful of new muskets were ordered from the Liège arms factory. Was the Tours Garde Citoyenne intended to assist the Committee in maintaining order, or was it a force designed to reassure the elites as much as to impress the popular elements? Similarly, in Auxerre, only 200 muskets intended to arm the local Garde Nationale were obtained from military stocks in Metz and immediately stamped 'Auxerre'. In contrast, the municipal authorities of Angers agreed to spend large amounts of money – nearly 16,400 *livres* – to arm their gardes nationaux as adequately as possible. The same was true in Mirecourt, a small commune in Lorraine, where 'quite considerable' expenditure was made on 5 October 1789.[47]

In the countryside, the situation was even less brilliant. In the summer of 1789, weapons available to the village gardes sometimes came from requisitions following visits to aristocrats' homes. Their members often had to make do with agricultural tools, scythes and forks. For lack of anything better, pikes were forged. In some communes, as in Bondoufle in July 1789, the local notables shared in the advances made for the purchase of muskets.

---

47   Archives Communales de Mirecourt (ACM): BB29: Registre des délibérations municipales.

THE GARDE NATIONALE 1789–1815

Cortège révolutionnaire, défilé de patriotes, watercolour by Etienne Bericourt. Only a handful of villagers donned the uniform of the Garde. The blue coat with red lapels allows us to date the watercolour to around 1790–1792. Pikes and peasant instruments are drawn in all their diversity. In the background, women armed with pikes and horsemen can be seen. The Garde Nationale was definitely a massive phenomenon. (Musée Carnavalet)

Ammunition was also lacking, so much so that in Limours, each garde had only one cartridge to carry out his patrol and an untimely shot could be worth a fine of up to 10 *sous*. Nevertheless, according to historian Serge Blanchi, the situation varied from one region to another.[48] The Breton communes thus seem to have been fairly well equipped with weapons.

A year later, the lack of arms remained chronic. The gardes nationaux wished to be armed, so the departmental administrations urged the Ministry to do what was necessary, but their hopes were quickly disappointed since the promised arms were almost exclusively distributed to the towns. Nevertheless, the Epinal Garde Nationale complained to the Vosges administrators that they had received only 334 muskets to equip no less than 4,000 gardes nationaux. Also, it asked that a complement be promptly dispatched to it, accompanied if possible by six artillery pieces and the appropriate ammunition. At the same time, investigations of the local authorities showed that weapons available to the village gardes nationaux consisted of a few muskets belonging to private individuals, hunting rifles and muskets bought with community money. Villages near the eastern borders of the kingdom asked in vain for war weapons, mostly muskets and pikes, in order to eventually face the enemy and maintain order in the countryside.

---

48   Bianchi, *La Garde Nationale entre nation et peuple en armes*, p.382.

PLATE SECTION 1

The Marquis de La Fayette, coloured engraving by Nicolas Hoffmann. The artist depicts La Fayette in the uniform of *Commandant General* of Paris' Garde Nationale. He is wearing the first regulation uniform from the summer of 1789. Note in particular the large epaulettes and the Order of Cincinnatus awarded to La Fayette. (Yves Martin)

Paris Garde Nationale by Nicolas Hoffmann. This garde is wearing the first uniform of the Garde, with a scarlet collar and white cuffs. Hoffmann has depicted the scarlet cloth naves applied to the turnbacks. The white pompom indicates that this guardsman belongs to Paris Garde Nationale's 3rd Division. (Yves Martin)

113

THE GARDE NATIONALE 1789–1815

Chartres Garde Nationale, 1790. This engraving by Nicolas Hoffmann matches perfectly the description of the uniform given in the *Almanach National pour l'année 1790*: 'royal blue coat, celestial blue lapels and cuffs, red piping and collar, white jacket and breeches, gilded copper buttons'. (Yves Martin)

Dreux Garde Nationale, 1790. When the Revolution began, Dreux had just over 5,000 inhabitants. Its gardes nationaux were dressed in a rather austere blue coat. (Yves Martin)

PLATE SECTION 1

At the beginning of the Revolution, many Gardes Nationales took on a red uniform. This is the case, for example, of the Gardes of Anet in the Eure-et-Loir (left) and of Hennebont in the Morbihan (right). Anet had about 1,500 inhabitants in 1789, but it still had a Garde Nationale. (Yves Martin)

115

THE GARDE NATIONALE 1789–1815

Garde and *sergent* of Brest's Garde Nationale, 1790. These two prints by Nicolas Hoffmann show the attention to detail of this Hessian artist who had been living in Paris since 1776. His depictions perfectly match the Brest Garde Nationale's uniform description as given in a letter dated 24 August 1789. (Yves Martin (left) and Anne S.K. Brown Military Collection (right))

PLATE SECTION 1

In 1789, the Nantes Garde Nationale formed two battalions subdivided into 10 companies of 100 men each: two of grenadiers, the same number of chasseurs, and six of fusiliers. Hoffmann accurately depicted the blue uniform with yellow lapels piped in scarlet. However, the bearskin plate bears a nave, symbol of Paris. (Yves Martin)

Parthenay Garde Nationale, coloured engraving by Nicolas Hoffmann. The gardes were dressed in a smart white uniform. In March 1790, they quelled the movement blocking the removal of grain from the city. (Yves Martin)

THE GARDE NATIONALE 1789–1815

Depicted by Nicolas Hoffmann, this grenadier is dressed in the uniform decreed during the course of July 1791. His white and blue plume indicates that he belongs to the 6th Division of the Garde Nationale Parisienne. (Yves Martin)

Garde Nationale drummer. His uniform is abundantly adorned with tricolour braids. The bearskin cap plate hardly corresponds to the most common models. (Librairie Historique Teissèdre)

PLATE SECTION 1

Garde Nationale veteran, coloured engraving by Nicolas Hoffmann, 1791. This veteran is dressed in the uniform regulated on 13 July 1791. The hat, the white epaulettes and the sash are noteworthy. The weaponry consists of a pike carried with confidence and a sabre whose appearance remains questionable. (Librairie Historique Teissèdre)

At first glance, few elements distinguish this Garde Nationale gunner from his counterparts in the line army. The soldier is dressed in a royal blue uniform with scarlet facings. Cannon adorn the turnbacks. (Librairie Historique Teissèdre)

THE GARDE NATIONALE 1789–1815

On Friday 23 July 1790, at around 2:00 p.m., the 11 delegates, their 11 substitutes and the 100 gardes nationaux who represented the Orléans Garde Nationale at the Festival of the Federation, made their way back to their town. Carried at their head by *Sergent-Major* Francheterre, was the banner given by the Paris Commune to each departmental delegation. (Original artwork by Jean-Claude Colrat)

This white silk taffeta banner was offered by the Paris Commune. On 14 July 1790, it was blessed by Talleyrand, bishop of Autun, during the Festival of the Federation. The next day, it was displayed in the National Assembly's session room. (Original artwork by Jean-Claude Colrat)

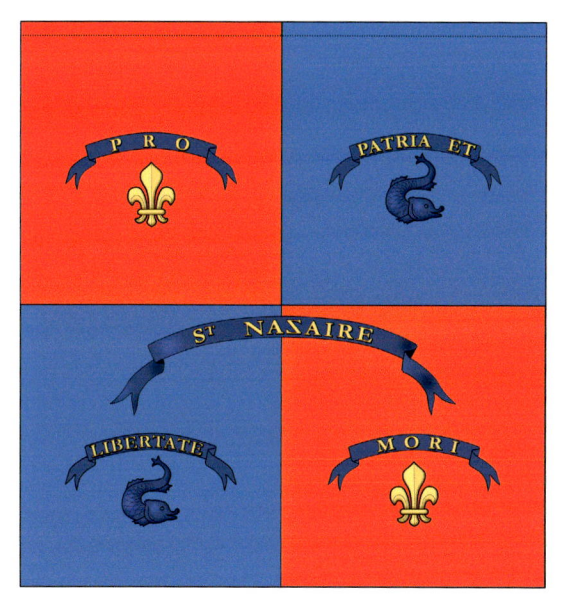

PLATE SECTION 1

Flag of Saint-Nazaire en Royans Garde Nationale, 1789. (Original artwork by Jean-Claude Colrat)

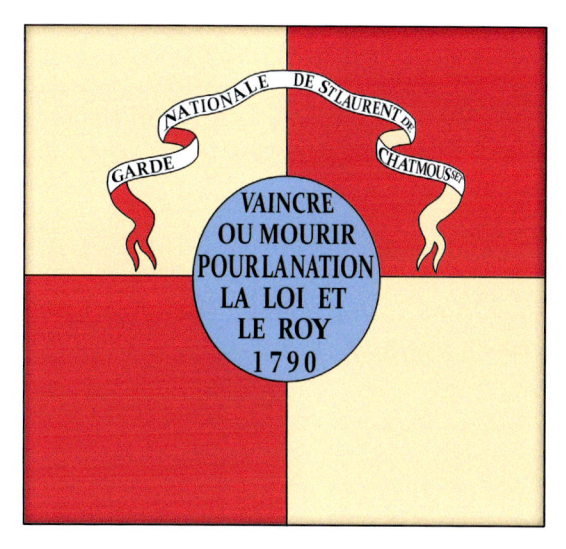

Flag of Saint-Laurent de Chamousset Garde Nationale, 1790. This flag in silk taffeta was made in 1790. Note the spelling error on 'Chamousset'. The flag was discovered when the town hall was moved in 1990. It was restored in 1994 and classified as a historical monument in 1995. (Original artwork by Jean-Claude Colrat)

Flag of the Garde Nationale of Echigey and the three Tards, 1790. (Original artwork by Jean-Claude Colrat)

Olonzac Garde Nationale flag. This silk flag, of which only the reverse is reproduced, uses the white cross of the royal colours. On the obverse, a Phrygian cap and the inscription 'Constitution-Liberté' appear. This emblem is currently on display at the Musée de l'Empéri in Salon-de-Provence. (Original artwork by Jean-Claude Colrat)

121

THE GARDE NATIONALE 1789–1815

Autezat Garde Nationale flag, 1791. This large flag, inspired by the infantry colours of the Ancien Régime, is made of silk and has a white cross delimiting two azure and two red cantons. This emblem, now held in the Musée de l'Armée (Paris), is surprisingly embroidered on one side only. (Original artwork by Jean-Claude Colrat)

Varennes Garde Nationale flag, 1791. Following the King's arrest at Varennes, the Constituent Assembly decided on 18 August 1791 that each garde of the commune would be given a musket and a sabre. The Garde Nationale would also receive two cannon and a flag which was seized by Prussian troops in 1792 and deposited in the royal arsenal in Berlin. (Original artwork by Jean-Claude Colrat)

Dieppe Garde Nationale flag. It was probably made in 1791. The reverse is exactly the same. This flag was exhibited at the 1889 Universal Exhibition in Paris. (Original artwork by Jean-Claude Colrat)

Gumbrechtshoffen Garde Nationale flag, 1791. This flag has been kept since the nineteenth century in the Château de Chantilly. It is unclear how it came into the Prince de Condé's ownership. In 1838, the municipality of Gumbrechtshoffen unsuccessfully requested that this emblem be returned. (Original artwork by Jean-Claude Colrat)

PLATE SECTION 1

Carouge Garde National flag. After Sardinian troops failed to invade the Mont Blanc region in October 1792, Carouge remained a French city until 1814. This flag, now kept in the Musée d'Art et d'Histoire de Genève, belonged to the local Garde Nationale. Is this the flag blessed on 30 June 1793 and mentioned in contemporary sources? (Original artwork by Jean-Claude Colrat)

Mont Blanc Garde Nationale flag; 1804–1814. (Original artwork by Jean-Claude Colrat)

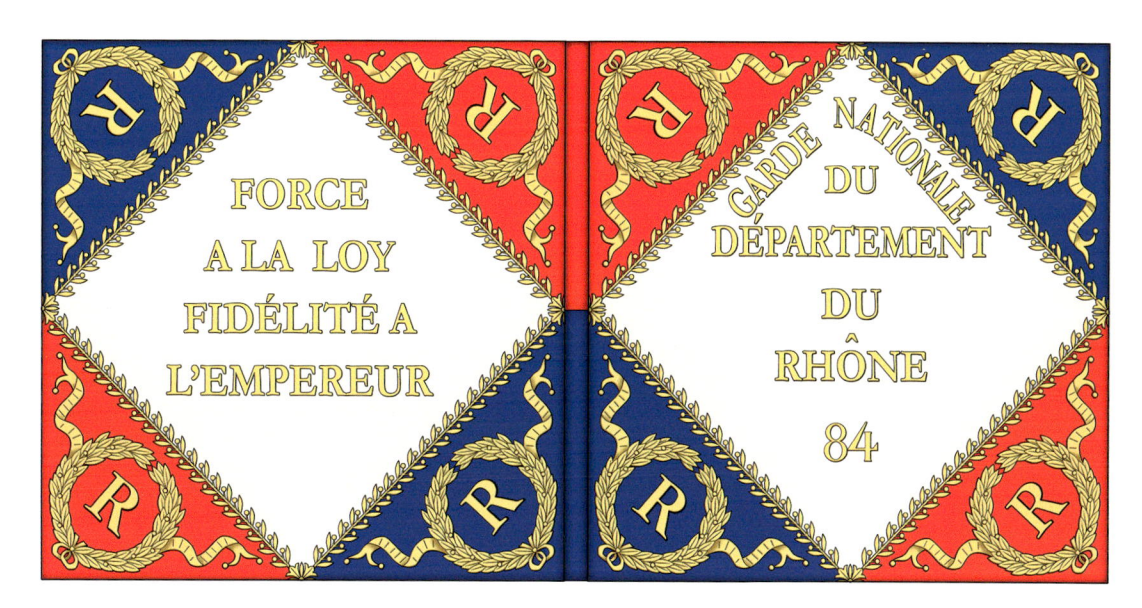

Rhône Garde Nationale flag, 1804–1814. This flag is topped by a pike, instead of the regulation eagle. It is currently preserved, in a very degraded state, in the Musée de l'Armée, Paris. (Original artwork by Jean-Claude Colrat)

THE GARDE NATIONALE 1789–1815

Flacq Garde Nationale flag. This silk taffeta flag is currently preserved in the Musée de l'Armée, Paris. The corner wreaths have no inscriptions. (Original artwork by Jean-Claude Colrat)

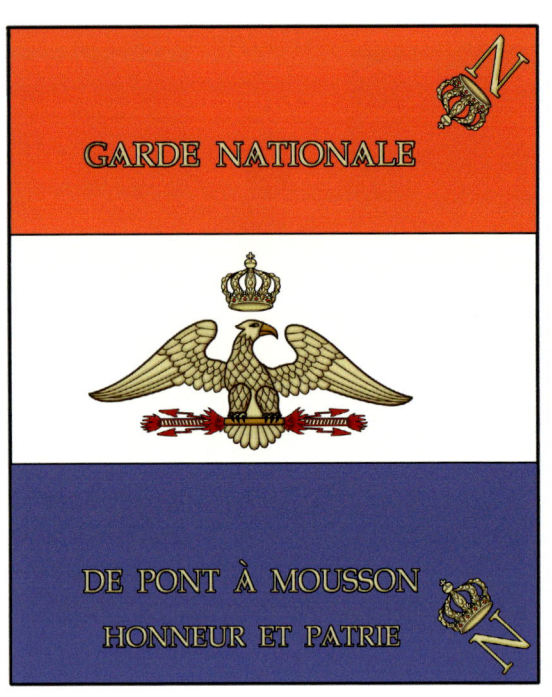

This pennant of Pont-à-Mousson's Garde Nationale (1810–1814) is said to have been seized during the campaign of France in 1814. In 1925, it became part of the collections of the Museum of History and Culture of Kama Sarapul, in Udmurt Republic, Russia. (Original artwork by Jean-Claude Colrat)

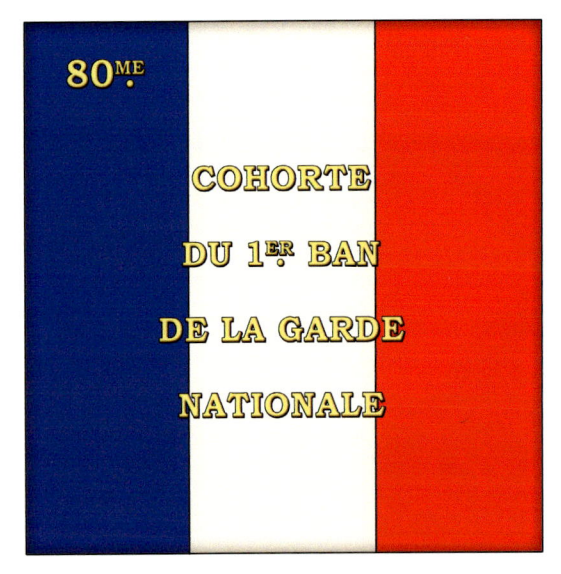

The Garde Nationale's 80e Cohorte was used to form the 150e Regiment d'Infanterie de Ligne in February 1813. Its flag was taken from a military storehouse by Allied troops in 1814. This 97 centimetres square flag had no inscription on the reverse. It also lacked fringes and cravats. It was mounted on a black-painted staff with an iron pike on top. (Original artwork by Jean-Claude Colrat)

1812 pattern flag of the 153e Regiment d'Infanterie de Ligne. The reverse was devoid of battle honours. (Original artwork by Jean-Claude Colrat)

PLATE SECTION 1

Morbihan Garde Nationale flag, 1815. All embroidery is in silver. This example is currently on display at the Wellington Museum in Waterloo. (Original artwork by Jean-Claude Colrat)

Elba Garde Nationale flag. It was ordered in spring 1815 and seized by Prussian troops the same year in Paris. Shortly afterwards it was sold to an English gentleman, Mr Cureton. At the beginning of the twentieth century, it was displayed in the Tussaud Museum, until it was destroyed by a fire in 1925. A colour engraving of it remains, published in England by Mr Cureton in 1823. It was used to create this illustration. (Original artwork by Jean-Claude Colrat)

Flag of the Seine-et-Oise Garde Nationale, 1815. Obverse and reverse are illustrated here. (Original artwork by Jean-Claude Colrat)

4

From Gardes Nationaux to Volontaires Nationaux

1789–1794

Both the royal army and the Garde Nationale were involved in the revolutionary process from the outset. Mainly composed of military personnel, most of whom were in favour of national sovereignty, the Military Committee of the fledgling Constituent Assembly was concerned very early on with the relationship between the two entities and with the organisation of the armed forces. As early as the autumn of 1789, it prepared, jointly with the Ministry of War, a report on military organisation and recruitment. It was presented on 19 November and, on 12 December, the debate began in the Assembly. Two opposing theses clashed in the Salle du Manège in Paris.

Lengthy Parliamentary Debates

A patriotic aristocrat and soldier by vocation, Dubois-Crancé presented a particularly remarkable report, inspired by the theses of the philosopher Rousseau. He spoke of a national, universal and compulsory conscription, aimed at all active citizens; around 1,200,000 men. Furthermore, he suggested dividing the military forces into three parts, following a pyramidal logic. The third line – the Garde Nationale – would include every man and voter capable of bearing arms. Each garde would have his own musket and sabre and would meet once a year with the other gardes of his commune. The second line, totalling 150,000 men, would be formed by the provincial Milices composed of all active and unmarried citizens between the ages of 18 and 40, registered as part of the active army. They would be under the orders of their municipality and canton, and their commanders would be appointed by the Garde Nationale. In the cities, these Milices would exercise once a week in summer and would ensure the safety of their fellow citizens. In wartime, they would supplement the army, which would first take on the older men. The village Milices would not serve. Their weapons were to be collected in the chief town of the canton and handed out only in case of absolute necessity to fill the gaps in the urban formations. However, six men, chosen from each of these Milices, would be armed to assist the police. Such precautions undoubtedly betrayed the concerns of the patriots in the face of the uncontrolled and contagious violence that had shaken the rural world on the occasion of the 'Great Fear'. The first line would consist of 150,000 men from the regiments of the royal army, professional soldiers recruited by voluntary enlistment. War, in fact, could not be improvised. At the end of their engagement, these professionals would train and supervise the departmental Milices, so that the military quality of the gardes nationaux could only progress rapidly. Dubois-Crancé stressed the urgency of following his views. The new principles being applied in France could not but arouse the hostility of the other European monarchies. War seemed inevitable to him and France had to give itself the necessary means to win.[1]

Yet Dubois-Crancé's views were far from being widely held. Instead of welcoming the patriotic impetus embodied by the gardes nationales, many deputies were suspicious of their proliferation and the fragmentation of their municipal organisation, which could revive old local rivalries. Even within the Military Committee, Dubois-Crancé's colleagues feared this massive and uncontrolled armament, which they perceived as a potential cause of disorder. In fact, the Duc de Biron, the Baron de Wimpffen and the Comte de Custine all advised for the retention of the traditional system. In his *Réflexions sur l'établissement des milices nationales*, Custine was in favour of a professional army recruited through voluntary enlistment and supplemented by militiamen drawn by lottery. Convinced of the so-called manoeuvring superiority of other European permanent armies, first and foremost the Prussian infantry, many of his colleagues believed that the Garde Nationale would never reach this level of efficiency. Giving it too much importance was suicidal. On the contrary, it should be confined to police duties and made into a sort of reserve from which the royal army could, in wartime, draw a number of pre-prepared reinforcement units and above all detachments to guard supplies, coastal works and inland fortresses.[2]

In their respective speeches, Dubois-Crancé and Custine had both used the expression 'national Milices', without giving it the same meaning. A radical like Dubois-Crancé made it the vector of a refoundation of the military organisation of the kingdom. A moderate like Custine used it to justify a reform of the old provincial Milices. The Assembly refused to make a decision, backing neither Custine nor Dubois-Crancé. On 16 December 1789, it confined itself to voting on a decree which stipulated that 'French troops, of whatever arm they are, other than the gardes nationaux and Milices, will be recruited by voluntary enlistment'.[3] During the debates, the deputies had denounced the abuses of the recruitment system, but failed to abolish the mechanism that led to them. Nor had they resolved the problem of the reserve, whose existence had until then been based on the lottery

---

[1] Dupuy, *La Garde nationale*, p.216.
[2] Madival & Laurent (eds), *Archives Parlementaires*, vol.X, p.555.
[3] Madival & Laurent (eds), *Archives Parlementaires*, vol.X, p.620.

for provincial militiamen. This particularly unpopular practice had been denounced by a large proportion of the cahiers de doléances, which openly called for the abolition of the militia draw.

The discussions highlighted the difference of nature, as well as the complementarity, between the Garde Nationale and the army. The former defended freedom, the latter could be a threat to it. But by taking the right to bear arms and to organise themselves as troops, the citizens placed themselves, at least in appearance, on the same level as the soldiers. Indeed, some thought that they could therefore be employed for the same tasks, including the external defence of the kingdom. The idea, at any rate, was in vogue. Nevertheless, before proceeding to a definitive organisation, it was necessary to fix the attributions of the army and the Garde Nationale with respect to the executive power. In January 1790, the deputies agreed that the gardes nationaux would be responsible for maintaining the future *Constitution*. The army was to defend the state from external enemies. From then on, rather than organising these two large forces and clarifying the logic of their coexistence, the Assembly was irresolute and lost itself in procrastination.

By 1790, however, the royal army was close to dissolution. Set at 150,000 men, its actual strength peaked at 120,000 in August, but it fell to only 98,000 men three months later.[4] Officers resigned en masse or emigrated. Desertion among the troops reached rarely seen levels. In addition, the year was punctuated by mutinies and riots which culminated in August with the Nancy Mutiny and by the disturbances affecting elements of the royal navy in Brest. The Assembly remained passive when faced with these revolts which were harshly repressed by the officers, even those who professed liberal ideas or belonged to Freemasonry. It was more a spectator to the re-establishment or attempts at re-establishing discipline than it was directing the movement. In September, it nevertheless adopted a series of decrees imposing new rules of discipline, establishing military tribunals, but liberalising the rules of promotion. The widespread mutinies of the royal troops were only one aspect of a serious political destabilisation. At the same time, the kingdom of France was confronted with the beginnings of a real religious war that was brewing in the departments of the Midi.

In this context, it became urgent to define and organise this public force which the deputies had so often mentioned, either to deplore its weakness or to fear its power. Faced with this legal vacuum, the Assembly resolved to examine the *Rapport général sur l'organisation de la force publique* presented on 21 November 1790 by their colleague Rabaut Saint-Etienne, on behalf of the Military Committee and the Constitution Committee. Such a text finally gave a definition to the public force. Legally, it corresponded to 'the union of the force of all the citizens' and was divided into three main parts. According to Rabaut Saint-Etienne, the Garde Nationale was 'nothing other than the nation' or, more accurately, it was a gigantic armed force residing in the nation. However, it was not a 'military corps', but only 'the determination

---

4   Albert Meynier, 'L'armée en France sous la Révolution et le 1er Empire', *Revue d'Etudes Militaires*, 19:5 (1931), p.7.

FROM GARDES NATIONAUX TO VOLONTAIRES NATIONAUX

of the mode in which citizens should assemble, form and act when required to perform their service'. The 'armed corps for internal service', such as the Gendarmerie instituted in January 1791 to replace the old Maréchaussée, were to act 'against those who disrupt order and peace'. Finally, it was the army's responsibility to 'act against external enemies'.[5]

Nevertheless, many patriots did not despair of assigning military functions to the Garde Nationale, especially as its organisation was suitable for this. Drafted by the Military Committee, the *Instruction du 1er janvier 1791* distinguished in this respect between the Garde Nationale in 'their usual state', whose aim was the internal policing of the kingdom, and 'in their accidental situation', whose aim was 'the external defence of the kingdom'. Conceived to normalise the evolutions of the gardes nationaux, this *Instruction* prescribed to make them manoeuvre in battalions, but also to instruct them in column on the march.[6] That same month, 100,000 muskets marked 'AN', for 'Arme Nationale', were distributed to the gardes nationaux of the frontier and maritime departments. This decision showed the firm resolution of the Military Committee to compel the mass of citizens to support the line army troops.

Soldier of the Regiment d'Aquitaine and gardes nationaux, 1791. (Original artwork by Patrice Courcelle)

On an idea of Deputy Alexandre Lameth, the Committees of the National Assembly proposed to extract a national Milice force from the Garde Nationale. On paper, it was a question of organising a corps that could quickly set off 'at the moment when the Nation in danger would call for its help'.[7] Each canton was to provide a company of volontaires of 30 to 50 men. These companies were to be grouped together at the rate of one battalion per district and, at each level, the volontaires were to elect their officers. The whole was to total a reserve of about 250,000 men. But on 28 January, a majority of the deputies of the Assembly rejected this project, preferring to stick to the raising of 100,000 auxiliaries which would complete 30 line

---

5   Madival & Laurent (eds), *Archives Parlementaires*, vol.XX, p.598.
6   Anon., *Instruction pour les gardes nationales, arrêtée par le Comité Militaire et imprimée par ordre de l'Assemblée Nationale* (Paris: Imprimerie Nationale, 1791), p.63.
7   Madival & Laurent (eds), *Archives Parlementaires*, vol.XXII, p.535.

infantry regiments. In accordance with the principles voted on 16 December 1789, these were volontaires aged between 18 and 40 who signed up for a period of three years. They did not leave their homes, were only required to undergo a bi-annual review and had to join their regiments in wartime. They received, even in peacetime, an allowance of three *sols* per day and continued to enjoy their rights as citizens. In a way, they were the successor to the Ancien Régime Milice recruited by lottery and which was definitively abolished on 20 March 1791. It was not until 4 June that the beginnings of their organisation were sketched out.

The radicalisation of the revolutionary movement certainly favoured the objectives of the patriotic military. The affair of the German princes who owned land in Alsace, the repression of the Brabant Revolution, the agitation of the emigrants at the borders as well as the internal divisions commonly attributed to the actions of the counter-revolutionaries, argued in their favour. As the months went by, the shadow of the looming war considerably altered the conceptions that were then held by the vast majority of French people and most of their representatives. The Revolution appeared threatened both from the inside and the outside. Also, in December 1790, the departmental authorities of the Var had sent 600 volontaires to the border. On the 12th of that month, a decree passed that allowed the commanding officers and the Maréchaussée to request and then move the gardes nationaux in order to prevent a possible Austrian invasion from the Netherlands or Luxembourg.

In late January, the Assembly had effectively managed to bury Alexandre Lameth's proposal. This success was short-lived, since in the spring it was literally besieged by petitions requesting the creation of armed forces from the gardes nationales. It resisted as much as it could, especially as the supporters of a military reserve composed of gardes nationaux had obviously not given up their project. On 8 March, the Assembly – at the request of deputy Merlin de Douai – ordered that a report 'on the measures to be taken for the defence of the State' be submitted to it.[8] This was done on 10 June, at a time when the internal situation was worrying and the army in complete collapse. While the emigration of officers continued at a steady pace, petitions from patriotic clubs such as the Jacobins were now openly calling for the dissolution of the royal troops. If the deputies refused to pronounce themselves on either the dismissal of the officers or the dissolution of the army, they nevertheless took account of the scale of the popular initiatives. The next day, rightly concerned about the threat posed by the emigrant army on the borders of France, the Constituents conscripted one in 20 of the gardes nationaux of the departments. It was neither more nor less than a call for volontaires. In truth, the deputies had been preempted by the initiatives of several towns and departments. On 4 February, the Paris municipality had already decided to open a register in which volontaires could enlist. Nevertheless, enthusiasm moderated and a large part of the press found this initiative dangerous. But it did not matter. That same month of February, the Puy-de-Dôme patriots asked for the opening of registers, which was granted the following month.

---

8   Lacroix, *Actes de la Commune de Paris*, vol.V, p.74.

In May, the department of Gironde followed suit. The men called up by the Assembly elected their officers but awaited orders from the central power to do so. Moreover, they would only be paid when the needs of the State required it and would go into action when war broke out. It was therefore only a precautionary measure, with no immediate effect, concerning around 110,000 men. No one could have imagined then that, eight days later, this national armed force would become a reality.

The 1791 Levy of Volontaires

The King's Flight, a Game-Changing Event

On 21 June, the King's escape abruptly changed the situation. Informed of what it called the 'kidnapping' of Louis XVI and the royal family, the Assembly took control of the government and, over the course of 21 and 22 June, issued no fewer than 30 decrees. On the evening of the 21st, Alexandre Lameth passed a decree of capital importance without discussion. First of all, this text ordered that the function of the gardes nationaux of the kingdom was to 'provide for the internal and external safety of the State and the maintenance of the *Constitution*'.[9] In addition, it called for the raising of the largest possible number of men in the border departments of the east, and that of 2,000 to 3,000 men in all the others. Such a decree finally confirmed that these volontaires would elect their officers and NCOs, whose conditions of eligibility were strictly fixed and that they would receive a pay of 15 *sols*, twice as high as that paid to the infantrymen of the royal army. During the summer, while the *Pillnitz Declaration* increased the fear that war would break out very quickly between the still peaceful France and the main European powers, the Constituents gradually specified the terms of this first levy of men by the decrees of 22 July and 4 August. Many departments were then assigned a specific number of battalions to organise according to their population. In many cases, the total number of men they had to muster did not reach the figure of 2,000 or even 3,000 men initially requested. On 17 August, the number of men to

Volontaires Nationaux infantryman and drummer, 1791–1792, gouache by Henri Boisselier, based on documents from the Henin and Würtz collections. (Yves Martin)

---

9   *Révolutions de Paris*, 103 (1791).

be raised finally came to 100,450, divided into 175 battalions of 568 men each, distributed into eight companies of 71 men. On the indication of their comrades, eight men of tall stature were to be extracted from them to make up a grenadier company. From then on, a battalion of volontaires consisted of nine companies of 63 men each.

Table 6. Volontaires Nationaux company. Organisation of August 1791

Capitaine	1
Lieutenant	1
Sous-lieutenant	1
Sergent-major	1
Sergent	2
Caporal	4
Tambour	1
Grenadier/Fusilier	52
Total	63

The 1791 Volontaires, Facts and Myths

It was necessary to create a real recruitment service to form the first battalions of volontaires. The departmental directorates appointed commissioners in each district to centralise the enlistments. In Lorraine, explains historian Jean-Paul Rothiot, they were generally members of the department's general council, almost all of whom were judges of their district court.[10] In the Eure, according to historian Jean Vidalenc, they were former officers, retired for the most part, and knights of Saint-Louis.[11]

A geography of attitudes towards the raising of the Volontaires Nationaux was sketched out from 1791. There was a France of apathy, a France that responded to enlistments without excessive passion but without reluctance either and, finally, a France of enthusiasm. In Lorraine, explains Rothiot, the 1791 levy was carried out promptly and the objectives set were quickly achieved and even exceeded.[12] The Vosges provided five battalions instead of the four requested, the Meurthe, seven battalions and the Meuse, eight. Similarly, the Nord and the Pas-de-Calais had to raise three battalions each, an objective that these two border departments achieved in barely two months. The Pas-de-Calais even had a surplus of 426 men which enabled it to form the cadre of a fourth. In contrast, some departments in the Massif Central and the southwest did not even participate in the levy, while others were extremely slow to respond. Several departments in the west took nearly five or six months to pay their voluntary tribute.

---

10   Jean-Paul Rothiot, 'De la milice à la Garde nationale en Lorraine, 1750–1792', in Serge Bianchi and Roger Dupuy (eds), *La Garde nationale entre Nation et peuple en armes* (Rennes: Presses Universitaires de Rennes, 2006), p.354.

11   Jean Vidalenc, 'Les volontaires nationaux dans le département de l'Eure', *Annales Historiques de la Révolution Française*, 114 (1949), p.119.

12   Rothiot, 'De la milice à la Garde nationale en Lorraine, 1750–1792', p.355.

This is how the first military corps from the Nation came into being. Although they were supposed to alleviate the recurring manpower problems of the line army, they were no longer intended, like the auxiliaries, to supplement it. However, although many patriots publicly suspected the army of counter-revolutionary sentiments, the Assembly did not seek to establish a new army to replace the royal troops. It is true that the volontaires had a different uniform and pay from the army. Carried by a *sergent-major*, their tricolour flags, on which were inscribed the name of the department and the number of the battalion, were specific to them. But on the frontiers they had to defend, as on the battlefields, the volontaires, to whom the rules of military discipline were applied albeit in a more relaxed manner, would operate alongside the army and be placed under the orders of generals. The desire to bring the battalions of volontaires closer to the regular army was obvious, so as to facilitate their implementation and command.

The Assembly hoped to control these Volontaires of 1791. In the first place, they were recruited from among the Garde Nationale, which was theoretically made up of active citizens and their sons. In addition, the volontaires were grouped into battalions, which were small units and therefore relatively easy to monitor. Until the departure from their home department, each battalion remained under the almost total control of the civilian authorities: in this respect, the departmental and district directorates had the upper hand in the raising of Volontaires of 1791, from their inscription on the registers opened by the municipalities to the formation of the units. This was, in a way, the implementation of the principle of the supremacy of civil power over military authority. Finally, the election of officers by their men was a definite innovation, albeit one that was carefully supervised and controlled. The decree of 4 August specified that one of the two *lieutenant-colonels* – the highest rank in the battalion – was required to have served as a *capitaine* in the royal army. The other officers were also expected to have served in the army. This was obviously to keep out the incompetents. If they did not come from the regulars, Volontaires officers had to have been Garde Nationale officers previously. Moreover, the elections and their results in a number of departments confirmed that, at least as far as the Volontaires' command was concerned, the intentions of the Constituents were fully satisfied. The deputies wanted a bourgeois levy: this was achieved by the officers' background. Elections were held under the control of the local bourgeoisie and resulted in the appointment to the higher ranks of notables, sons of the middle class or the nobility, most of whom had some experience of the profession of arms.

In 1791, the Volontaires levy took place in peacetime. However, it had an immense impact and its course gave rise to various myths. The first of these opposed the volontaires themselves, whose enrolment was based solely on patriotism and was totally pure, as it was free of all material and financial considerations, to the 'mercenaries'. Such a pejorative term ended up reflecting on the professional soldiers. They too had in theory enlisted voluntarily, but they had turned their enlistment into a profession, or at least a means of earning a living. The myth obviously proved to be a hard one, as French historian Jacques Godechot testifies: 'The Volontaires of 1791 were undoubtedly the most authentic of the volontaires raised during the Revolution. No coercion was exerted on the Garde Nationale to obtain enlistments.'[13]

However, the way in which the 1791 levy was carried out demonstrates the deceptive nature of the legend. Each volontaire was required to dress, equip and arm himself at his own expense, which represented a considerable expenditure. This was probably the reason why the pay allocated to volontaires was so high. However, many of the active citizens had modest fortunes. Also, in this period of economic crisis, even the most sincere patriots could find the pay attractive. As proof, the recruitment of the battalions of volontaires completely dried up that of the auxiliaries, which was organised simultaneously. Those who had initially joined the auxiliaries 'deserted' en masse to join the battalions of volontaires. The authorities readily acknowledged that it would have been difficult not to prefer the pay allocated to them compared with the three *sols* paid to the auxiliaries, which was five times less. But it is not easy to distinguish between the motivations of the volontaires: the auxiliaries remained at home until the declaration of war, while the volontaires headed for the frontiers. For a patriot, this circumstance could prove decisive. The Constituent's lack of understanding of these realities almost compromised the results of this first levy. It undoubtedly delayed the departure of volontaires in some departments. Forcing volontaires to dress and equip themselves at their own expense should, it seems, have been enough to keep out the poorest citizens, but many passive citizens had been serving as gardes nationaux since the beginning of the Revolution. On 4 September 1791, the Assembly drew the extreme consequence of this situation by authorising the departments to grant impecunious volontaires the necessary advance, reimbursable from their pay, to acquire clothing and equipment. As far as the social origin of volontaires was concerned, the wishes of the deputies of the Assembly had been exceeded.

War and the New Call for Volontaires

France declared war on Austria and Prussia on 20 April 1792. Things turned out badly for the royal armies. Faced with the Austrian advance, and especially that of the Prussians, the issue of manpower became crucial once again. If the rhythm of the levies of men increased, it was not yet time to consider instituting a new armed force.

A Series of Legislative Measures
On 5 May, Lacuée presented a report on volontaires. Long before the famous decree of 23 August 1793, it envisaged a *levée en masse* for a revolutionary war which was to have as its motto 'Liberty or Death'. The next day, the creation of 31 new battalions of volontaires was decided. Twenty of them would be raised in 10 departments which had not provided a contingent in 1791, in other words Cantal, Aveyron, Tarn, Lot, Lot-et-Garonne, Ardèche, Lozère,

---

[13] Jacques Godechot, *Les institutions de la France sous la Révolution et l'Empire* (Paris: Presses Universitaires de France, 1968), p.137.

FROM GARDES NATIONAUX TO VOLONTAIRES NATIONAUX

Départ d'un volontaire pour les armées révolutionaires, gouache by Lesueur. No detail is missing from this depiction of a volontaire happily leaving his home, along with his spouse and children. It is not uncommon for them to leave only after the first stage of their journey. Then came the most emotional farewells. (Musée Carnavalet)

This other Lesueur gouache depicts another departure of a volontaire, certainly more bourgeois, as suggested by the elegance of the women, the young man's powdered hair and his father's breeches. (Musée Carnavalet)

135

Gers, Dordogne and Haute-Loire. The 11 others would be distributed, thereafter, 'in the departments of the interior of the kingdom which offered to raise them and which, by their population, will be able to provide them more easily, without harming trade and industry'.[14] This same law increased the strength of the battalions of volontaires from 574 to 800 men. France now had 214 battalions of volontaires, amounting to some 171,200 men. This levy differed from the one carried out in 1791: it was ordered by the government, whereas the previous one had been preceded, in some departments, by a spontaneous movement. The law of 31 May ordered the formation of 54 Compagnies Franches, units of light troops composed of 200 men each including officers. On 8 June, at the instigation of Servan, Minister of War, the Legislative Assembly decided to raise 20,000 gardes nationaux fédérés to protect Paris, a measure which the King vetoed. In July, the situation became so threatening that, on the 11th, the Assembly proclaimed 'la Patrie en danger'.[15] The law of 22 July ordered the raising of the Volontaires of 1792: 42 battalions in all, of which the 33,600 men would once again be drawn from the Garde Nationale. At the same time, this law called for 50,000 men to join the line army and reinforce it. Such a figure proved to be considerable and the incorporation of these men changed, long before amalgamation, the appearance of the royal regiments. On 23 July, a decree approved the initiative of Lamorlière, *general-en-chef* of the Armée du Rhin, who had requested 40,000 gardes nationaux in the communes under his territorial command. The next day, the Assembly authorised the army generals to request, in the departments close to the armies, up to half of the grenadiers and chasseurs registered in the elite companies of the Garde Nationale.

Once again as Minister of War after 10 August, Servan did not change much of the principles that had prevailed previously. The limits of voluntary service then became clearer, even if the deputies of the Assembly did not necessarily perceive the practical obstacles that weighed heavily on the result of the levies. By the summer of 1792, the barrier between active and passive citizens had been shattered. Contrary to what the Assembly claimed, the volontaires were, less than ever, able to assume the costs of their commitment. It is certain that, for many of these men, the duty to arm themselves became one of the rights of the citizen before becoming his supreme right. Meanwhile, this principle was confronted with very harsh economic and social constraints that explained the complexity of the operations.

The impetus for the levy was, moreover, very gradual. From May to July, a third of the expected battalions were not raised. Recruitment accelerated with the events of August, namely the publication of the *Brunswick Manifesto*,[16] the successes of the coalition armies and the fall of the monarchy. In reality, the 'war wind' did not reach its peak until September when the threat of invasion became tangible. But even then, it barely touched some departments,

---

14   Madival & Laurent (eds), *Archives Parlementaires*, vol.XLIII, p.15.
15   Madival & Laurent (eds), *Archives Parlementaires*, vol.XLVI, pp.335–336.
16   The *Brunswick Manifesto* was produced by émigrés who had gathered outside France under the banner of the allied armies in 1792. It was essentially a threat directed against the revolutionaries in Paris.

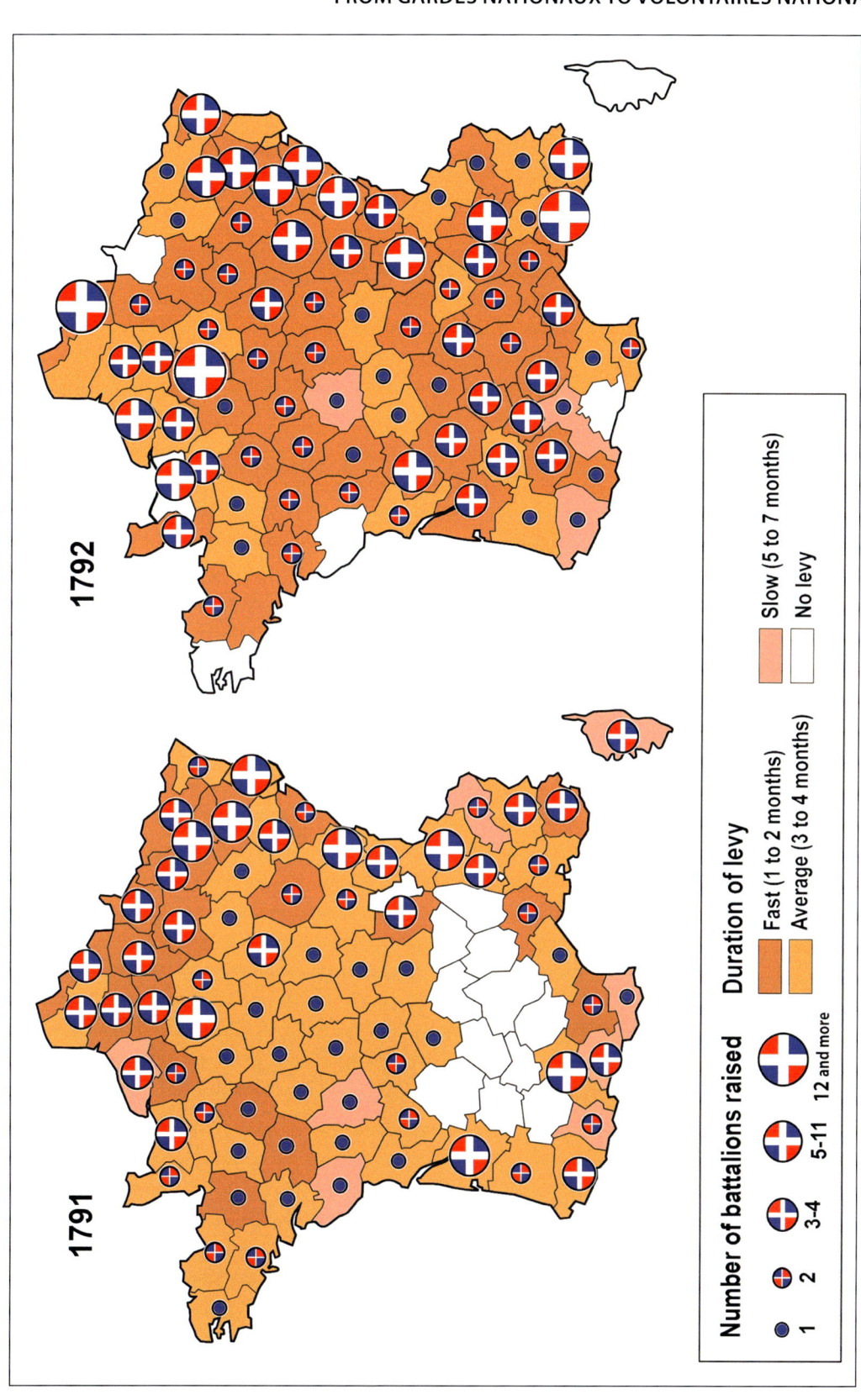

FROM GARDES NATIONAUX TO VOLONTAIRES NATIONAUX

Map 5. The Volontaires' levies in 1791 and 1792.

137

or only starting in November and December. The Aude, the Tarn, the Basses-Pyrénées, the Pyrénées Orientales and the Landes thus waited until November and sometimes the end of December to finally deliver the last battalions expected of them. In central France, the Indre, the Allier and the Cher were also latecomers. In addition, the levies of 1792 confirmed the existence of marked contrasts between departments but also within them, between rural and urban cantons.

How to Recruit Volontaires in 1792?

Once they had been informed of the number of men to be provided, the municipalities summoned the citizens. The decree implementing the law of 11 July clearly implied that the volontaires, just as in 1791, were to be drawn from the Garde Nationale, which was assembled. Although volontaires presented themselves in sufficient numbers in the border zones and in departments such as Paris, Seine-et-Oise and Seine-et-Marne, elsewhere practices were developed that undermined the image of the 'pure' volontaire or demonstrated how simplistic this image was. Much more so than those of 1791, the Volontaires of 1792 were married and fathers. They were reluctant to go away since they were leaving a family behind. They often only agreed to leave their land on the express condition that the village communities pay them compensation or give it to their relatives. They did not consider themselves mercenaries. The action of the municipalities in this respect was approved by the district and departmental authorities, who were much more realistic than the National Assembly. In fact, they noted that the problems of arming, equipping and clothing these men were even more crucial than a year earlier. The action of the village communities was also a sign of collective solidarity and the beginnings of a war effort that would soon mobilise the entire nation.

As the number of volontaires gradually dwindled, other practices appeared, not unlike those observed during the raising of the Milice or the soliciting of troops under the Ancien Régime. Elections were used here and there, but the authorities soon realised the use the citizens were making of them. Here, men physically unfit for the military were designated; there, absent men who, once they returned, contested the election. One did not hesitate either to hand over men who bothered the communities: 'lukewarm' or, on the contrary, sans-culottes. One sometimes proceeded to the lottery. It is true that a quota had been fixed by districts and by cantons, even if it indicated the amount of recruits as desirable, not obligatory, to reach. Lotteries caused a stir in the assemblies. Some departmental authorities, such as those of the Puy-de-Dôme, were opposed to a measure which recalled 'a mode adopted under a regime whose operations breathed only servitude'.[17] However, lotteries avoided measures that were even further from voluntary service, such as resorting to recruiters. Such men, who were soldiers in the line army, took charge of the requisitions carried out by the generals. As for the municipalities or departmental administrations, they employed civilian

---

17 Francisque Mège, *Les bataillons de volontaires 1791–1793* (Paris: A. Claudin Libraire-Editeur, 1880), p.162.

recruiters. In Ille-et-Vilaine, they were 'intelligent young people' who were promised three *livres* per recruit and an officer's place at the formation of the battalion.[18] In Brittany, constitutional priests became recruiters. Practices that the authorities wanted to believe had disappeared forever were used by some. In the Côtes-du-Nord, for example, some recruits complained of having been drunk and pressured into signing a 'voluntary' pledge. This form of recruitment required the payment of sometimes large sums of money to the recruiters and no doubt to the recruits. The authorities taxed the communes that had not provided volontaires in September and October. A 'list of infamy' was drawn up by the department, with the municipalities having to 'equip, arm and pay for the entire campaign a number of volontaires equal to that which had been requested of them'.[19] This coercive measure was used throughout France, for example in the Massif Central and in Brittany. Taxation was sometimes accompanied by additional measures: the communes which did not pay would receive so-called 'garnisaires'. It went as far as imprisoning all unmarried men who were fit to bear arms and who refused to volunteer. In September, when 30,000 new volontaires were requested from the departments surrounding Paris, some young men forced others of their own age to sign up with them. In Seine-et-Marne, the employees of the administrations of the districts and the department, the journeymen millers and bakers, the workers of the pike factories, whom their activity theoretically made safe, admitted afterwards that they had enlisted under constraint. The heads of the administrations had to get the Minister of the Interior to intervene to bring them back. These arrangements coexisted with the undeniable patriotic enthusiasm that rushed men to the tricolour platforms to go and defend their country and freedom.

Officer of the Garde Nationale Parisienne, by Henri Boisselier. This officer most probably belonged to a Parisian Volontaires unit. He is of the finest patriotic elegance. He is armed with a sabre *à garde tournante* and a brace of pistols carried at the belt. (Yves Martin)

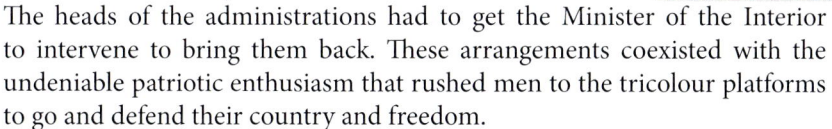

A Social Portrait of Volontaires and Officers in 1792

The social profile of the Volontaires of 1792 was generally more modest than that of their counterparts of 1791. There were more rural dwellers and, in particular, poor peasants. In addition, the leadership was less 'bourgeois' than in 1791. In 1792, the elections took place within the framework of local authorities renewed by the appearance of patriotic militants from less privileged social strata. They were sometimes held within popular societies rather than municipalities and the pressure of the notables was much

---

18   Jean-Paul Bertaud, 'Enquête sur les volontaires de 1792', *Annales Historiques de la Révolution Française*, 272 (1988), p.157.
19   Bertaud, 'Enquête sur les volontaires de 1792', p.157.

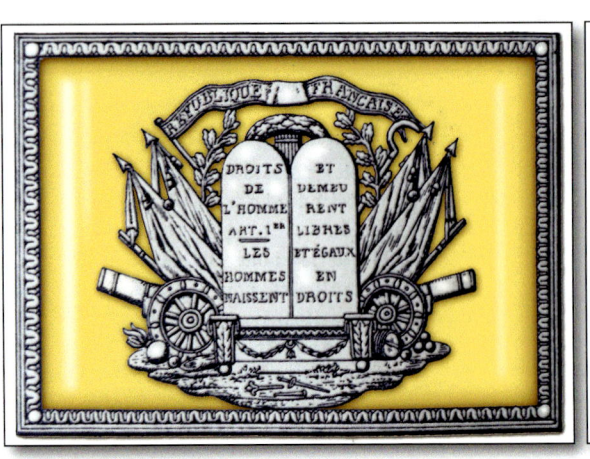

Volontaires Nationaux officer's belt plates. (Coloured by Jean-Claude Colrat)

weaker there. They also sometimes took place en route to the frontline. The petty bourgeoisie, that of talented people, clerks, small legal practitioners, sometimes heads of workshops or shops, werre better represented than the year before.

Among the officers of 1792, the presence of peasants of modest origin was also greater than in 1791. These men were, in most cases, militarily less experienced. The research carried out at a regional level gives nuance to this picture and provides some guidelines. In addition to the 'sans-culottes' officers of the numerous Parisian battalions or those of cities such as Marseilles, some noble officers commanded battalions in the provinces. In certain departments such as those of the Massif Central, the southeast or Brittany, the methods of electing officers in the summer of 1792 remained similar to those observed the previous year. Volontaires usually voted by acclamation, and thus very quickly elected their *lieutenant-colonels*. For the lower ranks, the two-round ballot was more common. However, the rivalry between the competitors was never very intense and volontaires quickly rallied around the names of candidates who seemed to be sponsored in advance by local notables who had controlled power since 1791. This is in fact what the future *Colonel* Bial, enlisting as a volontaire in the Bas-Limousin at the age of 19, explained. His *Memoirs* provide a vivid description of the patriotic impulse at the time and relate the speeches made on this occasion by political leaders who expressed the wish that all ranks should be awarded naturally to educated young people from well-to-do families, the only ones capable of being in command. Bial confessed that he did not share this opinion, since, according to him, it was also necessary to have 'zeal, devotion, love of liberty, and the desire to sacrifice one's life to the salvation of the Fatherland'.[20] In September and October 1792, the situation changed here and there, and well-known militants from the popular societies were then appointed.

---

20   Gabriel Soulié (ed.), *Mémoires du Colonel Bial ou Souvenirs des Guerres de la Révolution et de l'Empire 1792–1814* (Brive: Lachaise, 1929), p.36.

Amalgamation

In the autumn of 1792, the French armies launched a counter-offensive and then conquered Belgium and the left bank of the Rhine with almost 400,000 men. Less than two months later, their strength had fallen to fewer than 220,000 men. This was partly due to the fact that many Volontaires of 1791 had left their battalions after the battles of Valmy and Jemmapes. They relied on an ambiguous provision of the decree of 28 December 1791, which became law on 3 February 1792, and seemed to give them the right to leave at the official end of the campaign, that is, the following 1 December. The fact that volontaires of 1792 followed them in this desertion 'within the country', whereas nothing in the law of 22 July authorised them to do so, was indicative of the particular role that these men intended to play: they felt that they were citizens who had temporarily gone to assist the line army. It also corresponded to the initial conception of the auxiliary force envisaged by the revolutionary assemblies' politicians. However, this picture must be qualified. It is true that contemporaries described roads crowded with volontaires who, at the end of the campaign, headed back home. Nevertheless, the registers show that 'desertion' was hardly generalised and that it varied greatly according to the homogeneity of the battalion, the ascendancy taken by the commanding officer, but also according to regional and social origin. In the winter of 1793, the loss of manpower, coupled with the formation of the first coalition following the execution of Louis XVI, made the search for new men once again of prime importance.

But before solving this thorny problem, the difference between the battalions of the line army and those of the volontaires had to end, otherwise the army would break up. The juxtaposition of two distinct types of troops, adopted in June 1791, had not stood the test of conflict. On 7 February 1793, Dubois-Crancé proposed co-brigading as a means of amalgamation. This proposal had technical reasons (to give more coherence and efficiency to the military forces of the Republic), not to mention political reasons (to obliterate the identity of the royal army). It was a practical measure to create a single, coherent, manageable structure by juxtaposing existing units, two battalions of volontaires and one line battalion, within a new unit: the demi-brigade. The draft organisation called for 198 of these, each with 2,437 officers and men. Each demi-brigade would be composed of a staff commanded by a *chef de brigade*, three field battalions (eight companies of fusiliers and one of grenadiers), an artillery company with six 4-pounder guns, and, in wartime, an auxiliary company which formed a depot.

The uniform, pay and discipline were unified. The election of officers was more or less generalised, but a certain amount of promotion by seniority nevertheless remained. Amalgamation was intended to overcome the opposition, which only partially corresponded to reality, between the soldiers of the line army, deemed competent but indifferent to the fate of the Republic, and the volontaires, judged to be motivated by the purest patriotism but poorly trained. It was to avoid the dispersal of volontaires in the line army's regiments, which would have weakened the spirit that animated them, and the creation of new units in which the volontaires would have overwhelmed the professional fighters by their numbers, preventing the latter from passing on their experience. Finally, amalgamation was to overcome the *esprit de corps* inherent in a professional army but also regional particularities. The smallest unit of a battalion of volontaires, namely the company, was made up of men coming from the same canton. The demi-brigade, on the other hand, juxtaposed citizens of all geographical and social origins. The intermingling made it necessary to use the French language rather than regional dialects.

Dubois-Crancé's plan was partially adopted on 21 February. As it happened, the formation of the demi-brigades was adjourned on 31 March 1793 due to the approaching campaign season. Their composition was further clarified in a decree of 12 August 1793, particularly in terms of the composition of the staff, and how the amalgamation would actually be accomplished: each company was to be made up of a third of regular soldiers. On 8 January 1794 (19 Nivôse Year II), a decree was issued finally enacting the reform proposed 11 months before. Amalgamation, which was led by a *representant en mission*, was the occasion for a real civic mass. Surrounded by the population of the nearby communes, the troops were reviewed. The flags were placed in bundles, as were the weapons. The *representant* then harangued the troops, reminding them of the advantages of fraternity and the benefits of a republican government. The ranks broke and cries of 'Long live the Republic!' were heard. At a drum roll, everyone was back in his place. The *representant* named the staff officers, had the flags distributed before swearing the republican oath, which was taken wholeheartedly by the men of the demi-brigade. After the officers had been recognised, the battalions paraded.

Requisitions and *Levée en Masse*

The first levy of men ordered by the Convention occurred on 24 February 1793, as the situation worsened with the formation of the first coalition on 1 February. The law still called for 'volontaires', although volunteering was a mere fiction. In reality, it was a requisition of single men and childless widowers between the ages of 18 and 40, a provision that was certainly reminiscent of the former Milice. It was still by no means a question of universal service, since only 300,000 men were drawn from all those required. Nor was it an egalitarian service. Replacement was authorised and numerous cases of exemption were provided for, firstly for physical incapacity, but also in favour of employees of the administrations, municipal officers and workers whose job was considered essential to the good material and financial organisation of the war. Finally, it was not a matter of personal service, as the obligation was collective, which also revived the principles of the Milice. For the first time since the Revolution, each commune was assigned a contingent which was compulsory, and no longer merely desirable, to raise. Rural dwellers were unable to escape the common burden and the departments most apathetic to volunteering could no longer shirk it, even if the contribution to be levied was still not very precise. The designation of the quota was left to the choice of the communes, which could rely on the young men themselves to determine

FROM GARDES NATIONAUX TO VOLONTAIRES NATIONAUX

the method. The lottery did not cause too many problems, even if, in some departments, the results were undoubtedly rigged. On the other hand, the designation gave rise to numerous disputes which reflected the resistance that the levy encountered in many departments. The levy of 300,000 men in fact led to multiple movements of discontent and, above all, to the outbreak of civil war in western France.

The levy of 300,000 men was a kind of half measure which, by the summer of 1793, had provided only 150,000 men, perhaps a little more. Like their predecessors, the deputies of the Convention were reluctant to require compulsory service from citizens. Under pressure from the Parisian people, the *levée en masse* was finally decreed on 23 August 1793. To achieve this, the young Republic had to be threatened in its very existence: six months of almost uninterrupted defeats since the battle of Neerwinden, all the borders crossed by the coalition armies, not to mention a desperate internal situation marked by the war in the Vendée and the federalist revolts against the Convention's authority. The *levée en masse* concerned at least 450,000 young men and introduced a first step towards compulsory personal service. Indeed, the measure was aimed above all at young single and widowed men without children between the ages of 18 and 25, consequently destined for the battlefield. As citizens were called up on a personal basis, there was no

Lesueur sets this scene in early April 1793, shortly after *Général de division* Dumouriez's betrayal. The artist emphasises the enthusiastic mood of the 'volontaires'. However, at that time, only some of them were actually volunteers. The presence of money is noteworthy. An officer, perhaps a recruiter, urges a reluctant young man to join his comrades. Finally, alcohol was also used to stimulate the warrior's ardour. (Musée Carnavalet)

143

THE GARDE NATIONALE 1789–1815

Left: *Requisitionnaire* by Henri Boisselier. This man was hastily dressed and equipped. His outfit is a mixture of civilian elements – including the famous *carmagnole* – and military effects, such as the bonnet de police, knapsack, giberne, sabre-briquet and musket. (Yves Martin)

Below: *La retirade des Français*, engraving by Seele, 1796. Seele was a southern German artist who extensively illustrated military subjects. He shows here the fairly shabby appearance of the soldiers of a line infantry demi-brigade. (Anne S.K. Brown Military Collection)

longer a quota assigned to each commune. Replacement was no longer allowed either. The exemptions still existed for the married men of the corresponding age groups and for those who worked with the manufactures of war or who drove the military carts. The deputies certainly envisaged the *levée en masse* as an emergency measure to safeguard the Republic, not as a lasting institution. In the decree of 23 August 1793, no indication was given that a regular renewal would be ensured and that each year a new age group would replace the oldest in the army. So, when the salvation of the fatherland seemed assured and the struggle turned into a war of expansion, the requisitioned left en masse and desertion became the scourge of revolutionary armies.

As early as 1789, the Garde Nationale's fate was linked to that of the line army. Their history was intertwined. Even what divided them ultimately tended to bring them together. Thus, the Garde Nationale was born in July 1789 to deal with the threat posed by the royal army's foreign troops. By means of volontaires nationaux, however, the Garde provided, from June 1791, the elements of a truly national armed force. Historian Georges Carrot wondered whether the Volontaires of 1791 were aware of the decisive turn they were making in the Revolution.[21] They were certainly an original force, whose mindset was probably more civic than military. In any case, the raising of such volontaires met the army's needs. In 1792, as there were insufficient volontaires, revolutionary political leaders gradually turned to restrictive solutions, which heralded the generalised conscription of 1798. However, neither the levy of 300,000 men nor the *levée en masse* could be considered as such. Volontaires gradually lost their own identity through the effect of amalgamation. As for the mobilisation of young people aged between 18 and 25 from the *levée en masse*, it certainly completed the evolution towards a national army made up of citizen-soldiers and no longer just soldier-citizens. These troops gave the Republic its greatest successes, from the Champagne to the banks of the Rhine, as well as the Italian plains. These successes were costly, with little consideration for casualties. They were also dangerous, in that they widened the armies' scope of action and gave rise to new enemies, thus requiring ever greater manpower.

Volontaires, Get Dressed!

A Crisis Situation
When the first battalions of volontaires were formed in the late summer of 1791, war had not yet been declared. Nothing about the material aspects had been planned. The departmental authorities therefore had to act quickly to prevent the volontaires from giving up on serving a country that was unable to treat them decently. Volontaires were gardes nationaux and therefore had to provide for their own clothing and equipment. While this was conceivable for active citizens, who were originally the only ones allowed to join the Garde Nationale, such an expense was impossible for passive citizens, who were by definition less fortunate. However, the latter had been present in the Garde since its inception, as recognised by the decree of 6 December 1790 relating to the organisation of the public force. As a result, many volontaires were unable to obtain the slightest item of clothing or equipment and therefore lacked everything. They had only the clothes they were wearing at the time of their enlistment. The battalions had been organised in late August and early September 1791, when the weather conditions were suitable, if not pleasant. The clothing records that have been preserved reveal the under-equipment of such units a few weeks after their creation. Even at best, no battalion was uniformly equipped and there was considerable variation from one company to another. However, some measures were taken to deal with this. In departments where resources were notoriously inadequate, the authorities allowed merchants to travel to Paris or

---

21 Carrot, *La Garde nationale*, p.113.

THE GARDE NATIONALE 1789–1815

Under the guidance of a NCO, *sectionnaires* or volontaires are practising a core exercise for any infantryman: handling the musket. None of the three men at the drill has been given a full uniform. The scene is set during the Republican period, but it could just as easily have taken place in the summer of 1792, during the proclamation of 'la Patrie en danger'. (Musée Carnavalet)

any other city that could provide what was needed. Since volontaires could not wait indefinitely to receive their clothing, deadlines for obtaining the necessary supplies were set. The battalions included workers who were employed by the units' councils of administration to set up manufacturing workshops, in accordance with the instructions of the departmental administrations. Despite these difficulties, many battalions were ready to march to the borders when war broke out in April 1792.

Table 7. Clothing and equipment for the two Volontaires Nationaux battalions of the Eure to be provided by the department according to a report dated 1 October 1791

	1st Battailon	2nd Battalion	Total
Coat	431	467	898
Waistcoat	461	496	957
Breeches	952	990	1,942
Bonnet de police	485	481	966
NCO hat	16	–	16
Soldier hat	313	414	727
Shirt	492	656	1,148
White collar	810	829	1,639
Black collar	466	465	931
Shoes	793	806	1,599
White gaiters	463	488	951
Grey gaiters	475	490	965
Black yarn gaiters	469	489	958
Handkerchiefs	603	733	1,336
Stockings	514	755	1,269
Knapsack	471	791	962
Haversack	484	482	966

FROM GARDES NATIONAUX TO VOLONTAIRES NATIONAUX

The Volontaires of 1792 and the Requisitionnaires of 1793
The battalions raised in the summer of 1792 experienced the same kind of difficulties as their predecessors, so that many units were not operational when, in February 1793, the Convention decreed the 300,000-man levy. Each department had to dress, equip and arm a much larger number of men than those assembled in the battalions of Volontaires of 1791 and 1792. It was feared that the citizens of the 300,000-man levy would suffer the same burdens as their predecessors. The authorities did struggle to obtain quality goods and supplies at a price far removed from speculation. Nevertheless, new recruits were quickly able to reach the frontiers. The experience acquired from previous levies, the enrichment of the legislative arsenal and the acuteness of the military crisis forbidding any procrastination undoubtedly explained this situation. In order to provide for clothing, the administrative bodies were in fact authorised to take all measures deemed appropriate. Tailors, shoemakers and workmen could for example be requisitioned. They were no longer required to work for private individuals and were placed under the control of commissioners appointed for this purpose.

A Wartime Economy
While the clothing, equipment and armament of the 'voluntary' recruits of the 300,000 men were not yet completed, the *levée en masse* was decreed on 23 August 1793. The number of those required was almost twice that of the recruits of February. A war economy was de facto set up, in which the state was heavily involved in organising manufacturing and production. In other words, the state determined what was to be manufactured, set the quantity, the methods, the quality and the price of each object. The satisfaction of the army's needs took precedence over all other considerations. A significant proportion of the uniforms and equipment of volontaires of the 1793 levies came from donations or loans from sedentary gardes nationaux, pensioners and veterans, and even from collections organised in the autumn by popular societies and surveillance committees, with whom local merchants and craftsmen were associated.

Headgear
Volontaires favoured the black felt hat, edged with a woollen braid of the same colour, worn 'en colonne' or 'en bataille'. In wartime, a calotte made of two iron blades was theoretically to be placed on the form. Seldom distributed or quickly lost, it was in fact rarely worn on the battlefield, where it offered only relative protection against enemy sabre blows. A woollen braid held in place one of the two cockades that volontaires received when they entered the battalion. This cockade made of basin, which could be up to 14 centimetres in diameter, displayed colours that varied from one to the next. In a public space saturated with symbols, was this not an excellent way of displaying patriotism? In a gusset sewn under the cockade, a small plume was inserted, often tricoloured but of which contemporary iconography – whether in the sumptuous gouaches of Lesueur or in German engravings – recalls that numerous variants naturally coexisted. As for the red plume, it identified the grenadiers at first glance. Less expensive woollen tufts were

THE GARDE NATIONALE 1789–1815

Above: This rare example of a revolutionary cap represents a type known as the bonnet de police, which was typically adorned with revolutionary imagery. The headband is embroidered with a Phrygian cap mounted on a pike, and fasces, a symbol of unity and authority in Ancient Rome. (The Metropolitan Museum of Art, New York)

Below: Miniature portrait of a young *fourrier* of the grenadier company of the 3rd Battalion of Volontaires of the Côte d'Or, 1793. He has the distinctive *fourrier* braids on the upper part of each arm. (François Vinot-Préfontaine's collection)

also used. Some volontaires units were issued unpopular infantry helmets.

Easy and inexpensive to make, the bonnet de police, fashioned *à la dragonne*, was very popular with volontaires. Piped in white or scarlet, its long blue flame ended with a tassel with scarlet or tricoloured fringes. Cut from scarlet cloth, the headband was edged with a white wool braid and decorated with an embroidered badge, a modest reminder of the political transformations that took place in France between 1791 and 1793. Typical of the Constitutional Monarchy, the motto 'La Nation-La Loi-Le Roi' was amputated of its last term, and even replaced by other watchwords such as 'Liberté-Egalité' or 'Vivre Libre ou Mourir' with the advent of the Republic. Moreover, the badge was often replaced by embroidery combining a Phrygian cap, fasces, flags and floral motifs. A small-diameter cockade might also have been affixed to the headband or to the flame. When not in use, the bonnet de police was held under the cartridge box by two bleached buff straps.

The 'Blue Uniform'

As for the headdress, the 'blue uniform' immediately distinguished the volontaires from the line infantrymen, who wore the 'white uniform' until the end of the summer of 1793. In reality, it was the Garde Nationale's coat, regulated by the Constituent Assembly on 19 July 1790 to put an end to the variegation observed five days earlier at the Festival of the Federation. It had to be cut from royal blue cloth. Lapels and cuffs were scarlet, while the collar, in white cloth, was also piped in scarlet. Lesueur's gouaches repeatedly depict this short-lived uniform, because the gardes nationaux barely had time to have it made before a new decree was issued in mid-July 1791. The modifications led to a more harmonious distribution of the three national colours and mainly concerned the collar, now in scarlet cloth piped with white, and the lapels, in white cloth with scarlet piping. A few appropriate changes were enough to bring the 1790 uniform up to date. In September 1791, the officers of the 2nd Battalion of the Côte d'Or had scarlet lapels of their men's clothing

FROM GARDES NATIONAUX TO VOLONTAIRES NATIONAUX

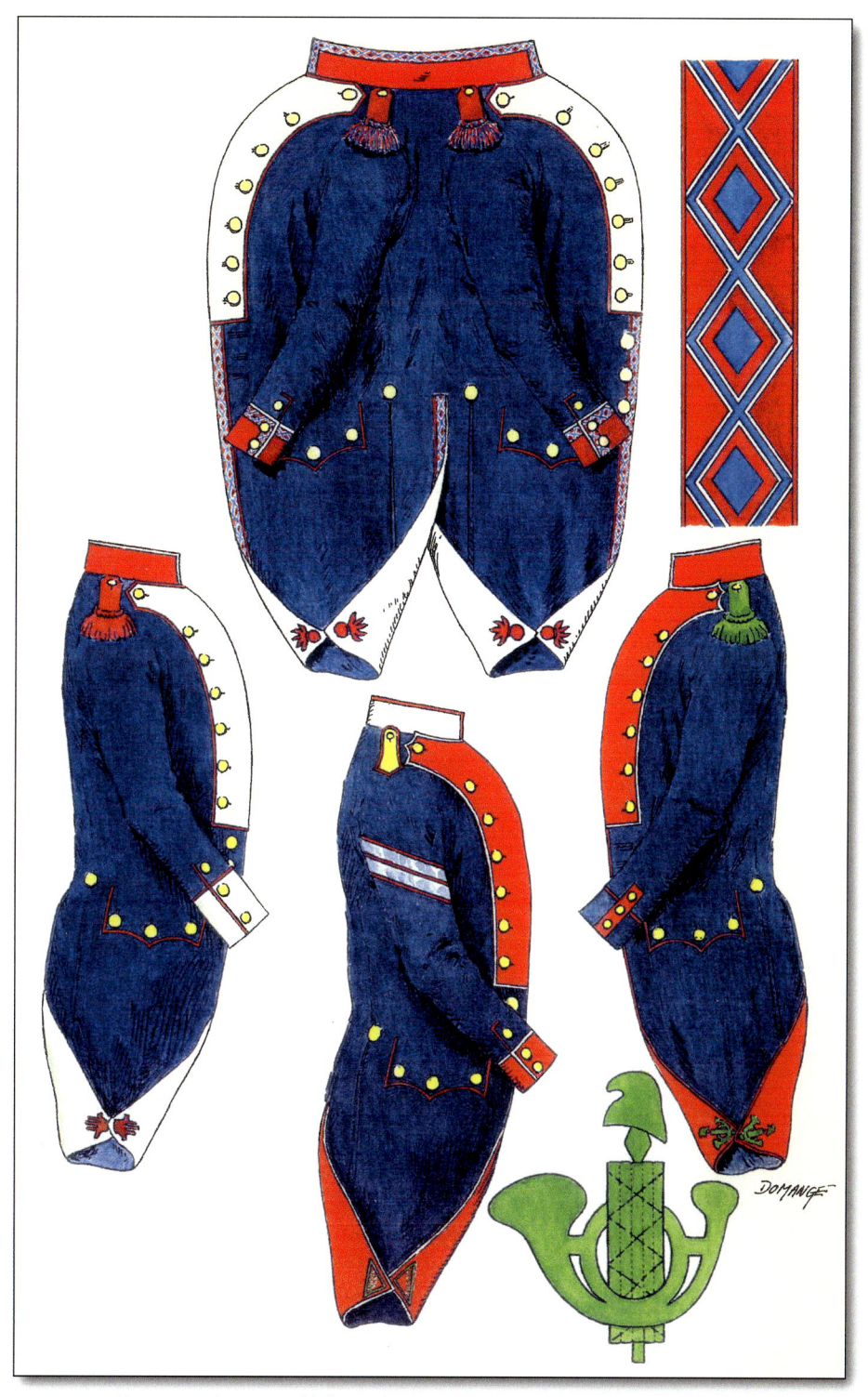

From top to bottom and left to right: Drummer's coat of the Bataillon de l'Arsenal.
Habit of the Garde Nationale Parisienne adopted in 1789 and worn by some Volontaires Nationaux units in 1791.
Fusilier's uniform of the Garde Nationale Parisienne according to the decree of 19 July 1790.
Coat of Nicolas Masson, a chasseur franc de l'Egalité, born in Paris in 1769. Masson joined the unit at its creation and was killed in Calabria on 4 July 1806 whilst serving in the 1er Regiment d'Infanterie Légère. (Original artwork by Jacques Domange)

covered with white *droguet*, which they bought at their own expense. In the summer of 1792, as the volontaires made their way to the frontiers, scarlet lapels had not completely disappeared. When they existed, the shoulder straps, made of blue cloth piped in scarlet, were attached by a button sewn as close as possible to the collar. If the local authorities had the financial means to do so, the grenadiers' clothing was adorned with red woollen epaulettes. A vest with one or two rows of buttons was worn under the garment.

Although, according to the law, the uniform was the same for everyone, local authorities, driven by economic imperatives as well as by a parochial spirit, did their best to differentiate their battalions by using specific colours and attributes. In 1791, the Lorient Volontaires' lapels were made of pink cloth. The following year, those of their counterparts in the 3rd Hérault Battalion were made of a sea-green cloth previously used to dress the coastguard gunners. Variety characterised the turnbacks ornaments – small pieces of cloth bearing high convictions and commitments. Fleur-de-lys, hearts and flaming grenades, but also triangles of scarlet cloth embroidered with a Phrygian cap and the words 'Liberté' or 'Constitution', can be found, for example, on the clothing of the first battalions organised in 1791. At that time, Parisian Volontaires wore a stylised version of the nave, the symbol par excellence of their city. Buttons could be studied in their own right. Alongside regulated models, there were indeed infinite variants. Stamped with the name of the district and the words '(La Nation) La Loi et Le Roi', Garde Nationale buttons, twice regulated in 1790, adorned the uniforms of the first Volontaires units in 1791. In 1792, new models appeared with various references, such as 'Département de …', 'Volontaires Nationaux', 'République française', but also the battalion number or the motto 'Liberté-Egalité'. The Phrygian cap, which varied in size, also appeared on many of them. On 4 October 1792, the Convention finally standardised the button for all the troops of the Republic. Adorned with fasces, the Phrygian cap and the words 'République française', this generic model was undoubtedly widespread from the winter of 1792–1793.

Pantaloons, Gaiters and Footwear
Upon enlistment, each volontaire received two pairs of white knitted breeches, which were soon replaced by striped pantaloons of various colours. They also received three pairs of gaiters, one white, one grey and one in black cheesecloth. Volontaires were subjected to continuous marches rather than combat, and at best they received two pairs of buckled shoes, a key element of their clothing and a cardinal concern of both the command and the public authorities. While it was possible to fight without a full uniform or all the equipment, it was difficult to do without shoes. But sometimes, in defiance of official decrees, men were given only one pair or, worse, were forced to use clogs or even to go barefoot. In September 1791, the council of administration of the 1st Battalion of Eure Volontaires stipulated that shoes had to be 'made from calf and have soles with 20 nails and heels with 15 nails', but they were usually hastily made and allowed

moisture to penetrate.[22] In December 1793, a decree of the Convention ordered that all shoes must have a square toe. Only soldiers were henceforth allowed to wear them. However, the square toe sole did not fit the shape of the feet and the poorly finished heel made walking difficult and caused recurrent injuries.

Weapons and Equipment

Equipped with a bayonet, which volontaires generally handled with ease, the musket was the main weapon of these men. The archives clearly show their chronic shortage and the disparate nature of the battalions' armament. Thus, one found 1763 and 1777 model muskets. In 1793, hunting weapons requisitioned from individuals and seized from so-called 'suspects' were also added. However, this state of affairs differed from one region to another. In the summer, the municipalities of the Ain department deplored their inability to equip their young volontaires with anything other than 'a few bad hunting rifles', so that only a minority of the departmental contingent was properly armed when it left for the borders. The departmental authorities of Eure had, by contrast, managed to provide willy-nilly for the needs of the volontaires and then the requisitioners. A maximum price had been determined and was set at 40 *livres* for the 1763 model musket and 48 *livres* for the 1777 model musket fitted with its bayonet. In addition, gunsmiths, blacksmiths, locksmiths and workmen had been requisitioned. When the volontaires had a musket, they often had to cope with an ammunition shortage. Powder and lead, which were necessary to make bullets, were scarce. Oil and grease were commonly lacking to keep the musket in serviceable condition. The musket's frizzen became worn and therefore had to be frequently replaced. Although iconography readily depicted volontaires with 'mineur' swords, the reality was far more nuanced. In 1792, due to a shortage of weapons, grenadiers were the only ones equipped with a 1767 model sabre-briquet.

Made of strong blackened cowhide, the cartridge box was closed by a wide, unadorned *patelette*. This was the most important piece of equipment as well as ammunition it contained everything else necessary for the use of the musket (ball extractor and turn-screw). It was supported by a banderole made of bleached buff leather to which a bayonet scabbard was normally fastened. A cowhide knapsack and a haversack completed the equipment.

---

22 Archives Départementales de l'Eure (ADE): 42 L 14.

THE GARDE NATIONALE 1789–1815

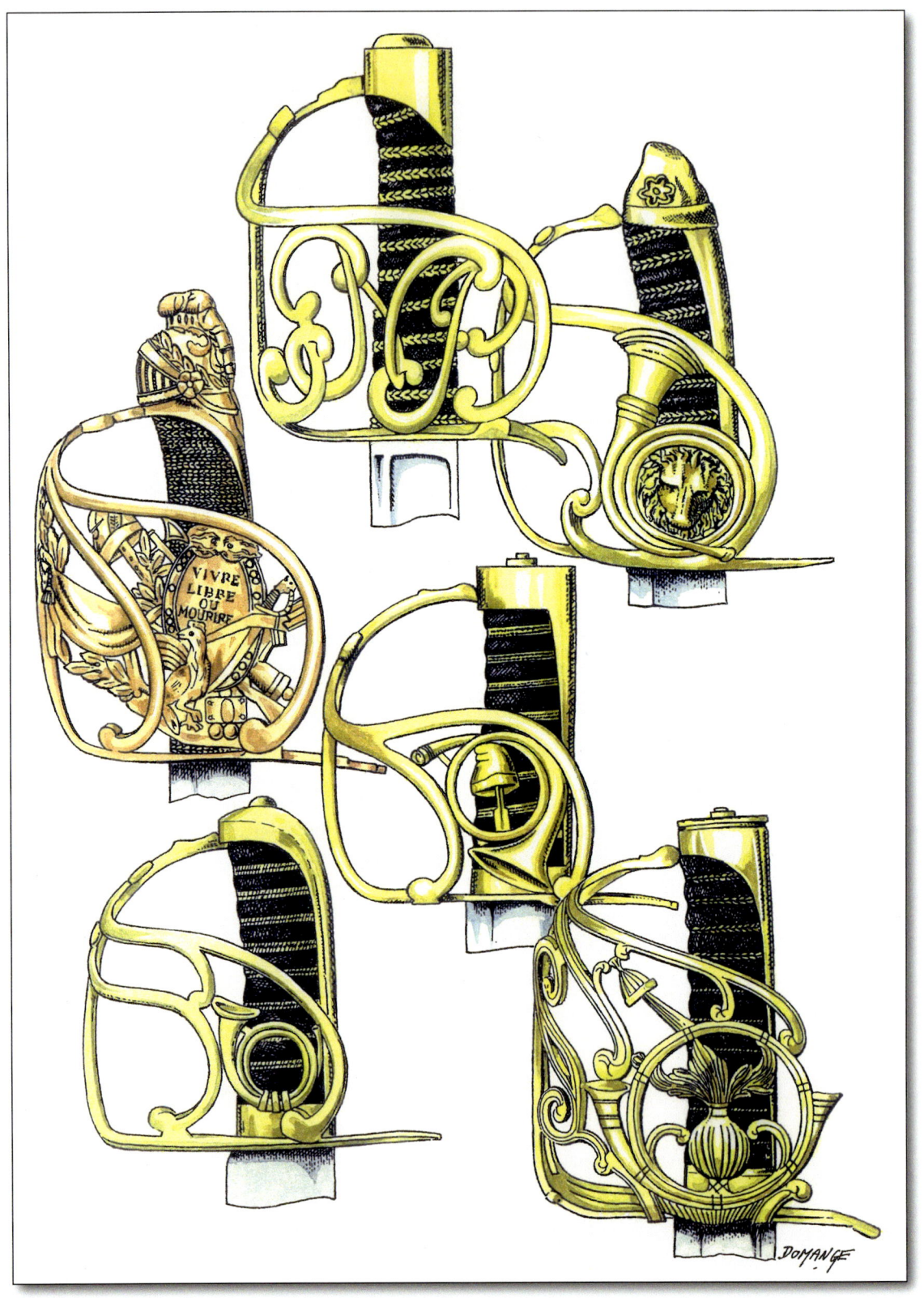

Sabres 'à la Montmorency' attributed to Volontaire officers. Original drawing by Jacques Domange. (Yves Martin)

5

The Federations Movement and the Garde Nationale Flags

1789–1790

The early days of the French Revolution were marked by an atmosphere of great anxiety and emotional intensity. There was an undeniable hope for change as well as a fear of unrest and even the development of a counter-revolution. The spread of the 'municipal revolution' led to the overthrow of the Ancien Régime authorities. It was therefore up to the active citizens to set up new administrative regulations but also to ensure a return to order. If the Kingdom of France had experienced numerous uprisings in the pre-revolutionary crises of 1788, the first year of the Revolution was certainly characterised by its share of local anti-nobility revolts, recurrent fears and movements related to subsistence, not to mention the panics of the 'Great Fear'. Faced with the amplification of these disturbances, the gardes nationaux did not restrict their action to the limits of their commune, but instead quickly sought to federate. These federations allowed them to affirm their mutual solidarity, to form a common revolutionary front and to maintain a certain cohesion in an unstable context.

The First Gatherings

Faced with a political scene threatened by anarchy, the organisers of the first federations sought above all to establish a counterpoint by working towards local unity. As early as 21 July, the Garde Nationale of Montpellier, which had just been created, drew up a pact of solidarity grouping together the towns of Nîmes, Sète and Aigues-Mortes. Several historians have seen this as the first concrete manifestation of the federative process of the summer of 1789. In the following weeks, the example of Montpellier was in any case followed by other towns: the mayor of Cherbourg thus tried to federate the Milices of the Cotentin peninsula. On 2 August 1789, the small town of Luynes, in the Loire valley, celebrated the union of the new municipal authorities with the local Garde Nationale. Presented – for the first time – as a 'patriotic confederation', the event was punctuated by several oaths to 'the Nation, the Law and the King', to 'the rights of Man' and to 'public security', to which all participants subscribed.[1] More importantly for later developments in the movement, the Luynes federates printed a brochure outlining the proceedings and content of their ceremony. Such a decision ensured that their event would receive wide publicity, which the fledgling local revolutionary press and correspondence networks were happy to relay. The descriptions of the festival soon inspired other ceremonies, also called 'confederations', which were also intended to affirm the unity of the Gardes Nationales and local administrators. They went beyond the strict framework of the towns of the Loire and concerned the entire kingdom. Three weeks after that of Luynes, a federation appeared in Largentière, in Ardèche, and another in Saint-Sauveur, in Haute-Saône, two towns separated by more than 500 kilometres. In Saint-Sauveur, the organisers formed a committee of correspondence. In both cases, the ceremonies were designed to be applicable and transposable everywhere and therefore widely shared. In mid-August, the military committee of the town of Angers conceived a very ambitious project. On 18 August, it addressed all the already organised Milices of the kingdom to encourage them to set up a solid network of correspondence between the local Milices and the provincial capitals, but also between the latter and the Garde Nationale in Paris. Although this first attempt at national organisation was well received, it did not have an immediate impact. It did, however, point to the interest of uniting the forces of the various Milices on a regional scale.

The power of such events lay mainly in the number of participants and the collective affirmation of shared goals. Therefore, the organisers wanted to extend the size of the event and to specify its content. The end of the summer of 1789 marked the end of the first phase of the federative movement, that of the essentially local federations that had sprung up in the countryside in the wake of the 'Great Fear'. From then on, the movement entered a new phase going beyond the provincial framework, that of regional and interregional federations, which became widespread from the end of September 1789, only to grow during in the course of October and concern the Pyrenean valleys, the Cévennes (a Protestant bastion), Beaujolais and Forez, but also Burgundy and Franche-Comté. The most decisive gathering took place in Bourg-l'Etoile, between Montélimar and Valence, on 29 November 1789. Over 12,000 gardes nationaux from the Vivarais and Languedoc gathered there and sought to project the power of the movement forward, a will that was illustrated by the oath taken that day: 'We, French citizens from both banks of the Rhone, swear to be always united and to fly to the rescue of our brothers in Paris or in any city of France where liberty would be in danger.' Faujas de Saint-Fonds, former Vice Senachal of Montélimar, spoke up to affirm that 'We are no longer Dauphinois. You are no longer

---

1 Anon., *Acte de confédération patriotique et de Constitution provisoire de l'Administration et de la Milice citoyenne de la Ville et Cité de Luynes* (Place and publisher unknown, 1789), p.3.

Languedocians. We are French!'[2] He was warmly applauded as his words perfectly summarised what the gardes were feeling. It was decided to develop the movement through even larger and more open federations. The commander of the Montélimar Garde Nationale therefore invited the members of the Dauphiné and Languedoc communities to meet again two weeks later, so that on 13 December the town of Montélimar hosted the first interregional confederation. About 6,000 participants gathered there, half as many as at the Etoile federation. However, the presence of delegates from the neighbouring regions of Dauphiné, Provence and Languedoc proved very significant with 97 communities sending delegates. In addition, the federations attracted the interest of the national press for the first time. In a faithful transcription of the Constituent Assembly's debates, an article in *The Moniteur Universel* evoked the Montélimar event as 'a revolution as surprising as ours', in which 'the people are armed, but the arms bring peace'.[3] The regional federation of Valence, which was to consolidate the dynamic of two months earlier in Montélimar, took place on 31 January 1790. Its organisers, wishing to attract a large audience, chose a field outside the city limits used for military parades. The initial objective was achieved as 9,000 gardes nationaux – more than in Montélimar but less than in L'Etoile – and a crowd estimated at 30,000 spectators came to attend a 'very imposing spectacle'.[4] With 14 rallies organised between January and February 1790, the Rhone territories were at the forefront of the federation movement. The fear that the Kingdom of Piedmont-Savoy – which was then home to the Comte d'Artois and other openly counter-revolutionary aristocrats – would launch an invasion across the Alps probably pushed the local revolutionaries towards more cooperation, solidarity and fraternity. The desire for new and larger federations also manifested itself in western France, and two federations were held in the Breton town of Pontivy within a month of each other. If the first, held in mid-January 1790, was made up of 'young people' from 69 communes, the second, organised a month later, involved the gardes nationaux and the municipal administrators of 129 communes in Brittany and Anjou. This second gathering aimed to 'accelerate the execution of the decrees of the National Assembly', but also to sign a federative pact whose final oath explicitly echoed the one pronounced in Etoile nearly two and a half months earlier. 'We solemnly declare that, being neither Bretons nor Angevins, but French and citizens of the same kingdom, we renounce all our local and particular privileges and that we abjure them as unconstitutional', the participants repeated in chorus.[5] They were also called upon to extend the movement and to 'spread the feelings of union and fraternity in all the provinces'. The project was transformed from one of local solidarity and mutual assistance into a movement with broader ambitions.

---

2   *La Vedette des Alpes*, 9 (1789), p.71.
3   *Moniteur Universel*, 24 décembre 1789.
4   *L'Observateur provincial*, 7 (1790).
5   Roger Dupuy, *La Bretagne sous la Révolution et l'Empire 1789-1815* (Rennes: Éditions Ouest-France, 2004), pp.43–46.

THE GARDE NATIONALE 1789–1815

Provincial Federative Festivals: An Anatomy

From late winter to early spring 1790, the intensity, number and size of the federative gatherings increased. Each one was part of a process and provided an opportunity to send letters and proclamations to other provinces or to invite participants to join future confederations. In this way, a real federative network developed, incorporating ever larger territories into a national project. From April to July, the Kingdom of France lived to the rhythm of the federations, which multiplied at a rate never seen before. Rochefort on 6 April, Poitiers and Grenoble on the 11th, Troyes on 8 May, Tours on the 16th, Lyon and Montpellier on the 30th, Lille on 6 June, Chartres on the 9th, Nantes on the 24th and Toulouse on 4 July: these were the most important milestones in this vast movement which, starting from the districts and ending in the regional capitals, was constantly gaining ground.

Spread all over France, these gatherings had strong similarities, the origin of which did not fail to raise questions among historians. 'Except for a few variations in detail, the same inspiration from the capital's cenacles was to be found everywhere', judged Georges Carrot.[6] 'Perhaps we should recognise an intention to centralise on the part of the government', asked Odile Lesaffre-Ramette with greater caution.[7] Thus, the parade of gardes on their way to the federations, especially when they passed through towns and villages, became an event in itself. In the Norman town of Evreux, it even led to a general fraternisation. On the other hand, the organisation of such ceremonies was far from easy. The question of accommodation for the participants, in particular, often became controversial because of the very limited number of local people willing to host the visitors. In many cases, municipalities had to decide that bourgeois and shopkeepers should host several participants, on the condition that they could choose which ones.

In order to reach larger crowds than ever before, organisers sponsored various events before and after the main festival and did not hesitate to spend considerable funds. In Orléans, for example, participants danced in the city's main square after the event, while in Troyes, the 9 May federation was placed at the heart of a four-day sequence of popular festivities that cost a whopping 30,000 *livres*. The organisers also realised that in order to ensure maximum public participation in the federative festivities, a processional route had to be set up that drew on well-established traditions dating back to antique festivals – such as Roman triumphs – seen as timeless models. The procession through the city

In 1790, Marc Dolle (1754–1831) was *lieutenant-colonel* of the Grenoble Garde Nationale, in which his younger brother was a *capitaine*. He was one of the instigators of the federative festival organised in Grenoble on 11 April 1790, which brought together 8,000 gardes fédérés, most of whom came from the Dauphiné. His physiognotrace portrait was probably engraved the following July. (Musée Carnavalet)

---

6   Carrot, *La Garde Nationale*, p.86.
7   Odile Lesaffre-Ramette, 'Une fête révolutionnaire provinciale et ses aménagements: La Fédération de Lille, le 6 juin 1790', *Revue du Nord*, 254–255 (1982), p.794.

THE FEDERATIONS MOVEMENT AND THE GARDE NATIONALE FLAGS

Fédération de Lille, print by Helman after a drawing by Watteau, 1790. Most of the festival took place on the esplanade of the Champ de Mars, a large open area between Lille's ramparts and Vauban's citadel reserved for military exercises. In the background of the engraving, one can make out the tower of Sainte-Catherine, the cupola of the Madeleine, the Minimes, Saint-André and the Carmelite convent. (Musée Carnavalet)

was intended to introduce festivity and jubilation into all districts and to bring together, as far as possible, the urban population's various social strata. It traced an ideal route resulting from a judicious study and featured symbolic places and stations where the highlights of the ceremony took place.

The vast majority of the federative camps in the provinces – in Lille, Lyon and Strasbourg – had the same essential characteristics. The camp was vast and had to contain a large crowd. Easily accessible, it was located outside the city but nevertheless in its immediate periphery. It was to be flat and undeveloped, allowing for both collective and individual creation of an imaginary space. Its oval shape was criticised on the grounds that the circle would have been more egalitarian. In any federation, which was a grandiose and theatrical production, the natural element played a key role. The city was often used as a backdrop, while the art of gardening made a necessary contribution to the festivities. The design of the festive space itself was often entrusted to a renowned architect who mainly used light and ephemeral materials (wood, plaster, stucco or painted canvas). These materials were quick and easy to use, but still had a certain appearance of solidity.

The enclosure was generally delineated by a material barrier – such as a palisade – or a human barrier – a cordon of gardes nationaux, for example – to facilitate its appropriation. In fact, the military aspect of the federative celebrations cannot be overlooked. The garde national and the king's soldiers were key in this regard, as perfectly understood and vastly memorialised by men of letters and artists. Carefully organised, the gardes represented a maximum mass of 9,000 men during the first spring federations. At the end of May and the beginning of June, their numbers had certainly multiplied, since one counted nearly 60,000 in Lyon and several tens of thousands in Lille. In Lyon, female units marched for the first time and, 'sword in hand', joined ranks with the participants.[8] Similarly, units of teenagers mingled with adults.

Throughout France, speeches, patriotic songs and oaths read by representatives of the various authorities characterised these rallies. However, the federative celebrations were not only euphoric: they were also openly religious. Were they not presided over, at least in part, by a priest? Many included a blessing of the flags and a mass. Moreover, the altar of the Fatherland, the essential place of the ceremonies, focused the attention of the participants. One had to climb a few flights of stairs to reach it. This elevation was intended to make it more visible but also to prove its symbolic importance and dignity. In Lyon, it was developed to the point of being called a 'mountain' by the protagonists.[9] In any case, most of the witnesses did not see any contradiction between the Catholic ceremonies and the revolutionary celebrations, like the orator who saw the Dijon federation as a 'magnificent harmony between religion and politics'.[10]

Built around the altar of the Fatherland, the tiers, usually of wood, made the public both actors and spectators of the celebrations. This arrangement therefore eliminated the distinction between all participants. The multitude participated in the festivals and at the same time saw them. Such a logic symbolically echoed the new political order that had been established during the recent municipal revolution. Moreover, the spectators now greatly exceeded the number of gardes nationaux. Thus, according to the brochures, the Nancy federation of 19 April attracted 'an infinite number of people of all ranks, ages and sexes'.[11] The Lille federation of 6 June welcomed no less than 100,000 people while, a week later, 75,000 onlookers converged to attend the Strasbourg rally. Paradoxically, while the largest gatherings had undoubtedly reached an unprecedented scale, the revolutionaries were beginning to feel cramped and were more convinced than ever that the whole of France needed to come together in a collective act.

Paris Comes into Play

Paris had been in the vanguard of the Revolution many times, but was nevertheless slow to react to the phenomenon of federations. At the end of

---

8 Anon., *Relation du camp fédératif sous les murs de Lyon du 30 mai 1790: Supplément du Courrier de Lyon* (Lyon: Publisher unknown, 1790), p.2.
9 Emil Kaufmann, *Trois architectes révolutionnaires: Boullée, Ledoux, Lequeu* (Paris: Editions de la S.A.D.G., 1978), p.27.
10 Jean-Baptiste Volfius, *Discours prononcé le 18 mai 1790, à la cérémonie du serment fédératif prêté sous les murs de Dijon, par MM. les Députés des départements, ci-devant province de Bourgogne, par M. l'Abbé Volfius* (Dijon: P. Causse Imprimeur, 1790), p.28.
11 *Affiches des évêchés de Lorraine*, 1790.

THE FEDERATIONS MOVEMENT AND THE GARDE NATIONALE FLAGS

1789 and the beginning of 1790, the idea of uniting the provinces by means of a great national ceremony did not enthuse either the high officials of the municipality or the deputies of the National Assembly. La Fayette was also cautious. As early as August 1789, anxious to avoid accusations of Caesarism, he had declined the offer of the city of Angers, which wished to entrust him with the command of all the Milices of the kingdom. In January 1790, Abbé Fauchet's proposal to have him appointed *generalissimo* did not get his approval either: it seemed premature. 'It is not a good policy to put in the hand of only one man such a wide command of citizen troops', he had prudently answered.[12] The following month, a new attempt by the undaunted Abbé was met with similar reluctance.

Within this context, Paris decision-makers had long considered festivities connected to the *Constitution* yet to be finalised. In mid-January 1790, they began to plan an oath-taking ceremony for 14 July, but only for young men aged 21 who were starting their service in the Garde Nationale. It was only under constant and effective pressure from the provinces on Paris, through the distribution of brochures, newspapers and letters, that the idea of a nationwide federative celebration finally made headway. Once it had proved itself in the provinces, the federations' programme was now able to establish itself in the political heart of the nation.

Le serment des districts parisiens, gouache by Lesueur, 1790. In February 1790, the Parisian districts took an oath to the *Constitution*, which was then being drafted. Such an oath was a rehearsal for the Federation oath, sworn almost five months later. This gouache was undoubtedly produced after July 1791, since the gardes nationaux wore the uniform with white lapels, scarlet collar and cuffs regulated at that time. (Musée Carnavalet)

---

12   Lacroix, *Actes de la Commune de Paris*, vol.III, p.517.

The provincial fédérés' wishes echoed the concerns of many deputies in the Constituent Assembly who argued, in order to avoid alliances outside the central state, that it was necessary to control this movement by merging it into a vast national federation. On 20 March, the arrival of a Breton-Angevin delegation from the Pontivy federation, heartily welcomed by the Constituent Assembly, provided the opportunity desired by all. The same evening, the Society of the Friends of the Constitution, sitting in the Jacobin convent, pronounced itself in favour of a national federation of all the Gardes Nationales. According to them, it would make it possible to organise a general monitoring of the aristocrats and all the 'bad citizens' in order to nullify all their liberticidal projects. On 29 March, the Breton and Angevin delegates went together to the Jacobins to present a radical address declaring that 'a general federation is the only way to strengthen the Revolution'.[13]

In April, interest in the federations grew within the 60 Parisian districts. On 22 April, the Saint-Honoré district thus presented the Paris city council with a project for a 'national confederation' explicitly inspired by the Breton-Angevin federation. Its originality lay in the fact that it would only involve populations living within a day's walk of Paris. Despite the municipality's lack of decision, the Saint-Eustache district sounded out the kingdom's towns to gauge the interest of a 'general federation of provinces in the capital'.[14] A few weeks later, this same district on its own initiative sent a delegate to the huge federation of Lyon in order to bring back as many details as possible on how to organise such a large-scale event. The aim was also to create links with the fédérés in the provinces. In short, in Paris, as previously in the provinces, the campaign was led by local organisations.

As the project of a national federation without central control from Paris gained ground in the provinces, the National Assembly received on 11 May a letter from Arras announcing two twin confederations, one in Arras, the other in Lille, and further intended for the departments of Nord and Pas-de-Calais. Its authors also called for a date to be set for 'one general confederation so that all of France's gardes nationaux could simultaneously take the same oath in the administrative centres of their departments'.[15] This proposal was unanimously applauded by the deputies and immediately submitted to the committees of the Assembly without any follow-up. As for the Parisian municipality, it announced on 15 May its intention to solemnly invite the municipalities, the Gardes Nationales and all the line regiments to send delegations to Paris to celebrate the first anniversary of the storming of the Bastille on 14 July. Despite many accounts praising the regional federations, such a decision did not fail to raise a series of questions and even concerns. What would such a flood of provincials produce? Would the aristocrats not take advantage of the situation to carry out attacks and plots? The facts seemed to prove the municipal authorities wrong.

---

13   *Les Révolutions de Paris*, 38 (1790), p.18.
14   Archives Municipales de Sens (AMS): 2 D 2 41.
15   Madival & Laurent (eds), *Archives Parlementaires*, vol.XV, pp.488–489.

Extensive Preparations

In any case, the proposal was not discussed in the National Assembly until 5 June. The scale of the provincial mobilisation, with massive gatherings, had finally compelled the Constituent Assembly to organise a national federation in the capital together with the Paris municipality. 'Everything is changing around us. Almost all the regions in the kingdom have formed their own federation', declared Paris mayor Bailly on this occasion. 'Honour your vote and finish your work with a great national gathering,' he said.[16] Certainly, some conservative deputies objected that the time of the gardes could be better used. However, the motion met few opponents. The deputies claimed to be representing national sovereignty. In fact, a national federation could only take place under their control, in Paris, the 'revolutionary capital of the kingdom'.[17] Planned for 14 July 1790, one year exactly after the storming of the Bastille, the celebration under preparation was deliberately on an unprecedented scale, even by comparison with the largest regional federations. The project for a stadium more than 800 metres long and capable of accommodating no less than 250,000 spectators on the Champ de Mars was approved. It was to be surrounded by embankments, the centre of which would provide the parade ground. The size of the chosen site was certainly impressive, but there were calls – though without any success – for the Festival to be held in an even larger place: the Plaine des Sablons, which could hold 800,000 to 900,000 people. Various projects revolved around the idea of a series of simultaneous celebrations, both in Paris and in outlying towns across the country, on 14 July 1790. No less than 2.5 million guardsmen would attend. Each municipality was to organise its own celebration. 'On the same day, at the same hour, let a general cry, a unanimous cry be heard in all parts of France!' was the official proclamation of the National Assembly.[18]

It was a real challenge to complete the construction and be ready for 14 July. The situation became extremely worrying when the workers responsible for building the stadium threatened to strike, refusing to work day and night until the work was completed. Faced with the immensity of the task and the short time remaining before the fateful date, the Parisian sections – in a great show of solidarity – mobilised tens of thousands of volunteers to complete the construction of the esplanade. Then a simple garde national himself the future general, Paul Thiébault, recounted in his *Memoirs* how the gardes nationaux went *en masse* to the construction site,

> drumming, with pennants at the rally's departure. But the gardes nationaux paid and drew men to join them. That was not all: officers on leave in Paris, monks even, and finally the most elegant women, mingling with people of all ages, ranks and sexes, crowded the avenues of the Champ de Mars from midday until dinner

---

16   Madival & Laurent (eds), *Archives Parlementaires*, vol.XVI, p.118.
17   Pascal Dupuy, *La Fête de la Fédération* (Rouen: Presses Universitaires de Rouen, 2012), p.7.
18   Pierre Moithey, *Le Défenseur de la Liberté, ou Histoire de la Révolution de Mil Sept Cent Quatre-Vingt Neuf* (Paris: J. Bigot Imprimeur-Libraire, 1789), vol.I, p.101.

time and even after dinner, with carriages, horse-drawn carriages and cabriolets! Everyone arrived with his shovel or his pickaxe and wheelbarrows were sent from all sides.[19]

The 125,000 volunteers who, according to estimates, crowded the site, undoubtedly surpassed the needs. Although he indicated that a few accidents occurred during construction, Thiébault insisted above all on the general good humour that reigned on this immense site. Emotional connection with the federative project was a prime motivating factor. And in fact, the city of Paris took on the appearance of 'a vast patriotic workshop'.[20] The demonstration of goodwill by tens of thousands of men and women enabled the Festival of the Federation to have a far greater effect on the population than any directive. This 'week of wheelbarrows', as it was later called, left a vivid mark in the memories of those who took part. Contemporary iconography also perpetuated the memory.

The mobilisation for the Paris Federation had gradually spread throughout the country with the election in each municipality of gardes nationaux delegates for the national event. The Assembly had decided to cover the transportation costs of the delegates to the tune of 300 *livres*, but for the representatives of many regions, the journey to the capital also meant several weeks' absence and consequently lost work. Nevertheless, the event attracted a large audience from all over France. Participants were warmly welcomed by municipalities along the routes to Paris and were offered board and lodging.

The gardes nationaux fédérés of the departments met in an assembly on 10 July and once again asked that La Fayette be appointed commander general of the Gardes Nationales of the kingdom. He refused, agreeing only – and unwillingly – to preside over their assembly. On the afternoon of the 13th, in torrential rain, nearly 14,000 of these provincial gardes nationaux massed in Place Louis XV and then paraded through the Tuileries gardens before King Louis XVI. Some 20 of them then joined La Fayette in presenting an address to the National Assembly. If the Nation was in enthusiastic expectation of the new *Constitution*, the enlightened will that guided it was 'already creating a new order', the 'hero of two worlds' explained on this occasion. The festival that was coming up, he continued, would be complete if it allowed new revolutionary ideals to be proclaimed. La Fayette also took the opportunity to reassure the deputies that the Garde Nationale was, to his mind, revolutionary enthusiasm within the law. 'The banner of liberty will never become that of licence', he concluded.[21] Such a speech was warmly applauded and, in spite of the atmosphere of division which had surrounded the first debates over organising a national federation, all the deputies declared that they were publicly committed with undisguised enthusiasm to the ceremonies. The delegates of the gardes nationaux then headed to the Tuileries for a royal

---

19 Fernand Calmettes (ed.), *Mémoires du Général Baron Thiébault* (Paris: Plon, 1896), vol.I, pp.258–259.
20 *L'Observateur provincial*, 22 (1790).
21 Madival & Laurent (eds), *Archives Parlementaires*, vol.XVII, p.77.

audience. Louis XVI took this opportunity to express his confidence in them and asked them to make known to the provinces the affection he felt for all his subjects, especially the poorest and most unfortunate.

The Parisian Festival and its Aftermath

Wednesday 14 July 1790. The rain had been pouring down on Paris since dawn, but it had hardly deterred an impressive parade from setting off from the faubourg Saint-Antoine towards Place Louis XV at around 7:00 a.m. The Garde Nationale Parisienne led the way with its cavalry, music and drummers, followed by its grenadier companies. The municipality and the presidents of the districts came after them, preceded by a children's battalion. Elderly men closed this Parisian prologue of approximately 8,000 individuals. Then came the 15,000 gardes from the departments with their own music, their own flags, and banners they had been given the day before. The crowd cheered them even more than the Parisians. It also gave a standing ovation to detachments of soldiers and NCOs representing the royal army. The showering rain did not disturb the prevailing good mood. The long procession to the Champ de Mars was enlivened by crowds on balconies and at windows, who threw bread and distributed brandy to the participants. A garde national from the Marne village of Sézanne, visiting Paris for the very first time, wrote that he had been touched by 'friendship that all the Parisians kept showing by applause and the redoubling of 'Vivent nos frères! Vivent nos camarades!'[22] Another provincial described the festival as a moment 'not only imposing by its beauty, but also uplifting from the seeds of union and fraternity brought by the deputies'.[23]

The regional federations' model was strictly adhered to. The vast space between the École Militaire and the Seine was covered for the occasion with stands. A gigantic triumphal arch and a tribune, intended to welcome officials, had also been erected there. In the centre, framed by antique-style torches and surrounded by the flags of the 60 Paris Garde Nationale battalions, stood a circular altar of the Fatherland. Under the roofed platform leaning against the Ecole Militaire, the King was to sit surrounded by the royal family, the municipality and the ambassadors. While tens of thousands of gardes nationaux marched in the centre of a huge stadium filled with 300,000 spectators, thousands of others found themselves unable to join the festival and had to secure the area surrounding the Champ de Mars.

La Fayette, in full dress uniform, arrived on a white horse, stepped onto the platform and, in the name of the gardes nationaux fédérés, was first to swear the oath. A true political manifesto, it therefore deserves to be reproduced in full:

---

[22] Nicolas Frérot, 'La Fédération du 14 juillet 1790 (Souvenir d'un délégué de la ville de Sézanne)', *Annales Historiques de la Révolution Française*, 8 (1931), p.164.
[23] Pierre de Vaissière, *Lettres d'« aristocrates »: La Révolution racontée par des correspondances privées, 1789–1794* (Paris: Perrin, 1906), p.173.

THE GARDE NATIONALE 1789–1815

1er événement du 14 Juillet 1790, coloured print by Janinet, 1790. Janinet depicts the passage, on the Quai de la Conférence, of provincial gardes nationaux. At the head of the delegation is the banner offered by the Paris Commune. Janinet shows the consensus between the crowd and the armed forces. (Yves Martin)

THE FEDERATIONS MOVEMENT AND THE GARDE NATIONALE FLAGS

2e événement du 14 Juillet 1790, print by Janinet. This engraving depicts the Garde Nationale's entry on the Champ de Mars. The entrance was marked by a triumphal arch designed by architect Cellerier. The flag flying on the left of the print hardly corresponds to one of the 60 Parisian battalions. In the right foreground, veterans march past. Their uniforms are incorrectly depicted: on 14 July 1790, they were lapel-less. (Yves Martin)

> We swear to remain forever faithful to the nation, to the law and to the king, to maintain with all our power the *Constitution* decreed by the National Assembly and accepted by the king, and to protect, in accordance with the laws, the safety of the people and property, the circulation of grain and foodstuffs within the kingdom, the prescription of public contributions in whatever form they exist, and to remain united with all Frenchmen by the indissoluble bonds of fraternity.[24]

Around 3:00 p.m., as soon as the King arrived from Saint-Cloud, Talleyrand, Bishop of Autun, celebrated mass before oaths were taken: the President of the Assembly did so on behalf of the deputies and electors, before Louis XVI himself appeared. When 40 successive cannon shots were heard, it was clear that the King had fulfilled his office and the audience rejoiced as if the Revolution had reached a final and fraternal fulfilment. The spectators, exhilarated by the music and the roar of the cannon, cheered not only Louis XVI but also La Fayette. 'There was much hugging and much weeping', as historian Roger Dupuy notes.[25]

In Paris, the festive celebrations continued for a week, precisely until 20 July and the departure of most of the gardes nationaux fédérés. Following the main ceremony, the participants dispersed to a series of banquets organised locally by the 60 Garde Nationale Parisienne battalions to honour their provincial guests. Some sections erected vast pavilions on the outskirts of the city, surrounding the Champ de la Fédération and extending to the Champs-Élysées, with dancing and fireworks. La Fayette offered several banquets to delegations where he delivered his speech on respect for laws, property and morals. As for the festivities, Bailly did not spare the Paris Commune's funds. In addition to the pleasures of the table and dancing, there were nautical jousts on the Seine, theatrical performances, illuminations and fireworks. These multiple festive occasions were intended, like the civic festivals of Ancient Rome from which they were inspired, as a way for people to escape from their daily routine and experience an exceptional moment. And in fact, the participation hardly diminished as the days went by. The last celebrations were at least as popular as the first. The review of the Garde Nationale Parisienne organised at the Champ de Mars on 18 July attracted as many spectators as the Festival of the Federation itself.

Cohesion and Communion?

As a concerted movement that affected the whole of France from the summer of 1789 to the summer of 1790, the federations were an eloquent testimony to the emotional force generated by the early days of the Revolution. Beyond their initial motivations, which ranged from mutual defence to open citizenship and egalitarianism, the small-town revolutionaries invented a radically new form of popular engagement that quickly spread across

---

24 Louis Rondonneau, *Collection Générale des Lois depuis 1789 jusqu'au 1er avril 1814* (Paris: Rondonneau et Decle Libraires, 1817), vol.I, p.340.
25 Dupuy, *La Garde nationale*, p.70.

THE FEDERATIONS MOVEMENT AND THE GARDE NATIONALE FLAGS

The Festival of the Federation gave rise to scenes of communion and fraternisation. This plate from Noirmont and Marbot's monumental work on the French army's history depicts this very moment. Pictured here, from left to right, are gardes from Avignon, Pont-Saint-Esprit, Maintenon, Chartres and Brest. To their right stand gardes nationaux of the Théâtins district, with their distinctive flag. (Yves Martin)

THE GARDE NATIONALE 1789–1815

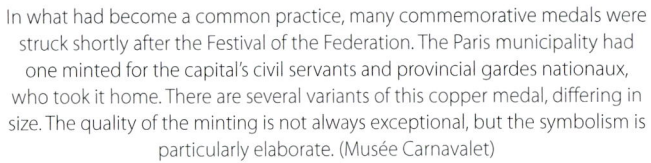

In what had become a common practice, many commemorative medals were struck shortly after the Festival of the Federation. The Paris municipality had one minted for the capital's civil servants and provincial gardes nationaux, who took it home. There are several variants of this copper medal, differing in size. The quality of the minting is not always exceptional, but the symbolism is particularly elaborate. (Musée Carnavalet)

Bellac Garde Nationale officer, miniature portrait, 1790. On 24 June 1790, the gardes nationaux of the canton of Bellac, in the Haute-Vienne, met there to appoint delegates who would travel to Paris for the Festival of the Federation on 14 July. Painted by miniaturist Goutel shortly after this event, this *capitaine* in a blue uniform, with red lapels and collar piped white, certainly took part. (François Vinot-Préfontaine's collection)

the country, involving ever greater numbers of participants. For many revolutionaries, the federative ceremonies soon proved to be indispensable: they provided the local elites with a method of consolidating popular support for their action and of demonstrating the Garde Nationale's strength. In addition, the federative celebrations allowed peripheral France – that of the provinces – to play a significant role. However, such public ceremonies could not be considered as pure novelties, as they drew on the many legacies of the Ancien Régime society.

Preparations for the various federative festivals hardly took place in an idyllic atmosphere. Local rivalries remained strong and were sometimes reinforced by the new division of the French territory into 83 departments. Ideological conflicts were not absent from such meetings, as were disputes over precedence and financial disagreements. Thus, the people of Toulon refused to invite the Garde Nationale of Montauban, which was perceived as factious. In Châteauneuf, the gardes of Grasse and Antibes had come to blows, and while in Grenoble tensions arose over the swearing of the oath. The summer of 1790 was, for its part, marked by resistance to the Revolution. For example, the south-east of the territory was still affected by the age-old struggles between Catholics and Protestants. In August 1790, the counter-revolutionaries of the Vivarais – a region which had played a central role in the early days of the federation movement – organised a show of force on the small plain of Jalès. The demonstration brought together between 20,000 and 45,000 participants, including the mayors of the southern Ardèche, their municipal officers and, above all, the gardes nationaux who came with their flags. In the name of protecting the Catholic religion, the audience openly defended the monarchy against the power of the Assembly. This 'camp de

THE FEDERATIONS MOVEMENT AND THE GARDE NATIONALE FLAGS

Right: Alleged portrait of Marius Pommerol, delegate from Marseilles to the Festival of the Federation, 1790. This *sous-lieutenant* is armed with a 'petit Montmorency' sabre of personal purchase and adorned with a tricolour sword knot. The Federation commemorative medal is pinned to the left lapel of his coat, decorated with a pair of trefoils in gold lace. (Musée Carnavalet)

Below: On this engraving by Louis Le Coeur, easily identifiable are La Fayette's oath at the altar of the Fatherland, departemental Gardes Nationales' banners, as well as some Paris Garde Nationale colours – such as that of the faubourg Saint-Marcel – are readily recognisable. Also of note, in the foreground, is the young boy in a chasseur uniform. (Musée Carnavalet)

Jalès' demonstrated that large gatherings based on collective emotions were just as suitable for revolutionary projects as for the most conservative causes.

No matter. Attendees of the National Federation of the Champ de Mars memorialised the moments they experienced. Such writings show to what extent their authors found themselves in a kind of emotional fusion, mixing their sensations and experiences with the description of the festival. 'One can only imagine it by seeing it,' wrote the Comte de Seneffe.[26] 'Nothing could be greater, more imposing and more majestic', reported one of the Avignon delegates in a letter to the authorities of his city.[27] 'The picture I had before my eyes for 12 hours could not be rendered, either with the brush, nor with the pen, or with the tongue', assured Prussian-born deputy Anacharsis Cloots. 'The cannon, the music, the applause, made the sky and the earth tremble', 'the triumphal arch, the bridge over the river, the stylish altar, the Roman style palace with all the flags, all the banners, offered an enchanting sight', he added.[28] And indeed, witnesses were impressed by the innumerable spectators, the shimmering uniforms and the beauty of the flags, which became commonplace in the iconography of Parisian and provincial festivals.

Paris Garde Nationale Flags

True Artworks

The origin of the 60 flags which, brandished by the Garde Nationale Parisienne, rose into the sky on 14 July 1790, dated back to the previous summer. On 27 July 1789, it was officially decided that each Parisian district would have its own Garde Nationale battalion as well as a flag bearing a motto. Thus, 'a spontaneous creation of Paris, the Garde, born at the time of the storming of the Bastille, wanted to have its flags along with its uniforms and 60 emblems were invented in turn for the 60 battalions' as undeniable markers of identity.[29] In reality, as early as 17 July, when Louis XVI went to the Hôtel de Ville, two districts were already flying their own flag, that of Notre-Dame with the motto 'le salut de la Patrie' (the Salvation of the Nation) and that of the Mathurins, which proclaimed 'Liberté'. According to the deliberation registers of the districts, the flag arrangements were taken into account in the first week of August. However, far from respecting them scrupulously, the districts instead gave free rein to improvise. Nevertheless, this practice was more of a continuity than a novelty: the royal army's flags, which were also freely composed, fulfilled their role of gathering and guiding the men of the unit all the better. It was with remarkable care and attention that each district took it upon itself to produce a work that was both original and individual.

---

26   Pierre de Vaissière, *Lettres d'« aristocrates »*, p.173.
27   Archives Municipales d'Avignon (AMA): 4 H 1 11: Lettre du 16 juillet 1790.
28   Georges Avenel, *Anacharsis Cloots: L'orateur du genre humain* (Paris: A. Lacroix, Verboeckhoven et Cie Editeurs, 1865), p.195.
29   Marcel Reinhard, 'Les drapeaux de la Garde nationale parisienne en 1789', *Études européennes: Mélanges offerts à Victor Louis Tapié* (Paris: Publications de la Sorbonne, 1973), p.525.

THE FEDERATIONS MOVEMENT AND THE GARDE NATIONALE FLAGS

Vieilh de Varennes composed a *Description des soixante drapeaux que l'amour patriotique a offert aux soixante districts de la ville et des faubourgs de Paris*.[30] A true testimony, full of emotions, hopes and patriotism, the text testified to the remarkable erudition of its author. All the flags were described with extreme precision. Size, explanation of the colours and all their nuances, deciphering of the allegories, symbols and words: nothing failed to escape the attention of this former Ponts-et-Chaussées engineer who had taken part in the storming of the Bastille. In addition, the author took care to indicate who made the flag, who decorated it and who were the generous donors who ensured its financing. A genuine work of art accompanied by 60 carefully water-coloured engraved plates, this book is all the more essential as the flags represented throughout its pages were destroyed in 1792 at the advent of the Republic.

Some districts did not hesitate to call on renowned artists to design their flag, which was considered a work of art. Thus, in Saint-Victor, Bourgoin, painter of the King's gardens, designed the district flag. The famous Gobelins factory was responsible for making the flag of the Saint-Marcel district. In Saint-Lazare, the flag was designed by Charpentier, an embroiderer established at the entrance to the faubourg. The painting was done by Nebel,

Nicolas Hoffmann is regarded as a scrupulous picture maker. The background of his plate depicting La Fayette features a flag of the Garde Nationale Parisienne with a gigantic ship at the bottom and fleurs-de-lys at the top. No such flag has ever been flown! (Yves Martin)

---
30 Raymond Augustin Vieilh de Varennes, *Description curieuse et intéressante des soixante drapeaux que l'amour patriotique a offerts aux soixante districts de la ville et des faubourgs de Paris, précédée de l'état-major général de la garde nationale parisienne* (Paris: Sorin, 1790).

THE GARDE NATIONALE 1789–1815

Bénédiction des drapeaux de la Garde Nationale Parisienne à Notre-Dame, le 27 septembre 1789, engraving by Berthault. At the end of September 1789, the Constituent Assembly decided on the general blessing of the flags of the Garde Nationale de Paris at a solemn ceremony in the church of Notre-Dame. The flags were blessed before a huge crowd by Monseigneur de Juigné and Abbé Fauchet gave a homily. (Musée Carnavalet)

painter and decorator, rue du Temple n° 150. Lorthiot, the King's painter, composed and produced the flag of the Oratoire. In these circumstances, the refinement of the ensemble and the beauty of the decorations should hardly come as a surprise, any more than the numerous references to ancient models.

As for the donors, variety prevailed. Flags were commonly donated by district officers: M. Royer for the Prémontrés or M. Crevecoeur for the Cordeliers. In other districts, as in Saint-Louis-en-l'Isle, Saint-Nicolas-des-Champs, Saint-Séverin, Saint-Lazare, Les Récollets or the Jacobins, the active citizens, members of the Garde Nationale battalion, contributed. No less than 11 flags were given by personalities: La Fayette himself offered, for example, the flag of the Sorbonne district and M. Lothier, the King's Prosecutor, gave Notre-Dame's. Nine rather fortunate individuals wanted to pay for the flag of their district, for example Dret, banker in the district of Mathurins, or Armet de Lisle, trader in the district of Saint-Nicolas du Chardonnnet. At the Carmelites, at Saint-Louis-la-Culture but also at the Blancs-Manteaux, the ladies of the districts took charge of financing the flags.

Such emblems were blessed in a relatively short period of time, between 17 July and 31 December 1789. At the end of the religious ceremony, the priest often gave a speech of 'fiery patriotism' in which he paid tribute to God for 'this life-giving revolution'.[31] In the popular faubourg Saint-Marcel, the blessing of the flag was – surprisingly enough – a peaceful and worldly ceremony where people went by invitation to hear all the new authorities and the citizen-king praised. The emphasis was on the need to provide children with a good education in order to reduce crime and to 'nurture talent'.

Flags' Design

What did these flags look like? Their size remained largely the same as the royal infantry's flags. Made of silk, they were 1.78 metres square, nailed to a flagstaff of between 2.9 metres and 3.24 metres, with a ferrule at the lower end. The top was decorated with a gilded copper spearhead. Most of the time, the cravats, 73 centimetres long, were made of white taffeta fringed with gold. However, some districts wore it in blue and red – the city's colours. Five of them decorated their flag with tricolour cravats, which anticipated the ordinance of 22 October 1790 by almost a year.

More than half of these flags were, like those of the royal infantry, structured by a white cross, which allowed four squares or cantons to be identified and colours and decorations to be organised in great diversity. Even though the cross remained, each district sought to assert its originality in relation to the initial model. Red, white and blue were widely used in the chromatic palette, although there was no precise order in which they were arranged. In fact, only two flags, that of the Blancs-Manteaux and that of the district of Saint-Thomas, displayed tricolour bands. Only 16 flags were mostly white, and only that of the district of Saint-Louis de la Culture was entirely white. Originally white, the flag of Saint-Jacques-de-l'Hôpital was modified in the course of 1790.

Flags' Messages

An overwhelming majority of the flags – no less than 54 out of 60 – included mottos that belonged to a long tradition dating back to Roman Antiquity. Above all, they turned the flags into mouthpieces for the districts. The writing of these short – given the limited space – and generally combative messages

Flag of the Saint-Marcel district, anonymous engraver, 1789. This flag was offered by the Gobelins Royal Manufacture. According to French historian Elisabeth Liris, 'the character hardly evokes a peasant and his clothing does not correspond to that of a countryman. Perhaps he evoked, in a slightly disguised way, one of the images of the Great Fear that was still so present in everyone's mind at the time?" (Musée Carnavalet)
* Elisabeth Liris, 'De la Liberté à l'Union dans l'iconographie des drapeaux des districts parisiens', *Annales Historiques de la Révolution Française*, 289 (1992), p.349.

---
31 Elisabeth Liris, 'Iconographie et épigraphie des drapeaux de la Garde nationale de Paris en 1789', in Serge Bianchi and Roger Dupuy (eds), *La Garde nationale entre Nation et peuple en armes* (Rennes: Presses Universitaires de Rennes, 2006), p.285.

THE GARDE NATIONALE 1789–1815

Flag of the 1st Battalion of the 1st Division (Saint Jacques du Haut Pas District). This flag is quartered into four blue cantons by a broad white cross throughout, on the model of the Gardes Françaises colours. In the centre of the flag is the representation of the Bastille fortress. Four liberty caps replace the four fleurs-de-lys featured on the flag of the Gardes Françaises. (Yves Martin)

was very neat, in capital letters and often in gold letters. A total of 254 words were written on the surface of the fabric. Within this corpus, liberty, mentioned 26 times, came out on top, well ahead of union (recorded 13 times), force (12), law (10), king (seven, including one in Latin), fatherland (four, including two in Latin), death (seven – six 'to die', one 'to perish') the nation (three, including two 'nation' and one 'national'). Moral values included virtue, prudence, vigilance, loyalty, fidelity, fearlessness, perseverance and firmness. The references remained rather timid in the political domain. If the citizens, the Commune, the people, justice and the *Constitution* were certainly evoked, fraternity was only mentioned on one occasion. There was a heavy and eloquent silence on equality. Nevertheless, the flags of the districts unquestionably affirmed real commitments: 'Pour la liberté' ('For Liberty') at the Récollets, 'La Loi et la liberté' ('Law and Liberty') at Saint-Joseph. They were imperative at Sainte-Élisabeth: 'Vaincre ou mourir' ('Win or Die'). They were also found in the form of maxims: 'Un roi juste fait le bonheur de tous' ('A just king makes everyone happy'), on the flag of the Tresnel district, 'L'union fait la force' ('Union makes strength'), in Saint-Honoré. Finally, four mottos were written in Latin. Did the majority of the gardes nationaux grasp their meanings? All these mottos were chosen by the battalion commanders, which explains certain omissions as well as the elitism of some of the inscriptions.

Table 8. The symbology of the Paris Garde Nationale's colours, as described on pages 28 to 31 of Vieilh de Varennes' book

Emblem	Symbol of…
Anchor	Hope
Scales	Justice
Cap	Liberty
Caduceus	Peace
Plough, ploughshare, spade, rake, scythe, sickle, pitchfork, billhook, plants, fruit	Agriculture and abundance
Broken chain, spread rings	End of oppression and slavery
Oak	Value
Rooster	Vigilance
Dove	Sweetness
Starry crown	Candour
Laurel wreath	Triumph, reward of virtue and valour
Cross or crosier	Clergy, Catholic religion

THE FEDERATIONS MOVEMENT AND THE GARDE NATIONALE FLAGS

Epigraphy openly favoured union and freedom. Nevertheless, since the latter was still fragile, the districts recalled its difficult conquest and the necessary vigilance to maintain it. To represent such values, the artists used traditional images which they did not hesitate to update according to their talents, their aspirations, but also the social tone of the district. To evoke and represent freedom in the sequence between the storming of the Bastille and the days of October 1789 was to translate into images an achievement, a conquest, a metamorphosis in which the Parisian districts were the actors. It also meant expressing the stakes, hopes and fears generated by the events themselves, in a political and social landscape in tumult. In this rather perilous process, the districts referred to both the past and the present: the old elements of flag decoration and the emerging revolutionary symbolism therefore coexisted.

Echoing the mottos, the images emphasised freedom and unity, combined with the obligatory presence of the city of Paris. Freedom was present in many forms in the speeches, gestures and images and was visibly embodied in the bonnet. In 1789, in the context of the freedom/servitude logic, reference was made not to the 'Phrygian cap' but to the *pileus*, which, in Greek Antiquity, represented for slaves the tangible sign of their emancipation and their accession to freedom. Red was far from being the 'official' colour. Indeed, the cap was grey on the flag of the Filles-Dieu district, crimson red at the Jacobins Saint-Honoré and the Carmes-Déchaussées, grey and white at the Feuillants, ochre at Saint-Louis and blue at the Sorbonne. On the flags, such a cap was automatically included in ascending patterns and surmounted – depending on the district – a sword, a pike, a beam or even a ship's mast.

Left: Flag of the 2nd Battalion of the 1st Division. (St Victor District). Elisabeth Liris explains that the colour features allegorical representations of Liberty, Justice and Concord, and an old farmer in rags, a realistic figure that may represent poor and populous boroughs. Liberty dominates the scene, freeing the old man from his chains and raising the liberty cap on a pike, as a triumphant challenge to servitude. (Yves Martin)

Right: Flag of the 10th Battalion of the 1st Division (Mathurins District). (Yves Martin)

THE GARDE NATIONALE 1789–1815

Flag of the 9th Battalion of the 6th Division (Champs-Élysées/Capucins Saint Honoré District). This blue flag was offered by the Duchesse de Bourbon. (Yves Martin)

The other image of freedom was an allegory of a goddess or a young woman. The union was expressed both by the mottos and by a tonic and abundant iconography, giving substance to a pugnacious discourse embodied mainly in the theme of the fasces, which appeared on a quarter of the flags, either as the main element or as a secondary motif. It was an attribute of the lictors in Roman antiquity and consisted of an axe surrounded by wooden sticks joined by a strap. In ancient Rome, it symbolised both the right to life and death (through the axe) and its necessary union. Alongside the symbols of freedom and union, the presence of Paris was shown on the standards either by allegories or by the presence of the nave, a symbol that has adorned the capital's coat of arms since the thirteenth century. In fact, this nave, solidly mounted, with an abundance of sails, sometimes sailing, sometimes anchored, appeared on 22 flags. Finally, Paris took on the face of Sainte-Genevieve, the capital's patron saint, honoured since the sixth century.

Beyond the cautious ambiguity of their message, these flags make it possible to understand, thanks to the polysemic value of symbols, one of the essential moments in the history of the Garde Nationale and that of the Revolution, within a remarkable originality and artistic research that war, from 1792 onwards, no longer allowed.

Flame and Flag Bearers of the Garde Nationale Parisienne

'It will be given to each battalion of the Garde Nationale Parisienne a flag of colour and legend to the choice of the district. This flag will be placed at the centre company, which will be the one paid, and kept by NCOs of the first, second, fourth and fifth unpaid companies. When the troops are not under arms, the flags of the 10 battalions forming a division will be deposited with the division chief', decreed *the Règlement pour la formation, organisation, solde, police et discipline de la Garde Nationale Parisienne*.[32] From the autumn of 1789, each of the cavalry companies had a standard. These were deposited with the cavalry divisional commander. On the march, they were carried by *maréchaux-des-logis* standard bearers.

'Each of the other four companies will have a flame, which will be carried by a *sergent* when the troop is under arms. Otherwise, it will be deposited at the home of the *capitaine* of each company', indicated the above-mentioned

---

32 Anon., *Règlement pour la formation, organisation, solde, police et discipline de la Garde Nationale Parisienne* (Paris: Lottin, 1789), p.15.

THE FEDERATIONS MOVEMENT AND THE GARDE NATIONALE FLAGS

Règlement.[33] Lesueur's gouaches are the sole iconographic source to reproduce its appearance: the flame was made up of three tricolour bands arranged horizontally. The gouache was accompanied by a note in ink stating that 'each company having its flame, it was very bright when the army was deployed'.[34]

In order to be able to carry their flag while marching, flag bearers of the Garde Nationale Parisienne were equipped – as revealed by a series of gouaches by Lesueur – with a special belt made of buff leather and fitted with a gusset designed to receive the heel of the staff. Was this a specific provision for the Garde Nationale, or did it already apply to the infantry of the royal army? In addition, flag bearers wore, across the chest, a cover that seems specific to them. Made of cloth or silk, sometimes very simple, sometimes fringed with gold, it was tied on the right hip and protected the flag from the elements when it was not deployed.

The 83 Departmental Banners

A few days before the Festival of the Federation, the Paris municipality offered each of the 83 delegations of the provincial gardes nationaux – 'as a token of alliance and fraternity' – a 'simple and unadorned' banner, according to journalistic accounts. Made of white taffeta, it was decorated on both sides with a civic crown of oak leaves – a symbol of patriotism – and the name of the department to which it had been assigned. Fleurs-de-lys were placed at the corners. The inscription 'Confédération nationale à Paris – 14 juillet 1790' appeared in gold letters on the obverse and 'Constitution' on the reverse. The banner was surmounted by a pike and tricolour cravats. During the ceremonies of 14 July 1790, such emblems were carried by the eldest member of each departmental delegation and served as a rallying point. On this occasion, after mass, they were blessed by Talleyrand, bishop of Autun, on the altar of the Nation. On 19 July, the National Assembly decreed that the banners would be 'placed in the location where the administration of each department would hold its sessions'.[35] Brought back by the gardes nationaux fédérés to their respective departments, these emblems were at the heart of local ceremonies organised with great pomp between the end of July and the

Paris Garde Nationale flag bearer and flame bearer, by Lesueur. Both are wearing the uniform regulated in 1791. This gouache is one of the few period representations of a flame bearer. (Musée Carnavalet)

---

33 Anon., *Règlement pour la formation*, p.16.
34 Musée Carnavalet (MC): D.9060: 'Suite de l'armée parisienne', c.1791–1792.
35 Madival & Laurent (eds), *Archives Parlementaires*, vol.XVIII, p.191.

This poster of 28 July 1793 reproduces the decree of the National Convention ordering the destruction of the banners distributed during the Festival of the Federation. (Musée Carnavalet)

beginning of August: presented to the curiosity of the crowds who had come in great numbers to admire them, they were then deposited in the room devoted to their reception. On 28 July 1793, in accordance with the request of the popular society of Auxerre, a decree of the Convention ordered that 'the banners of the Federation of 14 July 1790 will be burnt, as bearing the odious signs of royalty, and replaced by others bearing the symbol of the unity and indivisibility of the Republic, on 10 August of this year'.[36] The departmental authorities largely complied with this request, including those favourable to federalism. In Lyon, which was under siege at the time, the ceremonies of 10 August 1793 were marked by the erection of a stake on which the titles of feudal rights were symbolically burnt, as well as the banner given to the delegation of gardes nationaux from the Rhône three years earlier. In fact,

---

36 Madival & Laurent (eds), *Archives Parlementaires*, vol.LXIX, p.608.

only a banner fragment from an unidentified department remains today, preserved in the Musée Carnavalet in Paris.

Flags in the Departments

The existence of flags within the Garde Nationale was by no means specific to the city of Paris. In fact, such standards formed the most sensitive link between the gardes and their commune. Blessed by a priest shortly after their creation, they were then placed in the choir of the churches. Many flags were made, sometimes at great expense, at the instigation of the municipalities in anticipation of the various federative celebrations that punctuated the life of the kingdom from the summer of 1789 to the summer of 1790. Paradoxically, these town flags often disappeared after the proclamation of the Republic, burnt on the orders of a *représentant en mission* as emblems tinged with monarchism.

L'état des Gardes Nationales de France is therefore a valuable aid in imagining their appearance. In this respect, the book reveals that the Epinal Garde Nationale had two flags. The silk was divided into four quarters – two blue and two pink – dotted with fleurs-de-lys and separated by a white cross in the centre. The coat of arms of both the city and the King appeared on it, together with the motto 'Pro Rege et Patria' (for king and country) for the former, 'Prius Mori Quam Fidem Jallere' (rather die than ignore the faith) for the latter. In Chartres, two flags were also made – one white, the other red – bearing the motto 'Vive la Nation, Vive le Roi'. In Hennebont, Brittany, the flags were tricoloured and decorated with the motto 'La Liberté ou la Mort' (liberty or death).

In Puteaux, a small town in the Paris region, the municipal deliberations indicate that on 3 June 1790, after mass, Guillaume Nezot, mayor of the commune, managed to convince his constituents to allocate 150 *livres* to the making of a flag, which was blessed on 4 July by Louis Noel, the parish priest. It was accurately described in the municipal register:

> The flag is made of white taffeta and is decorated on the right-hand side with the crowned coat of arms of France, a rosebush and other ornaments. It is written 'Garde Nationale de Puteaux'. On the left side is a well. Above the well is the sun in which is the eye of surveillance. On the right side of the well is a plough and a sheaf of wheat. On the left side of the well is a vine with its fruit on it.[37]

This flag, which contained 'some signs of royalty', was burnt on 27 March 1793 during a patriotic celebration. It was replaced by a new flag offered by Julien Gohin, a local patriot.

As early as 1789, the municipality of Saint-Nazaire en Royans, in the Drome, had a flag of 1.44 metres by 1.59 metres made. Composed of four

---

[37] Archives Municipales de Puteaux (AMP): Registre des délibérations du conseil municipal de la commune de Puteaux, 1790.

THE GARDE NATIONALE 1789–1815

quarters with opposing colours, it is decorated on both sides with two large fleurs-de-lys and as many dolphins, and bears the motto 'Pro Patria et Libertate Mori'. The date – 1789 – appears on the obverse only. The flagpole was mounted on the upper edge, a position rarely seen elsewhere.

In 1790, the Garde Nationale of Echigey and the three Tart (Tart l'Abbaye, Tart le Haut and Tart le Bas) totalled 203 men. On 16 May, they all took the oath at the federative festival in Dijon. The four communes had also joined forces to commission a painted silk flag measuring 1.80 metres square. It was decorated with fleurs-de-lys at the top corners and a radiant sun representing royal authority. It also featured a ploughman in the centre, a symbol of the people in action, wearing a tricolour cockade on his hat. The flag thus symbolised the alliance between the king and the nation, but also the revolutionary enthusiasm of the peasantry in the smallest rural communities. The latter were ready to defend freedom dearly, as was assured both by the federal oaths taken in 1790 and by the unequivocal motto 'Vincere aut Mori' ('Win or Die') painted between two cannon on the fabric of their flag. Finally, the central scene provides useful information about the agricultural techniques used in this region of the Saône Valley. The ploughboy is handling a wheeled plough, apparently made of wood and harnessed to two horses. On the left is a sheaf of wheat into which a sickle is planted, and on the right, vines. The soil of the three Tarts, which was difficult to plough – hence the choice of horses over oxen – produced wheat and oats, which were harvested with the sickle until the middle of the nineteenth century, but also an excellent white wine. While the Festival of the Federation was in full swing in the capital on 14 July 1790, the flag took part in the one organised in Aiserey, the chief town of the canton. When the Republic was proclaimed, it was hastily brought up to date: the fleur-de-lys in the left-hand corner was smeared to remove its representation.

The commune of Arc-sur-Tille sent 12 delegates to the federative festival of Dijon. On their return, they recounted that several cantons of the vicinity had presented themselves at the meeting with flags. Also, the municipality of Arc-sur-Tille decided as of 20 May to acquire one, for the rather high sum of 127 *livres* and six *sous*. The flag was ready in record time. On 3 June, it was solemnly blessed by Abbot Terguet – also mayor of the village – then placed at the head of the Corpus Christi procession. It is a white silk flag. In the middle stands a pike passing through a civic crown and surmounted by the cap of liberty. A blue ribbon joins a golden sceptre to the pike. Further down, a relaxed bow is depicted. Against the pike, two cornucopias pour fruit and wheat. On the right, water – a symbol of fertility – flows from an urn. Thanks to this fertilising source, an olive tree laden with fruit and a lily in blossom are growing. The olive tree probably referred to peace and the lily to the constitutional monarchy in the making. At the bottom of the flag lies a broken yoke. Two scrolls were inscribed with the words 'Ton règne, Liberté, ramène l'abondance, anime l'industrie et détruit la licence' (Your rule, thy Liberty, brings back abundance, enlivens industry and destroys licence). The flag was certainly that of the Garde Nationale, but it was also that of the municipality, which had allocated the necessary funds for its creation. The mayor had had it stored in the sacristy, while the gardes nationaux asked, on the contrary, that it be deposited with their commander. On 5 July, Terguet asked his constituents to decide on the question. It was finally agreed that the flag would be kept in the sacristy, but that it would be taken out whenever the needs of military service justified it. This was only a temporary measure, as the flag was to be housed in the town hall which was under construction. Although local historians claimed that it was flown on the Champ de Mars on the occasion of the Festival of the Federation, this assertion is not very convincing. On the other hand, it is certain that it was raised during a federative festival organised in Dijon on 14 July 1791 and formed the rallying point for the 22 gardes nationaux of the Arc-sur-Tille delegation. The day after the celebrations, it was brought back to the town hall, where the municipality could check that it was intact. It was then decorated with a gold fringed tie. In addition, a belt and a gusset had been made for the flag bearer. Following the proclamation of the Republic, the flag underwent some minor changes. For example, the fleur-de-lys at the end of the sceptre was mutilated as part of the destruction of the royal symbols. It was later replaced, albeit in an awkward manner. A new flag, probably more in keeping with the new republican iconography, was acquired in early 1793.

A flag was also made in 1790 in the small Rhone commune of Saint-Laurent de Chamousset. Measuring 1.60 metres by 1.80 metres, it was composed of four parts of taffeta, two scarlet and two white. On the obverse, a circle of sky-blue cloth has the new *Constitution* in its centre. Behind this legislative text, a sceptre and a hand of justice, two attributes of royal power, are crossed. The date '1790' appears at the bottom of the circle. On the reverse side, the motto 'Vaincre ou mourir pour la Nation, la Loi et le Roy 1790' (Win or die for the Nation, the Law and the King 1790) adorns the blue circle.

6

The Pivotal Years

Summer 1790–Summer 1792

While representing only a fleeting pause in the eventful history of the French Revolution, the Festival of the Federation of 14 July 1790 made a powerful impression on the minds of contemporaries. This great celebration of fraternity can in fact be interpreted as a political operation, promptly embellished by literature and, even more so, by an overabundance of iconography. These historic weeks in the summer of 1790 undeniably marked the triumph of La Fayette, the strongman of the moment. The provincial gardes nationaux, most of whom came from bourgeois families and were the only ones able to afford the cost of a long journey to Paris, were enthusiastic, almost hysterical, about him. The profile of the Commander-in-Chief of the Garde Nationale Parisienne was engraved on thousands of sabres acquired by his subordinates, thus implicitly proving their devotion to him. His famous white horse was hugged. Better still, street publications, patriotic refrains and allegories to the glory of La Fayette spread his name throughout the kingdom and confirmed his popularity at its peak.

The Federations, from Crisis to Decay

Before separating to return to their departments, the fédérés adopted a declaration in which they deplored that La Fayette had not been appointed their supreme leader. In addition, on 24 July, the gardes nationaux who were prolonging their stay in the capital laid the foundations of a Société des gardes nationaux des départements whose main objective was to establish a continuous correspondence between the gardes of the main cities of the kingdom. La Fayette gave them his support and, not surprisingly, was appointed honorary president. The 'hero of two worlds' no doubt hoped to find a counterweight to the attacks he had been facing since the completion of the Festival of the Federation. His prominent position made him a prime target for some of the press. There were numerous libels and petitions from sections hostile to the centre companies or the aides-de-camp of the

Commandant General. The latter would have prevented the commemoration of 14 July, would not have given the 'Victors of the Bastille' their rightful place in the original parade and would have allowed himself to be worshipped like an idol by provincial gardes nationaux.

On their return from the Festival of the Federation, the fédérés found several regions in turmoil. Despite good wheat harvests, there was a simmering food crisis. A new episode of 'Great Fear' hung over the north and east of France, while the south-east of the kingdom was agitated by fierce religious quarrels between Catholics and Protestants. Nevertheless, in August 1790, La Fayette felt that he had strengthened his hold on the country through the Festival of the Federation. He could therefore continue to work towards the establishment of a constitutional monarchy, which he saw as the only viable solution for the future of the kingdom. Moreover, he hoped to be successful in what he himself considered to be a difficult challenge: to convince a million citizens to accept a common discipline and principles.

However, he was concerned about the revolt of several regiments of the royal army, as he confessed in a letter to his mentor, US President George Washington. Indeed, since the spring of 1790, seditions marked by assassinations of officers, the theft of regimental coffers and the creation of committees of soldiers and NCOs had developed in many garrison towns. Despite his personal reluctance, the Minister of War authorised the regiments of the royal army to participate in the Festival of the Federation. It was hoped that such a decision would channel the revolts. But such a calculation turned out to be erroneous. The regimental delegates, who had returned from Paris, were convinced that they had to ensure the triumph of revolutionary principles in an army marked by divisions between the troops and the officers. In this struggle for influence aimed at getting the most reactionary officers to resign, they frequently received the support of the gardes nationaux and the patriotic clubs established in their garrison towns. The irregular payment of wages – delays sometimes reaching several months – also crystallised discontent. The Constituent Assembly had, of course, decided to increase the pay of troops, but the measure was delayed and several regiments put pressure on their commanders. Some complied, but most complained to the minister about growing indiscipline, which they attributed to bad habits contracted in Paris, to the harmful influence of members of patriotic clubs, and to the bad example set by the gardes nationaux. The fortress of Metz was thus affected on 4 August. A week later, a similar conflict broke out in Nancy, which at that time housed a garrison of some 5,000 men. On 11 August 1790, the Swiss of the Regiment de Châteauvieux unsuccessfully demanded the accounts of their unit from their officers; in addition, the leaders were whipped. However, the soldiers of the other two French regiments of the garrison, who had obtained satisfaction with their accounts, took up the cause of their comrades and rose up. All of them could rely, if not on the support, at least on the benevolent neutrality of the local Garde Nationale.

Determined to stem a movement that could potentially destroy the royal army, the Assembly promptly reacted by dissolving the soldiers' committees by decree. As for the Minister of War, he gave the Marquis de Bouillé, military commander in Metz, very strict orders. Such instructions were transmitted to him by an aide-de-camp of La Fayette, whom his chief had also charged – illegally – to coordinate the action of the gardes nationales there. Strengthened by his recent Parisian apotheosis, La Fayette believed that he could exploit the 'Nancy affair'. He therefore asked the Constituent Assembly to appoint inspectors to assess the situation on site. In addition, he was aware of the need to curb disorder and to make the Garde Nationale the instrument of the desired pacification. In this respect, he instructed the gardes nationaux of Nancy to back up Bouillé's action. It was above all, in his eyes, a symbolic action intended to discourage insurrection. But the situation escaped La Fayette and deteriorated tragically. On 31 August, the Swiss having refused to leave Nancy as Bouillé had demanded, the latter took action at the head of 2,400 men whom he had the wisdom to have preceded by 800 gardes nationaux coming from Metz and Toul. Moreover, he refused to negotiate and imposed his conditions. The two French regiments and the majority of the gardes nationaux present in Nancy submitted, but the two battalions of the Regiment de Châteauvieux and a few gardes nationaux who refused to abandon them entrenched themselves in one of the fortified city gates. The clash was harsh, especially as the defenders wanted to fire cannon at the assailants. André Desilles, a young Breton *lieutenant* in the Regiment du Roi, tried to stop them by lying down on the gun, but only delayed the firing. He was seriously wounded and died a few weeks later. This discharge of grapeshot also caused the death of 31 assailants, including the commanders of the Gardes Nationales of Toul and Metz. In the end, half of the Swiss were killed, and the rest were captured. The repression could then begin, and it was terrible. Considered as criminals, the insurgents were punished according to martial law. Twenty-one were hanged, another was tortured on the breaking wheel, while 50, condemned to the galleys, were sent to the penal colony of Brest. The 'Nancy Affair' certainly caused a great stir throughout the country and soon throughout Europe. For the first time, revolutionary unrest had simultaneously affected several units of the royal army. The episode also demonstrated that the gardes nationaux, often divided and ineffective when acting under municipal control, could on the contrary perform excellent services when placed under military command.

On 2 and 3 September, rallies of several thousand people gathered around the Tuileries to denounce the cruel fate of the Swiss of the Regiment de Châteauvieux and demand the ministers' dismissal. The amount of security deployed by Bailly and La Fayette showed that both had the situation well in hand. It especially dissuaded the demonstrators from marching on the Château de Saint-Cloud, where the King was then staying. Unimpressed by popular pressure, the Assembly congratulated Bouillé on 11 September and celebrated the martyrdom of young Desilles. This agitation in the capital confirmed La Fayette's diagnosis: the whole affair was a plot to prevent the Assembly from calmly completing the writing of the *Constitution*. If properly exploited, the example of the martyrs of Nancy gave La Fayette an excellent opportunity to strengthen the unity of the Garde Nationale. On 12 September, 600 delegates of the Garde Nationale Parisienne, 10 from each battalion, met at the Hôtel de Ville and voted an address of thanks to the gardes nationaux who had helped restore order in Nancy. On the 20th, a funeral service was

Pompe funèbre, au Champ de Mars, en l'honneur des citoyens soldats morts à Nancy en septembre 1790, engraving by Berthault after a drawing by Jean-Louis Prieur. (Musée Carnavalet)

organised at the Champ de Mars, on the very spot of the Festival of the Federation. The aim was to counter the popular demonstrations in favour of the Swiss mutineers and to silence the rumours of collusion between La Fayette and his cousin Bouillé. The provincial gardes nationaux were equally unanimous and many organised masses in memory of their colleagues from Toul and Metz who had lost their lives in Nancy. La Société des gardes nationaux des départements, which actively supported La Fayette, was no stranger to such efforts.

By the autumn, the Cordeliers and the Jacobin left launched an undermining action against the mayor of Paris and the commanding general of the Garde Nationale Parisienne. It was a twofold offensive against the key elements of the so-called 'La Fayette system': the centre companies and the Société des gardes nationaux des départements. Composed of former soldiers and NCOs of the Regiment des Gardes Françaises, the centre companies were undoubtedly the spearhead of the Garde Nationale Parisienne, but were also among the most sensitive elements to seditious propaganda. They were therefore worried by the rumour that the King was to be provided with a Garde Constitutionnelle of 6,000 men, from which the Gardes Françaises who had joined the Garde Nationale would automatically be excluded. The newspaper *Les Révolutions de Paris* added with some perfidy that 'one aimed to degrade them to the low status of the Ancien Regime's Guet'.[1]

In the provinces, the municipalities were generally renewed during the autumn in a way that favoured the patriots. The latter took advantage of this to carry out a purge of the local Gardes Nationales' officers. For example,

---

1   *Les Révolutions de Paris*, 70 (1790).

THE GARDE NATIONALE 1789–1815

Marc-Antoine-François Mazois, *colonel* of Bordeaux Garde Nationale, physiognotrace portrait, 1791. Mazois began his business career as a merchant immediately after completing his studies. He settled in Bordeaux in 1788. The following year, Mazois made his mark as a patriot and by his dedication to the popular cause. In fact, he was elected *colonel* of the city's Garde Nationale in 1790, then *adjudant-general* the following year. (François Vinot-Préfontaine's collection)

the Garde Nationale of Nancy, reorganised following the events of August, passed back into the hands of the Jacobins. The same occurred in Le Mans. The 'Marseilles La Fayette', Lieutaud, had to withdraw after he tried in vain to mobilise the gardes nationaux against the mayor and the patriotic clubs. In Brest, the Garde Nationale teamed up with the Society of the Friends of the Constitution to demand that there be no supreme chief of the Garde Nationale and that its ranks be open to all citizens.

Given this context of latent war, La Fayette intervened in the Assembly on 18 November 1790 to request the adoption, as soon as possible, of an official and definitive statute for the Garde Nationale, which would specify the latter's missions. The vote of this fundamental law was, according to him, to 'close a long period of empiricism and uncertainty'.[2] From July 1789 onwards, there had been a succession of partial and provisional measures which could encourage the most hazardous initiatives and above all facilitated the permanent contestation of a command which was likewise partial and temporary. As for the Société des gardes nationaux des départements, La Fayette wanted to give it an official existence. To this end, he asked the National Assembly to invite every month at least two gardes nationaux from the departments to stand guard in front of the Assembly as well as the Tuileries palace. However, such a project came up against the strong opposition of Charles de Lameth, President of the Assembly. Denounced on 30 November by Jacobin orator Fréron, it scandalised the left side of the Assembly. All saw in it a kind of defiance against the Garde Nationale Parisienne. It was asserted at the bar of the National Assembly that the gardes nationaux of the departments had no particular right to represent the latter, given that the deputies of the National Assembly were supposed to do so. The fédérés bowed and the Société was transformed into a simple 'correspondence office of the gardes nationaux', soon renamed 'the 83-department club'.[3] La Fayette, reluctantly, accepted this failure and quickly suffered two further setbacks. On 6 December, a decree authorised passive citizens who had already served in the Garde Nationale to remain in it. The next day, La Fayette did not oppose the vote on a decree which cancelled all the measures against the Nancy insurgents. This legislation was nonetheless a clear repudiation of his earlier policy.

In sum, La Fayette's strength now lay solely in his influence over the Garde Nationale Parisienne. He limited his strategy to the Parisian area in order to reassert his authority and his principles. But he was aware of the weakness of his position and the need to deal, against his will, with the forces of disorder. On 13 November, following a duel between Charles de Lameth

---

2   Madival & Laurent (eds), *Archives Parlementaires*, vol.XX, pp.522–523.
3   Georges Carrot, *La Garde nationale*, p.94.

and the young Duc de Castries, the crowd invaded the latter's hotel in his absence and ransacked it from top to bottom. Despite the 36,000 men under his command, La Fayette did not dare to prevent the building from being ransacked – the furniture and silverware were thrown out of the windows – and arrived late at the scene. Moreover, no rioter was arrested. The *Commandant General*'s apparent irresolution provoked sharp criticism from the moderates. On 19 November, the Palais-Bourbon and Beaumarchais' home were threatened with looting, a threat to which La Fayette responded minimally by doubling the patrols and reinforcing the fixed posts.

Shooting at La Chapelle: The Chasseurs aux Barrières on Trial

The year 1791 began on the same basis. Almost 18 months after the destruction and burning of a large number of the octroi barriers throughout Paris, the conflict over taxes had by no means died down. The new Parisian municipality had not given up on these indirect taxes, which were in any case necessary for its proper functioning. Moreover, it wished to enforce the rules, including outside the capital, by fighting against fraudsters and smugglers. In this context, a unit of Chasseurs aux Barrières had been set up, which was specifically charged with monitoring the octroi. However, fraud and smuggling were hardly considered illegal acts, but rather a means of subsistence by a large part of the population.

Jean-Louis Prieur begins the year 1791 of his series *Tableaux Historiques de la Révolution française* with this drawing. The artist seems to depict this tragic event as accurately as possible. Despite appearances, Prieur clearly took sides against the Chasseurs aux Barrières but also against the Paris Garde Nationale, which in his eyes was guilty of a hesitant attitude and of having arrived late at the scene of the shooting. (Musée Carnavalet)

On 24 January 1791, two sub-brigadiers employed by the Ferme Generale – the organisation in charge of collecting taxes – accompanied by about 20 chasseurs aux barrieres, arrived in La Chapelle Saint-Denis, a modest village north of Paris. There they made a routine house call on a wine merchant who had contraband tobacco in storage. Such a visit was carried out without a requisition from the civil authority, in this case the mayor of the village of La Chapelle, a certain Portefin. Left at liberty, the merchant stirred up a few fellow smugglers. The crowd grew and one of the sub-brigadiers asked for the mayor's help, but he refused to come. At the scene of the seizure, the tension rose again: a man called Lecamus opened fire and mortally wounded Morin, a chasseur aux barrières. His comrades immediately returned fire and the shooting began as the village population gathered in the church square. The toll was relatively heavy, with three dead – two gardes nationaux from the village of La Chapelle and a chasseur aux barrieres – plus a dozen wounded, mainly villagers. The mayor finally understood that the situation could deteriorate rapidly. He therefore asked the Garde Nationale Parisienne for help. The latter arrived in the village too late, however, as the dead and wounded were already littering the main street. After the shooting, they nevertheless succeeded in calming things down and bringing back some peace.

At first sight, the incident in the village of La Chapelle looked like a banal event that had tragically degenerated. It quickly became more than a simple local event with wider repercussions. Indeed, the fatal clash quickly highlighted the conflicting relations between the sections and a large part of public opinion on the one hand, and the Parisian municipality on the other. While the former were outraged by this tragedy, the city's magistrates supported the Chasseurs aux Barrières, who were nevertheless described by the patriotic press as 'brigands who do not hesitate to murder the people',[4] or even as 'an impure group of cutthroats, in the pay of the Commune and under the orders of the Ferme Generale'.[5] It was no longer just the taxes at the entrances to the city that were being questioned by the sections, but the disastrous political management of the leaders of the municipality and of La Fayette, who was accused of having campaigned for the formation of this unit of Chasseurs aux Barrières. The differences that arose on this occasion only accentuated the gap between the two rival camps.

28 February 1791: La Fayette's *Folle Journée*

Nearly a month after the tragic events at La Chapelle, two other cases re-established La Fayette's ascendancy among his supporters. On 28 February, a rumour ignited the faubourg Saint-Antoine: the work undertaken by the Paris Commune at the Chateau de Vincennes was in fact concealing a plot for the King to escape! A tunnel would join Vincennes to the Tuileries Palace and weapons were said to have been stored there. About 4,000 demonstrators,

---

4   *L'Ami du Peuple*, 342 (1791).
5   *Les Révolutions de Paris*, 81 (1791).

Affaire de Vincennes, le 28 février 1791, engraving by Pierre-Gabriel Berthault after a drawing by Jean-Louis Prieur. In the foreground, La Fayette, bareheaded, is surrounded by Vincennes' municipal officers, who are needed to request armed force. While La Fayette is speaking, the demolition of the dungeon nevertheless goes ahead. Perhaps Prieur was suggesting that the Marquis and his men's power was no longer as effective as it had been. (Musée Carnavalet)

most of them armed, were determined to destroy the dungeon of Vincennes, which they considered a 'new Bastille'.[6] Santerre, who commanded the Battalion of the district of Enfants-Trouvés, tried to prevent the worst, but he could not convince his fellow citizens to give up their project. So, he followed the rioters more than he stopped them. It was, as historian Roger Dupuy wisely comments, 'a kind of replay of October 1789, when La Fayette left for Versailles with his gardes nationaux'.[7] La Fayette, in fact, had the greatest difficulty in intervening. Several battalions in the faubourgs refused to obey his orders, while others were more than suspiciously lax. By the end of the afternoon, when he finally reached Vincennes with the centre companies and some artillery pieces, the destruction of the dungeon had already begun. Doors, bars and mattresses had been thrown out of the windows. The watchtower on the terrace and the battlements on the parapet had been knocked down. La Fayette managed to rally most of Santerre's men and ordered the workmen to stop the demolition. On their refusal, he opened fire after the customary summons. A few demolition workers were killed and 64 of them were arrested. Returning to Paris, La Fayette found the gates of the faubourg Saint-Antoine closed. The Barriere du Trone was guarded by men

---

6   Victor Fournel, *Les Hommes du 14 Juillet: Gardes-Françaises et Vainqueurs de la Bastille* (Paris: Calmann Lévy, 1890), p.301.

7   Dupuy, *La Garde nationale*, p.78.

mostly in Garde Nationale uniforms, with whom shots were exchanged. La Fayette had to threaten to use his cannon to obtain passage without having to release his prisoners.

As soon as he reached the Hôtel de Ville, La Fayette learned that the Tuileries had been invaded by 300 to 600 armed nobles, soon to be renamed the 'chevaliers du poignard'. Judging the situation to be threatening, they had decided to position themselves as close as possible to the monarch. At the head of several battalions of the Garde Nationale, La Fayette went to the royal residence and had the nobles who had been unable or unwilling to flee expelled. He especially attacked the royal household, which had tolerated the presence of these intruders whose exact intentions remained unclear. Louis XVI, for his part, claimed not to know what these men were doing in his apartments. Contemporaries did not fail to cry conspiracy. Had the excitement around the dungeon at Vincennes served to keep La Fayette away from the Tuileries? Was it to get the royal family to leave Paris? Historians remain divided on the interpretation of these events.

In any case, they strengthened La Fayette's popularity, especially as it had enabled him to strike successively at the Parisian extreme left and the right, symbolised by the aristocrats. Despite the insistent demands of some Parisian sections, no legal proceedings were finally instituted against the 'chevaliers du poignard' captured on the evening of 28 February and all were released by 13 March at the latest. On this occasion, it was opportunely suggested that there might be connections between the two extremes of the political spectrum. As for the Vincennes affair, it proved that La Fayette was still able to impose his authority, even if it meant using arms to do so. It was also an eloquent testimony to the process of decomposition affecting the Garde Nationale Parisienne. Indeed, some of the most radical battalions continued to believe that the supreme authority remained the people and that the Garde Nationale should not oppose the insurrection. Moreover, the day of 28 February 1791 had displeased the extremes, so much so that La Fayette suffered numerous attacks on both facets of his person: the soldier who commanded the Garde and the politician. In particular, he was at loggerheads with Santerre, who felt that he had been slandered in an order of the day drawn up by the staff of the Garde Nationale Parisienne. Following a trial with many twists and turns, the plaintiff was finally absolved.

Enforcing the *Civil Constitution of the Clergy*

Adopted on 12 July 1790, the *Constitution Civile du Clergé* (*Civil Constitution of the Clergy*) caused, from the first quarter of 1791 onwards, an increasing number of incidents in which the Garde Nationale was routinely involved. This legislative text redefined the status of priests, who became public servants paid by the state and elected by the citizens. The decree of 29 November 1790 required priests, as indeed all public officials, to take an oath of loyalty to the *Constitution*. The priests who accepted the oath were called constitutional priests. Those who refused were called refractory priests. Nationwide, only half of the parish clergy agreed to take the required oath.

In the contact areas between Catholic and Protestant communities, particularly in Lozère, Aveyron, Gard and Hérault, the implementation of these contested reforms sometimes contributed to the transformation of the Garde Nationale into an instrument serving a party. It oversaw the installation of sworn-in priests and the tracking down of refractory priests. In the already tense context of the south of France, only the patriotic and often Protestant companies agreed to maintain order in the event of a conflict over the religious question. The arrival of a sworn priest was a very delicate moment. Though there are many examples of this, the case of Saint-Affrique is emblematic. In this small town in the Aveyron department, a Catholic mayor was elected following a massive mobilisation of the most modest voters. The Protestants were present en masse in the ranks of the Garde Nationale as well as in the patriotic society of the Friends of the Constitution. At the end of July 1791, the arrival of a sworn-in priest was the trigger for particularly serious unrest. The mayor and several municipal officers chose to leave the commune, so that it fell to the Protestant elected representatives to install the new priest. Their presence in the church and the provocative attitude of the Catholic notables, who turned their backs on the altar, led to a demonstration of discontent by the population. The ceremony quickly turned into a riot. The municipal officers were overwhelmed and called in the gardes nationaux from neighbouring communes to restore order. The arrival of these detachments from the communes of Millau and Camarès – two towns with large Protestant communities – quickly took on the appearance of a punitive expedition. Guided by patriotic inhabitants of Saint-Affrique, the guardsmen invaded the houses of the Catholics, whose women were brutally expelled. The latter were beaten and humiliated in the public square and sometimes thrown into the river. These violent acts, which lasted three long days, caused several families to flee the town, and ended with a great farandole dance led by the Garde Nationale of Millau, with their sabres drawn. They left a deeply traumatised town, families humiliated and two religious communities more antagonistic than ever and almost irreconcilable. Called in to bring order to a troubled town, the gardes nationaux had deliberately diverted their mission, as they were driven by a partisan spirit.

Refractory priests were quite numerous in Paris. A tolerant man, La Fayette, who referred to North American society and the *Déclaration des Droits de l'Homme et du Citoyen*, did not understand the obligation of the oath. On his orders, the gardes nationaux protected the churches where the Constituent Assembly had authorised the refractories to celebrate mass. This decision exasperated the Jacobins, who saw refractory priests as counter-revolutionaries trying to turn the 'little people' against the patriots and the Constituent Assembly.[8]

This conflictual context led to a surprising event on the eve of Easter 1791. As Louis XVI was about to leave for the palace of Saint-Cloud to receive Easter communion from a refractory priest and then spend the summer there, a mob blocked his carriage, preventing the departure of the

---

8   Dupuy, *La Garde nationale*, p.80.

royals, who were accused of plotting and wanting to join the Marquis de Bouillé. Warned, La Fayette and Bailly went to the scene and harangued the demonstrators. Despite the threat of the proclamation of martial law, the latter – among them the gardes of the duty battalion! – would not listen to either the mayor nor the general. Should force be used in the presence of the royal family? After two hours of waiting, during which Louis XVI had left La Fayette to judge the situation, the King wisely returned to the palace, probably satisfied with proving publicly that he was indeed the prisoner he claimed to be. On 21 April, mortified by his failure and scorned in his authority, La Fayette presented, according to a now well-known logic, his resignation to the Parisian municipality. Immediately, his supporters, from 57 of the 60 battalions of the Garde Nationale Parisienne, demonstrated noisily outside his mansion to get him to reverse his decision. This was certainly not the unanimity of the previous summer, and the democratic newspapers claimed that only a few officers had spoken out and that the ordinary guardsmen had a different opinion. In the days that followed, pleas poured in from all over France deploring La Fayette's decision. Demonstrations and supplications by armed forces were contrary to the decree of 6 December 1790 and were denounced by the Club of the Cordeliers as well as by a large number of Parisian sections. These testimonies of fidelity comforted La Fayette, however, and he withdrew his resignation on 27 April.

21 June 1791: When the King Took Flight

On 21 June 1791, shortly after 5:00 a.m., Lemoine, one of the King's valets, discovered that his master's bed was empty. The Tuileries palace was in an uproar, as it was discovered that the Queen, the royal children, but also Madame Elisabeth – the King's sister – the Comte de Provence and his wife, had disappeared. The entire royal family had vanished in the night! In a few hours, all of Paris learned the unbelievable news in disbelief. Unbelievable, because although rumours of a possible escape had been circulating for several weeks or even months, no one imagined it possible. Was the Garde Nationale not in charge, day and night, of the surveillance of the royal family?

The officers on duty had immediately warned La Fayette, who left his private mansion in a hurry and was greeted by a crowd threatening him with their fists and shouting 'Traitor!'[9] He then met Bailly at the Tuileries, as well as Beauharnais, President of the Constituent Assembly. La Fayette asked them if the arrest of the King was necessary for the public safety of the kingdom. On their affirmative answer, he wrote a letter

Jean-Louis Romeuf, undoubtedly La Fayette's favourite aide-de-camp. On 21 June 1791, Romeuf was sent in pursuit of Louis XVI, who was finally arrested that evening in Varennes. Romeuf had a successful military career under the First Empire and died as a *général de brigade* at the Battle of Borodino. His brother Jacques-Alexandre also served as Lafayette's aide-de-camp. (Author's collection)

9 Louis Hastier, 'La Fayette et la fuite du roi', *Revue des Deux Mondes*, 4 (1955), p.674.

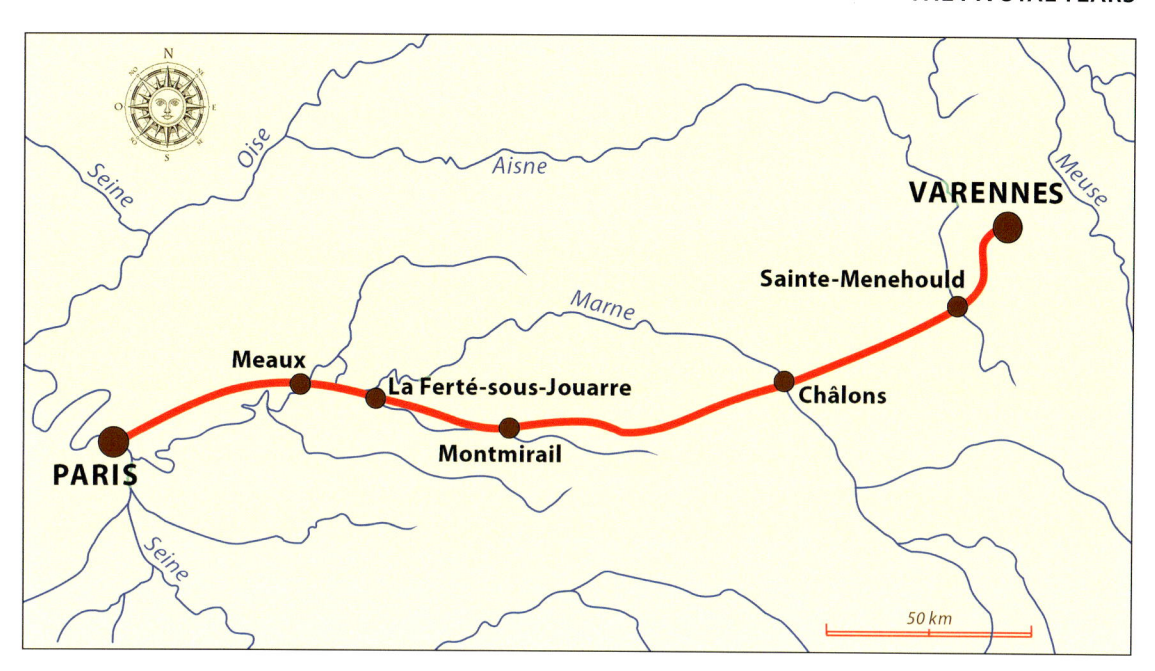

Map 6. The King's Flight, 21 June 1791.

to the battalions of the Garde Nationale explaining that the King and his family had just been 'abducted' by the 'enemies of the Nation' and that all the gardes nationaux and all the citizens were ordered to arrest them.[10] This was an immediate endorsement of the kidnapping theory, which was very convenient because it saved time and did not immediately call into question the institutions. Around 11:00 a.m., couriers carrying La Fayette's orders set off in all directions. On the road to the eastern frontier, where the Marquis de Bouillé and his cavalrymen were awaiting their arrival, the heavy berline carrying the royal family and the small cabriolet hosting the chambermaids were several hours behind schedule. At about 8:00 p.m., the vehicles stopped in front of the relais de Sainte-Menehould, whose postmaster, Jean-Baptiste Drouet, had stayed at Versailles. According to his own account, Drouet saw a man in the back of the carriage – the King was disguised as a valet – and was struck by the resemblance of his face to the effigy of a 50-*livres* assignat. He did not react immediately, however, and only set off in pursuit of the berline when La Fayette's couriers announced that Louis XVI had fled. At around 9:00 p.m., Jean-Baptiste Drouet and his friend Guillaume mounted their horses and set off towards Varennes-en-Argonne, where they thought the royal carriages were heading to. They arrived there less than an hour later and immediately informed the grocer Jean-Baptiste Sauce, the commune's procurator, that the escaped royal family's carriages had stopped at the upper end of the town. The bridge over the river Aire was hastily barricaded and the Varennes Garde Nationale was put on alert. Its commander, the future *Général de Division* Etienne Radet, also had two cannon brought near the bridge. The two carriages were in fact immobilised well before the barricade, under the vault

---

10   Lacroix, *Actes de la Commune de Paris*, vol. V, p. 20.

THE GARDE NATIONALE 1789–1815

This engraving by Laurent Guyot evokes the royal family's arrest on the night of 21–22 June 1791. It highlights the decisive action of the Varennes Garde Nationale, which stopped the fugitives' heavy carriage under the vaults of the Eglise Saint-Gengoult. Note also the presence, to the left, of the artillery set up by the village's Garde commander, Radet. (Musée Carnavalet)

of the church Saint-Gengoult. At the sound of the *tocsin*, Jean-Baptiste Sauce forced the travellers to get out of the carriages and took them into his home. At about 12:30 a.m., judge Destez, who had lived long enough in Versailles, formally recognised the King and the surgeon Mangin mounted his horse to carry the news to Paris. At the same time, several thousand peasants and gardes nationaux converged on Varennes. At about 8:00 a.m. on 22 June, the patriots of Varennes, in agreement with the envoys of the Assembly, Bayon and Romeuf – both officers of the Garde Nationale Parisienne – decided to send the royal family back to Paris. Alerted by the *tocsin* that was ringing everywhere, a huge crowd came to line the road, followed by the procession of 'prisoners' flanked in particular by the Varennes Garde Nationale.

At the same time, three deputies were sent by the Constituent Assembly to escort the royal family to Paris. On the 25th, the King and Queen returned to the capital through the Porte de Pantin, where La Fayette and his staff were waiting for them. 'A huge crowd covered both sides of the road, without shouting or violence, watching the procession pass with a disgruntled air but in perfect order', commented the general in his *Memoirs*.[11] A double line of guardsmen contained this silent but hostile crowd. Rabaud Saint-Etienne and Pétion both observed that the gardes carried their weapons with the butt in the air, subverting the only known practice of this gesture: during the funerals of very high dignitaries, the troops, lined up in a guard of honour, mourned by covering the drums with a black crepe, with pikes and flags pointed at the ground and muskets with the butt up. This was the protocol

---

11 Marie Joseph Paul Yves Roch Gilbert Du Motier, marquis de Lafayette, *Mémoires, correspondances et manuscrits du général Lafayette: Révolution française* (Paris: H. Fournier, 1837), vol.II, p.246.

observed by the Gardes-Suisses for two centuries when the remains of the king or queen were taken to Saint-Denis. At the end of June 1791, far more than a signal to the crowd that there would be little zeal in maintaining order, the Garde Nationale undoubtedly signified the symbolic death of a King who had become illegitimate in its eyes. Everything continued on like this until the Tuileries, but as the carriages stopped and the passengers were about to get out, insults were hurled, especially at the Queen. The lines of gardes nationaux were pushed aside, demonstrators tried to open the carriages and the escort came to blows with the aggressors who were repulsed with difficulty. La Fayette and his cavalrymen formed a protective screen which allowed the royal family to enter the palace quickly behind the closing gates.

The news of the King's departure took a week to spread to the furthest reaches of the Kingdom of France. Some learned of it from the official mail of the Assembly, others from the Parisian press, and still others from the rumours that were spreading. The flight to Varennes certainly had a profound effect on the population. The event was one of the few that moved the entire country, a country that experienced anxiety, outbursts of violence and panic at the thought of imaginary invasions. In this respect, the Normandy countryside is an emblematic example. The anxiety caused by the King's flight awakened old fears there. Despite the abolition, albeit partial, of feudalism and the abolition of the nobility in June 1790, the 'aristocratic plot' still haunted the peasants' imaginations. As soon as the announcement of the royal flight to Varennes was made, the rural municipalities and the Garde Nationale were immediately called upon to search the surrounding chateaux. On the afternoon of 23 June, a crowd of men from the communes of La Motte-Fouquet and Magny-le-Désert set off for the chateau of the Marquis de Falconer. Led by the mayor of Magny-le-Désert, the search was carried out 'without any dishonesty' and the weapons were quickly handed in.[12] The next day, in Laval, the departmental authorities sent a detachment of gardes nationaux to the château de Lancheneil in Nuillé-sur-Vicoin, where rumour had it that there was an arms depot. In Mayenne, the Garde Nationale requisitioned the arms and cannons stored at the chateaux of Oisseau and Evron. The departure of some chatelains, such as those of Niafles, was interpreted as desertion and treason: the Craon Garde Nationale stopped their carriages and put them under house arrest for six weeks. In the Sarthe, the editor of the *Journal Général* was told that all the chateaux around Mamers had been searched and their occupants forced to go to town to be under surveillance.

Bloody Sunday: The Champ de Mars Massacre

By fleeing to the borders, the King had obviously chosen his side. Should he be stripped of his rights? Should he be replaced by a new monarch, for example his cousin, the Duc d'Orléans? Was proclaiming a Republic a viable

---

12 Archives Départementales de l'Orne (ADO): L 2613: Attentats contre les personnes et les propriétés, troubles, désarmement des suspects (juillet 1791–germinal an III).

option? Since the return of Louis XVI to Paris, the capital had been agitated by one single question: would the sovereign remain on his throne, at the head of the executive power? From Luxembourg, where he had sought refuge, the Marquis de Bouillé attempted to mitigate the responsibility of the monarch by a letter in which he assumed full responsibility for the kidnapping. He had organised everything and had to put pressure on the King to leave, he said. This letter was timely, and on 16 July the Assembly voted a decree exonerating the King from the flight of 20 June. In other words, Louis XVI was reinstated in his functions. However, the damage had been done, as La Fayette lucidly acknowledged in his *Memoirs*. 'This departure for Varennes deprived the King of the confidence and goodwill of the citizens forever', he regretted in retrospect.[13]

Indeed, while the upper-class areas of the right bank of the Seine approved of the Assembly's votes, the same clearly did not apply to the rest of the Parisian population, particularly in the faubourgs Saint-Antoine and Saint-Marcel, where the deputies' votes outraged the inhabitants. As early as 15 July, upon learning that the Assembly was considering making the King's escape look like a kidnapping and that there was talk of adopting a decree that would restore Louis XVI to all his prerogatives, the members of the Cordeliers club and nearly 12,000 people gathered at the Champ de Mars to sign a petition on the altar of the Fatherland denouncing the foregoing measures. But as the six commissioners carrying the petition, surrounded by a crowd of demonstrators, approached the Salle du Manège where the Assembly was sitting, the cavalry dispersed them. As a result, they went to the Palais-Royal and accounted for their actions to the members of the Jacobin Club. The latter had also drafted a petition expressing their opposition to Louis XVI's restoration, which was to be sent to all the departments. The Cordeliers also called for a parade to be organised on 17 July between two highly symbolic places: the ruins of the Bastille and the Champ de Mars. Admittedly, this demonstration was intended to be peaceful and unarmed – sticks and knives were banned – but many of the participants nevertheless stuffed their pockets with stones to fight the gardes nationaux, whom they hated, if necessary. La Fayette, who had been warned of the Cordeliers' project the day before, had caught them unaware. The bridges were guarded and the patrols easily dispersed the barely gathered militants. Aware that the anticipated march could not take place, the demonstrators went to the Champ de Mars in dispersed order. As the Jacobins had withdrawn their petition, as much because of the Assembly's vote as because of the fear of a bloody repression, a new text was drafted on the spot and proposed to the citizens for signature. However, this sunny morning was brutally marred by a trivial and bloody incident. Two voyeurs wishing to take advantage of the parade of women coming to sign the petition on the platform under which they were hidden, were discovered and lynched without further ado, before their two decapitated heads were taken through the streets to the outskirts of the Palais-Royal. In the meantime, witnesses warned the municipality and the

---

13   Lafayette, *Mémoires*, vol.V, p.122.

Publication de la loi martiale au Champ de Mars, le 17 juillet 1791, print after a drawing by Jean-Louis Prieur. The Champ de Mars massacre was in some respects the bloody epilogue to the flight towards Varennes. The day soon turned violent, as Prieur perfectly captured. (Musée Carnavalet)

Assembly that atrocities were being committed on the Champ de Mars and that heads were being carried on pikes. In response, Bailly dispatched three commissioners accompanied by a detachment of gardes nationaux under the orders of La Fayette. They were met with stones at one of the entrances to the esplanade, while rows of citizens – many of whom were gardes nationaux themselves – crowded around the Altar of the Fatherland to sign the petition. La Fayette confined himself to deploying his forces in a sufficiently dissuasive manner to calm the most exalted demonstrators momentarily. The crowd, however, objected to the interruption of the petition signing.

In the early afternoon, calm seemed to reign again on the Champ de Mars. However, completely contradictory news continued to reach both the National Assembly and the Hôtel de Ville. Faced with the impatience of the deputies who were indignant that nothing was being done to stop the disorder, Bailly resolved, at around 5:00 p.m., to proclaim martial law. The now famous red flag was flown from one of the windows of the Hôtel de Ville. Determined to end it all, the gardes nationaux headed for the Champ de Mars, greeted by applause in some streets, by boos in others. They reached the area around the altar of the Fatherland in a cloud of dust which prevented some of the petitioners from discerning the red flag of martial law. A tense face-off began between the gardes nationaux, tested by the hostility displayed towards them for weeks, and a disparate crowd with no real leader, exhausted by a whole day spent between exaltation and exasperation. The first detachments were indeed greeted by insults and stone-throwing which injured several grenadiers. Without any warning being given, the front ranks fired into the air without succeeding in stopping the throwing of stones. Then the exasperated gardes nationaux, without waiting for any command, began to fire on the demonstrators grouped around the altar. Another column caught the citizens in the rear and cavalrymen pursued the fugitives and sabred them. The shooting caused panic and dozens of bodies lay lifeless when the gardes withdrew. Other guardsmen, who had arrived via the École Militaire, intervened and tried to limit the confrontation, while artillery officers prevented their men from using their guns. The next day, Bailly claimed that 12 protesters and two gardes had been killed. The democratic press, putting forward the figure of 2,000 dead, spoke of a massacre, while historians' estimates put the death toll at around 50 and the number of wounded at around 600.[14] In an apparent paradox, the 'bourgeois' gardes nationaux had opened fire, while the paid gardes had remained disciplined. The lack of professionalism and the fear of overflow combined with the need to fight back after weeks of accumulated tension. Fear had played its usual role on unprofessional armed groups.

A Major (Re)organisation Movement

The Establishment of Repressive Measures

The Champ de Mars massacre led to a clear rupture between the most radical patriots and the moderate deputies who had a majority in the Assembly. On 18 July, the latter voted to congratulate the Garde Nationale Parisienne while a repressive wave fell on the democratic movement. The press was muzzled, the Cordeliers club was closed and 200 people were arrested. Whereas Camille Desmoulins had deemed it prudent to take refuge in the suburbs on the morning of the 17th, Danton fled to London for a while and Marat temporarily suspended the publication of *L'Ami du Peuple*. The moderates considered that stopping the Revolution was necessary.

On 14 June 1791, the Le Chapelier Law prohibiting the assembly of workers and journeymen, as well as the organisation of strikes, was passed. This law placed all obstacles to economic freedom in labour and industry under martial law. In fact, it was not only the workers' movement but the entire popular movement that was targeted by a repressive legislative apparatus. Decisions taken in the aftermath of the Champ de Mars shootings confirmed this state of affairs. The law of 27 July retained martial law and summarised its successive amendments. It also made the protocol more flexible, defined the form of legal summonses and reduced their number, a provision probably resulting from the aforementioned shootings. Finally, its proclamation defined any gathering of more than 15 adult males as a seditious demonstration.

---

14 Timothy Tackett, *When the King Took Flight* (Cambridge: Harvard University Press, 2004), p.150.

That same day, the deputies discussed the problems related to the use of the forces of law and order and their respective missions. The Gendarmerie was always to be used primarily against bands of robbers and rioters. When the size of the crowd made it impossible to use the Gendarmerie alone, the paid Garde Nationale would be called upon in urban areas, or the Garde Nationale of the canton in the case of rural communes. If the Gendarmerie and local gardes nationaux were unable to restore public order, the district or departmental elected magistrates were entitled to call in the line troops, or the available gardes nationaux, including those from outside the troubled department or departments.

The Law of 14 October 1791

Once they had confined the action of the Garde Nationale, envisaged as an auxiliary force, within supposedly prudent limits, the deputies could now organise it definitively without inconvenience. Indeed, for more than two years, the institution had been operating within a temporary organisation modified by successive decrees imposed by urgent political circumstances. The summer of 1791 was therefore marked by the desire to finally organise the Garde Nationale on a kingdom-wide scale.

The debates resumed at the end of July, after three months of adjournment, and proved to be less stormy than the previous ones held at the end of April. On 20 April, the first real debate on the Garde Nationale had opened. It was amplified during the sessions of 28 and 29 April. The left, mainly represented by Robespierre, Buzot and Pétion, demanded that all citizens be armed. As for the right, it affirmed that if one wanted to arm everyone, one would end up arming no one. As the moderate majority of the Constituent Assembly was worried about an over-armament leading to an excess of violence, the provisional texts of the previous years were still used. The fact remains that in just two days, on 28 and 29 July, the rest of the Military Committee's draft, which Rabaut Saint-Étienne presented and defended, was validated, with the adoption of a few amendments on minor issues. On 16 August, title IV of the future *Constitution* with the sober title 'About public force' was examined. In 13 articles, it brought together the various fundamental provisions adopted, as events dictated, since 1789. Despite the deputies' commendable effort to synthesise the text, it was still relatively disjointed. The first six articles clearly endeavoured to limit the influence of the Garde Nationale in the political life of the nation, particularly in regard to maintaining order. The first article defined the fundamental missions of the public force: to defend the borders and ensure internal order and law enforcement. As for article 2, it clearly demonstrated the desire to undermine the role of the Garde Nationale by granting it only a minor role. The next three articles specified that the Garde Nationale was not allowed to decide on its own whether to intervene. On the other hand, it elected its leadership with some uniqueness. The officers exercised their functions for a limited time and could not be re-elected to equal or higher rank until they had become ordinary fusiliers again. Finally, no one could command 'the Garde Nationale of more than one district'. In case of border aggression, the King was to command 'all parts of the public force': this was the result of a single, tersely worded article. Four articles were needed to define terms for the use of the Garde within the kingdom. It was up to 'civil officers' to initiate the use of public force. If the disorder exceeded the limits of a department, the King could make necessary decisions, but he had to inform the legislature.[15] This was certainly an inefficient and conflict-ridden system.

According to historian Roger Dupuy, the Garde Nationale appeared unquestionably as 'an immense organism composed of juxtaposed cells, without unity of command, condemned to intervene only very locally and as a last resort, to maintain order within the kingdom'.[16] The cautious but uninspiring constitutional principles were developed by a fundamental decree of 29 September 1791, which became a law on 14 October after Louis XVI approved it. Adopted during the penultimate session of the Constituent Assembly, on the eve of its final disbandment, this law theoretically put an end to a long series of provisional decrees and debates announced and postponed. Never repealed, all subsequent regulations and laws referred to it. The text was organised into five main sections.[17]

The first section specified that only active citizens, that is, those who were eligible to vote and had been continuous residents for more than a year, could serve in the Garde Nationale. Passive citizens who had served continuously since the beginning of the Revolution and who were judged to be of good intent could continue to appear on the registration register. The sons of active citizens who had reached the age of 18 also had to be registered. This service was a privilege but also an obligation without financial compensation. Not being registered, however, meant that citizen's rights were not exercised, and missing even one day of service required the payment of a tax equal to two days' work. In addition, those who skipped their service three times in a single year were suspended for one year from service and from the right to vote or stand for election.

The second section focused on the organisation of the Garde Nationale. In the countryside, it was divided into cantons and districts, rather than municipalities. In the towns, the basic element of the system remained the electoral section or district. Each canton, section or district provided the manpower for at least one battalion of four companies. At the district level, the battalions were grouped together in a legion or even in a combination of legions. The basic unit was the company: in the cities, it aggregated citizens from the same neighbourhood and in the countryside, citizens from the most neighbouring communities. Companies of veterans, 'young citizens' under the age of 18, cavalrymen riding at their own expense and sections of gunners were organised. On the second Sunday of May each year, the active citizens registered in the companies met without uniform at the canton's chief town to elect their officers and NCOs up to the rank of *caporal*. Once elected, the officers and *sergents* chose the battalion's commanding officer and his assistants by an absolute majority. The company officers in turn met

---

15 Anon., *La Constitution française, présentée au Roi le 3 septembre 1791 et acceptée par Sa Majesté le 14 du même mois* (Paris: Imprimerie Nationale, 1791), p.103.
16 Dupuy, *La Garde nationale*, p.99.
17 Madival & Laurent (eds), *Archives Parlementaires*, vol.XXXI, pp.625–632.

Attributed to Jean-Jacques Hauer and probably painted between October 1791 and spring 1792, this family portrait shows three gardes nationaux. On the left, is the father, wearing the uniform prescribed in July 1791. Standing on the right, are presumably his two sons. One is probably an officer commanding the artillery detachment attached to a Garde Nationale battalion. The other is a chasseur. (The Metropolitan Museum of Art, New York)

to elect the legion staff at the chief town of the district. All these commanders were elected for a one-year term only.

The third and most important section set out the role and forms of action of the Garde Nationale. The gardes nationaux were responsible for maintaining order and ensuring obedience to the law. They could dispel 'all popular riots and seditious gatherings', arrest and bring to justice 'those guilty of excesses and violence', and use 'force of arms' under martial law. The other clauses were much more restrictive and proved the deputies of the Constituent Assembly's distrust of armed citizens. With the exception of patrols, ordinary and daily service or exercises, the chiefs could not take any initiative. They could only act on special requisition in quiet periods. These requests for intervention were only addressed to them if there were not enough gendarmes, paid gardes or line troops available. The commanders had to carry them out without discussion, but could demand that they be written down. Without a legal injunction, the officers could not assemble their

THE GARDE NATIONALE 1789–1815

troops and, without orders, the citizens could not assemble either. It was forbidden to go in arms to an electoral or political assembly. The federal oath took place every year on 14 July at the district chief town. The organisation of any particular federation was considered an attack against 'the unity of the kingdom and the constitutional federation of all the French'. Article 12 provided that in the event of an invasion of French territory by foreign armies, the King would send his orders to the number of gardes nationaux that he deemed necessary. There was thus the possibility of using citizens against an external enemy. In the event of military action by the gardes nationaux, the senior commander would always be a gendarme or a line officer.

The fourth section determined the order of service and the rank of the companies, which were fixed annually by lot.

The fifth and final section dealt with discipline. Elected officers were required to behave 'as citizens commanding other citizens'. No force could be used against recalcitrant officers who refused to submit to their obligations. Disobedience, abandoning one's post, disrespect and insubordination were punishable by arrest or imprisonment for a maximum of eight days, regardless of rank. It was possible to refuse the punishment, but this entailed the loss of citizenship rights and the payment of a replacement tax.

Portrait of an *adjudant sous-officier* of a Garde Nationale grenadier company painted by E. Lussigny and dated 1791. This NCO is dressed in the third uniform of the Garde. His bearskin plate, dating from the end of the Ancien Régime, was transformed at the beginning of the Revolution then hastily brought up to date in the summer of 1792. In this respect, the fleurs-de-lys have been hammered out. (Musée Carnavalet)

As with the *Constitution*, the decree of 29 September 1791 did not provide for a central organisation to lead, control and direct these armed citizens. The King was only involved through his Minister of the Interior. It was up to the administrations of the departments and districts to ensure that it was applied and to report any infringements to the Assembly. Such provisions denoted the general embarrassment of the deputies in the face of the Garde Nationale. Since 1789, the revolutionary politicians had limited themselves, according to circumstances and political calculations, to channelling this immense force and adapting this instrument of undeniable military potential to the various situations. On the eve of the separation of the Constituent Assembly, the deputies' distrust towards the Garde Nationale continued to prevail. As proof, they had waited until the penultimate session of the Constituent Assembly to adopt the decree finally organising the Garde Nationale and specifying its missions, its recruitment, its management, its armament and its uniform. In short, the deputies were worried about the Garde, but they could not disavow it. Passive citizens, the least favoured Frenchmen, had been deliberately eliminated from it. Armed citizens were relegated to second-class tasks and remained under strict control. In addition to mistrust, there were many contradictions. Service was compulsory and therefore demanding for the citizens. The burden was heaviest for the less fortunate who needed time

Reorganisation of the Garde Nationale Parisienne

In the summer of 1791, legislative measures led to the establishment of a Garde Nationale subject to the same regulations, discipline and uniform. However, within the Garde Nationale Parisienne, some units were paid up while others were not. The King's flight brought the entire Garde Nationale into activity, and the distinction between the paid and unpaid Gardes was no longer relevant. It was abolished by the decrees of 3, 4 and 5 August 1791 which became law on 28 August. Thus, with the paid infantry companies of the Parisian Garde Nationale – nearly 9,000 men in all – new units of the line army were formed. These were a division of foot Gendarmerie (the 29th, with 912 men), a division of mounted Gendarmerie (the 30th, with 912 men), to which were added three line infantry regiments (the 102nd, 103rd and 104th, with 5,634 men) and two battalions of light infantry (the 13th and 14th, which numbered 1,622 men). The whole force was placed under the orders of seven *chefs de corps* and three *adjudants-generaux*. Some significant advantages were granted to the former paid gardes nationaux. The promotion of NCOs was thus accelerated and their pay remained higher than that of the line army and the Gendarmerie. The law recognised that it was absolutely necessary, until the *Constitution* was consolidated, for the newly created corps to form part of the armed force of the capital to maintain order and tranquillity. These almost 10,000 men now represented a permanent intervention force which was seemingly more available than when they were distributed among the centre companies. However, what was gained in terms of immediate intervention potential was lost politically in terms of the moderating influence exerted in the 60 former districts of Paris by these same companies genuinely devoted to La Fayette.

On 12 September, the Assembly decreed that the Garde Nationale Parisienne would still consist of six divisions, called legions, each with 10 battalions. Each battalion comprised four companies, 'not including the grenadiers, which would be drawn from the other four'.[18] The chasseurs were omitted. The position of *commandant general* was abolished. Each

Mounted gendarme, coming from the Parisian Garde Nationale cavalry. His uniform is similar to that of the Gendarmerie, as regulated by the law of 16 February 1791. (Musée Carnavalet)

---

18   Anon., *Code de la Garde Nationale contenant tous les Décrets sanctionnés et acceptés par le Roi* (Paris: Devaux Libraire, 1792), p.112.

THE GARDE NATIONALE 1789–1815

legion chief was to carry out the functions 'for one month, in turn'. This responded to the fears of seeing the Garde Parisienne transformed into a praetorian legion for the benefit of a single man, just as La Fayette had done. The separation between sections and battalions was maintained, however.

La Fayette's Farewell to the Garde Nationale Parisienne

That same 12 September, the King announced that he would accept the *Constitution*. La Fayette took the opportunity to indicate that he would voluntarily resign from office the following month. In fact, he considered that the adoption of the *Constitution* marked the end of his mandate. On 8 October, he bid farewell to the Garde Nationale Parisienne, not at one of his favourite reviews, but during a visit to the Paris municipality where he gave a speech in the presence of the Parisian councillors and several officers of the Garde. The General obviously no longer hoped to provoke the demonstrations of enthusiasm that occurred the previous summer. He then limited himself to sending a letter to all the Parisian battalions, whom he thanked for their loyalty and determination to uphold the law in spite of the pressures they had been subjected to 'in the midst of the storms of twenty-seven months of revolution'. He also urged them to remain vigilant and not to believe that 'all the seeds of despotism are destroyed', because, according to him, freedom remained fragile.[19] The following day, all the Garde Nationale Parisienne companies sent a delegate to the Hôtel de Ville to discuss ways of showing their gratitude to La Fayette. It was decided that 'in recognition of his good and loyal command since the Revolution, they would present him with a sword on which this inscription would be engraved: "À La Fayette, l'Armée parisienne reconnaissante, L'An 3e de la Liberté" [To La Fayette, the grateful Parisian Army, Year 3 of Liberty]'. On 14 October, *Les Annales Patriotiques* reported that the 'hero of two worlds' had just refused 'the military command of the departments of Meurthe and Moselle' and that he was retiring to his land in Auvergne, 'until the dangers of the fatherland called him back to lead the Garde Nationale'.[20] For his supporters, this departure could only constitute a simple parenthesis, as his presence seemed indispensable. The radical left-wing press, on the other hand, laughed at this departure on the sly.

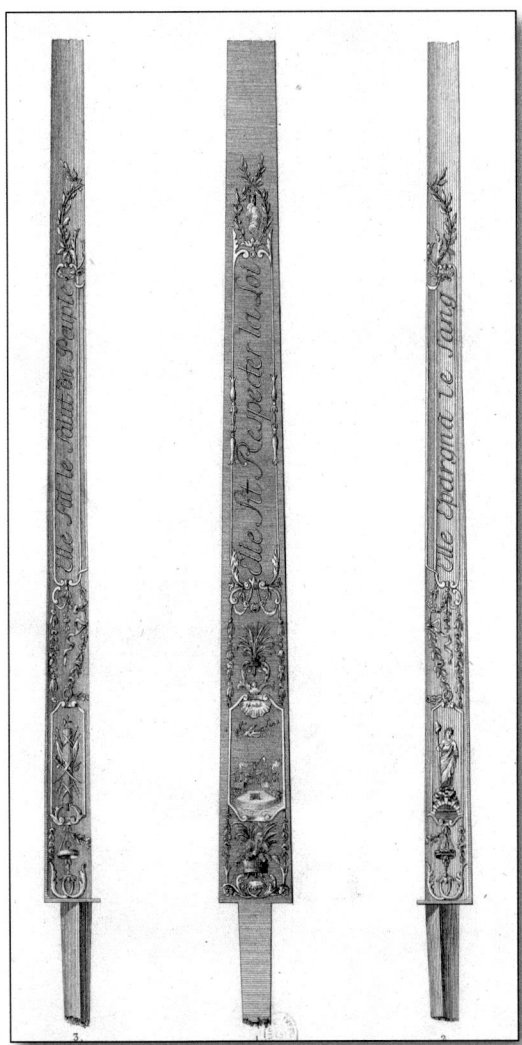

Engraving representing the sword's blade which the Garde Nationale Parisienne gave to La Fayette in October 1791. Forged from the iron locks of the Bastille prison, the blade represents the Bastille and various allegorical subjects linked to its seizure and subsequent destruction. (Musée Carnavalet)

---

19 Bernard Sarrans, *La Fayette et la Révolution de 1830: Histoire des choses et des hommes de juillet* (Paris: Thoisnier Desplaces, 1833), p.36.
20 *Les Annales Patriotiques*, 742 (1791), p.2072.

Implementation of the Law of 14 October 1791

In the autumn of 1791, the King had accepted the *Constitution* and the majority of the Assembly sincerely wished to see it applied. A public force existed to ensure its enforcement and a legislative arsenal had been developed to crack down on public order offenders. Some thought that the Revolution was over. However, the truth was not so. The Constituent Assembly had only produced texts and decided on a series of theoretical principles. Opposition was temporarily curbed after the shootings at the Champ de Mars, but it gained strength again. It emerged in the first days of October in connection with the liquidation of the paid Paris Garde Nationale, which was intended to form new units in the line army. Many of their soldiers lived in Paris, had married and ran small businesses there. They feared to be moved away from it. Under pressure from the sections, the Assembly had to recall that the units to which it had given birth could only be removed from the capital by virtue of an express decision of its own. The same desire to spare the opposition is apparent in the decision concerning the chasseurs volontaires companies. The laws of September and October 1791 had only kept the grenadier companies, and the chasseurs petitioned to be maintained or organised into light companies attached to each battalion. Despite the support of Gouvion, a former right-hand man of La Fayette who had meanwhile become a deputy, they only obtained, by a decree of 11 February 1792, to continue their service until May 1793.

In Paris, the new organisation of the Garde Nationale was nonetheless implemented from October onwards. The operations ended on 14 November with the designation of the six legion chiefs who, in turn, were to assume the general command for a period of one month at first, then two months. La Fayette was elected by the battalions of the 4th Legion, but he immediately declined this command, which was far inferior to the one he had held for the past two years and from which he had resigned on 8 October. In truth, he had other ambitions and hoped to regain control of the capital's Garde Nationale through his election as Paris mayor, convinced that he would retain the support of the majority of the capital's wealthy citizens. But he was deluding himself. His taste for pomp and a certain nonchalance which led him to delegate his powers were detrimental to him. His main rival, Pétion, was seen as a tireless worker and could count on an undeniable oratorical talent that La Fayette lacked. Moreover, on his return from Varennes, Pétion had shown himself to be in favour of putting the King on trial and then had supported the republican petition movement of July 1791, which had earned him immense popularity in the capital. Last but not least, the monarchists campaigned against La Fayette. In fact, Pétion was elected thanks to a coalition of extremes and the support of all those disappointed by Fayettism. The election was held on 13 November 1791 and Pétion won by 6,728 votes, compared to 3,126 for La Fayette. Participation proved derisory: less than 10,000 active citizens had voted out of a total of 80,000.

In the departments, the law of 14 October was applied with a certain delay, due to more or less sharp local dissensions related to divergent economic interests, religious differences but also to centuries-long antagonisms. The Garde Nationale was barely legally stabilised and found itself back in the situation of its beginnings. In the midst of an economic malaise, a subsistence crisis and a social uprising, it once again entered the political arena, and its actions are at least as complex to interpret as in 1789. In many cases, the Garde Nationale actively supported the popular movement. In the rural areas of the Beauce and northern France, they provided the manpower and leadership for the bands of tax collectors who looted markets, stopped grain convoys and occasionally massacred some local notables. In a number of localities, the gardes retained an undeniable autonomy vis-à-vis the requisition orders. They also frequently refused to crack down on popular uprisings, as in Dunkirk on 13 and 14 February 1792. In Étampes, on 3 March, the Garde Nationale did not intervene either to protect Mayor Simoneau, who was opposing the rioters' demand to legalise the maximum tariff for wheat and bread. After unsuccessfully proclaiming martial law, the mayor was killed. Faced with the divisions of the Garde, the authorities preferred to resort to line troops, admittedly undisciplined and sometimes reluctant to intervene against the protesters, but nonetheless more effective because they were less involved in local quarrels. In Evreux, Périgueux and Montauban, the urban gardes mobilised successfully in the face of what appeared to be a new 'Great Fear'. In accordance with the Le Chapelier law, the armed force was sent to suppress the gatherings of the labourers and winegrowers of Joigny, the floaters of the Yonne or the lumberjacks of Morvan.

In Avignon, the struggle between supporters and opponents of the reunion of the Papal States with France led, on 16 and 17 October, to the massacres of La Glacière, named after one of the towers of the Palais des Papes where the bodies of 60 aristocrats, or supposed to be so, were piled. They had just been arrested after the murder, in a church, of Nicolas Jean-Baptiste Lescuyer, one of the city's notorious patriots, who had been accused by furious churchgoers of having made a statue of the Virgin cry. The gardes nationaux had been the willing executioners, turning the place of detention into a sinister slaughterhouse. The Cévennes remained another hotbed of religious antagonism in the kingdom. As a consequence of the law of 14 October, the reorganisation of the Gardes Nationales provided the Catholics with the ideal opportunity to get rid of Protestant and patriotic officers. In February 1792, the turn of events in Mende even forced the Legislative Assembly to dissolve the new Garde Nationale, which was regarded as 'aristocratic and fanatic'.[21] Meanwhile, Protestant gardes nationaux converged towards Jalès where their Catholic counterparts had gathered. The clashes, which were to be repeated the following summer, resulted in a number of deaths. As in the previous year, the gardes nationaux intervened to enforce the *Civil Constitution of the Clergy*. In the West, those of the towns continued their expeditions against the villages in which refractory priests were active.

---

21   *Gazette Nationale ou Le Moniteur Universel*, 91 (1792), p.764.

The Radicalisation of the Garde?

In 1792, the consequences of the dismantling of the Garde Nationale of Paris as organised by La Fayette became clearer. While the constitutional option had always prevailed over the previous two years, the political choices of each section influenced the behaviour of the Garde Nationale battalions. The institution was undoubtedly undergoing an internal weakening as food shortages and the threat of war worsened.

A new food crisis hit the capital. It was no longer confined to daily bread, but also concerned colonial foodstuffs. While colonial goods remained a luxury for most of the kingdom, cane sugar and coffee had become commonplace in Parisian working-class circles. The consumption of coffee with milk had become widespread since the 1760s in the faubourg Saint-Marcel. On the evening of 20 January 1792, crowds stormed several sugar warehouses in the faubourg to protest against the sharp rise in the price of this product, which

Charles-Alexis Alexandre (?) protégeant une cargaison de sucre à Paris en février 1792, oil on canvas by Bizard, 1792. A working-class woman threatens an officer of the Garde Nationale Parisienne seeking to prevent the looting of a sugar shipment. Note that sugar loaves are scattered on the ground. The identity of the officer, dressed in the uniform prescribed in mid-July 1791, remains unclear. (Musée de la Révolution française, with permission)

merchants attributed to the unrest that was then sweeping through the sugar island of Saint-Domingue. In October 1791, this product was worth between 25 and 30 *sous* a pound, but it rose to nearly 60 *sous* at the beginning of January. This vertiginous rise exasperated the masses and women in particular. All denounced the speculation of the merchants whose shops were full but who preferred to sell their precious merchandise piecemeal. The warehouses were broken into, but they were not looted: sugar was sold at 25 *sous* a pound, the same price as in previous months. On the night of 13–14 February, still in the faubourg Saint-Marcel, a convoy transferring sugar from a warehouse just rented by two entrepreneurs in partnership to buy and resell sugar at high prices was stopped by demonstrators. Once again, the sugar was sold at a price that the protesting consumers found acceptable. Mayor Pétion demanded that the gardes nationaux be summoned to protect the shops of the two speculators, but most of the companies in the faubourg Saint-Marcel refused to march: they certainly did not want to favour the manoeuvres of the two acolytes. A reinforcement was eventually sent by *Commandant en Chef* Aclocque. The area around the shop was cleared and the sugar returned to its warehouse. The next morning, however, the unrest resumed with even greater vigour than the day before. Hundreds of demonstrators sought to break down the doors of the warehouse and barricades were erected in the adjacent streets. Finally, at around 7:00 p.m., Pétion himself intervened at the head of 1,200 guardsmen from other parts of the capital. The demonstrators were dispersed and a few dozen of them arrested. The affair caused a stir in the press for several weeks. As for the Garde Nationale, each battalion responded to the actions of the rioters according to what was happening in its own district. Thus, the question of sugar had an importance for the working-class population of the faubourg Saint-Marcel which was misunderstood by other Parisian sections as well as by the rest of the kingdom. The gardes of the faubourg refused to crack down on the rioters in order to oppose an abuse of the freedom of trade, although they did not accept the violation of the right to property. It did allow Pétion to intervene against the riot, but later showed support for the defendants to obtain their release. It obviously tried to reconcile obedience to its hierarchy's orders with neighbourly solidarity.

At the end of the winter and during the spring of 1792, popular societies, in which democratic values were taught, flourished in the capital. Consequently, they played a prevalent role in the civic education of citizens. A certain discipline prevailed. Weapons were banned, intemperance and coarse language were prohibited. Several societies were located in the barracks of the Garde Nationale, which gave the impression that the latter endorsed the democratic discourse and demands of the militants. Although pikes were provided to a growing number of passive citizens, they would have had great difficulty in prevailing against district battalions. The leaders of the democratic party therefore had to rally as many gardes nationaux as possible to the people's cause in order to obtain the support of these battalions or, if not, their neutrality. In this context, popular societies proved to be essential.

Nonetheless, the spring of 1792 was above all marked by the war which was declared with fairly general enthusiasm to Francis II of Austria. It had certainly been brewing since the summer of 1791 but only began on the following 20 April. It quickly turned into a litmus test forcing all fractions to choose sides. The more patriotic hoped for a massive mobilisation of the popular masses so that the king would give up his right of veto. According to them, the war was also intended to uncover the latent treachery of the generals and the ulterior motives of the moderates. While his entourage thought the war was lost in advance, Louis XVI imagined that he would be able to play the role of protector of his subjects against the invaders and regain his then shaky authority. Still numerous and influential, the Fayettists thought that military operations would be likely to reunite the unanimity of 14 July 1790 and impose respect for the *Constitution* on the King. Moreover, a military victory would put them in a strong position. As for the economic circles, they hoped for a resumption of business orders and the opening of new markets. To varying degrees, everyone relied on the immense reservoir of men constituted by the Garde Nationale either to force victory or to minimise the initial setbacks.

The disastrous beginnings of the operations on the border of Austrian Netherlands led to a new patriotic fever and the launching of another federative movement. On 4 June, *Maréchal de Camp* Joseph Servan, Minister of War, proposed the creation of a camp in the immediate vicinity of Paris, bringing together 20,000 gardes nationaux volontaires. In all the cantons of each department, five gardes would be chosen to be sent to Paris. They were to celebrate the anniversary of 14 July and defend the capital. At the same time, it was a question of putting pressure on the Parisian political circles and preventing a royalist *coup de force*. The Garde Nationale Parisienne did not appreciate this suspicious intervention by the provincials. The Fayettists saw it, no doubt rightly, as a manoeuvre aimed at neutralising the general staff and consequently circulated a petition which collected more than 8,000 signatures. After vehement parliamentary debates, the measure was finally adopted on 8 June. Louis XVI, who had just had his Garde Constitutionnelle dissolved, vetoed it. He also blocked a decree providing for the deportation of refractory priests. On 12 and 13 June, Ministers Servan, Roland and Clavière were dismissed. Louis XVI got rid of troublesome personalities in the perspective of a victorious foreign invasion and replaced them with figures of no real stature. Three days later, the King's obstinacy determined several sections to warn the municipality of their intention not only to go and demonstrate in arms before the deputies, but also to force Louis XVI

Mademoiselle Méricourt en habit militaire, gouache by Lesueur. In March 1792, Anne-Josephe Terwagne, known as Théroigne de Méricourt, requested permission to organize a women's Garde Nationale. Claiming to be citizen, she asked that women be armed to defend Paris in case of foreign invasion. It was her whom Lesueur depicted in an 'amazon uniform'. (Musée Carnavalet)

to reverse his successive vetoes and recall the patriotic ministers. The departmental authorities enjoined the mayor of Paris and the commander of the Garde Nationale to take all necessary measures to prevent the success of this illegal initiative. However, the protesters apparently did not reverse their decision.

During the night of 19 to 20 June, people slept little in the sections of the faubourgs and the centre of the capital. There was a concerted effort to overcome the last reluctance and, above all, to specify the routes of the mobilisation. The rioters could count on the tacit support of the municipality. At 5:00 a.m., the *generale* was drummed to bring the citizens together and no one objected. The mobilisation nevertheless remained partial and hesitant. In the faubourg Saint-Antoine, for example, only 1,500 demonstrators and gardes nationaux under the command of Santerre headed for the Assembly. The crowd that joined them along their route grew rapidly, so that the procession probably numbered 20,000 men when it reached the gates of the Assembly. To contain these thousands of armed demonstrators, Romainvilliers, the *Commandant General* of the Garde Nationale for the month of June, had only been able to muster 23 incomplete battalions out of the 60 in the capital, amounting to about 13,000 men.

This was theoretically sufficient, since the only organised force of the demonstrators was reduced to the six battalions of the faubourgs Saint-Antoine and Saint-Marcel, totalling about 2,500 men. But he did not give them any precise orders, especially as he only managed to meet Pétion at around 11:30 a.m. The latter then presented him with an order from the municipality to associate his battalions with the demonstration. From then on, nearly 8,000 people marched for two hours in front of the deputies of the Assembly and generously conspired against the aristocrats and 'Monsieur Veto', that is, the King. Among them were many guardsmen from the faubourgs, but also hundreds of others who had come individually, especially from the working-class districts in the centre of the city. When the crowd finally left the Assembly, the battalion commanders hoped to bring the gardes nationaux back to their respective sections. However, the gunners' companies, grouped on the Place du Carrousel, demanded to enter the Tuileries Palace. Headed by Lazowski, who commanded the gunners of the Gobelins section, they led the crowd and a battalion of gardes nationaux who broke down the gates. In the meantime, Santerre arrived and the gates of the Tuileries were attacked without Romainvilliers' battalions making the slightest opposition. Lazowski even had a cannon hoisted on the first floor of the royal residence and aimed it at the salle des Cent-Suisses. For his part, Louis XVI was physically protected by a few guardsmen in uniform and by Aclocque, who commanded the Legion of the faubourg Saint-Marcel.

On 20 June, the Garde Nationale Parisienne displayed its deep divisions and great weakness. The battalions which had agreed to maintain order found themselves unable to prevent the Tuileries from being invaded. Mixed with the sans-culottes, other battalions demonstrated in arms and with their leaders. Some commanders had resolved to follow the crowd in an attempt to reason with them, but in the heat of the moment they were overwhelmed by emerging leaders. For diverse reasons – physical stature, vocal power, allure and panache, generosity and humanity – these influential men from different social backgrounds had initially seduced the neighbourhood assemblies, creating cohesion and therefore effectiveness. These determined figures took the popular discourse in hand and, at the right moment, formulated demands that had previously been made in a more eruptive style.

The invasion of the Tuileries and the attacks on the King's person were very serious matters. On the 21st, the Assembly voted a decree prohibiting the submission of petitions by armed citizens. Thirty-three departments also protested against this clear violation of the royal residence. On the 24th, Louis XVI took advantage of the situation and mounted his horse. Accompanied by the Dauphin in national uniform, he was cheered on the Champs-Elysées by the gardes nationaux of the faubourg Saint-Germain. The initiative, which came far too late, was not unrelated to La Fayette's action. On 26 June, after announcing his intention to keep the army out of the conflict, La Fayette went to Paris in an attempt to involve the Garde Nationale in a *coup de force* against the Jacobins. The next day, Pétion forbade the review of the 1st Division of the Garde, headed by Aclocque, which La Fayette intended to organise. On the 29th, La Fayette only managed to gather a handful of officers at his home. A rally planned for the very same evening on the Champs-Élysées brought together barely a hundred guardsmen. La Fayette left Paris on 1 July without having found the support he had hoped for amongst his former troops.

The objectives of the revolutionary *journée* of 20 June 1792 were to convince the government to enforce the Legislative Assembly's rulings, defend France against foreign invasion and preserve the spirit of the *Constitution of 1791*. In the afternoon, the King appeared before the crowd, accompanied by a few persons. Surrounded by gardes nationaux who formed a barrier against the mob, Louis XVI remained calm and firm. (Musée Carnavalet)

At the beginning of the summer of 1792, the Garde Nationale Parisienne still seemed politically divided. Without firm leadership and faced with a revolutionary municipality, it was no longer able to play the temporising role it had fulfilled since 1789. And yet, in July, events were accelerating. Members of the patriotic clubs and section activists were busy convincing the gardes nationaux fédérés converging on Paris for the 14 July celebration of the need for a new revolutionary *journée*. According to them, it was a question of putting an end to Louis XVI and the intrigues of his court. On 12 July, the fédérés who had already arrived in Paris demanded that the Assembly make the King resign before they left to fight on the borders. The next day, Louis XVI asked the departmental authorities to suspend Pétion for not having prevented the *journée* of 20 June, but the Assembly immediately reinstated the mayor of Paris in his functions. On the 14th, gardes nationaux and citizens marched from the Place de la Bastille to the Champ de Mars and the ceremony proved to be a triumph for Pétion. The day after the commemoration, a number of fédérés did not hurry to Soissons where they were to regroup or categorically refused to go. Still others, coming from the south-east and particularly from Marseilles but also from Brittany, continued to flock to Paris where the reception conditions proved to be precarious.

On 22 July, at the sound of the *tocsin*, the decree proclaiming 'La Patrie en Danger' was officially promulgated. It caused an intense emotion and led to the enlistment of 4,000 Parisians in just 48 hours. Pikes were mass-produced, especially since, from 17 July, the Parisian municipality accepted in the ranks of the Garde Nationale all the citizens who were equipped with them. At the bar of the Assembly, Carnot requested 300,000 pieces of this very crude weapon which was erected as a symbol of revolutionary enthusiasm. On the 23rd, 300 fédérés from Brest arrived, soon followed by 500 Marseillais welcomed by Santerre himself and 200 gardes nationaux from the faubourg Saint-Antoine. That same evening, a violent brawl took place on the Champs-Élysées between the Marseillais and the gardes nationaux of the moderate section of the Filles-Saint-Thomas, who had gathered for a banquet. Such a bloody confrontation worsened the already extreme tension of the Parisian political climate. On 25 July, Austrians and *émigrés* issued the *Brunswick Manifesto*. This incendiary text revived popular anger and reinforced patriotic unanimity. On 1 August, following an initiative of the Quinze-Vingts section, the sections of the capital declared themselves permanent. The same day, a decree legalised on a national scale the opening of the Garde Nationale in favour of the passive citizens. In addition, the municipalities had to take charge of the production of pikes. These were to be distributed 'to all the citizens in a state to bear arms and who were not already provided with a weapon'.[22] They were stamped 'AN' (for 'Arme Nationale'). This marking was intended to allow for more effective control of the production of weapons, as it concerned pikes, muskets and sabres. Any weapon without a mark was to be confiscated. It was therefore a police measure whose ultimate objective was to control popular emotions and to supervise revolutionary *journées*.

---

22 Madival & Laurent (eds), *Archives Parlementaires*, vol.XLVII, p.363.

THE PIVOTAL YEARS

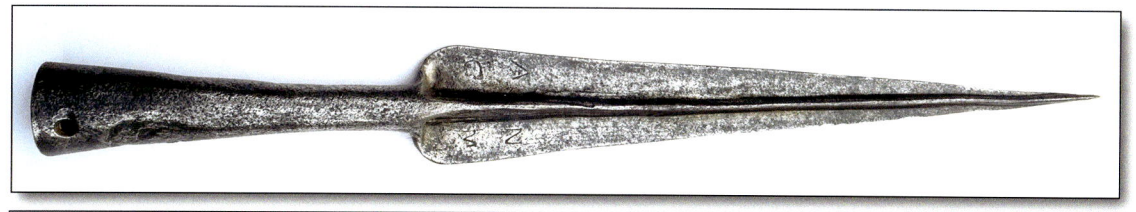

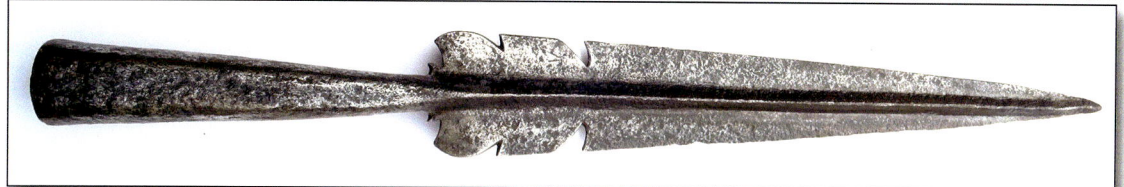

In the capital, the sans-culottes tried to control all the sectional assemblies, which, on 6 August, allowed them to request from the Assembly the removal of the King and his dynasty. They also demanded the dismissal of the general officers appointed by the King, the dismissal of the general staff, the prohibition of nobles as commanders in chief, but also the renewal of the departmental administrations. La Fayette was to be arrested and tried promptly. Meanwhile, the Girondin deputies felt that the sections had gone too far and demanded only that Louis XVI accept the return to office of the patriotic ministers. On 8 August, the Assembly finally ruled on the crimes of which La Fayette was accused, and the deputies acquitted him of all charges. As for the sections, they had formed an insurrectionary committee and 2,000 to 3,000 provincial fédérés were determined to support the Parisian revolutionaries. The confrontation was now inevitable.

Pikes were suitable for both military and civilian use. The iron spearhead had to be mounted on a wooden handle that 'may not be less than eight feet long, nor more than ten feet' – that is, from about 2.5 metres to just over 3 metres. In fact, the pikes made in 1792 and 1793 were no more than two metres long, far less than the law required. (Fabien Pacaud's collection)

Uniforms and Flags

A Unified Uniform

Following the Festival of the Federation, the colourful uniforms of the gardes nationaux did not meet with unanimous approval. Amongst the Assembly, some deputies, such as Regnault de Saint-Jean d'Angély, affirmed that it was necessary to 'authorise each municipality to choose the uniform to be worn by the Garde Nationale of its territory'.[23] However, as early as 18 July, other voices were in favour of a common uniform for all guardsmen of the kingdom. D'André asked that the Constitution Committee consider, for the next day's meeting, 'the determination of a common uniform', which was done.[24]

On the 19th, the session opened with discussions on various minor points. Imagining that 'the gardes nationaux would one day be employed to repel the enemy', Deputy Dupont de Nemours proposed that they be given distinctive lapels, on the grounds that 'the general should be able to know which unit was coming in'. The debates then focused on the coat's turnbacks.

---

23   Madival & Laurent (eds), *Archives Parlementaires*, vol.XVII, p.185.
24   Madival & Laurent (eds), *Archives Parlementaires*, vol.XVII, p.185.

THE GARDE NATIONALE 1789–1815

Miniaturist Jean-Louis-Dominique Duvaucel de Marsoeuvre (1749–1830) spent much of his artistic career in Bordeaux. In 1790, Marsoeuvre was a *sous-lieutenant* in the staff of a unit of the Bordeaux Garde Nationale, the Regiment de Saint-Maixent. He was appointed *aide-major* shortly afterwards. The officer portrayed here was perhaps one of his superiors. (François Vinot-Prefontaine's collection)

Officer of a Garde Nationale chasseur company, wearing the uniform with scarlet lapels defined in the summer of 1790. Note the buff leather gloves and the so-called 'Corsican belt'. (Osenat, with permission)

De Foucault asked in this respect that the motto 'La Loi, Le Roi' ('The Law, The King') be stitched on them. Barnave proposed that the word 'Constitution' be substituted for 'Loi'. In his view, the word 'Loi' only 'presents a vague idea, whereas the word "Constitution" has the advantage of including the Law and the King'. His colleague Martineau then pointed out that the word 'Constitution' had too many letters in view of the smallness of the turnback badges. De Toustin preferred to read 'Défenseurs de la Liberté' ('Defenders of Liberty'). Noting that 'almost all the uniforms were blue', Démeunier alluded to the need to 'establish external signs of fraternity between all the citizens', although he did not specify his thoughts.[25]

As a result of these sometimes futile discussions, a decree was issued stating that all the gardes nationaux in the kingdom had to wear the same uniform by 14 July 1791 at the latest, the anniversary of the Festival of the Federation. Deputy Brillat-Savarin even proposed to postpone this deadline until 14 July 1792. During this year-long interval, 'the guardsmen who have adopted a uniform other than the one prescribed may continue to wear it.'[26] Aware of the considerable expense involved in acquiring a uniform, the

---

25   Madival & Laurent (eds), *Archives Parlementaires*, vol.XVII, pp.190–191.
26   Madival & Laurent (eds), *Archives Parlementaires*, vol.XVII, p.191.

Assembly in fact allowed the gardes nationaux to equip themselves over time, according to their finances. The new uniform consisted of

> a royal blue coat, scarlet lapels and cuffs, white piping. White collar and scarlet piping. Yellow or gold epaulettes. The coat's turnbacks would be scarlet. On one of the turnbacks, the word 'Constitution' shall be written in yellow or gold letters, and on the other lapel, the word 'Liberté'. White waistcoat and breeches.[27]

The Quarrel of the Buttons

A few weeks later, the design of the buttons was standardised. Coats of arms and mottos disappeared in the process. On 5 September 1790, the Assembly decreed that the button of the gardes nationaux of the kingdom would henceforward bear the words 'La Loi, Le Roi' placed in the middle of a civic crown. On the outer edge of the button, the name of the district to which the garde belonged was also to appear. In districts with several sections, the latter would be distinguished by a number placed after the district. Article 3 of the decree – which appeared to have been written by specialists – provided for and authorised different types of buttons: gilded, mounted on bone or wood, solid. This ensured that each garde remained in control of the quality of manufacture that best suited him and allowed his level of wealth to show discreetly. Moreover, it allowed a greater number of factories to run.

Garde Nationale buttons, 1790. Buttons bearing the words 'La Loi, Le Roi' were theoretically only produced for a time span of less than four months. On 23 December 1790, the term 'Nation' was added. (Private collection, France)

---

27   Madival & Laurent (eds), *Archives Parlementaires*, vol.XVII, p.191.

However, one important word was missing: the Nation, the source of sovereignty. A fierce debate began immediately and continued throughout the autumn. The radicals feared it was evidence the Garde Nationale would be used for counter-revolution. In their view, the controversial deployment of gardes nationaux to suppress the revolt in Nancy argued for this. On 23 December 1790, the deputies – on a report from the Agriculture and Commerce Committees – finally recognised their mistake. The central inscription was changed to include three words: 'La Nation, La Loi, Le Roi'. In addition, it was to be 'of yellow or gilt copper, mounted on bone or wood with gut string attachments'.[28] This reversal was explained, according to the deputies, by the fact that the previous formula was truncated and no longer conformed to the new political situation. In fact, these politicians declared it truly conservative and banned it. The trade issue cannot be overlooked. It was really a question of preventing the importation of large quantities of mass-produced buttons made by British factories much more cheaply than their French counterparts. French workers, however, had real expertise in the production of buttons mounted on bone or wood and therefore had no reason to fear competition from across the Channel. It is no surprise that the decree recommended this method of production. Finally, in order not to penalise French manufacturers who had already complied with the decree of 5 September 1790, a draft decree reported by Dubois-Crancé suggested on 13 January 1791 that the previously defined model remained authorised until 14 July 1792. Such a proposal was ratified on 15 January following 'lively discussions'.[29] In truth, the uniform button crystallised wider issues that had begun long before and continued long after the design of the button had been fixed.

A 'Definitive' Uniform

On 13 July 1791, a new uniform was 'definitively' regulated, as the decree itself put it.[30] It took the form of a blue cloth coat with white lapels piped in scarlet, and scarlet collar and cuffs. For once – and this is rare enough to note – this situation lasted. Contemporary with the creation of the first Volontaires Nationaux units, this habit became the 'national uniform' and eventually clothed the French line infantry. Grenadiers wore distinctive red woollen epaulettes and chasseurs had green epaulettes and blue breeches.

The Cavalry

The uniform of the Garde Nationale cavalrymen was regulated in July 1790: a blue coat with scarlet lapels and cuffs with white piping, white collar and turnbacks piped in scarlet, a yellow epaulette trefoil and aiguillette, plus white breeches. The saddle cover and holster-covers were made of scarlet cloth with yellow braiding. At the end of September 1790, 728 muskets

---

28 Duvergier (ed.), *Collection Complète des Lois*, vol.II, p.119.
29 Paul Bordeaux, *La Garde nationale et les volontaires de Beauvais et de l'Oise au début de la Révolution: Leurs boutons d'uniformes* (Beauvais: Imprimerie de la Société Académique de l'Oise, 1913), p.339.
30 Anon., *Code de la Garde Nationale*, p.43.

THE PIVOTAL YEARS

intended to arm the cavalrymen were supplied by the Maubeuge arms factory. The Parisian municipality was responsible for transporting them to the capital. In 1792, some modifications occurred. The coat was similar to that of the foot gardes nationaux which had been regulated the year before. However, the turnbacks were scarlet instead of white. In addition, the cavalrymen wore a yellow woollen aiguillette over the shoulder.

Veteran units

A Lesueur gouache is the sole source representing the veterans' uniform according to the July 1790 provisions. As for the other gardes nationaux, the lapels were made of scarlet cloth. However, the collar is scarlet, whereas one would expect it to be white. The law of 14 October 1791 allowed the formation, in each canton, of a company of veterans composed of men over 60 years old and dressed in the 'same uniform' as the rest of the Garde Nationale. They were still distinguished by a white sash and a Henri IV-style hat, which Hoffmann accurately depicted on a plate. Lesueur opted for the traditional felt hat. In Paris, the veterans wore distinctive white epaulettes. Lesueur pictured this feature in one of his famous gouaches. These men were provided with a spontoon.

Artillery and Sappers

The law of 14 October 1791 also stipulated that 'communes owning guns may attach two to each of their battalions of gardes nationaux, either sedentary or volunteer intended for the defence of the borders. In this case, each battalion would be assigned a detachment composed of an officer, two *sergents*, two *caporaux* and twelve gunners'.[31] After recognising that 'the number of 17 men is not enough for the daily service of two artillery pieces', a decree of 18 March 1792 acted on the formation of a gunner company assigned to the service of these pieces.[32]

The gunners received a uniform reminiscent of both the Garde Nationale and the artillery. It consisted of a blue coat, scarlet collar and cuffs with white piping, white lapels piped scarlet. The turnbacks were adorned with cannons and grenades. The buttons were 'like those of the gardes nationaux'. A blue waistcoat with scarlet piping and blue breeches completed the outfit. The dirty nature of their duties led the gunners to adopt blue cuffs and lapels piped in scarlet, a provision confirmed by the decree of 18 March 1792. This law granted the gunners a musket, a pair of pistols and a sabre. The leatherwork was black and the cartridge box was absolutely similar to that of the other gardes nationaux.

Garde Nationale cavalryman in the uniform regulated in July 1790, watercolour by Henri Boisselier. (Yves Martin)

---

31 Anon., *Code de la Garde Nationale*, pp.146–147.
32 Duvergier (ed.), *Collection Complète des Lois*, vol.III, p.82.

THE GARDE NATIONALE 1789–1815

The law of 18 March 1792 also attached four sappers to the Garde Nationale's artillery companies. These were armed with a sabre, an axe and a brace of pistols. They wore a characteristic fawn leather apron. Such companies were gradually organised. It was not until September that this happened in Cambrai. On 21 September, 114 swords with curved and strong blades, 98 black belts with copper plate, 16 white harnesses for sappers, 16 sapper's axes and sheaths, 16 tan leather aprons, 16 bearskin caps for sappers, two drum cases and two drummer's coats were purchased. In Auxerre, the artillery company was effectively formed in December, when it was provided with guns. Two men were then taken from each company to become gunners and two grenadiers per company to become sappers.

Garde Nationale Flags, 1791–1792

In accordance with article 1 of the law of 23 September 1791, the battalions of the Garde Nationale de Paris retained their flag. The words 'Le Peuple français' and 'La Liberté ou la Mort' were to be added during a ceremony mentioned by journalist Prud'homme in his newspaper *Les Révolutions de Paris*. In the provinces, the Garde Nationale of Pézenas received its first tricolour flag in July 1791. It was offered to them by Monsieur de Steinauer and bore the motto 'La Liberté ou La Mort'. This anticipated article 27 of the decree of 29 September of the same year, which stipulated that the words 'Le Peuple français' and 'La Liberté ou la Mort' should be embroidered on the flags of the Garde Nationale. The making of such flags represented a considerable expense for the municipalities. Thus, on 25 March 1792, the gardes nationaux of Mortagne-au-Perche called a town council meeting. They asked for 'the acquisition of a flag in the proportion of their fellow gardes nationaux of Paris, which would be paid for out of the expenses of the municipal office'. Parts of the existing flag were kept to make up the new one. 'However, the unconstitutional parts were to be given to the municipal authorities'.[33] On 4 April, Lamireau, an upholsterer, took charge of cutting up the flag and recovering what could be used to make the new one. In Milhars, in the Tarn, the decision to acquire a flag in conformity with the legislative prescriptions of autumn 1791 came belatedly, precisely on 26 June 1792.

Chasseur and sapper of the Garde Nationale, 1791–1792, Lesueur's gouache. This is one of the very few representations of a sapper assigned to the Garde Nationale's artillery companies. He is wearing a bearskin cap, is armed with a sword and pistols and carries his axe on his shoulder. (Musée Carnavalet)

---

33 Joseph Besnard, *Histoire religieuse de Mortagne* (Mortagne: Pichard-Hayes Libraire-Editeur, 1891), pp.149–150.

7

The Garde in the Republican Era

August 1792–Spring 1795

On the evening of 9 August, the King was informed that massive gatherings and preparations were taking place in the capital, harbingers of alerts for the night. Once again, Louis XVI appealed to the constituted authorities and summoned municipal officers to the Tuileries palace, as well as Roederer, the elected magistrate of the Seine department. In short, he sought to surround himself with personalities capable of guaranteeing his protection and, he thought, holding a certain influence over the people of Paris. These attempts were in vain, as an electric atmosphere hung over the city.

Assault on the Tuileries Palace

Faced with the risk of crowd outbursts and violation of the royal residence, Mandat, the new *commandant en chef* of the Garde Nationale Parisienne, set about strengthening the defence of the Tuileries. This Fayettist, consequently convinced of the need to respect the *Constitution*, immediately tripled the number of gardes nationaux allocated to the protection of the palace. These 2,000 to 2,500 men came from 15 battalions. Among them, that of the Filles Saint-Thomas: 550 men commanded by *Chef de Bataillon* Tassin de l'Etang, who, after having made their entry into the gardens by the gate of the Pont-Royal, were placed along the terrace, its right side leaning against the Porte du Manège. A dozen cannon, placed in the courtyards, outside the palace, came to reinforce them. In addition, there were 900 to 1,000 mounted Gendarmes Nationaux from the former cavalry of the Garde Nationale, a little less than a thousand Gardes-Suisses and several hundred gentlemen – often former Gardes du Corps – who, since 20 June, had been taking turns with the King to reinforce the internal security of the palace. In total, between 4,500 and 5,000 well-armed and trained men. However, there was still an unknown factor: would these gardes nationaux agree, when the time came, to open fire

THE GARDE NATIONALE 1789–1815

Jeunes hommes allant s'exercer au canon, gouache by Lesueur. These young men handling a gun undoubtedly belong to a Garde Nationale artillery company. Three of them are dressed in more or less regulation uniforms. The others are dressed as sans-culottes, the only uniform element being the bonnet de police. The number of gunners and the size of the gun suggest it is a 1764 model 4-pounder. (Musée Carnavalet)

on other gardes nationaux? The incidents that had occurred on the Champs-Elysées, on the occasion of the arrival in Paris of the fédérés from Marseilles 10 days earlier, suggested that a certain number of companies – following the example of the grenadiers of the Filles Saint-Thomas Battalion – were indeed determined to fight. Finally, some gardes nationaux were also entrusted with the surveillance of the main bridges over the Seine in order to prevent the rioters in the faubourgs from gathering. Others were kept in reserve on the Place de Grève. Mandat foresaw that they would be able to catch the attackers from the rear. Pétion, mayor of Paris, told anyone who would listen that if the Tuileries palace was attacked, it would be defended. But after coming in person to visit the defensive perimeter, he slipped away in the darkness.

The attackers counted on about 2,000 fédérés from Brest and Marseilles. To this were added battalions from a dozen sections mainly located in the two working-class faubourgs of Saint-Antoine and Saint-Marcel or in the centre of the capital. In all, probably 5,000 men were immediately available. This total did not include all the citizens who could join the insurrection. Armed only with the pike, they would be most useful in case of a stampede or a partial rallying of the palace garrison. But nothing was obvious in the camp of the insurrection, everything remained dependent on the degree of mobilisation of the gardes nationaux of certain battalions. However, the situation evolved very quickly. Thus, around 8:00 p.m. on 9 August, only the Quinze-Vingts section seemed determined to take action and attack the Tuileries. By 10:00 p.m. however, agitation had gained ground: 30 sections out of 48 began to assemble, promising to be ready to march within two hours. On the eve of the confrontation, the preparation of the artillery was another fundamental point of the armed mobilisation. Several orders show that the sections sought at all costs not only to have additional guns and powder, but above all to get various ammunition. At midnight, at the sound of the *tocsin*, sections and battalions of the Garde Nationale had to choose

THE GARDE IN THE REPUBLICAN ERA

Groupe de citoyens combattant aux Tuileries, le 10 août 1792, Lesueur gouache, circa 1792–1794. This small group of *sectionnaires*, including young and middle-aged men, advances towards the enemy with pikes held horizontally, in accordance with drill books. Pikes allowed the crowd to push against a line of crossed bayonets and the shock should cause the opponent to disperse. All these fighters are wearing the unavoidable carmagnole. (Musée Carnavalet)

their side, the choice of which depended greatly on the influence of the officers on their men. A dozen battalions responded to Mandat's orders, but others split up. The grenadier company of the Gravilliers Battalion decided in this respect for the defence of the Tuileries, while the other companies opted for the insurrection.

The sections each appointed three commissioners from among the most energetic patriots. All were determined to act. Gathered at the Hôtel de Ville, they constituted, at about 3:00 a.m., an insurrectionary committee which promptly took the place of Pétion's municipality. To reach each other, the forces of the faubourgs Saint-Antoine and Saint-Marcel had to cross the Seine, whose bridges Mandat had taken care to guard. However, in response to the insistent demands of the commissioners, the Parisian municipality ordered the battalion of the Henri IV section, responsible for guarding the Pont Neuf, to withdraw its cannon: this deprived it of the only effective means of resisting the summons of the insurgents. Moreover, in order to disorganise the command for sure, the insurrectionary committee summoned Mandat in the early hours of the morning. After some hesitation, he agreed to go to the Hôtel de Ville. He was promptly and illegally dismissed and replaced by Santerre, a prominent figure in the faubourg Saint-Antoine. For good measure, Mandat was arrested and sent to the prison de l'Abbaye. But no sooner had he left the Hôtel de Ville than his escort abandoned him to the hands of the infuriated crowd, who massacred him with pikes and sabres. The assassination of Mandat certainly deprived the gardes nationaux assigned to the defence of the Tuileries of precise orders at a most delicate moment, as many of them did not accept having to obey to the officers of the Gardes-Suisses or the royalists.

At the same time, Roederer refused to proclaim martial law, which Louis XVI had been calling for. At about 8:00 a.m., the King wanted to review the battalions of gardes nationaux, hoping to exalt their loyalty. His hopes were soon disappointed. Although a few cheers were heard as he passed, many of the gardes remained silent. Those posted in the gardens shouted 'Vive la Nation!' but also insults aimed at the sovereign and his entourage. Disconcerted, the King returned to his palace and agreed to Roederer's proposal to place himself under the protection of the Legislative Assembly. Such a decision had far-reaching consequences for further events.

On reaching the outskirts of the Tuileries, the insurgents were at first impressed by the number of battalions massed ahead of them. After the passage of the King through the ranks of his supposed defenders, the fédérés from Brest and Marseilles nevertheless advanced to rally the Tuileries' defenders. The gendarmes withdrew and the gunners passed with their guns into the ranks of the rioters. Other units, however, still hesitated. The departure of the King for the Assembly created a stir which was put to good use by the assailants, who broke through the perimeter gates and ran towards their counterparts to embrace them. No sooner had these scenes of fraternisation begun that they were brutally interrupted by firing from the windows of the Tuileries by the Swiss, who had decided to accept the fight. After having discharged their muskets, the latter pursued the fugitives and pushed back the gardes nationaux of the faubourg Saint-Antoine. The affair seemed quite compromised. The fédérés from Brest and Marseilles were the first to recover and stopped the progress of the Swiss who, faced with the ardour of the new arrivals, had to withdraw and take cover behind the walls of the palace where the crowd of attackers pursued them to their deaths. The human toll was particularly heavy: nearly 400 attackers were killed – including about 90 fédérés – and 800 to 1,000 among the defenders. In addition, several hundred people were wounded. Both sides showed great determination. Everyone sensed that the day would be decisive: hence, no doubt, the fierceness of the fighting and its epilogue.

On 10 August, the gardes nationaux were, like the Gardes-Suisses, the main protagonists of the fighting at the Tuileries. However, the relentlessness with which the Gardes-Suisses were massacred masked the lack of unanimity that characterised the attitude of the gardes nationaux during this revolutionary *journée*. Embodying the people of Paris in arms, the gardes had indeed fought on both sides: some to storm the Tuileries Palace, others to protect it alongside the Swiss. Some of those assigned to defend the palace – including the men of the Filles Saint-Thomas Battalion – did not react after the Swiss volley. In a report to the administrators of his department, the commander of the Brest fédérés even suggested that some of these gardes had fired on their fellow citizens. In addition, a number of gardes nationaux, led by determined leaders, had formed the core of the forces launched against the executive power. On the evening of 10 August, the people in arms imposed on the Legislative Assembly the decisions dictated by the orators who were supposed to represent the wishes of the popular strata, foremost among

THE GARDE IN THE REPUBLICAN ERA

The storming of the Tuileries Palace was a genuine battle, as this engraving clearly reveals. Aiming to exalt the importance of the event, the artist chose a bird's eye view: in fact, the palace occupies the entire width of his picture. Moreover, he shows the patriots – sans culottes, provincial fédérés and Parisian gardes nationaux intermingled – attacking in line, amidst the smoke of musket and artillery fire. (Musée Carnavalet)

which was the suspension of the King. In this context, the Garde Nationale – or more precisely the units that supported this intrusion justified by the right to resist oppression – played an essential role.

The Armed Sections

Table 9. Armed section companies. Organisation of 19 August 1793

Capitaine	1
Lieutenant	1
Sous-lieutenant	2
Sergent-major	1
Sergent	4
Caporal	8
Tambour	2
Citoyens	107
Total	126

On 11 August, the deputies decided that all distinctions between active and passive citizens were definitively abolished, which necessarily led to changes in the conception and organisation of the Garde Nationale. On the same

THE GARDE NATIONALE 1789–1815

Sans-culottes en armes, Lesueur gouache. Two gardes nationaux on duty. The uniformed officer on the left is a wig-maker. Remains of hair powder cover his shoulders, a detail that the artist perfectly observed. On his right, the guardsman is undoubtedly a bourgeois wearing breeches and silk stockings. (Musée Carnavalet)

day, the section commissioners suppressed the Garde Nationale staff, which had shown itself to be favourable to Mandat. The day after, they replaced the 60 battalions inherited from the former districts by 48 armed sections corresponding to the 48 electoral sections. The concordance between the sections and the battalions of the Garde Nationale that the law of 21 May 1790 had destroyed was thus re-established. However, it took almost a week before a law legalised the reduction of the 60 battalions to 48. Such a decision implied that the units of the Garde Nationale would be closely dependent on the sectional authorities. They were no doubt the symbol of the autonomy of the sections, which were now in control of their armed force. Each section had a flag 'to the colours of the Nation with the inscription "Liberté–Egalité"' and 'a commander-in-chief, a second-in-command, an adjutant and a flag bearer'.[1] It included a number of companies proportional to its population, so that it could generate the equivalent of several battalions and count several companies of gunners, to which were attached a certain number of workers 'drawn from the citizens armed with pikes to be employed in the manoeuvres and in the defence of the entrenchments'.[2] This was a subtle way of reinforcing the military weight of the sections considered to be democrats against those perceived as moderate or even reactionary. In fact, the reorganisation of the Garde Nationale preceded the transformation of the political framework of the capital, because it was in its battalions that the census of all citizens was carried out. The Garde became an integral part of sectional democracy. The sans-culottes put into practice the principles of equality and fraternity in the battalions: even if replacement remained, the personal obligation to serve was to erase social differences. The union of patriots was expressed through fraternisation between battalions or participation in national and sectional festivals. The sans-culottes also attached great importance to the election of their officers, and the appointment of the section commander mobilised a usually negligent electorate more than any other. After 10 August, the leaders of the Garde Nationale were quite radically renewed. The command of the battalions, until then mostly held by nobles, passed into the hands of men from Parisian industry and commerce and from the new bourgeoisie. The election of officers and NCOs by the entire population also allowed the patriots to impose their authority on the territory of a section by carrying out all the necessary controls, disarmament and arrests.

---

1 Anon., *Collection générale des décrets rendus par l'Assemblée Nationale* (Paris: Baudouin Imprimeur, 1792), pp.182–183.
2 Anon., *Collection générale des décrets*, pp.182–183.

Guilty Inaction: The September Massacres

In the aftermath of 10 August, Paris was marked by a general atmosphere of suspicion and a police frenzy. Under the control of the sectional assemblies, the Garde Nationale carried out numerous house visits, hunting down the survivors of the fighting in the Tuileries, whether they were Swiss or aristocrats who supported the King, but also refractory priests, moderates and hypocrites. Such behaviour particularly concerned the Sans-culottes section – formerly the Jardin des Plantes section – which, on the night of 29–30 August, provided nearly 600 men to take part in a general search throughout Paris for suspects and hidden weapons, as well as making an inventory of all the available horses.

On 2 September, after the fall of the Longwy fortress and the announcement of the imminent surrender of Verdun – one of the greatest fortresses of north-eastern France – the Commune ordered the following message to be posted throughout Paris: 'To arms! The enemy is at our gates!'[3] It sent delegates to all the sections to discuss the urgent measures to be taken. In addition to the need to fortify the walls, many sections wished to guard against a possible conspiracy in the prisons, which were well filled since 10 August. The massacres began a little later. After murdering a group of prisoners who were being transferred to the prison de l'Abbaye, the mob, armed with swords, axes, pikes and sticks, entered this prison and then the nearby Carmes prison, systematically executing the inmates, whether they were political prisoners or common criminals. Until 6 September, the Conciergerie, the Salpêtrière, the Châtelet, the Bernardins, Saint-Firmin, the two prisons of La Force and the prison-hospital of Bicêtre were stormed. After five days of carnage, between 1,100 and 1,400 people – about half of the incarcerated population – had been killed. Danton and Roland, respectively Minister of Justice and Minister of the Interior, let the massacres happen. Robespierre and Marat had remained silent. According to historian Roger Dupuy, the Garde Nationale did not join the killers, but did nothing, at least for three days, to oppose this punitive violence.[4] The abundant contemporary iconography also depicts the presence at the scene of the massacres of gardes nationaux who, although armed with pikes, let the massacres take place. In the same vein, the Gobelins section, which had become the Finistère section, waited until 5 September to order its battalion of gardes nationaux to oppose the return of the murderers to Bicêtre, where 170 inmates had been exterminated the day before. American historian Timothy Tackett postulates that while the exact identity of the murderers remains an enigma,

> many of them were undoubtedly Parisian gardes nationaux and provincial fédérés who had remained in the city since their arrival in July. Most of these men had thus risked their lives three weeks earlier in the capture of the Tuileries, and were soon to leave to fight the enemy armies. In their mind, which had been heavily

---

[3] Timothy Tackett, 'Septembre 1792: De la rumeur au massacre', *L'Histoire*, 458 (2019), p.65.
[4] Dupuy, *La Garde nationale*, p.132.

influenced by dozens of rumours circulating for weeks, the September massacres were probably both an act of revenge and a service to the city, ensuring the safety of its citizens on the eve of their departure.[5]

Similar scenes also occurred outside Paris. Prisoners from Orleans on their way to the capital, where they were to be brought before the special tribunal set up to judge the crimes of 10 August, were thus massacred in Versailles, right in front of their escort of gardes nationaux, by the crowd and volunteers preparing to join *Général de division* Dumouriez's army. On 9 September, in a climate of intense tensions still exacerbated by fear, massacres occurred in Lyon during which a crowd of rioters savagely murdered, in the city's prisons, no less than nine cavalry officers suspected of royalism as well as three refractory priests. Dispatched to the Pierre-Size prison in the afternoon, the gardes nationaux were instructed to open fire in case the crowd became too threatening, but the growing mob ended up seizing the prisoners and massacring them, without the gardes being able to stop them. On the other hand, in the prison of Roanne, three battalions of gardes nationaux succeeded in securing the prisoners and dispersing the onlookers who were mixed up with the rioters. Minor massacres also took place in Gisors, Lorient, Marseille and Toulon. The Garde Nationale had hardly taken part in them, but had allowed them to be committed.

The Garde, at the Heart of Ideological Conflicts within France

Apparently unable to deal with the rioters and to provide serious policing, the Garde Nationale also proved particularly weak when it had to oppose foreign armies. In July 1792, when France was declared to be 'in danger', there was indeed a concern to count the gardes nationaux in order to provide them with arms, powder and ammunition. Similarly, it was up to the municipalities to call in the Garde Nationale if 'a seditious movement or a gathering of brigands and thieves' occurred in their commune, to conduct patrols 'to ensure the preservation of properties' and to check travellers' passports.[6] Led by Prussian, Austrian and *émigré* troops, the invasion of France effectively began on 19 August. In spite of the slowness and the little ardour of the German troops, the soldiers of La Fayette and Luckner did not manage to contain them. In Longwy, on 23 August, then in Verdun, on 2 September, the Garde Nationale discouraged the defenders from resisting any further and opened the drawbridges of the two fortresses to Prussian troops. Was this decision linked to the unenviable fate of the gardes nationaux in the *Brunswick Manifesto*? It threatened to treat them as rebels. The laws of war would not be applied to them, and they would have been severely punished if they had been caught in arms. It also made them responsible for the peace and safety of people and properties. It is worth noting, however, the conduct

---

5   Tackett, 'Septembre 1792: De la rumeur au massacre', p.65.
6   Archives Départementales des Vosges (ADV): 3H1: Arrêté du district de Neufchâteau, 20 juillet 1792.

THE GARDE IN THE REPUBLICAN ERA

of Lille's guardsmen during the siege of their city in September and early October 1792. The city of Lille was a key location in northern France's defensive system. On 9 September, Austrian troops began siege operations. On the defenders' side, the garrison was insufficient and the warehouses were empty. Nevertheless, the city's Garde Nationale Legion, under *Colonel* Briant, numbered 8,000 men divided into 12 battalions. Added to this were two companies of the city's gunners, under the command of *Capitaines* Niquet and Ovigneur. On 29 September, the Duke of Saxe-Weimar ordered the town to surrender, but this was refused. The shelling began the same day and lasted until 5 October. The Austrians ran out of ammunition and lifted the siege on the 7th. Throughout the siege, Lille's gardes nationaux served on the ramparts and also manned fire pumps: two suburbs were indeed hit by fires, while two others were destroyed by the bombardment.

Santerre, Commandant de la Garde Nationale Parisienne en 1792. Engraving by Bonneville, c. 1793. An entrepreneur in the faubourg Saint-Antoine, brewer Santerre became one of the most prominent figures in the revolutionary *journées* that ultimately led to the fall of the royalty. On 10 August 1792, he was appointed *Commandant General* of the Garde Nationale Parisienne, a position he held until his departure to the Vendée in May 1793. (Musée Carnavalet)

In the aftermath of the September massacres, a new National Assembly – the Convention – was set up. The monarchy was abolished on 21 September and the Republic was proclaimed the following day. From the outset, the Convention had to fight to preserve its existence in the face of internal and external counter-revolution. Moreover, the action of this new constituent assembly was hampered by the existence of factions, the Girondins and the Montagnards being the main ones. Obviously, the Garde Nationale Parisienne remained at the very heart of the debates. Indeed, some deputies, starting with those of the Girondin majority, felt, at best, at the mercy of popular movements that the Garde Nationale was no longer able to contain, at worst, prisoners of the Parisian crowds. In addition, from the very first sessions of the Convention, the Girondins wished to protect it – and their own selves – from the threats of the Commune as well as the injunctions of the sections. They also wished to preserve the Garde-Meuble from systematic looting that was facilitated by the lax supervision of these same sections. They therefore proposed the creation of a paid garde from the departments. On 23 September, Roland, Minister of the Interior, made such a request. A commission charged to study the modalities was immediately created. At the next day's session of the Convention, Buzot, another major figure of the Girondins, asked for the creation of a 'public force' recruited from the 83 departments. This would be capable of counteracting the influence of Paris on the Assembly and would be specifically charged with ensuring its security. Many departments also denounced the hegemony of the capital. The parliamentary debates were particularly tense, with the Montagnard deputies pretending not to understand the merits of their colleagues' proposals. In this affair, the Parisian sections were in great danger of losing their monopoly on law enforcement in the capital. As usual, they drafted a number of petitions. The Girondins persisted in their project, which definitely alienated the Parisian people. On 8 October, Buzot – in the name of the Convention's Military Committee – presented a draft decree providing for the arrival in Paris, by 1 December 1792 at the latest, of 3,500 gardes nationaux reinforced by 1,500 mounted gendarmes, all chosen by the general councils of the 83 departments. Receiving the pay allocated to the Gendarmerie, they would be stationed in Paris and commanded by an officer-general appointed by the Convention. Not surprisingly, the draft decree was not voted on. On 18 October, the camp formed outside Paris in the course of August was removed by order of the Convention. It had, until then, served to justify the maintenance of the gardes nationaux fédérés from the provinces on whom the Girondins counted to counteract the hostility of the Parisian sections towards them. Despite Santerre's wrath, however, fédérés battalions continued to flock to the outskirts of Paris and asked to serve alongside the Garde Nationale Parisienne. The sections hoped to keep them away from Paris and demanded that they be sent to fight on the borders. On 10 November, after a heated debate, the Convention finally decided to keep them there. At the beginning of 1793, there were still nearly 2,500 of them, poorly organised, with little discipline and undeniably won over by extremist propaganda. In short, the Girondins had tried to restore the influence of the departments by planning to raise forces there dedicated to the protection of the Convention. But their failure gave rise to the idea that they were anti-Parisian and this fiction would have serious consequences a few months later.

In the departments, the autumn of 1792 was marked by recurring clashes between the bourgeoisie, supporters of economic freedom, and the popular classes who wanted to regulate the markets. In the Yonne, Touraine and Loiret regions, armed bands stopped grain convoys and taxed them arbitrarily. The delegates of the Convention were frequently subjected to violence and vexation by the mob, without the Garde Nationale intervening. On the contrary, the Garde frequently chose to collude with the rioters. From mid-October 1792 to mid-January 1793, the trial of the King, organised by and at the Convention, mobilised opinion. It allowed the left side to accuse the Gironde of wanting to save the King by appealing to the popular sanction of the verdict. Nevertheless, capital punishment, voted by part of the Girondin deputies, led to a kind of momentary unanimity.

The King's Execution

The execution of Louis XVI was set for 21 January 1793. The Paris Commune, as well as certain sections along the route from the Temple prison to the scaffold, carefully prepared the security arrangements. Indeed, how would the people react to this unprecedented act in French history? Would not a final royalist *coup de force* attempt to save Louis XVI along the route to the guillotine? Those suspected of being too sympathetic to the King, or even sensitive and sympathetic to his plight, were kept away: the royalists, of course, but also women, whose moods were supposedly more amenable to mercy. 'Any man who cries for mercy or who agitates without consideration

THE GARDE IN THE REPUBLICAN ERA

This engraving, from *Les Révolutions de Paris*, shows King Louis XVI's final moments. 1,200 guardsmen (25 from each section) escorted him to the Place de la Révolution. They had to be armed with a musket and know how to properly manoeuvre. They wore an identity card at the buttonhole, as indicated in Santerre's orders. (Musée Carnavalet)

will be arrested and taken to prison. Women will not leave their homes. The sections will be in arms at their various posts', proposed the Gravilliers section in a decree immediately taken up to the comma by the neighbouring sections.[7] In addition, the entire Parisian armed force was mobilised. At that time, it involved more than 116,000 men divided into 886 companies, an average of 2,400 men per section. Such an operation was a success for Santerre, its commander. In truth, any absence was considered a counter-revolutionary act.

'Since 5:00 a.m., one could hear the dull roll of the cannons and caissons, the trot of the cavalry and the regular pace of the troops. It was an event that was being prepared', wrote a student at dawn on 21 January 1793.[8] Louis XVI, in his last glimpses, certainly only saw men at arms. From the night of 20 to 21 January, about 12,000 gardes nationaux, shoulder to shoulder, lined the route from the Temple prison to the Place de la Révolution, on which the scaffold had been set up, to give the ceremony all the space and solemnity required. A favour was granted to the King: he went to execution in the Paris mayor's coach, not in the cart of those condemned to death. The journey, through streets still half-obstructed by snow patches, took more than two hours, at the slow pace of the horses of the 100 Gendarmerie cavalrymen who preceded the carriage, as well as the 100 Garde Nationale cavalrymen who followed it. On the Place de la Révolution, the guillotine was surrounded by several battalions preventing the public from approaching it. The immediate vicinity of the Place was also occupied by a tide of blue uniforms: 80,000 men, gardes nationaux and gendarmes, accompanied by 84 guns, were deployed

---

7   *Courrier de l'Egalité*, 157 (1793), p.666.
8   Gaston Maugras (ed.), *Journal d'un étudiant pendant la Révolution* (Paris: Plon, 1910), p.316.

on that icy morning of 21 January. The whole thing gave the impression of general support for the ex-King's punishment, but what allowed this one-day of unanimity was that the execution had been desired by the Convention, not demanded by the Commune and the Parisian sections.

The execution of Louis XVI and the annexation policy of the Republic, mainly in Savoy and Belgium, were real challenges to monarchical Europe. On 1 February 1793, France declared war on Britain and the United Provinces. In the Convention, the facade of unanimity displayed following the death sentence of the ex-King hardly lasted. The Montagnard deputies claimed that the *appellants*, in other words the partisans of the appeal to the people to sanction the Convention's verdict, could only be masked royalists. The war against most of the European states required the raising of 300,000 men. In the spring, however, this led to unrest in the Côte d'Or, the Yonne and the Puy-de-Dôme. In the departments of western France, tens of thousands of peasants, refusing the principle of the lottery, revolted. Already strained by religious quarrels, the situation deteriorated particularly in the Vendée: from mid-March onwards, it turned into a dangerous insurrection that urban gardes nationaux struggled to contain. For example, around 11 March 1793, youth gangs supported by their communities gathered and converged on Nantes. On 15 March, some 10,000 insurgents met at the Pont du Cens, north of the Loire, and prepared to attack Nantes, which then had about 5,000 defenders. The next day, the gardes nationaux had to go out to break the siege, while other bands were already pouring in from the south. In March and April, the military situation deteriorated brutally in Belgium and the Netherlands. Defeated by the Austrian troops at the battle of Neerwinden on 18 March, *Général de division* Dumouriez deserted the cause on 5 April. Three weeks later, the indictment and acquittal of Marat by the Revolutionary Tribunal only served to inflame the quarrels between the Montagnards and Girondins. The latter were blamed for Dumouriez's treason – which they had supported for some time – but also for the uprising in the Vendée.

The Jacobin Republic Under Fire: Federalist Revolts

On 18 May, the Convention set up an ephemeral Commission of Twelve, mainly composed of Girondins. Charged with examining the acts of the Paris Commune, it decided to beef up the forces protecting the Convention with contingents of gardes nationaux taken from the 48 sections of the capital, hoping in this way to neutralise the influence of units devoted to the Commune and the Montagnards. On the 24th, it also decreed the arrest of Hébert, Deputy Prosecutor of the Commune but also editor of the famous newspaper *Le Père Duchesne*. The Parisian sections mobilised against this *coup de force*. As early as the 27th, the section of the Cité thus asked to be admitted to the bar of the Convention to denounce the Commission of the Twelve, which was disbanded for the first time that day, but re-established the following day. It was still active when, on 31 May, the Convention learned that the day before the Parisian sections had united in an insurrectionary committee. One of the first measures of that committee was to appoint

THE GARDE IN THE REPUBLICAN ERA

Hanriot, the commander of the armed section of the Sans-culottes, as *Commandant en Chef* of the Garde Nationale Parisienne, replacing the temporary commander provided for by the law. As soon as he took office, Hanriot took energetic measures, such as closing the gates of the capital. He also ordered the *tocsin* to be rung in all the churches and the *canon d'alarme* to be fired from the Pont Neuf. Although this signal could theoretically only be triggered by the Convention, Hanriot also had the *generale* drummed. On the morning of 2 June, the fate of the Girondin deputies was still not fixed. But, as soon as the session resumed at the Convention, around 10:00 a.m., addresses and petitions read in the gallery multiplied. At the same time, Hanriot had almost the entire available strength of the Garde Nationale, nearly 80,000 men reinforced by about 100 artillery pieces, surround the Convention's session room at the Tuileries. However, only the most reliable units, but also the gunners, were massed in the immediate vicinity of the Assembly in order to impose the required arrests. The others believed that the Convention was threatened by royalist gatherings reported on the Champs-Élysées! In the session room, where the deputies were more or less prisoners, the atmosphere was extremely tense. Robespierre and his supporters, with cruel irony, invited their colleagues to go outside to see that the people were watching over them, while a crowd of strangers, many of them women, were clogging the corridors and blocking the exits. When the deputies reached the outside, they were confronted by hedges of bayonets and pikes and then

Journées du 31 mai et du 2 juin 1793, engraving by Pierre-Gabriel Berthault. Parisian sections were heavily armed. On 2 June 1793, their guns pointed at the Convention prompted the deputies to order the arrest of nearly 30 of their Girondin colleagues. (Musée Carnavalet)

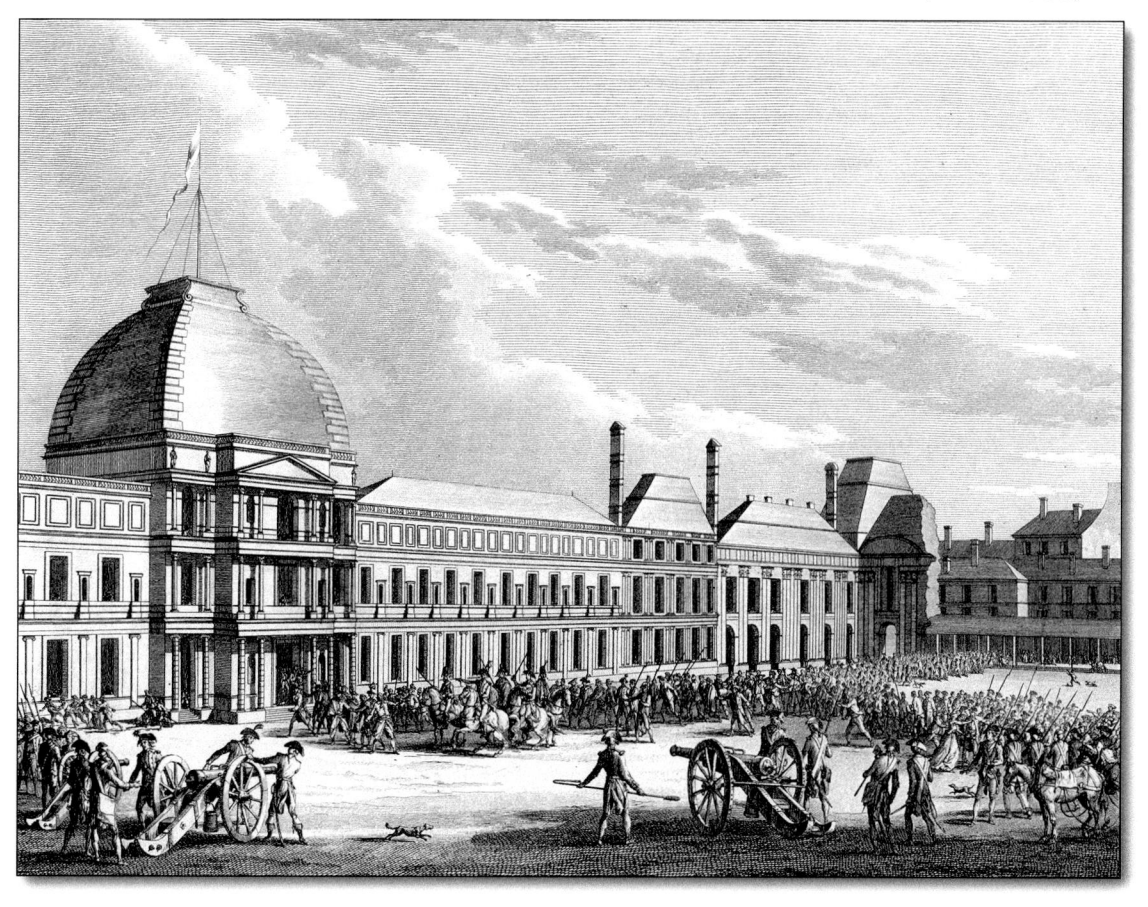

231

heard Hanriot instruct his men to prepare to open fire and the gunners to move to their guns. So, equally frightened and dismayed, they returned to their seats to vote on the decree for the arrest of 32 Girondins, including two ministers, Clavière and Lebrun. After six months of verbal jousting, the sans-culottes got the last word in a perfectly executed *coup de force*. Hanriot was the key man of this revolutionary *journée*, as he had decided on the massive mobilisation of almost all of the gardes nationaux of Paris, willy-nilly.

The Girondins promptly denounced the *coup*. Defeated in the capital, they nevertheless tried to resist by appealing to the support of the departments. Port cities, such as Bordeaux and Marseilles, and industrious cities, such as Rouen and Lyon, protested on their behalf. In fact, local merchants and notables had retained enough influence and clientele to compete for the sections with the Montagnard-friendly club members. At the end of June, the situation was critical for the Convention. Accused of the crime of 'federalism' – the fact of wanting to break up national unity and divide the patriots in the face of external and internal threats – the supporters of the Gironde seemed able to win in the west, the south-west, the Rhone valley and the Midi. However, the situation was highly confused and the Jacobin clubs network held out in medium-sized cities.

During this 'federalist crisis', which turned into a real civil war, the Garde Nationale was a key player in the confrontation and supplied the protagonists on both sides. 'In the first months of 1793, political power in Lyon depended on the ability of each faction to mobilise the battalions of the Garde Nationale for its cause', notes historian Bruno Ciotti.[9] As early as 29 May, the sections of this major city in the Rhône, largely controlled by the moderates, effectively relied on the Garde Nationale to overthrow the Montagnard municipality, which was nevertheless supported by the military. This success was obtained following a genuine street battle, at the cost of some 40 dead and nearly 120 wounded. In the west, in the Bordeaux region, but also in the Midi, the gardes nationaux of the bourgeois companies provided the backbone of the armed forces – sometimes called 'Armées Départementales' – in revolt against the Convention. On 7 June, the department of Gironde decided to raise such a force, intended to march on Paris.

By the turn of July and August, the Rhône-et-Loire department and the Lyon municipality sought to recruit gardes nationaux from the rural districts surrounding the city. This was to increase their forces in anticipation of a siege which was henceforth unavoidable, especially as the Lyonnais armed forces were then commanded by a large number of royalist officers. One of the first decisions of the ageing *Général en Chef* Perrin de Précy was to make the Lyonnais gardes nationaux the core of his meagre troops. Each battalion had a company of grenadiers, a company of chasseurs and two companies of fusiliers. Only the grenadier and chasseur companies – mainly composed of citizens who volunteered – were paid and quartered. With a maximum of 7,200 men, they nevertheless supported the majority

---

9   Bruno Ciotti, 'Servir dans la Garde nationale de Lyon en 1792', in Serge Bianchi and Roger Dupuy (eds), *La Garde nationale entre Nation et peuple en armes* (Rennes: Presses Universitaires de Rennes, 2006), p.330.

THE GARDE IN THE REPUBLICAN ERA

of the fighting against the besieging troops from August to early October. On the other hand, the staff had little confidence in the fusilier companies. Less disciplined and more reluctant to fight, they were therefore essentially confined to routine patrols.

The Armée des Alpes was given the task of putting down the Lyon rebellion. It was, however, reinforced by means of gardes nationaux raised in the rural departments on the outskirts of Lyon, such as the Ain, the Haute-Loire and the Puy-de-Dôme. If their recruitment was initially difficult, local counter-revolutionary threats, skilfully exploited by the republican authorities, rekindled the patriotic fever. In September, 35,000 gardes nationaux of questionable combat value were theoretically sent to Lyon. The case of the levies operated in the Puy-de-Dôme invites one however to relativize this estimate, because if 12,000 men effectively left the department, only approximately 5,000 arrived in Lyon. On the way, many detachments were left in garrison or employed in the surveillance of the Forez region, west of Lyon. In terms of symbolism, however, the objective was achieved: the numbers assembled proved not only the recognised legitimacy of the Convention's power, but also the permanence of revolutionary enthusiasm.

The Girondins failed to give shape to a provincial federation that would seriously worry Paris, and the various federalist movements came to naught. On 9 October, the Lyonnais laid down their arms and on 19 December, *Général de division* Dugommier recaptured Toulon. The Girondine rebellion had only been possible due to the existence of the Garde Nationale and the exaltation of resistance to oppression which the people of Bordeaux, Lyon and Marseilles had availed themselves of.

Lyon Gardes nationaux during the siege of the city, summer 1793. From left to right: *Capitaine* in regulation uniform – Garde national of a centre company, likewise in regulation uniform – Grenadier – Chasseur. This plate was drawn on the basis of items kept at the Musées Gadagne (Lyon), correspondence from the Armée Départementale de Rhône-et-Loire and the *Memoirs* of Jean-Baptiste Nolhac, a siege fighter. (Original artwork by Marc Morillon)

THE GARDE NATIONALE 1789–1815

The People's Armies

The crises of the summer and autumn of 1793 were hardly limited to the clashes caused by the protest against the *coup de force* of 2 June. Since March, the Vendée, born of the refusal to levy 300,000 men, had resisted all republican assaults. As for the coalition armies, they won victories in the east of the country, in Mainz, but also in the north, in Valenciennes and Dunkirk. The Montagnards faced up to this with determination and energy. The new *Constitution* was adopted after only three weeks of debates, on 24 June 1793. It settled the question of 'the forces of the Republic' in eight brief articles which mentioned the existence of the Garde Nationale without ever mentioning it by that name. It was probably a concession to the Cordeliers and the Hebertists. Several of their influential members, such as Bouchotte and Ronsin, held high positions within the Ministry of War and were deeply hostile to an institution which they considered to be irremediably corrupted by Fayettism and Moderatism. Moreover, the tone of the text of the new *Constitution* announced the *levée en masse* of 23 August to deal with the continuing deterioration of the military situation. For all that, the deputies of the Convention had not fully satisfied the sans-culottes. On 4 and 5 September, a new outbreak of fever inflamed the Parisians, whose leaders felt it necessary to obtain the revolutionary measures that were needed by successively invading the Hôtel de Ville and the Convention. On this occasion, Danton proposed that a vote be taken to create a so-called 'Armée Révolutionnaire'. The concept, which testifies to the fear and the

La patrouille révolutionnaire, counter-revolutionary engraving denouncing Ronsin's Armée Révolutionnaire, c. 1794. The Armées Révolutionnaires helped in supplying urban centres. They actively participated in the dechristianisation: they pursued refractory priests and closed churches. Finally, as in Lyon, they became repressive forces. Members of Ronsin's Armée Parisienne served as gendarmes at the trials and stood guard at the guillotine. (Musée Carnavalet)

punitive will of the working classes, had in fact emerged in the previous April to designate the gathering of sans-culottes paid through taxes levied on the rich and the malevolent. On 2 June, the Convention had indeed voted for the principle, but it had been careful not to ensure its realisation. The Armée Révolutionnaire was thus organised only as from September in Paris: it was to total 7,200 men, including 1,200 gunners taken by rotation from the armed sections. The Committee of Public Safety, dominated by Robespierre, would have liked that the command be entrusted to Hanriot. It nevertheless had to bow to the will of the Cordeliers and accept the nomination of Ronsin, a hobby general. The Armée Révolutionnaire played a significant role in the Paris area: it was responsible for ensuring the supply of the capital, which was essential for the safeguarding of order, by carrying out requisitions and protecting the arrival of grain. It also took part in the process of dechristianisation, which led to a profound change in the way people lived. In the departments, armées révolutionnaires appeared at the beginning of the autumn under the dual influence of *représentants en mission* and popular societies. They sometimes resembled private clans, or even bands of criminals. That of Crémieu, in Isère, numbered only 32 men, that of the Lot, nearly 3,200. In all, the 56 Armées, very different in the extent of their theatres of operation, brought together around 30,000 men. The liquidation of these formations was carried out in two stages. The decree of 4 December 1793 abolished the departmental and communal Armées and left only the Parisian Armée Révolutionnaire. This Armée, which had become a prime target for the moderates, enjoyed government support for some time, before the crisis of March 1794 finally dismantled it. Accused of having participated in a so-called conspiracy, its leaders, such as Ronsin and Mazuel, were guillotined alongside the Hebertists on 24 March. Three days later, the Armée Révolutionnaire, deemed 'vicious, dangerous and contrary to equality',[10] was definitively dismissed. Thus disappeared an outgrowth of the Garde Nationale, which had taken the motives and ideals of 1789 to its extremes.

The Garde in Limbo

From the summer of 1793 to the first months of the summer of 1794, the Garde Nationale was thus in limbo. In many departments, it had been compromised during the 'federalist crisis'. In the eyes of the Cordeliers and the Hebertists, it was necessary to replace it by Armées Révolutionnaires made up of authentic sans-culottes against the enemies of the interior and to have recourse to the *levée en masse* in the event of threatening attacks on the borders. However, it was felt at the Committee of Public Safety that the effectiveness of such military radicalism needed to be verified. On the other hand, the Garde Nationale remained useful for the military training of citizens.

---

10 *Journal des Débats et des Décrets*, 554 (1794), p.117.

THE GARDE NATIONALE 1789–1815

Above: *A Scene at St Pierre, Martinique, 1794*, original unsigned watercolour caricature. This watercolour evokes the surrender of Martinique, at the end of March 1794: a plenipotentiary brings the British ultimatum to a paunchy French officer, perhaps *Général de division* Rochambeau. In the background are infantrymen, most likely gardes nationaux. All of them are wearing the round hat and the red lapel coat typical of insular uniforms. (Anne S.K. Brown Military Collection)

Left: The son of servants, François Henriot became a *chef de bataillon* in the faubourg Saint-Marcel in 1792. Elected head of the Garde Nationale Parisienne on 1 July 1793, he gradually asserted himself in his functions. He avoided dramatizing the clashes that occurred in front of the shops because of lack of supplies or rising prices. Similarly, he was able to maintain a flexible but rigorous discipline within the Garde. (Musée Carnavalet)

THE GARDE IN THE REPUBLICAN ERA

Obligation de porter la cocarde tricolore/Arrestation d'un suspect, Lesueur gouaches, circa 1795. These two scenes, certainly drawn after 9 Thermidor, involve some members of Parisian armed sections. They portray the abuses of power these men may have been guilty of. Lesueur contrasts elegantly dressed, powdered-haired 'suspects' with the menacingly gesticulating sans-culottes. (Musée Carnavalet)

In the weeks following the *coup de force* of 2 June, the Montagnards sought to curb the popular momentum and maintain control of the armed force in Paris. They failed to get Raffet, a veteran of the American War of Independence and at the time commander of the moderate section of the Butte-des-Moulins, elected. The election resulted in an unprecedented turnout in the sectional assemblies. The results, proclaimed on 1 July, announced 15,354 voters. Hanriot received 59.3 percent of the votes. Raffet's score (39.7 percent) was proof that the mobilisation of both parties had been successful. The percentage of participants exceeded 10 percent, as in the election of the mayor of Paris. Hanriot was therefore confirmed in the position he had held since the end of May.

In the autumn, the Garde Nationale Parisienne proved to be unreliable in the political context of the moment. In the moderate sections, which were predominantly bourgeois, a certain distrust towards Hanriot prevailed. The manoeuvre of 2 June – that of mobilising the moderate battalions in order to better neutralise them – had not been forgotten, so the moderate sections were cautious before obeying the orders of the *Commandant en Chef*. In the democratic sections, the ranks of the Garde were largely filled with activists under the influence of the Hebertists or the Cordeliers. In fact, the Committee of Public Safety set out to regain control of the various battalions. Such an objective implied a patient and thorough work to influence the elections of the officers and to modify the composition of the surveillance committees of the various sections. It was also a question of bringing out new men and intimidating the personalities already in place when they opposed Robespierre. The task proved delicate, especially as Hanriot had neither the charisma of La Fayette nor of Santerre. He had the profile of a conscientious executor, able to avoid major conflicts and to manage with a certain skill the daily running of the Garde, which he associated with the regime's celebrations. In short, he developed a strategy of infiltration and sedation: the Garde Nationale Parisienne was mainly used for the daily routine of mounting

THE GARDE NATIONALE 1789–1815

Lesueur depicts a revolutionary celebration. In the foreground are elegantly dressed bourgeois guardsmen. The urban masses are more discreetly shown in the background. The citizen who has the honour of carrying the banner is likely to be a member of the Jacobin Club. From 1792 to 1794, the association between the bourgeoisie and the people was a reality: this allowed the advent, admittedly short-lived, of a radical Revolution. (Musée Carnavalet)

guards and providing escorts. On 12 March 1794, the arrest of the Hebertist leaders indeed provoked astonishment and disbelief within the sections. However, there was no revolutionary *journée* to obtain their release. Their execution on the 24th did not even lead to the beginning of a real protest, meaning that the strategy of infiltration was successful. It had certainly helped to break some of the strings of the sectional movement.

In the departments, the period was marked by a clear decline of the Garde. In the rural communes, the successive levies of men contributed to the regular drop in numbers. In Saint-Laurent de Chamousset, a small commune in the Rhône temporarily renamed Chalier-la-Montagne, a report stated that the officers of the Garde Nationale had become too numerous in relation to the number of fusiliers. The notables frequently withdrew from a command that no longer brought them much prestige. Absences and breaches of duty became more and more frequent, despite the maintenance of regulations. A report drawn up in Chalier-la-Montagne on 5 February 1794 (17 Pluviôse Year II) noted:

The departure of young men between the ages of 18 and 25 brings about a great change in the companies of the Garde Nationale. It would be useful to exercise the citizens regularly, on every decadal day. This would be a way of keeping them busy on that day, of preventing the effect of idleness and of maintaining republican ardour, because without exercise the men of the company will never have much ardour. It would be necessary to do two things: to have pikes made and to allow the commune to choose an ex-serviceman and to provide him with a salary.[11]

In the territories of western France confronted with the Chouannerie – a continuous threat to the partisans of the Republic – and devastated by the civil war, the gardes nationaux had initially to bear the brunt of the insurrection which they had struggled to curb. The army played a growing role, but did not completely supplant them. Sometimes organised as permanent troops, the gardes nationaux were responsible for guarding the forts, protecting public buildings and the trees of liberty, as well as convoys and the proceeds of requisitions. In addition, manhunts made it possible to recover barrels of grain and weapons and to kill 'brigands'. The gardes nationaux had to maintain liaison with the neighbouring towns, whose military garrisons would appear when the Chouans were busy attacking the patriots in a village. As for the anti-revolutionary commitment, it took a form very similar to the recruitment of the Garde Nationale. The parish chiefs were elected by their men, who followed their tactical decisions but imposed on them the duration and conditions of their mobilisation. In other words, the rural gardes nationales and the Chouannerie obeyed the same mobilisation rituals and operating constraints.

Born in 1751, Pierre-Aimé Joseph Martin, seigneur de l'Eclusette, served in Louis XVI's army before being appointed *capitaine* in the Garde Nationale at the beginning of the Revolution. Martin was sentenced to death for his correspondence with *émigrés* and guillotined in Cambrai in 1794. (François Vinot-Préfontaine's collection)

9 Thermidor: Three Commanders, one Garde

The months of April to June 1794 were marked by the consolidation of Robespierre's power, as well as that of the two major Committees. In addition, measures of a dictatorial kind were implemented, such as the law of 10 June, which further simplified the procedure of the Revolutionary Tribunal and nullified legal safeguards. At the same time, the French armies were pushing back the Prussians on the Rhine, the Piedmontese in the Alps, and the Spaniards in the Roussillon. When, on 26 June, the victory of Fleurus once again opened Belgium to French troops and legitimised the full powers of the revolutionary government, Robespierre could believe that he was

---

11   Archives Municipales de Saint-Laurent de Chamousset (AMSLC): Registre des délibérations du conseil municipal, an II–an III.

definitively in control. However, he still had to eliminate those who, within the Committees, were increasingly unhappy with his authoritarianism, as well as the 20 or so *représentants en mission* who had been recalled for misappropriation and abuse of authority. Less powerful than the members of the Committees, they knew that they were threatened by the next expeditious batches to the guillotine authorised by the law of 'Great Terror'. They succeeded in federating their fears with the pent-up hatred of many other deputies to overthrow Robespierre. In this context, controlling the Garde Nationale Parisienne became a vital issue.

On the morning of 27 July (9 Thermidor), as Robespierre prepared to unmask what he saw as the traitors at the Convention, the first decision of the Committee of Public Safety was to abolish the office of *commandant en chef* of the Garde Nationale. Hanriot was impeached and each legion commander would exercise command successively for 24 hours. Such a measure effectively put the conduct of possible military operations in the hands of the Committee of Public Safety. Hanriot was put under arrest at about 12:30 a.m. on Tallien's proposal, only a few minutes before Robespierre, and was finally apprehended at about 5:00 p.m. Two other *commandants en chef* – Fauconnier and Guiot, a soldier since 1759, a member of the 'Victors of Bastille' unit and a specialist of the *journées* – were appointed by one side or the other in the time leading up to his release at around 8:00 p.m. This testified to the obsessive importance of this local command to secure political and military control over Paris. While Hanriot returned to the Hôtel de Ville to dither over the conduct of operations, the Convention decreed him as an outlaw, which meant his death after confirmation of his identity. At the same time, it entrusted the general command of the Garde Nationale to Barras: the revolutionary *journée* of 9 Thermidor ended with the substitution of a deputy, who was also a former military officer, for the general commander provided for by law and chosen from amongst the legion commanders.

Throughout the day, the action of the Garde Nationale Parisienne proved to be most confused. At about 3:00 p.m., the Commune, remaining faithful to Robespierre, decided to sound the *tocsin* in the sections. The closest ones, namely those of the Temple, the Arcis, the Lombards and the Homme Armé, responded at once and their gardes nationaux assembled. Then Fleuriot-Lescot, the mayor of Paris, and Hanriot instructed the six legion commanders to close the gates of Paris, to send 400 men each to the Place de Grève and to come to the Hôtel de Ville to take orders from the Commune. Hanriot also ordered the gunners – some of whom had been removed from Paris under the pretext of national defence – to gather in the same Place with all the available cannon. It was too late. By 5:00 p.m. the 32 battalions of the four legions located in a large western half of the capital were hardly obeying the Commune's orders. In fact, two thirds of the gardes nationaux of Paris were thus removed from its authority. A few hours later, around 8:30 p.m., the balance of power was very different. While Hanriot and Robespierre had just been released, the Commune seemed likely to win. On the other hand, the defenders of the Convention, armed with a decree outlawing Hanriot and Fleuriot-Lescot,

THE GARDE IN THE REPUBLICAN ERA

This print, drawn by Monnet and engraved by Helman, depicts the night attack against Robespierre and his supporters gathered at the Hôtel de Ville on 28 July 1794. From a uniformological point of view, the gardes nationaux are particularly well dressed and equipped. One also notes a flag with vertical stripes in the left corner of the engraving. (Musée Carnavalet)

managed to neutralise the dubious sections. After sometimes violent verbal confrontations and a few clashes, 38 sections declared themselves in favour of the Convention. Only one, that of the Observatoire, clearly declared itself in favour of the Commune, while nine abstained from any meeting. Barras transmitted to all the commanders of section the order to defend the Tuileries, with half of their men accompanied by a gun. The other half was to remain in the sections as a reserve. At about 9:00 p.m., the detachments began to pour into the Place du Carrousel and two hours later, most of the sections had rallied the Convention. Those who had sent detachments to the Hôtel de Ville were trying to recover them. After midnight, the Commune, outlawed by the Convention, lost its support. Citizens were now afraid to oppose the Convention as the new and sole representative of the law. Towards 1:00 a.m. on 28 July, only 500 or 600 men mainly from the Finistère section remained in the Place de Grève, as well as the gunners of the Lombards, Popincourt and Quinze-Vingts sections. At 2:00 a.m., the men of the Convention invested the Hôtel de Ville to seize the insurgents. Robespierre was shot in the jaw with a pistol – it probably will never be known whether he tried to kill himself or whether the gendarme Merda was actually the one who fired the shot – and Le Bas committed suicide. Younger brother Augustin Robespierre and Couthon tried to imitate him. Since all these men were outlaws, the abbreviated procedure enabled Robespierre and 21 of his supporters, including Hanriot, to be guillotined at the Place de la Révolution at 6:00 p.m. The Garde Nationale Parisienne provided the orderly service at the execution.

The Garde Nationale of the Thermidorians

On 9 Thermidor, the armed sections saved the Convention in extremis. It was now necessary to prevent the latter from remaining at the mercy of an armed force which it did not control. A heterogeneous coalition bringing together a majority of moderates and a minority of former *représentants en mission*, the Thermidorians were concerned from the outset to take control of the Garde Nationale Parisienne in order to make it an effective protection force for the Convention. As early as 9 Thermidor, a decree had given it its name back and its former organisation into legions and battalions. Ten days later, another decree went even further in the sense of prudence, since it abolished the *commandant en chef* – it was essential to avoid the emergence of a new Hanriot – as well as the legion commanders. They were replaced by a staff of five section commanders who would lead the Garde Nationale of the capital for five days, under the authority of the oldest of them.

At the beginning of 1795, a freezing winter swept through the capital. It was all the more unbearable because of the lack of wood for the poorest of its inhabitants, who lived mainly in the two large faubourgs of Paris and in most of the city centre. In January and February, food prices skyrocketed, while bread rations provided by the authorities were drastically reduced. People were literally dying of misery and cold. Anger roared in the patriotic sections. People were indignant at the arrogance of the Muscadins, these bourgeois members of the gilded youth. On 12 March, an anonymous poster unambiguously called for insurrection. 'People, wake up, now is the time!', it proclaimed from the outset.[12] It caused a sensation and led to gatherings in the faubourgs Saint-Antoine and Saint-Marcel. On the 17th, a deputation of the faubourgs' inhabitants went to the Convention with threats. It demanded bread, the reopening of the popular societies and the application of the *Constitution of 1793*. In this electric context, the Committee of Public Safety had 400 muskets distributed to each of the 12 surveillance committees, which had succeeded the 48 revolutionary committees of the sections. These firearms, 100 per section, were to be entrusted by the battalion commanders to citizens worthy of receiving them. It was a disguised means of recreating, within each battalion of the Garde Nationale, the old compagnies du centre, prepared to intervene against possible disorders and compel the most subversive elements of the sections.

The insurgents took action at dawn of 1 April without any insurrectionary committee being organised. The slogans had circulated from one section to another, with no real overall plan. At about 11:00 a.m., a great mass of men and women flocked in great disorder to the surroundings of the Convention. Only a minority of the rioters were armed with muskets and no organised Garde Nationale unit had made the move. The young Muscadins, on whom many deputies were counting to protect the Convention, were nevertheless pushed around and, at around 1:00 p.m., the crowd burst into the session room. It remained there for about four hours, in a permanent tumult, and limited itself to exposing its wishes: the effective application of the *Constitution*

---

12   Loris Chavanette, *Quatre-vingt-quinze: La Terreur en procès* (Paris: CNRS Editions, 2017), p.182.

of 1793, concrete measures against the famine and the suppression of the bands of Muscadins. Meanwhile, the Committees organised their response. The Committee of General Security thus ordered the commanders of the Garde Nationale to mobilise the battalions of the 48 sections. The loyalist battalions, notably from the Mont-Blanc, Réunion, Champs-Élysées, Faubourg-Montmartre, Piques, Lepeletier and Butte-des-Moulins sections, began marching at around 5:00 p.m. to mass around the Convention. They were strong enough to clear it out without firing a single shot. The insurgents achieved nothing but did not insist as the balance of power was leaning significantly against them. In the evening and the following night, certain sections deliberated on whether to continue demonstrating, but nothing was decided. On the proposal of Barras, the Convention declared Paris to be in a state of siege. In the meantime, *Général de division* Pichegru, who had just distinguished himself in the Netherlands, was appointed military commander of the capital. It fell to him, from 2 April, to disperse the discontents.

In the weeks that followed, the Committees endeavoured to regain control of all the battalions of the Garde Parisienne. To do this, the same recipes as those of La Fayette were used. On 10 April, a decree ordered the disarmament of sectionnaires considered to be 'terrorists', who in fact found themselves excluded from the ranks of the Garde Nationale. In reality, this only affected a small number of individuals, perhaps 1,600 for all the sections. It therefore targeted the most compromised militants, more because of their apparent behaviour than their actual responsibilities. A decree of 17 April reorganised the Garde. Each of the 48 battalions had 10 companies: one of vanguard pikemen, one of rearguard pikemen and eight companies of fusiliers. The grenadier and chasseur companies were re-established, though they were not officially called as such. They had to dress, equip and arm themselves at their own expense. Such a prescription also applied to the cavalry, which numbered 2,400 men divided into three brigades with four squadrons. Each section had a company of gunners with two artillery pieces. The sans-culottes protested against this return to the past and denounced the reconstitution of 'the former army of La Fayette'.[13] In truth, only a few sections began recruiting elite companies.

Table 10. Organisation of Paris Garde Nationale infantry and artillery companies, Law of 28 Germinal Year III

	Fusiliers (8)	Pikemen (2)	Gunners (1)
Capitaine	1	1	1
Lieutenant	1	2	2
Sous-lieutenant	2	–	–
Sergents	4	2	2
Caporaux	8	4	4
Tambour	2	2	1
Hommes du rang	64	40	40
Total	82	51	50

---

13   Alphonse Aulard, *Paris pendant la réaction thermidorienne et sous le Directoire* (Paris: Cerf et Noblet, 1898), vol.I, p.676.

Table 11. Organisation of Paris Garde Nationale cavalry, Law of 28 Germinal Year III

Capitaine	1
Lieutenant	1
Sous-lieutenant	2
Maréchal-des-logis	2
Brigadier	4
Cavalier	89
Trompette	2
Total	101

The Garde Nationale Parisienne was not ready when, in May, unrest flared up again. Indeed, the food crisis was getting worse: the price of potatoes, for example, increased fivefold. Gatherings in front of bakeries were commonplace and posters demanding free distribution of the most necessary foodstuffs multiplied. The capital seemed, once again in the space of a few weeks, to be on the verge of an insurrectionary explosion. On 20 May, a pamphlet entitled *Insurrection du peuple pour obtenir du pain et reconquérir ses droits* (Insurrection of the people to obtain bread and regain their rights) gave the signal for the insurrection, which lasted two days. The first was marked by a disorderly and tumultuous occupation of the Convention and the assassination of Deputy Féraud. This gave the Committees time to organise their response and mobilise the moderate battalions. Finally, towards 10:00 p.m., the latter abruptly burst into the session room. The insurgents first feigned resistance, with an ensuing stampede little opposed by the loyalist forces.

However, during the night of the 20th to the 21st, turmoil continued to stir many sections: the *generale* was for example drummed in the middle of the night in the section of the Quinze-Vingts, while, at about 8:00 a.m., the *tocsin* resounded in the faubourg Antoine. As for the Committees, they ordered all the battalions to take up arms and protect the Convention. It was a question of preventing the insurrection by obliging the gardes to put themselves under the orders of their loyalist staff. Such recommendations made historian Georges Carrot write that, on 21 May, gardes from the moderate sections of western Paris faced each other with others from the more popular sections of the centre and east of the city.[14] In fact, many battalions converged on the Convention without letting their true intentions be known beforehand. Moreover, most of the units were ideologically divided, so that their members chose their side at the last moment, depending on the fluctuations in the balance of power. By 10:00 a.m., 24 battalions, or nearly 20,000 men, were occupying the area around the Tuileries. The most moderate had been placed in the immediate vicinity of the Convention, while the least reliable were relegated to the periphery. However, in the early afternoon, the three battalions of the faubourg Antoine challenged the position they had been assigned to and then marched on the Convention, pushing aside the battalions that tried to stop them. At about 3:00 p.m., they

---

14   Carrot, *La Garde nationale*, p.151.

THE GARDE IN THE REPUBLICAN ERA

Attaque du Faubourg St Antoine, le 4 Prairial An 3e de la République, print by Pierre-Gabriel Berthaut after a drawing by Abraham Girardet. The artist shows the disarmament of the faubourg Antoine, on 22 May 1795. This engraving perfectly captures the tension between loyalists and rebels. (Musée Carnavalet)

positioned themselves, with their cannon, in front of the Convention and the battalions that were protecting it. In a climate of heightened tension, loyalists and insurgents faced each other, while seeking to rally some of the opposing camp. Four hours later, other companies of gunners joined the insurgents. The balance of power had now shifted significantly in their favour. After considering confrontation, the Committees decided to play the fraternisation card. They were right to do so, because at around 10:00 p.m. the protesting battalions, confident that their grievances would indeed be taken into account, ended up joining their respective sections.

This second day of the insurrection had been a critical one for the Convention and the Committees. The defection of both the Gendarmerie and the gunners had put them in great danger. On the night of 21–22 May 1795, the Committees decided to convene all the 'good citizens' of Paris, to whom muskets were distributed. More than 20,000 men were thus mobilised. They were no longer to protect the Tuileries but to control certain sensitive points of the capital and to constitute a reserve in case of threatening gatherings. Above all, they were tasked to carry out a disarmament operation which took up the whole day of 22 May. In the morning, an operation targeted the home of Santerre, the former commander of the Garde Nationale. Simultaneously, the Convention demanded the surrender of the faubourg Antoine, along with the restitution of all the cannon. Once that news reached the faubourg's inhabitants, the streets were immediately covered with barricades. The Convention's informers indicated that the faubourg's three battalions of gardes nationaux intended to resist. As the hours passed, however, their fighting spirit waned, especially when they realised that no reinforcements from neighbouring sections were coming in. Five columns criss-crossed the faubourg at around 4:00 p.m. Involving several thousand gardes nationaux alongside the line troops led by *Général de division* Menou, the operation resulted in the handover of cannons belonging to the Popincourt, Quinze-Vingts and Montreuil sections. At 9:00 p.m. the operation was over: pikes and a few dozen muskets still in the hands of the ex-insurgents were collected as well. On 24 May, three other protesting sections, those of the Gravilliers, the Cité and the Panthéon, were also forced to surrender their guns. Shortly afterwards, the 42 other Parisian sections, now controlled by moderates, voluntarily gave up their artillery. 'Bad citizens' and 'terrorists' were also disarmed. In addition to this sectional purge, a military purge was carried out on the insurgents arrested on account of their actions or responsibilities during the first three days of the month of May. Among the nearly 3,000 individuals arrested, 136 were judged almost immediately. Seventy-three were condemned, of which 36 to death, 12 to deportation, seven to irons and 18 to a prison sentence. Among the condemned to death were six Montagnard deputies, 19 gendarmes accused of having rallied the insurgents, and four officers of the Garde Nationale for having pushed their men to the insurrection or for having read, within the Convention, the manifesto of the Prairial *journées*.

On 25 May, the Convention hastened to abolish the gunners. The gendarmes were also disbanded, but some of their men were taken over by the Légion de Police Générale, a municipal force of 7,000 men created on 27 June. On 29 May, under the pretext of 'coming to the aid of useful citizens', artisans, day labourers and less well-off labourers were completely exempted from service in the Garde Nationale Parisienne.[15]

Such a counter-revolutionary provision was confirmed by the decree of 16 June, which ordered the reorganisation of the Garde Nationale throughout France. Workers, itinerant workers and factory workers were only accepted in exceptional cases. As for the less fortunate citizens, they were only entered in the registers at their express request. This reorganisation more or less led to the exclusion of the former passive citizens. According to Deputy Baudin, it was necessary to entrust the arms 'only to pure hands' and not to 'distract the virtuous indigents from their work.'[16] Each battalion had 10 companies of 77 men each. The grenadier and chasseur companies were re-established and increased to 100 men by decree on 3 July. The election of officers was carried out each year, no longer within each company, but by all the citizens making up the battalions. Limited to the commune in 1789, to the district in 1791, the organisation was now extended to the department, in the form of a departmental division, eventually placed under the orders of a general officer temporarily appointed by the government.

---

15   Duvergier, *Collection Complète des Lois*, vol.VIII, p.158.
16   *Le Moniteur Universel*, 271 (1795), p.5.

THE GARDE IN THE REPUBLICAN ERA

Uniforms

The law of 14 October 1791 precisely regulated the uniform worn by the Garde Nationale. It simultaneously stated that 'in the countryside, it could not be required'.[17] 'In the summer of 1792, the uniform's regularity became a completely minor problem for the government, which was grappling with much more serious issues', Pierre Carles asserted.[18] In terms of clothing, the French Revolution was marked by two iconic items: the Phrygian cap and the carmagnole. The latter, a simple civilian jacket with shortened tails, sometimes with coloured lapels and cuffs, was a near-uniform for the republican armed sections.

In the summer of 1793, during the siege of Lyon, the city's Garde Nationale retained its uniform. However, contemporary texts stipulated that each soldier was 'free to dress as he deemed appropriate'.[19] The Lyonnais population remained largely attached to republican values. As a result, the troops wore the tricolour cockade. Yet some gardes carefully refrained from wearing it, substituting a white braid, considered, rightly or not, to be the royalists' sign of recognition. In his *Souvenirs de trois années de la Révolution à Lyon*, Jean-Baptiste Nolhac, a garde national himself, recounted that the elite companies were frequently dressed in civilian clothes. The usual uniform included a cotton carmagnole and pantaloons of the same fabric, with a wide belt. Hat pompoms and epaulettes – red for the grenadiers, green for the chasseurs – gave a slightly more military appearance to these troops. Nolhac added that their good appearance nevertheless made them look like line soldiers.[20]

The reform of 17 April 1795 (28 Germinal Year III) prescribed that the 1st and 8th companies of fusiliers of the Garde Nationale Parisienne had to wear the national uniform. The fusiliers of the 1st company donned red epaulettes, those of the 8th, green ones. The euphemism is noteworthy: it avoids referring

Drawing by Jacques Hilpert representing a wine-coloured carmagnole from the collection of renowned painter Maurice Orange (Colourisation by Jean-Claude Colrat)

17　Anon., *Code de la Garde Nationale*, p.142.
18　Pierre Carles, 'Dandys de la Garde nationale 1790-1792', *Gardes Nationales 1789-1871*, *Carnets de la Sabretache*, 50 (1979), p.136.
19　Georges Guigue (ed.), *Procès-verbaux des séances du conseil général du département de Rhône-et-Loire 1790–1793* (Trévoux: Jules Jeannin Imprimeur, 1895), vol.II, p.412.
20　Jean-Baptiste Nolhac, *Souvenirs de trois années de la Révolution à Lyon* (Lyon: L. Perrin, 1844), p.228.

THE GARDE NATIONALE 1789–1815

to the elite companies of grenadiers and chasseurs which were dissolved on 20 September 1793. The cavalrymen wore a yellow waistcoat and breeches, as well as a tricolour aiguillette. The law of 16 June 1795 (28 Prairial Year III), which reorganised the Garde Nationale in the departments, stipulated that the drummers should have tricolour epaulettes.

PLATE SECTION 2

Paris bourgeois militiaman, 13–14 July 1789. This figure is reconstructed using various period paintings and engravings. He wears a blue and red cockade to distinguish him from the protesters he was policing. (Original artwork by Patrice Courcelle Courcelle © Helion and Company 2022)

THE GARDE NATIONALE 1789–1815

General en Chef La Fayette and his aides de camp, 1790–1791. In the foreground, stands La Fayette, after a Lesueur gouache. Note the stapled lapels and the regulation tricolour plume. In the left background, one of his aides-de-camp, also from a Lesueur gouache. In the right background, another aide-de-camp, recognisable by his light blue and white plume, from a period portrait. La Fayette's aides-de-camp had no official distinguishing feature. The blue and white plume, as seen in Thévenin's *Fête de la Fédération*, must have been a makeshift one. (Original artwork by Patrice Courcelle)

PLATE SECTION 2

The Garde Nationale was a bourgeois guard that did not admit it. The men drawn by Patrice Courcelle are of good status and equal. The recruit wears the habit like his NCO, whereas in the army, the ordinary soldier exercised wearing a waistcoat. They move forward shoulder to shoulder and one feels the elegant and patient instruction. (Original artwork by Patrice Courcelle)

251

THE GARDE NATIONALE 1789–1815

From the beginning of the summer of 1790, Puteaux Garde Nationale had a flag. It was burnt in March 1793, but a description from three years earlier has enabled a reconstruction. In 1790, the flag was carried by *Sous-Lieutenant* Ponthaux. From the summer of 1790 onwards, it is likely that Puteaux's Garde Nationale members wore the blue uniform with scarlet cuffs and white collar
(Original artwork by Patrice Courcelle Courcelle © Helion and Company 2022)

PLATE SECTION 2

Parisian Garde Nationale veteran, circa 1790–1791, after a Lesueur's gouache. Note the white epaulettes and the medallion of *vétérance* on his chest. The coat has stapled scarlet lapels, a common feature in Lesueur's gouache series. (Original artwork by Patrice Courcelle)

253

THE GARDE NATIONALE 1789–1815

Pikeman of the Garde Nationale Parisienne, after a Lesueur gouache. This figure ostentatiously displays his revolutionary convictions. In some Garde Nationale units with radical beliefs, it was in good taste to shorten one's garb to resemble a proletarian outfit. The characteristic silhouette of the Samaritan pump can be seen in the background. (Original artwork by Patrice Courcelle)

PLATE SECTION 2

1791–1792 Volontaires Nationaux, front and rear view. They are wearing the 'national uniform' of the gardes nationaux which they belonged to. (Original artwork by Patrice Courcelle)

THE GARDE NATIONALE 1789–1815

When the siege of Lyon occurred in the summer of 1793, young Louis-Sébastien Rosaz (1777–1849) was only 16 years old. Yet he joined the chasseurs of the Bataillon de la Croisette. It is likely that, like many of the soldiers of the Armée Départementale de Rhône-et-Loire, he was dressed in civilian clothes. Only his epaulettes and hat pompom indicate that he was a chasseur. (Original artwork by Patrice Courcelle Courcelle © Helion and Company 2022)

PLATE SECTION 2

Armand Gentil, officer of the Paris mounted Garde Nationale, circa 1797–1799. This figure is drawn from a period miniature portrait. The coat is identical to the foot units, except for the aiguillette on the left shoulder. The headdress, a dragoon helmet, is specific to this troop. (Original artwork by Patrice Courcelle Courcelle © Helion and Company 2022)

THE GARDE NATIONALE 1789–1815

Garde National of the Garde Impériale, 1810. He could be Joseph Leplat, born on 20 April 1789 in Tourcoing, in the Nord department. This weaver joined the unit on 1 April 1810 and was integrated into the 1st Company of the 1st Battalion. However, he was discharged as early as 6 September 1811. (Original artwork by Patrice Courcelle Courcelle © Helion and Company 2022)

PLATE SECTION 2

Born in 1789 in La Ferté-Loupière, Yonne, Jean Moisson was a conscript of 1809. On 19 April 1812, this young carpenter joined the ranks of the 1st Company of the 1st Battalion of the 58e Garde Nationale Cohorte under number 48. In 1813, the 58e Cohorte was used to form 153e de Ligne. Jean took part in the campaigns of 1813–1814. Discharged on 4 August 1814, he married in 1816. (Original artwork by Patrice Courcelle Courcelle © Helion and Company 2022)

259

THE GARDE NATIONALE 1789–1815

Artist Patrice Courcelle based his artwork on a portrait of merchant and art collector Philippe-Balthazar Lenoir (1785–1867), painted by his friend Horace Vernet in 1814. In the background is a grenadier wearing a bearskin. (Original artwork by Patrice Courcelle – Private collection, USA)

PLATE SECTION 2

In January 1814, Napoleon appeared at a parade at the Tuileries Palace wearing a Garde Nationale colonel's uniform. The Emperor is mounted on his battle horse Nero. Napoleon's coat turns out to be of regulation cut and colour for the officers, namely long tails with silver buttons, embroidery and colonel's epaulettes associated with the Garde Nationale. The Emperor's uniform is still distinguished by the absence of regulation white piping on the collar. (Original artwork by Patrice Courcelle)

THE GARDE NATIONALE 1789–1815

Napoleon's Garde Nationale coat. (Original artwork by Patrice Courcelle)

8

The Decline of the Garde?

Summer 1795–Autumn 1799

Immediately after the Prairial riots, the Convention entrusted a Commission of Eleven, involving moderate republicans and constitutional royalists, with the task of drawing up a new *Constitution*, known as the *Constitution of Year III*. It was to replace the one sought by Robespierre and his supporters in June 1793, which the insurgents of Germinal and Prairial had demanded – albeit in vain – be applied. The new constitutional text was completed on 23 June and finally adopted on 22 August 1795. It was preceded by a *Declaration* enumerating not only the rights but also the duties of citizens. The right to resist oppression, which had been solemnly proclaimed by the two previous *Constitutions*, disappeared. Nor was there any mention of the duty of insurrection, which the sans-culottes considered to be the primary manifestation of popular sovereignty.

Contrary to the *Constitution of 1793*, which did not even mention it, the Garde Nationale was discussed at length in the 22 articles (articles 274 to 295) of title 9 of the new *Constitution*, soberly entitled 'Of the armed force'.[1] By synthesising the experiments conducted since the beginning of the French Revolution, this legislative text made the Garde Nationale the only legal public force. This armed force was 'instituted to defend the State against external enemies, and to ensure the maintenance of order and the execution of the laws within'. The text distinguished a sedentary Garde Nationale and an active Garde Nationale. If one sticks to the legislative provisions, the Garde Nationale was therefore everywhere.

Article 277 specified that 'the sedentary Garde Nationale was composed of all citizens paying a contribution and the sons of citizens in a condition to bear arms'. It corresponded not only to a military reserve from which the army could draw, but also to a non-professional police force, unlike the Gendarmerie. The next seven articles specified that its organisation was similar throughout the territory of the Republic and that no Frenchman

---

[1] Anon., *Constitution de la République française du 5 Fructidor an III* (Paris: Garnery Libraire, 1798), p.60.

THE GARDE NATIONALE 1789–1815

This engraving by Grasset Saint-Sauveur shows a grenadier of the Garde du Corps Législatif, a tiny unit tasked with protecting the two Assemblies of the directorial Republic, and a garde nationale. At the beginning of the Directory, the surviving Girondin deputies, reviving their 1792 ideas, planned for a while to have the Corps Législatif guarded by 1,500 gardes nationaux from the departments. (Author's collection)

could exercise the rights of a citizen 'unless he was registered with the garde nationale'. The links between citizenship and the carrying of arms were in fact explicitly underlined. The *Constitution* also stated that Garde Nationale officers were elected for a fixed time span and could only be re-elected after an interval. A citizen could not command the Garde Nationale of a department except on a temporary basis under the authority of the Executive Directory. The same applied to the command of the Garde Nationale of a town with more than 100,000 inhabitants. The constitutional text also recalled that the armed force intervening for the 'internal service of the Republic' could only act on a written order of the civil authorities concerned, either local or departmental, or under the authority of the Executive Directory, depending on the importance of the necessary interventions.

Article 292 set limits on the deployment of the armed force, which had to respect the administrative constituency: 'The public force can only be requested by the civil authorities within their territory. It cannot be moved from a canton to another, without being authorised by the administration of the department, nor from one department to another, without the orders of the Executive Directory'. This territorialisation of policing caused permanent problems for the civil and military authorities. Article 294 sought to regulate the deployment of armed forces in response to a mob whose size exceeded the means of the local public force: 'In the event of imminent danger, the municipal administration of a canton may request the Garde Nationale of neighbouring cantons. In this case, the administration which made the request, and the chiefs of the gardes nationaux which have been requested, are also obliged to report at the same time to the departmental administration'. This was a procedure that was as complex as it was slow, and certainly insufficient in practice. Finally, the *Constitution* stated that the public force was in essence obedient and could not deliberate under any circumstances. The modalities of the right of petition, the subject of several articles of the *Constitution*, clearly proclaimed that collective and armed protests in sectional assemblies or within popular societies were no longer an option.

13 Vendémiaire: Army versus Garde Nationale

However, such principles were challenged even before the new institutions of the Directorial Republic had time to take hold. In fact, the summer of 1795 had hardly been favourable to the Thermidorian deputies, who knew that they were less and less popular. How could it be otherwise? The value of the assignat was plummeting. Announced on 8 June, the death of Louis XVII had caused many monarchists to feel that the option of a constitutional monarchy had been neglected. In July, the mass executions of *émigrés* following their surrender at Quiberon outraged the ultra-royalists. An electoral debacle was inevitably looming. In addition to a first referendum on the acceptance of the *Constitution*, the Convention therefore decided to add a second one to apply, from the first vote, the annual renewal by thirds of future deputies to the two Councils provided for by the *Constitution*. For this first election, only one third of the parliamentary personnel of the Council of Anciens and the Council of Five Hundred would actually be elected. The remainder was provided by Convention members whose term of office would be extended. However, such a measure aroused strong opposition from public opinion, which rightly perceived it as a manoeuvre aimed at perpetuating the mandates of these men, ironically referred to as 'the perpetuals', by one or two years. The results were published on 28 September 1795 (6 Vendemiaire Year IV): the new *Constitution* was accepted by almost a million voters and rejected by just under 50,000. The decrees relating to the renewal of the deputies gathered the approval of 205,000 and were rejected by a little less than 109,000 votes. However, results were completely distorted by the decision of the Convention to count only the ballots which also included official voting results. In Paris, 47 out of 48 sections voted no, but 33 sections had not specified the exact distribution of votes, so the Convention refused to take them into account.

This crude manipulation of the results was unanimously condemned and caused an uproar in the sections. The Convention called for calm in Paris – without much success, needless to say – then threatened to withdraw to Chalons if its security was not assured. On 25 September 1795 (3 Vendémiaire Year IV), the Convention called line troops into the capital. Disregarding the Conventions' decrees and prohibitions, Parisian sections continued to agitate and to vote incendiary motions. The Convention could really only count on one section: that of the Quinze-Vingts, including the famed faubourg Antoine. The faubourg lacked gardes nationaux as a result of the disarmament measures for 'terrorists' enacted at the end of the events of Prairial. On the other hand, the armed Garde Nationale was to be found in the sections hostile to or very wary of the Convention. It was a question of votes and of forces: voting results were a flagrant demonstration that the capital was beyond the control of the central power. Also, on 3 October 1795 (11 Vendémiaire Year IV), the Convention launched an appeal to volunteers by inviting them to join the army, with nearly 1,500 men answering. The next day, they were formed into three battalions of 'Patriotes de 89', combining unarmed citizens, prisoners released from Parisian prisons for the purpose, and also relegated or unemployed officers. They were not in uniform, but received arms and food and, for greater efficiency, were placed under a common command with the line troops. The majority of these 'Patriotes de 89' were still under the repressive laws relating to the disarmament of 'terrorists' or were under house arrest. By forming such units, the Convention was certainly in blatant contradiction with itself, especially since the legality

THE GARDE NATIONALE 1789–1815

Investissement de la section Lepelletier par les troupes de la Convention, ink drawing by Jean-Jacques François Le Barbier. (Musée Carnavalet)

of these 'Patriotes' groupings with a more than sulphurous reputation was highly doubtful. To keep appearances, the Convention immediately repealed the respective laws. This action implied a tacit disavowal of its policy of repression against the 'terrorists' and sounded like a promise of amnesty. As for the sections, they considered the formation of these units as further provocation. The news of the liberation and enrolment of these 1,500 'terrorist Jacobins' spread around the city and even caused a panic: the 'terrorists' had returned and were certainly preparing to take their revenge! Above all, it led to the mobilisation of a growing number of sections. Throughout the day of 12 Vendémiaire, the *generale* was drummed everywhere in Paris and one worried to protect his district against the anguishing return of the 'blood drinkers'.[2] In the evening, accompanied by the *Représentants du Peuple* Delmas, Laporte and Letourneur de la Manche, *Général de division* Menou, sympathetic to the insurgents, had three columns converge on the protester's headquarters, the convent of the Filles-Saint-Thomas (in the Lepeletier section). Laporte ordered Menou to charge the 800 sectionnaires lined up in front of the section's headquarters, but he preferred to parley with the insurgents. His position in the rue Vivienne was actually not the best, especially as armed sectionaires occupied all the windows. In the evening, several sections were emboldened and declared themselves in insurrection. In the early hours of the night, when the drums of the insurgent sections called to arms, Menou only ordered *Capitaine* Thiébault's cavalry to drive them out of certain streets. The Convention finally dismissed Menou a few hours later and appointed Barras to command the troops in Paris. In the meantime, the insurrection was becoming more and more radical, so a confrontation became unavoidable.

---

2   Aulard, *Paris pendant la réaction thermidorienne et sous le Directoire*, vol.I, p.293.

THE DECLINE OF THE GARDE?

Renowned French illustrator Jacques Onfray de Bréville (also known as 'JOB') chose to depict the gunfire in the vicinity of the church of Saint-Roch from the insurgent gardes nationaux' point of view. They had previously tried to regroup on the steps of the edifice before being swept away by the cannon set up by Bonaparte, which can be seen in the background. (Yves Martin)

It took place the next day, 13 Vendémiaire. For the occasion Barras called on the services of seven generals present in the capital, though without worry of their past relations with Robespierre or his representatives. Among them was *Général de brigade* Bonaparte, whom Barras knew from the siege of Toulon. He entrusted the command of the artillery to the Corsican general who sent *Chef d'Escadron* Murat with 200 horses to the camp of Sablons in order to seize the 40 guns gathered there. They arrived at the Tuileries about 6:00 a.m. and were welcomed. At this hour, the Convention had for its defence only the 4,500 infantrymen coming from the camp of Marly joined by the 1,500 'Patriotes de 89'. The opposing forces were numerically almost equal. The insurgents could certainly count on a mass of 30,000 men gathered in the sections, but only 7,000 to 8,000 determined gardes nationaux marched on the Convention. The rest remained under arms in their districts and limited themselves to patrols to defend against a possible *coup de main* by the 'terrorists'.

Barras and his generals transformed the surroundings of the Tuileries into a real entrenched camp. A double series of posts reinforced by cannon placed at strategic points lined the right bank of the Seine, facing the insurgent battalions grouped on the opposite bank. Other posts, entrusted to the 'Patriotes de 89' commanded by Berruyer, controlled the openings of the streets linking the Tuileries to the rue Saint-Honoré, while *Général de brigade* Brune ensured the close defence of the Tuileries, where the Convention and its government Committees were sitting. Between 3:00 and 4:00 p.m., the insurgents deployed to make contact with the Convention troops, particularly in the rue Saint-Honoré. In the belief that the soldiers who were opposed to them would not dare to fire on 'honnêtes gens' (honest people), they had orders to fraternise. Barras had given his troops the sole instruction not to fire first, but to make clear their refusal to fraternise. Such summons were greeted with boos. Shots rang out and, loaded with grapeshot, Bonaparte's cannon mowed down the sectional battalions which had sought to assemble on the steps of the church of Saint-Roch. *Général de division* Carteaux had also used his artillery. On this cold Vendémiaire day, the cannon had undeniably demonstrated its terrible efficiency in street fighting. For two hours the firing went on without interruption, then became sporadic. At nightfall, the soldiers and the 'Patriotes de 89', who had fought bravely, combed the neighbouring districts to disperse the last insurgents.

With fierce fighting in the streets around the Convention, the 13 Vendémiaire was particularly bloody. Historians estimate the losses at 300 dead and wounded on the side of the Convention forces, against 500 to 600 among the insurgent gardes nationaux.[3] It was, after 10 August 1792, the deadliest of the revolutionary *journées*. On this occasion, the army and the 'Patriotes de 89' had given a lesson to the gardes nationaux from the most conservative sections of the capital. They had shown no qualms about opening fire on a few hundred arrogant grenadiers wearing uniforms cut from fine cloths and on young muscadins from the wealthier western districts of the capital. The army had reinstituted one of its Ancien Régime

---

3   Bronislaw Baczko, 'Briser la guillotine: Une amnistie thermidorienne', *Crimes, Histoire et Sociétés*, 2:8 (2004), p.7.

functions: suppressing riots. In the aftermath of 13 Vendémiaire, it occupied Paris militarily. The troops camped in the Tuileries gardens, in the public squares and at the city gates. They patrolled the streets and policed them. The soldiers sometimes behaved as if they were in a conquered city. There was some raiding but, contrary to persistent fears and rumours, no systematic looting. The Garde Nationale Parisienne had, for its part, taken on a factious role with serious repercussions for the institution. Three days after the uprising, a decree definitively abolished the Garde Nationale Parisienne's staff, as well as that of the divisions and sections. The entire hierarchical organisation imagined by La Fayette to protect the constitutional regime and then preserved by Santerre and Hanriot to ensure revolutionary order was now reduced to a juxtaposition of battalions placed under the direct orders of the military command of Paris. The same decree also dismissed the grenadier and chasseur companies, seen as the backbone of the recent sectional uprising, as well as the gunners and cavalry. The epaulettes granted by the law of 28 Germinal to such companies were suppressed. It was forbidden to wear them, under penalty of one month's imprisonment and two years in case of recidivism. The Garde did not put up the slightest resistance to all these measures.

Sent shortly afterwards to the departments with extraordinary powers, the government commissioners tried to demonstrate that the provincial gardes nationaux were just as suspect as their Parisian counterparts. They therefore aimed to extend – more or less legally – the provisions originally applicable to the city of Paris alone to all the gardes nationales of the Republic. In this vein, the *representant* Jacques Reverchon, operating in the Ain department, was informed that 'the white ganses worn by the chasseurs of the Garde Nationale Sédentaire of Bourg, the chief town of the Ain department, were the cause of the movements that occurred there' during the month of December 1795 (Frimaire Year IV).[4] Pointing out the need to 'remove any sign of rallying which the malevolence could make use of', and relying on the suppression of the companies of grenadiers and chasseurs in Paris, he decreed that:

> Article 1. The companies of grenadiers and chasseurs of the sedentary Garde Nationale of the Ain department are dismissed.
> Article 2. They will return to the centre companies, where they will be of common service with the citizen-soldiers who compose them.[5]

In Frimaire Year IV, Merlin de Douai validated the decisions of the *representant* Fréron. Fréron had suppressed the companies of grenadiers and chasseurs of the Marseilles Garde Nationale.[6] He indeed suspected them of hosting members of the Compagnies du Soleil, an openly counter-revolutionary organisation.

---

[4] Archives Départementales de l'Ain (ADA): L 114: Registre de délibérations de l'administration centrale, Arrêté du 30 frimaire an IV.
[5] ADA: L 114: Registre de délibérations de l'administration centrale, Arrêté du 30 frimaire an IV.
[6] ANF: AF/III/32: Rapport au Directoire exécutif sur les opérations du commissaire du gouvernement dans le département des Bouches-du-Rhône, 12 frimaire an IV.

THE GARDE NATIONALE 1789–1815

The Gardes Nationaux, Instruments of the 'White Terror'?

In the weeks immediately following the installation of the Directory, the Ministry of the Interior sent a circular to the administrators of the Republic on 13 November 1795 (22 Brumaire Year IV). Included in a general survey on the current state of France, it asked them whether the Garde Nationale had been set up in their respective departments. The replies received from all over the country were most discouraging for a regime burdened by public order problems. The vast majority of them revealed that the Garde Nationale was more or less a lifeless corpse. It was unorganised or poorly structured, lacking food or equipment, and neglected in service. This situation was hardly new. In many places it dated back to the creation of the Garde Nationale in the early years of the Revolution. Nevertheless, the extent of the disorder that now plagued the country, exacerbated by the shortage of troops available to maintain order, made the reorganisation of the Garde Nationale an unavoidable priority. This problem seemed particularly acute in south-eastern France, from the Rhône to Provence. Acts of violence of a frequency and savagery rarely encountered elsewhere in the country had been raging there since the spring of 1795. Long grouped under the ambiguous term 'White Terror', they were, in light of the latest

Massacres dans le Fort Saint-Jean Marseille, le 1er Prairial An 3e de La République, engraving by Berthault. Since Robespierre's fall, Jacobins had been imprisoned in Fort Saint-Jean. They were insulted and promised certain death. On 5 June 1795, some 30 armed men began to massacre them. When the municipal authorities arrived on the scene, they counted 88 dead bodies. The municipality claimed that the prisoners had rebelled and slaughtered each other! (Musée Carnavalet)

advances in historiography, more likely to be perpetrated by so-called 'moderate' gardes nationaux – relatives or colleagues of the victims of the surveillance committees and other 'terrorist' entities – than by royalists or other counter-revolutionaries. Historians point to the fact that the murderers, who enjoyed almost total impunity, knew their victims by name and blamed them for the execution of a relative or friend.[7] Moreover, they never uttered royalist slogans or evoked any allegiance to Louis XVIII or the Pope. This was true in L'Isle-sur-la-Sorgue, Montélimar and Avignon, but also further north, in Lyon. On 4 May 1795 (15 Floreal Year III), a vengeful mob surrounded the Roanne prison, forced open the doors and savagely massacred a hundred or so prisoners, all of whom were known or claimed to be 'terrorists'. The Garde Nationale could certainly have intervened, but it hardly did so. It represented a city bruised by a painful siege and then by a ferocious repression and on this occasion communicated with the people of Lyon against the 'Mathevons', a nickname attached to the local sansculottes and to all those who had supported the 'terrorist' regime and the excesses of the repression.

The Mobile Columns

If some communes maintained the gardes nationales, the gardes more often served the factions than they ensured public security. A law of Nivose Year IV aimed to reorganise the institution in depth. The Directory considered it necessary to create, in rural areas, mobile columns within all the sedentary gardes nationaux. According to the decree of 6 May 1796 (17 Floreal Year IV), each canton municipality had to designate, for a six-month service, one out of six gardes nationaux, whether single or married. Gathered in detachments under the leadership of officers elected in advance, these guardsmen formed an auxiliary force which had to be ready to respond to the administration's requests and to carry out localised operations. Such an organisation was supposed to make the Garde Nationale more effective and reactive. It responded to an urgent demand for security – from both administrators and the population – in a country plagued by endemic banditry and high delinquency. The Ministry of Police, which was responsible for maintaining law and order, ensured that the legislative text was effectively applied, as attested by the numerous circulars it sent to the departments.

The Directory wanted above all to have precise and reliable means of intervention outside the army. In truth, the results were mixed and varied greatly from one region to another. In several cantons of Ille-et-Vilaine confronted with the Chouannerie, the mobile columns obtained, with clear understanding of the ground and great mobility, some encouraging albeit ephemeral results. On the other hand, in Provence, the authorities of the department of Vaucluse deplored the fact that the mobile column

---

[7] Dupuy, *La Garde nationale*, p.204.

was useless in the face of the insoluble problem of desertion, all the more so because 'the men who make up the column are the fathers, brothers, friends, relatives, and allies of the requisitioners, and it is to be feared that far from arresting the cowards the armies are demanding, they are encouraging their flight'.[8] In addition, the authorities hoped that the creation of mobile columns would keep the gardes nationaux out of political action. This hope was soon dashed, as the example of Provence testifies. In Aix-en-Provence, the mobile column, chosen by a municipality composed of former Jacobins, was mainly made up of men who had distinguished themselves as members of the sans-culottes battalion in Year II. In Marseilles, an anonymous correspondent told the Ministry of War that the mobile column of the city was composed of a large proportion of men 'with neither morals nor confession'.[9]

The tone was similar further north, in Mâcon, in the department of Saone-et-Loire. On the eve of the elections of Year V, the mobile column which operated in this area was portrayed as 'a detachment of the revolutionary army': 'it is an impure mass of foreigners, denouncers, anarchists, who have found refuge, safety, protection and power there. Some honest citizens, ashamed to be associated with such brothers in arms, have refused service in this column which guards the commune. We fear to encounter its frequent patrols, which are always ready to insult and strike'.[10] Although one must be wary of the distorting prism of partisan judgements, the mobile columns clearly offered no guarantee for public order and the fight against banditry. Worse, they were used as an active tool for rival factions within the Republic. Examples of intimidation, robbery, beatings and even murder committed by the mobile columns in the context of settling scores were commonplace. In a letter to the Ministry of Police, an administrator in Marseilles lucidly confessed that 'as the columns are composed of men who have suffered during the two reactions, most of them often use this means to offend those they believe to be of a different opinion. The mobile column only serves to increase the hatred that many have for the Revolution'.[11]

Taking into account the apparent uselessness of the columns, other arrangements were occasionally proposed. In Morbihan, faced with the recurrent activities of the Chouans, the central commissioner of the department, a man named Gaillard-Latouche, assigned the control of the territory to republican forces. He pleaded tirelessly against the columns and never failed to point out their excesses. He also asked for the cantonment of the troops, even if it meant establishing them in several communes.

---

8   ANF: F/7/7186: Lettre du commissaire du pouvoir exécutif du département du Vaucluse au ministère de la Police générale, 29 messidor an IV.
9   SHD: B13 72: Lettre d''un ami sincère de la République' au ministère de la Guerre, 14 brumaire an VI.
10   ANF: F/1/CIII Saône-et-Loire/8: Mémoire des citoyens de Mâcon à l'appui de leur pétition au Corps Législatif, avril 1797.
11   ANF: AF/III/579: Lettre du commissaire du pouvoir exécutif auprès du bureau central au ministre de la Police Générale, 1er pluviôse an VII.

The Issue of Elite Companies: Much Ado About Nothing

The constitutional royalists – or 'Clichyens' – won the elections in early April 1797 (Germinal Year V). They too were tempted to reorganise the Garde Nationale by abolishing the mobile columns in order to recreate elite companies of grenadiers and chasseurs, whose officers and NCOs would be elected. The discussion around this bill was spread over the months of July and August 1797. The oratorical jousts between the best specialists of the two parties made it possible to draw up an assessment of the eight years of activity of the Garde Nationale.

The confrontation crystallised around the elite companies. Republican deputies suspected the royalists of wanting to make available to local administrations, the majority of which were in favour of their cause, some sort of praetorian guards. The law was finally passed on 12 August 1797 (25 Thermidor V). First of all, article three closed access to the Garde Nationale to French citizens who did not meet the censal tax requirements. The succeeding article nevertheless radically modified such requirements by leaving open the possibility of an enlargement through replacement. Thus, although reserved for active citizens only, the roles of the Garde Nationale could be extended if needed to the entire male population from the age of 18. The legislative text also provided for the creation of cantonal legions and the re-establishment of the staffs suppressed following the insurrection of Vendemiaire Year IV. Article 20 concerned the organisation of the controversial elite companies of chasseurs and grenadiers. Finally, several articles dealt with the creation of national dragoon companies (Dragons Nationaux) with a minimum of 65 cavalrymen. These would serve on foot and on horseback, and would mount and equip themselves at their own expense. If so organised, the Garde Nationale could have ensured the success of a monarchist *coup de force*, especially as it would have been supported by the majority of the deputies of the two Councils. The institution was further strengthened by a law of 13 Fructidor Year V (30 August 1797) specifying its duties and discipline.

Table 12. Dragons Nationaux (Law of 25 Thermidor Year V)

Capitaine	1
Lieutenant	1
Sous-lieutenant	1
Maréchal-des-logis en chef	1
Maréchal-des-logis	4
Brigadier	8
Trompette	1
Dragon	48
Total	65

Unfortunately, such laws were never implemented. The *coup d'état* of 4 September 1797 (18 Fructidor Year V), led by the troops of the Paris Military Division commanded by *Général de division* Augereau, swept away the royalist majority in the Council of Five Hundred and the Council of Anciens. A law voted the day after the *coup de force* hastened to cancel the decisions of the preceding month. New elections of Garde Nationale officers were held in no less than 49 departments. They did not give incumbent officers any chance to stay in office. Finally, a law of 4 Vendémiaire Year V opened widely the ranks of the Garde Nationale: it was ordered to accept in its bosom 'any valid citizen in a state to make his service'.[12]

On the field, however, the republican authorities were aware that a semi-professionalization of the forces of law and order was a necessity. They therefore often defended the elite companies. In the department of Calvados, Commissioner Pierre Lévêque noted in Germinal Year VI that 'the grenadier and chasseur companies kept in the battalions in place of the mobile columns are firm supporters of the public good and animated by a strong *esprit de corps*'. According to him, they offered above all 'the advantage of being able to immediately dispose of an imposing public force to fight against the Chouans'.[13] The fact remains that in operations, the Garde Nationale was permanently confronted with the presence of the Gendarmerie, professional troops whose missions were similar to its own. It was not until the law of 17 April 1798 (28 Germinal Year VI) reorganising the Gendarmerie that the latter's pre-eminence over the Garde Nationale was established.

Conscription and the Eclipse of the Garde Nationale

After the *coup d'état* of Fructidor Year V, the Garde Nationale continued to exist but its decline was inevitable. It was increasingly difficult to fill officer positions. French historian Roger Dupuy notes for instance that during the last three years of the Directory, no one was available to command the armed citizens in several communes of Ille-et-Vilaine.[14] The Garde Nationale of the northern district of Marseilles, which was to be organised in May 1799 (Floreal Year VII), was so short of men that officer and NCO positions stayed vacant. In addition, political authorities were suspicious of the Garde, a suspicion correlated with its persistent politicisation and its instrumentalization by various factions. During the elections of Year VII in several places in the Bouches-du-Rhône and Vaucluse, for example, the gardes nationaux were used to intimidate their political opponents. Already practically non-existent in the countryside, the service was very poor in the towns. The citizens usually showed at best a certain apathy and carelessness towards their obligations as guardsmen, at worst a clear disgust. Indeed, they were of little help in maintaining calm and enforcing the respect of property. Complaints about their inefficiency and carelessness multiplied,

---

12 Anon., *Collection des Lois du Corps Législatif et des Principaux Arrêtés du Directoire Exécutif* (Douai: Lagarde aîné Imprimeur, 1800), vol.III, p.73.

13 Bernard Gainot, 'Quelle place pour la Garde nationale pendant le Directoire?', in Serge Bianchi and Roger Dupuy (eds), *La Garde nationale entre nation et peuple en armes: Mythes et réalités 1789–1871* (Rennes: Presses Universitaires de Rennes, 2006), p.407.

14 Serge Bianchi, 'Les gardes nationales en Ille-et-Vilaine et dans le sud de la Seine-et-Oise: Bilans comparés', in Serge Bianchi and Roger Dupuy (eds), *La Garde nationale entre nation et peuple en armes: Mythes et réalités 1789–1871* (Rennes: Presses Universitaires de Rennes, 2006), p.388.

and the circulars issued by the Ministry of Police urged the departmental administrators to act accordingly. But how could men be persuaded to spend their nights on patrol, guarding official buildings, chasing deserters, rebels and other refractory priests without compensation? Worse, in accordance with a decree of 2 December 1797 (12 Frimaire Year VI), the most well-off Parisian gardes nationaux could be replaced in exchange for payment of a tax equivalent to two days' work. An instruction of 2 May 1799 (13 Floreal Year VII) generalised this procedure to all sedentary gardes nationaux. A sort of paid Garde Nationale was formed in this way. It constituted a mediocre, poorly trained, barely disciplined corps, because it was inadequately supervised and thus hardly motivated. It was frequently used to form temporary detachments to guard fortresses or military establishments and to escort prisoners of war.

Jourdan, général en chef de l'armée de Sambre et Meuse et ensuite de l'armée du Danube, engraving by Gabriel Levachez. Jourdan and Delbrel prepared the project which led to the conscription law. Both were deputies of the Council of Five Hundred: Jourdan represented the Haute-Vienne and Delbrel, the Lot. They wanted to institutionalise the experiments of the Revolution. (Musée Carnavalet)

The Directory estimated that it needed approximately 550,000 men to ensure the security of the country and to carry out necessary military operations: 200,000 men on the Rhine, 100,000 in Italy, 100,000 to protect the Low Countries, 80,000 in the west, as well as 70,000 to guarantee the internal order of the Republic. Yet, between 1796 and 1798, the strength of the Republic's armies oscillated between 350,000 and 380,000 men. It was therefore a matter of urgently closing a deficit of nearly 200,000 men. However, no one thought of calling on the Garde Nationale. *Général de division* Jourdan, deputy of the Haute-Vienne in the Council of Five Hundred, and Delbrel, his colleague from the Tarn, were charged by the Councils to propose a law on recruitment. They worked it out on the principle that any Frenchman owes service to his fatherland. The law was definitively adopted on 5 September 1798 (19 Fructidor Year VI) and proposed that the army continue to be recruited by voluntary commitments, but that the complement would be provided by 'a mass levy of the youth'.[15] The solutions that had been proposed empirically since 1793 became a permanent institution and young Frenchmen were in fact obliged to perform compulsory military service. All Frenchmen who had reached their twentieth year were to be registered together, that is to say conscripted, on the army's recruitment lists. They were to remain there until the age of 25 and form five age groups, each comprising about 200,000 young people, of whom more than two thirds were recognised as fit by the recruitment councils. The conscripts were called up according to the order of the conscription lists, starting with the youngest of the first class. The initial text of the law did not mention the lottery or the possibility of being replaced. Nor was it intended that all Frenchmen should be drafted, but they should be mobilised according to need.

---

15   AN: AD XVIII B: Procès-verbaux du Conseil des Cinq-Cents, séance du 1er fructidor an VI.

THE GARDE NATIONALE 1789–1815

ADMINISTRATION MUNICIPALE

DU SEPTIÈME ARRONDISSEMENT

DU CANTON DE PARIS.

CONSCRIPTION MILITAIRE.

L'ADMINISTRATION Centrale du Département de la Seine, ayant, par son Arrêté du 18 Thermidor dernier, fixé au 5 Fructidor, préfent mois, la réunion des Citoyens qui, aux termes de la Loi du 14 Meſſidor dernier, ſont appelés à la défenſe de la Patrie, par les Lois de la Réquiſition & de la Conſcription.

Les Citoyens de cet arrondiſſement, qui ſe trouvent compris dans leſdites Lois, ſont avertis de ſe rendre ledit jour, 5 du préſent mois de Fructidor, huit heures préciſes du matin, à la Maiſon commune de cet arrondiſſement, rue Avoye, N°. 160, pour y répondre à l'appel général qui en ſera fait, & de-là ſe rendre ſous les ordres de l'Officier chargé de l'organiſation des Bataillons auxiliaires à Courbevoye, juſqu'où ils ſeront accompagnés par deux Membres de la Municipalité.

Paris, le premier Fructidor, an VII de la République Françaiſe.

Les Adminiſtrateurs Municipaux,
Signé WULLIEZ, *Préſident;*
MAIRE, NAURY & DELAPORTE.

Le Commiſſaire du Directoire exécutif,
Signé CHAPPE.

Par l'Adminiſtration municipale,
LAMBIN, *Secrétaire en chef.*

De l'Imprimerie de DESVEUX, rue Avoye, Maiſon d'Aſnières, N°. 160.

Conscription poster calling on Parisian conscripts to assemble, Fructidor Year VII (1799). (Musée Carnavalet)

In Vendemiaire Year VII, the totality of the first class and part of the second were effectively raised, for a total of approximately 200,000 men. However, this first levy proved to be disappointing in its results. Due to the difficulty of equipping them and a high rate of insubordination, only 93,000 young men actually left to join the armies. In the spring of 1799, the military situation having strongly deteriorated in Germany as in Italy, French forces obliged to retreat or locked in fortified towns needed to be reinforced. Moreover, in the interior, the royalist nobles wanted to strike a blow, particularly in the West. The Chouans reached the cities of Le Mans, Saint-Brieuc and Nantes, from which they were almost immediately driven out. To deal with these various perils, the government decided on 17 April 1799 (28 Germinal Year VII) to raise 150,000 men from among the classes already levied. Doing so, the law of 28 Germinal singularly undermined the apparent egalitarianism of the Jourdan law. It established the drawing of lots among the conscripts of the second and third classes. In addition, it gave those who had drawn the 'wrong number' the possibility of being replaced by young people aged 18 to 20 who would be paid for this. Then, partly because of the ever-increasing pressure of the victorious coalition forces, partly because of the weakness of the French armies, a third law was promulgated on 28 June 1799 (10 Messidor Year VII). This time, the measure was effectively similar to a *levée en masse*. To protect French territory from invasion, conscripts of all classes who had not yet been called up by the previous laws were put into service. The possibility of being replaced was also abolished. Moreover, conscripts would be organised into battalions before being incorporated, while wealthier citizens alone would borrow one hundred million *francs* to clothe, equip and arm them. Although some 300,000 men were raised in just two years – as many as in the worst days of 1793 – almost a million should have been provided.

As conscription was generally not well received, emergency solutions had to be found. An attempt was made to exploit the memory of 1791 by providing that those conscripts called up by the earlier laws, but who had not yet joined the army, as well as the 'new' conscripts, would be placed in departmental auxiliary battalions, not in the line forces. In the hope of increasing the number of troops, a law was also passed giving amnesty to deserters provided they returned to the army. Conscripts who agreed to go were used to reinforce the armies fighting on the borders. Those who refused fed the bands of brigands, causing further unrest to royalist uprisings, which the 200 gendarmerie brigades – a little over 10,000 men spread throughout France – struggled to cope with. Their leaders could certainly have been supported by the sedentary gardes nationaux, but this was usually deemed unnecessary.

In an attempt to increase the effectiveness of these sedentary gardes nationales, a final restructuration was devised, a recurrent theme under the Directory. On 20 July 1799 (2 Thermidor Year VII), deputy Garrau proposed to the Council of Five Hundred a project prohibiting replacement in the Garde Nationale, a provision accompanied by prison sentences for offenders. The creation of companies of 'young citizens' and gunners was also planned. During the debates that followed, Jourdan asked, as for him, that the elite companies of grenadiers and chasseurs be re-established on the grounds that they gave 'zeal, emulation and discipline to the gardes nationales'.[16] Destroying them had, in his view, led to the destabilisation of the whole institution. For his part, his colleague Delbrel considered them 'vicious, dangerous and contrary to equality'.[17] The majority was ready to re-establish such elite companies, with the exception of towns where they had proved dangerous by their counter-revolutionary action. Nevertheless, article 278 of the *Constitution of Year III* imposed a uniform organisation for the whole of the Republic, so Jourdan's project was effectively abandoned. A few weeks later, another plan imagined having the citizens train militarily three times a month, but such an eventuality was deemed unsafe, if not completely unenforceable, in a number of departments. The distrust of official circles and the state of disorganisation affecting the Garde Nationale justified such a decision.

Then Came the *coup d'état*...

In the troubled period of the Directory, the Garde Nationale was deprived of its substance. Described as neglected and therefore ineffective, its service was widely decried. In fact, such a situation constituted a major obstacle to the maintenance of public order and undermined the fight against crime and violence within the Republic. An institution with ill-defined attributions, constantly confronted with competition from a more professional, more efficient but also more mobile Gendarmerie, the Garde – in the shape of mobile columns – also suffered from its subordination to local authorities and proved very difficult to mobilise in emergency situations. In order to be effective in the pre-insurrection situations that it routinely had to deal with, it would have had to adopt a professionalised structure, leading to the resurgence of elite companies. Contested in Paris, even within the two Councils as deputies feared that a sort of praetorian guard would be formed, such a solution was frequently perceived as being viable by a large proportion of local commissioners of the executive power.

Moreover, from the summer of 1789 to the first months of 1795, the Garde Nationale had occupied a prominent place in France's political life. While a 'Great Nation' was gradually taking shape from the Rhine valley to the Po plain, news of military operations and diplomatic negotiations took centre stage in the news, sometimes to the detriment of Franco-French conflicts. As for the Garde Nationale – above all a defensive force – it no longer seemed adapted to the strategic context of the moment. It even appeared to be an obstacle to the unity of the Republic, weakening it by the fratricidal conflicts it fostered. At the same time, the army asserted itself as a patriotic community capable of overcoming its differences of opinion in the face of the higher interests of the Nation. However, in exceptional situations, such as in the dark days of the summer of 1799, the gardes nationaux showed that they not

---

16   *Gazette Nationale ou Le Moniteur Universel*, 305 (1799), p.1242.
17   *Gazette Nationale ou Le Moniteur Universel*, 307 (1799), p.1249.

only retained a great capacity to react, but also that they were occasionally capable of regaining their primary vocation of 'Milices Citoyennes'.

When the decisive days of November 1799 occurred, the Garde Nationale Parisienne – which had contributed to the success of most of the main revolutionary *journées* – was no more than an amorphous mass of citizens fulfilling mediocre missions, which they relieved themselves of as soon as they could by means of replacements. Under such conditions, was it possible to entrust them with an active mission? Article three of the decree passed on 9 November 1799 (18 Brumaire Year VIII) by the Council of Anciens placed under the orders of *Général de division* Bonaparte the 7,000 troops stationed in Paris, the 1,200 grenadiers of the Garde du Corps Législatif, but also the sedentary gardes nationaux of the 17th military division composed of Paris and its suburbs. In reality, only the Grenadiers of the Garde du Corps Législatif played a decisive role in expelling the deputies from their session room in the palace of Saint-Cloud. On the evening of the *coup d'état* and despite its absolutely insignificant role in the circumstance, the Garde Nationale Parisienne was not forgotten in the congratulations that Bonaparte, now Consul of the French Republic, addressed to the troops who had supported him. In reality, the aim was to win the support of the population by letting them believe that they had participated in the action through the Garde Nationale. In truth, Bonaparte was counting as much on his prestige with the people and the bourgeoisie as on a properly structured military caste, accustomed to discipline and possessing an undeniable *esprit de corps*. The support of the soldiers hardly failed him and ensured his success.

Nevertheless, the army and its leaders did not want to stop the Revolution and return to a monarchical regime. On the contrary, they aimed to secure the republican form of the state, with military society playing a prominent role. Similarly, they did not want the territorial conquests of the Republic to be abandoned. The men who took power in Brumaire had to consider this state of mind into account. This had serious consequences for France – now engaged in a war with ever-widening horizons – and for the Garde Nationale, one of the assets of this bellicose policy.

9

Of Purple Cloak and Battlefields

1800–1815

According to part of French historiography, it seems to be a foregone conclusion that following the *coup d'état* of 18–19 Brumaire Year VIII, the Directory – a time of disorder characterised by a failing administration and mediocre and generally corrupt politicians – gave way to the Consulate, a stable regime in which a return to order would allow a new France to be founded after the excesses of the Revolution. In truth, the facts are much more nuanced. The directorial republic bequeathed to the Consulate a large number of institutions developed, sometimes in an improvised manner, during the revolutionary decade: legislative assemblies, departmental administrations, correctional and criminal courts, central schools, but also a conscript army. While some were already worn out by events or reflected an outdated ideology, others had demonstrated their usefulness and modernity. At the dawn of the nineteenth century, it fell to First Consul Bonaparte, France's new strongman known for his pragmatism, to preserve what was worth passing on to the next generations.

The Garde Side-lined

After having been the symbol of the first months of the Revolution, then the guarantor of the constitutional laws and the great public liberties, the Garde Nationale appeared to be a prematurely aged institution. The consular government kept it anyway, and mentioned it in the *Constitution* hastily drafted in Frimaire Year VIII to give birth to the new regime. However, the Garde was mentioned only very briefly, even elliptically. To distinguish the two formations that made up the Garde, the *Constitution of Year VIII* hardly innovated and reused the same vocabulary as the *Constitution of Year III*, its predecessor: 'The active Garde Nationale is subject to the regulations of public administration. The sedentary Garde Nationale is subject only

Groupe de gardes nationaux venant au secours d'une voiture attaquée par des brigands, anonymous engraving, c. 1799–1800. (Musée Carnavalet)

to the law'.[1] Under the Consulate, no new law was promulgated to specify the organisation of the Garde Nationale, which therefore remained in the legislative and regulatory state left by the Directory. Consequently, the laws of 14 October 1791 and 28 Prairial Year III were still authoritative. In truth, more than the endless reorganisations of the Garde, the proper functioning of conscription was the real emergency of the moment. One novelty: following the administrative reorganisation that occurred in Pluviôse Year VIII, the Garde Nationale was placed under the authority of the prefects recently created by the First Consul.

In the spring of 1800, faced with the resumption of the Chouanne rebellion, the gardes nationaux of western France were given the task of 'taking up arms and driving the brigands out of their territory'.[2] At the same time, a consular decree ordered towns with more than 5,000 inhabitants to raise mobile columns. The prefects recognised their usefulness and decided to keep them and even increase their number. In May 1800, as the second Italian campaign was opening on the Alpine front, Jean-Baptiste Fauchet, the

---

1   Fleurigeon, *Code Administratif* (Paris: Garnery, 1809), vol.III, p.56.
2   Carrot, *La Garde nationale*, p.166.

newly appointed prefect of the Var, arrived in Antibes, which was threatened with invasion by *General der Kavallerie* Melas' Austrian troops. If missives dispatched to the Parisian authorities hardly concealed his pessimism, Fauchet nevertheless addressed to his fellow-citizens a stirring call to arms and called on the assembly in Antibes for his department's mobile columns. Between 1,000 and 1,500 men promptly joined him to repel the Austrian forces from Italy. These men did not have to fight and the help they brought militarily was negligible, but their movements along the river Var made the enemy believe in the presence of considerable reinforcements. They confirmed the idea that France was only trying to defend Provence. Melas thus neglected the threat posed to his troops by the so-called 'Armée de Réserve' assembled by First Consul Bonaparte. He therefore continued to mass his troops on the outskirts of Nice and tried to cross the Var twice. When he learned of the irruption of the French troops in Italy through the Saint-Bernard pass on 21 May, it was already too late for him to save his line of retreat and he hurried to evacuate Nice. For his part, Prefect Fauchet was dissatisfied with the service of his mobile columns. He took it upon himself to reorganise them differently to what prevailed under the Directory. The administrator specifically targeted singles and men under the age of 40, placed under the control of soldiers. Faced with complaints from his constituents, the prefect was obliged to justify himself to the Minister of the Interior and finally had to abandon his plans. In July 1800, the prefect of the Gard also resorted to mobile columns, but, judged to be expensive, not very effective and above all a source of abuse, the measure was disavowed. While the Minister of the Interior deplored the prevailing administrative anarchy, his counterpart in the Ministry of War sent in line troops available following the military successes in Italy.

Such experiments could not prevent the marginalisation of the Garde that prevailed throughout the Consulate. It was indeed perceived as potentially dangerous. If it finally went unheeded, a report drawn up in September 1800 provided for the abolition of elections in favour of the appointment of officers by the prefect. NCOs were appointed by the battalion commanders. More than dangerous, the Garde Nationale was above all perceived as impotent and prone to unforgivable errors. 'The Garde Nationale is a powerless means of maintaining order and preserving public liberties. Everything bad that has been done in France since the Revolution has been done without the Garde Nationale being able to prevent it, and it has been more or less a stranger to everything good that has been done', thus affirmed a scathing report from 7 July 1800 (18 Messidor Year VIII).[3]

Gardes nationaux were required to support many missions: guarding town halls and prisons, escorting prisoners and public funds, assisting military detachments in their fight against armed bands, and carrying night patrols in the countryside. Nevertheless, a paid Garde Municipale was created in Paris in early October 1802. With just over 2,000 infantrymen divided into two demi-brigades and just under 200 cavalrymen, its missions were very similar to those of the Parisian Garde Nationale up to that point. The First Demi-

---

3   ANF: F/9/339: Rapport du 18 messidor an VIII.

Brigade was thus specifically responsible for guarding the entrances to Paris, in other words the barriers and ports. As for the Second Demi-Brigade, it was responsible for guarding town halls, the prefecture and also the capital's prisons. Dragoons conducted patrols and performed honorary services for the mayors. Elsewhere in France, the government was also able to rely on reserve companies created at the very beginning of the Empire, by a decree of 14 May 1805. Composed of a few dozen conscripts drawn from the reserve and placed under the direct authority of the prefect and the commander of the local gendarmerie legion, they formed 'a police force stationed in the chief town to guard prisons, beggar's warehouses, powder magazines, public monuments and to patrol the roads'.[4] This is without counting the gendarmerie, whose strengths had been considerably reinforced since July 1801. It represented what the First Consul wanted: a unit organised militarily but carrying out civilian missions. 'It is a special organisation that does not exist in any country in Europe. It is the most effective way of maintaining tranquillity. It is a half-civilian, half-military surveillance, spread over the whole country, which gives the most precise reports', Napoleon, now emperor, congratulated himself.[5]

A Symbolic Role

Gendarmes were certainly more effective in their role as guardians of the population's safety than the gardes nationaux, who never materialised as true soldiers. The spirit of citizenship did not sit well with military discipline and the obligation of service on the streets. From the soldier, the gardes nationaux therefore had nothing but the uniform, but their mere appearance under arms made it possible to publicly display the harmony between the bourgeoisie and the new consular authorities. In fact, the Garde Nationale frequently became ceremonial troops, in particular to welcome a prefect, a bishop, a senior state official or even the First Consul himself. When Bonaparte passed through Amiens at the end of June 1803, two companies of 30 cavalrymen belonging to the most affluent circles of this Picardy town, a company of gunners, an auxiliary company of chasseurs, and an elite company of the sedentary Garde Nationale accompanied by a band dressed to the nines for the occasion, were waiting for him. The Garde was most often invited to take part in the great republican festivals preserved by the regime and enhanced their splendour. In Year VIII, in the Pas-de-Calais, the procession formed for the celebration of 14 July and the Fête de la Concorde included, in addition to all the civil, judicial and military authorities of the department, two detachments of gardes nationaux. However, relying on orders from Paris, the prefects did their utmost to eliminate as much as possible 'any service or post of honour that was not indispensable', as the prefect of the Meurthe noted in 1802.[6]

---

4   Duvergier, *Collection Complète des Lois*, vol.XV, p.201.
5   Napoléon I, *Correspondance de Napoléon 1er publiée par ordre de l'Empereur Napoléon III* (Paris: Plon, Dumaine, 1863), vol.XII, p.377.
6   Carrot, *La Garde nationale*, p.168.

The Garde gradually fell into a state of lethargy but was nevertheless given a sort of symbolic revival with the proclamation of the Empire in 1804. A decree of 10 July 1804 (21 Messidor Year XII) provided that each department would send to Paris a delegation of 16 gardes nationaux, that is to say four officers, four NCOs and eight fusiliers to attend the coronation of Napoleon in Notre-Dame Cathedral on 2 December 1804. Three days later, these delegations received, like the line troops and the Garde Imperiale, new tricolour flags symbolising the cohesion of the nation and revolutionary continuity. This ceremony was organised at the Champ de Mars, the same place where La Fayette had organised the Festival of the Federation on 14 July 1790. Thus, the Garde Nationale continued to enjoy the aura of its origins and its myth endured. The new imperial regime had not dared to abolish it. On the contrary, it preferred to keep it as a reserve of legitimacy that it might need. Indeed, the Garde was part of Napoleon's desire to associate the notables with the new monarchy. Above all, it allowed him to build an additional bridge between revolutionary and imperial legitimacy.

Gardes Nationaux Levies and Requisitions, 1805–1808

In addition to its symbolic function, the Garde Nationale had, in Napoleon's mind, a secondary yet important use. It appeared to him as a sort of territorial reserve army, the genesis of which undoubtedly dated back to the summer of 1805. In August, the Emperor, under the pressure of events, had decided to abandon – at least temporarily – his planned invasion of Britain. The campaign that was opening up forced the Emperor to order the march of his troops from Boulogne and Holland towards Germany. The decision was taken on 26 August and was effective just three days later. Appropriately renamed 'the Grande Armée', imperial troops left Boulogne and headed east towards the Rhine. In fact, the northern coasts of the French Empire were vulnerable to a British attack or landing. The military vacuum created by the movement of the 'Grande Armée' also meant that the Garde Nationale had to be thoroughly reorganised. Time was short. The urgency of the situation made it impossible to follow the usual lengthy legislative procedure, so the issue was brought directly before the Senate. On 24 September 1805, a sénatus-consulte supplementing the law of 14 October 1791 decided that the gardes nationaux would henceforth be reorganised by means of imperial decrees. Moreover, article 4 regulated their missions: 'the gardes will be employed to maintain order on the inside and to defend borders and coasts. Fortresses are especially entrusted to their honour and bravery'.[7]

Bolstered by this constitutional authorisation, Napoleon soon signed from Strasbourg two implementing decrees. Dated 30 September, the first included some 30 articles and structured the Garde Nationale very differently compared to its revolutionary antecedent. Of course, the obligation for all able-bodied Frenchmen between the ages of 20 and 60 to serve was

---

7 Fleurigeon, *Code Administratif* (Paris: Valade Imprimeur, 1806), p.292.

maintained. The same applied to the existence of companies of chasseurs and grenadiers and the tricolour flag. However, although the Garde Nationale had hitherto been organised on a purely municipal basis, the decree specified that it could be convened at the departmental level. Legions were created in order to accentuate the Roman references of the imperial regime while erasing the memory of revolutionary insurrections. These brought together several cohortes, a term deliberately chosen to distinguish them from the army's battalions. Above all, the decree eliminated the main legacy of the 1789 organisation, namely the election of officers. From then on, officers, who were 'citizens with the necessary capacities to dress and equip themselves at their own expense', were directly appointed by the Emperor upon presentation by the Minister of the Interior.[8] It was up to them to designate NCOs. Finally, article 20 of the decree provided that the gardes nationaux required to perform military service outside of their home area would receive road, stage and accommodation allowances provided to line troops for such purpose. This prescription, which suggested worrying extensions in the guardsmen' activity, gave the impression that they could occasionally replace the army. In practice, it merely developed the measures enacted in article 4 of the aforementioned sénatus-consulte.

At the outset of the First Empire, Strasbourg's Garde Nationale was responsible for defending the main Rhine crossings. The authors of Alsatian paper soldiers represented Strasbourg's gardes nationaux in their collections. They represented a *tambour-major* in addition to the *caporal-tambour*. On the left, Boeswillwald's interpretation, on the right, Carl's. (Original artwork by Jean-Claude Colrat)

Table 13. Garde Nationale Company, September 1805 Organisation

Capitaine	1
Lieutenant	1
Sous-lieutenant	1
Sergent-major	1
Sergent	4
Caporal-fourrier	1
Caporal	8
Tambour	1
Garde National	132
Total	150

---

8   Louis-François Portiez, *Cours de Législation Administrative* (Paris: Garnery Libraire, 1808), vol.I, p.234.

These general scope provisions only applied in departments designated by Napoleon. Everywhere else, the former organisation was maintained. In truth, the imperial authorities did not want to deprive themselves of the Garde Nationale, but they feared that it would be fully resurrected. If difficulties arose, could the royalists, for example, not use it to launch an insurrection? Nevertheless, on 30 September 1805, a second decree ordered the immediate organisation and requisitioning of the Garde Nationale in four groups of departments on the borders of the Empire: those facing Britain, those on the left bank of the Rhine, those in Alsace and those adjacent to Switzerland. Each of these groups was placed under the orders of a *maréchal* or a *général* chosen among the senators: Kellermann and Lefebvre, Rampon and D'Aboville. They were responsible for the organisation of the gardes nationaux of the 12 departments of the north and east of the Empire (Somme, Pas-de-Calais, Nord, Lys, Röer, Rhin-et-Moselle, Mont-Tonnerre, Haut-Rhin, Bas-Rhin, Doubs, Jura and Léman), as well as the assembly of grenadier and chasseur companies intended to protect the borders, and for supplying the garrisons for Strasbourg, Besançon, Mayence, and the Saint-Omer camp. In the absence of clear and concordant instructions, the four senators tackled the most urgent. Charged with raising protective troops quickly and from scratch, they negotiated the necessary numbers – around 20,000 men, at the very least – directly with the prefects. The Nord, for example, was asked to contribute 2,800 men, while the Somme gathered 1,200 men. As for the grenadiers and chasseurs, they were chosen by a council based on nominative lists drawn up by the municipalities. These relatively well-off men largely took advantage of the possibilities of replacement which were offered to them. Moreover, they were usually posted to fortresses or garrisons close to their homes. Their service was temporary and they were relieved at short intervals, often for a month. Despite this, desertions were frequent. At the end of 1805, however, the prefectural authorities made very moderate use of the repressive measures at their disposal: they preferred to remind deserters of their duties and grant amnesty to those who returned voluntarily. In the Pas-de-Calais, such a policy was implemented by prefect Lachaise, with regard to deserters in the Saint-Omer camp.

Table 14. Organisation of the Garde Nationale in the northern French Empire departments, September 1805

Department	Number of Legions	Legion Number	Town
Nord	14	1	Lille
		2	Tourcoing
		3	Douai
		4	Dunkerque
		5	Bergues
		6	Cambrai
		7	Le Quesnoy
		8	Hazebrouck
		9	Seclin
		10	Avesnes
		11	Armentières
		12	Saint Amand
		13	Le Cateau
		14	Valenciennes

OF PURPLE CLOAK AND BATTLEFIELDS

Department	Number of Legions	Legion Number	Town
Pas-de-Calais	8	1	Arras
		2	Béthune
		3	Boulogne
		4	Saint Omer
		5	Montreuil
		6	Aire
		7	Bapaume
		8	Saint Paul
Somme	6	1	Amiens
		2	Abbeville
		3	Péronne
		4	Montdidier
		5	Doullens
		6	Mollien-Vidame
Lys	3	1	Bruges
		2	Bruges
		3	Ypres

Unsurprisingly, the services rendered by the gardes were of mediocre quality. In fact, these men had received poor training. This was not helped by the poor military education of their officers, relatively old bourgeois who were wealthy enough to dress and equip themselves at their own expense. At best, they plugged a few important gaps in the imperial military structure. After the victory of Austerlitz, on 2 December 1805, and the peace of Pressburg signed shortly afterwards, the reasons for their mobilisation were a thing of the past. Unconvinced of their effectiveness, Napoleon sent them very terse thanks in January 1806, then urged his Minister of the Interior to send them back home. 'It costs me a lot of money and is useless to me', he complained in a letter dated 8 February 1806.[9] This first call for gardes nationaux at least had a positive consequence. By serving in a legion, these men had become aware of their common interests: they were serving in a unit that protected their homes, families and property against Britain.

Napoleon had certainly not been convinced of the usefulness of putting the Garde Nationale into operation. However, at the end of the summer of 1806, the opening of hostilities against Prussia made him change his mind. On 20 September, just five days before leaving France to lead his troops, he decreed the requisition of the troops already raised in 1805 and their subsequent concentration in Strasbourg and Mainz. In addition, the Saint-Omer camp was reactivated: 6,000 men of the northern departments were to be gathered there. On 23 October, as he was heading into Poland, the Emperor ordered that 3,000 grenadiers and chasseurs should be assembled in Bordeaux and employed to protect the French south-west shores. Eight days later, another 3,000 guardsmen from the Seine-Inférieure were assembled for similar duties in Dieppe and Saint-Valéry. 'This will be a means of giving bread to many men and a way of providing for the security of these regions', Napoleon wrote to his Minister of the Interior.[10] In fact, this letter from

---

[9] Napoléon I, *Correspondance de Napoléon*, vol.XI, p.645.
[10] Napoléon I, *Correspondance de Napoléon*, vol.XIII, p.500.

THE GARDE NATIONALE 1789–1815

Garde Nationale grenadier and chasseur *sergent*, 1806, watercolour by Henri Boisselier. (Yves Martin)

Napoleon showed that he had given up on involving the good bourgeoisie in internal defence.

As the levies became routine, it became necessary to fix some rules, which until then had remained empirical. This was set out in a decree signed in Berlin on 12 November. Hardly aimed at a general reorganisation of the Garde Nationale, it was intended to make the provisions adopted on 30 September 1805 more effective. It confirmed the need for all French citizens between the ages of 20 and 60 to serve in the Garde, with the possibility of being replaced in the service. The grenadier and chasseur companies brought together the most able-bodied men, if possible aged between 20 and 40. Intended to form the active part of the Garde, such companies could be called upon to perform domestic service in towns of more than 5,000 inhabitants or military service. In the latter case, they were assimilated to the line troops in terms of pay, rewards and discipline.

It was clear that the imperial regime did not want the gardes nationaux to be a permanent system, but rather envisioned them as a reserve force from which it could draw, if necessary, the cadres of a small territorial army intended to protect the Empire's territory. The service therefore continued under these conditions until the peace treaty of Tilsit of July 1807 with Prussia and Russia. The first dismissals occurred in August and concerned the gardes nationaux assigned to the surveillance of the Rhine. At its 1807 session, the General Council of the Pas-de-Calais hoped 'that the glorious peace of Tilsit would allow His Majesty to send back to their homes the 2,000 elite men in charge of the defence of the coasts of the Ocean, or that at least he would find it fair to have this burden shared by a greater number of departments'.[11] Their wish was granted in the spring of 1808. As a reward, some officers were offered *sous-lieutenant* positions in the line army.

On the other hand, a decree of August 1807 maintained in activity 3,000 gardes nationaux raised in October 1806 in seven departments of the southwest: Gironde, Landes, Gers and Aude in particular. This unpopular decision encouraged desertions. These became even more frequent from June 1808 onwards when, faced with the worsening situation in Spain, these gardes nationaux provided detachments to the garrison of Pamplona, before

---

11   Archives Départementales du Pas-de-Calais (ADPC): N 5: Session de 1807.

OF PURPLE CLOAK AND BATTLEFIELDS

taking part in the siege of Saragossa the following year. For the first time, guardsmen had intervened in foreign territory. At the same time, a battalion was raised under the responsibility of the prefects in the department of Ariège and another in that of Haute-Garonne. These motley troops fought the incursions of the Spanish guerrillas on the Pyrenean border as best they could.

Overseas Gardes Nationaux: Defenders of a Quixotic Ambition

As soon as he became Consul, Napoleon, convinced that foreign trade was one of the main keys to prosperity, undertook a takeover of the French colonial empire. However, the territories of which it was composed were either under revolt or occupied by British troops. Signed in March 1802, the Peace of Amiens offered a very short-lived reprieve, since war with Britain resumed in May 1803. As Emperor, Napoleon fruitlessly prolonged this war overseas: in just a few years, the French colonial empire was completely swallowed up. In this context, the Garde Nationale was one of the most prominent players in this largely forgotten conflict.

In 1802, the Peace of Amiens had indeed allowed some military reinforcements to be sent to the French colonial possessions. However, the *capitaines generaux* appointed to the colonies – *Amiral* Villaret-Joyeuse to Martinique, *Général de division* Ernouf to Guadeloupe and, as he had not been able to take possession of the French trading posts in India, *Général de division* Decaen to the Ile de France – all noted the weakness of their position. They therefore undertook to strengthen it by relying on the Garde Nationale.

Gardes nationaux of the mobilised cohortes in the 10th and 11th military divisions, Peninsular War. Henri Boissellier depicts a grenadier, a chasseur and an officer. From 1808 onwards, both shako and hat were worn. (Guillaume Bretegnier)

Dealing With What Exists

When he arrived in Martinique on 3 September 1802, just as an epidemic of yellow fever was wreaking havoc among the line troops, Villaret-Joyeuse reorganised the local Garde Nationale – until then called the 'militia' by the British, who had occupied the island since 1794 – by a decree issued on 14 October 1802. The *Capitaine Général* divided the island into six military districts, each of which was to raise a battalion of gardes nationaux. Comprising a grenadier company, a chasseur company, as many companies

289

of fusiliers and a company of dragoons, each battalion was made up of all white men between the ages of 15 and 55, as well as free blacks of good repute. In April 1803, Villaret-Joyeuse lucidly wrote to Decrès, Minister of the Navy and the Colonies, that 'the gardes nationaux of the colony can be divided into two classes: that of the towns, which are highly trained and which, in military exercises, almost rival the line troops, and that of the countryside, which generally lack practice and instruction. I ordered the commanders of the districts to train them every Sunday'.[12] Armament remained a thorny problem, as the British had provided the Martinique militia with low-quality weapons.

As for *Général de division* Ernouf, who was appointed *Capitaine Général* of Guadeloupe and its neighbouring islands – Les Saintes, Marie Galante and La Désirade – he landed in Guadeloupe in May 1803, when war with Britain resumed. His meagre forces consisted of two, then three, battalions of the 66e Regiment d'Infanterie de Ligne, a few artillerymen and a handful of cavalry. To support them, Ernouf reorganised the local Garde Nationale. This aggregated all inhabitants of European origin and free Afro-Caribbeans between the ages of 16 and 55. Each of the six battalions he organised had companies of European fusiliers, companies of Afro-Caribbean chasseurs and a company of European dragoons. The small islands dependent on Guadeloupe also had their own gardes nationaux company.

In the summer of 1803, a new *Capitaine Général, Général de division* Decaen, arrived in the Indian Ocean. After renouncing the recovery of the French trading posts in India, he fell back on the Mascareignes, where he brought the news of the rupture of the peace with Britain. Also aware of his lack of military means, Decaen proceeded to mobilise local forces and reorganised the Garde Nationale, starting with that of his capital, Port Nord-Ouest. On 21 October 1803, he issued a series of decrees. The Port Nord-Ouest Garde Nationale Legion would consist of a battle corps formed from the white population and composed of an artillery company, two grenadier companies, six fusilier companies, a company of chasseurs à cheval, plus a reserve formed from men aged between 40 and 60. A battalion of chasseurs nationaux would incorporate free blacks. It would be composed of a carabinier company, four chasseur companies and a reserve corps of men aged 40 to 60. On 11 November, the Garde Nationale was reshuffled in all the other arrondissements or districts of the island.

A Long Last Stand

For the gardes nationaux serving overseas, the first years of the Empire were like a *baroud d'honneur* (last stand). In Martinique, the blockade became increasingly tight from 1808 onwards. As food supplies began to run short, the mobilisation of the Garde Nationale was restricted so that no rations would have to be issued. During the winter of 1808–1809, the British forces assembled an expeditionary force in Barbados to seize Martinique. With

---

12   Didier Davin, 'La Garde nationale de la Martinique, 1802-1815', <http://frederic.berjaud.free.fr/Articles_de_Didier_Davin/Garde%20nationale%20Martinique/La%20garde%20nationale%20de%20la%20Martinique.htm>, accessed 11 September 2022.

12,000 soldiers, it set sail on 28 January 1809 and, after two days at sea, reached Martinique's shores, where three simultaneous landings were made. Only 2,400 men reinforced by the Garde Nationale were facing them. Villaret-Joyeuse adopted a defensive system consisting of concentrating the weak forces at its disposal in a radius of a few kilometres around Fort Desaix, its main fortified point, and the large redoubt which communicated with it through an underground gallery. In the first days of the confrontations, the Garde Nationale stood by. However, a proclamation issued by the British opportunely stipulated that any colonist caught with his arms in hand would be imprisoned, deported and his property confiscated. As for the free blacks of the Garde Nationale, they would simply be sold as slaves. The Garde therefore deserted en masse during the night of 2 to 3 February. From then on, the line troops locked themselves up in Fort Desaix and the great redoubt, and resisted for three weeks. Villaret-Joyeuse finally capitulated on 24 February.

Following the fall of Martinique, Guadeloupe was left hopelessly isolated. From 1808 onwards, the island had been regularly attacked by the British and subjected to an effective blockade. In March 1808, the British had also seized the neighbouring islands of Marie Galante and La Désirade, which were weakly defended by tiny garrisons with a few guardsmen. In the summer of 1809, a cyclone ravaged the plantations, which only reinforced an already unbearable famine. As for the coastal batteries, they were short of ammunition while enemy raids intensified. By the autumn of 1809, Ernouf knew that the island was completely surrounded and that the landing of a British expeditionary force was imminent. This finally took place at the end of January 1810. Rather than repelling the opposing landings on the beaches, Ernouf chose to retreat to the mountains, relying on the rugged topography of Guadeloupe. The Garde Nationale supported the line troops as best it could. After an honourable but costly resistance – the line troops and the Garde Nationale lost nearly 400 dead and wounded – Ernouf surrendered on 4 February 1810.

The French failure was just as obvious in the Indian Ocean. With the few troops at his disposal, either arriving with him or locally raised, *Général de division* Decaen had nevertheless done better than resist British invasion

It seems that the 'national uniform' was worn by the Guadeloupe Garde Nationale. In 1807, British officer William Loftie drew an officer wearing it, but with white collar and cuffs, instead of red. Nearby islands such as the Saints, Marie-Galante, St Martin, and La Désirade also had their own Garde Nationale units, on which no information survives. (Yves Martin)

attempts for several years. At the end of November 1810, a British fleet landed nearly 25,000 soldiers – a mixture of European troops and native regiments of the East India Company army – on the northern shores of the Ile de France (today's Mauritius). Decaen could only muster about 4,000 men, including the Garde Nationale. These were largely concentrated around Port Napoléon, the island's capital. Solidly entrenched, imperial troops tried to resist the pressure of their adversary, but only delayed it. On 1 December, aware of the low morale of the gardes nationaux and fearing that his positions would be turned, Decaen gave up the sortie he was planning. The next day, noting the arrival of many new British reinforcements in front of his positions, Decaen judged it preferable to capitulate.

Walcheren 1809: The Garde Nationale at the Forefront

In April 1809, Austria gave in to British proposals and declared war on France once again. For this new campaign, Napoleon concentrated a large number of troops in Germany and found himself obliged to somewhat reduce the defence of his empire's territory. In doing so, 6,000 gardes nationaux from four departments in northern France were called up for active service, according to a well-established system quite familiar to Senator (and *Général de division*) Rampon. In order to lighten the obligation, the contingents of gardes nationaux provided by the departments were to be half renewed every three months.

Gathered in the Saint-Omer camp, these active gardes nationaux allowed the French command to hastily oppose some troops to the 40,000 British soldiers who landed on the island of Walcheren on 29 July. This was certainly insufficient if one wanted to effectively repel this expeditionary force commanded by Lieutenant General Lord Chatham and supported by 36 ships of the line, 16 frigates, 42 sloops and many smaller ships. However, other French forces were swiftly mobilised and immediately dispatched to the theatre of operations. On 2 August, despite the opposition of Clarke, Minister of War, Fouché, Minister of Police, who was also acting Minister of the Interior, additionally decided to raise the number of gardes nationaux in 15 northern departments, which made it possible to field 30,000 additional men. Such a decision was taken 'in the name of the Emperor', who was by then in Austria, far from the theatre of operations. Some in government circles feared Napoleon's reactions, but to their astonishment he approved the measure, which he made official in a decree signed at Schönbrunn on 6 August 1809. Received in Paris six days later, it legalised the activation of 30,000 gardes nationaux in eight military divisions located north-west of a line Le Havre-Rouen-Metz-Wesel. On 22 August however, absorbed by the peace negotiations with Austria, the Emperor created two armies commanded by prestigious chiefs: that of the Tête des Flandres, under *Maréchal* Moncey and that of Anvers, with *Maréchal* Bernadotte at its head, although the latter had been disgraced following the recent Battle of Wagram. As soon as he took command, Bernadotte addressed an uncompromising report to the Minister of War in which he affirmed that 'one will be able to take advantage of the old cohortes. But as for the newly raised gardes nationaux, they are almost useless units. More than half of them have already deserted. What remained were badly armed, lacking cartridge boxes and uniforms. If within two or three days I can gather 12,000 fit men in the vicinity of Antwerp, I will consider myself very happy'.[13] From his headquarters, *Général de division* Rousseau, commander of the island of Cadzand, also deplored that 'the troops under my orders, from Liefkenshoek to the Sluis Ecluse, comprise 2,300 men of line troops and 4,000 newly-raised and poorly equipped gardes nationaux, who embarrass me more than they serve me'.[14] On 28 and 29 August, Napoleon transmitted his instructions to his *maréchaux*. With regard to 'the kind of troops' that both commanded, it was necessary 'not to risk a battle' but, on the contrary, to remain on the defensive, to make exert, discipline and harden the troops.[15] Moreover, worried about the sanitary situation in the swampy marshes of Zeeland, the Emperor recommended that the soldiers be billeted in healthy locations. The Armée d'Anvers and the Armée de la Tête des Flandres contributed to locking the British in the island of Walcheren where the Polders fevers, an insidious, unforeseen and deadly enemy, finally forced them to retreat before the onset of winter.

After reproaching Clarke for his mistrust in the mobilisation of the Garde Nationale, Napoleon instead congratulated Fouché on his decisiveness. His position was strengthened by this explicit approval and, using the necessities of public security as an excuse, the minister ordered the Parisian sedentary

Brun-Lavaine, just 18 years old, was the 1st Legion d'Elite's chief of music. According to his *Memoirs*, the musicians had two sets of uniforms. The small dress, sometimes hidden by the greatcoat, was made of blue cloth and braided with silver lace. The full dress was white, with blue collar, cuffs and piping. In this case, the musicians wore a Polish-style chapka. (Yves Martin)

---

13   Léon de Lanzac de Laborie, *La domination française en Belgique Directoire-Consulat-Empire 1795–1814* (Paris: Librairie Plon, 1895), vol.II, p.153.
14   Robert Ouvrard, 'Les Armées de la Tête des Flandres et d'Anvers (Août-Septembre 1809)', Napoléon Histoire du Consulat et du 1er Empire (11 janvier 2019), <https://www.napoleon-histoire.com/les-armees-de-la-tete-des-flandres-et-danvers-aout-septembre-1809/>, accessed 11 September 2022.
15   Adolphe Thiers, *Histoire du Consulat et de l'Empire* (Paris: Furne, Jouvet et Cie Editeurs, 1873), vol.XIV, p.678.

Garde Nationale to be activated in the form of 24 cohortes (22 for Paris, two for its suburbs). The decision, which was issued on 18 August, was political and was not carried out without strong reservations on the part of the senior officials responsible for its enforcement. From 6,000 men initially, Fouché increased the strength of the Parisian Garde Nationale to 12,000, 24,000 and finally 30,000 men. He hardly called them to effective service on the shores of the Empire, but limited himself to call for voluntary service accompanied by a premium of 300 *francs* paid by the departmental authorities of the Seine. On 22 August, the minister created two cavalry squadrons, under the name of 'chevau-légers' and personally chose their officers amongst the young men of the liberal aristocracy. He had the unit escort him to the horse races organised at the Champ de Mars.

At the beginning of September, relying on alarmist reports concerning the British fleet in the Mediterranean, he undertook to generalise the measure of mobilisation of the gardes nationaux, until then limited to the northern part of the Empire, to Languedoc, Provence, but also Piedmont. The prefects of these territories proved to be quite embarrassed. The Gardes Nationales had not been organised for a long time, especially in the countryside. In some Italian departments, they had never even been formed. Moreover, the ministerial circulars did not specify under which legal regime they should be set up. Was it necessary to rely on revolutionary legislation or on the more recent laws of 1805 and 1806? Worse still, no imperial decree had authorised such levies. Faced with such questions, the prefects were cautious and contented themselves with launching recruitment operations while requesting additional instructions.

Such excitement caused serious concern which reached the Emperor's ears. It also revealed a number of recent flaws. In the summer of 1809, the Belgian departments had reacted with a certain lukewarmness, and not without murmurs, to the levies which affected them. In this respect, the correspondence between Latour du Pin – prefect of the department of the Dyle – and the services of Minister Fouché revealed the mutual misunderstandings between Brussels and Paris. On this occasion, the prefect recalled the magnitude of the work done. As there was no Garde Nationale in the Belgian departments until then, it had to be created in record time from scratch. Furthermore, Latour du Pin also admitted to the lack of enthusiasm among the population to defend their own coastline. As a result, the patriotic proclamations had only limited effect on a population that was submissive, but not really deeply rallied to France. The prefect nevertheless contrived to raise the department's gardes nationaux and to assemble, at least on paper, the 740 men required from Brussels, by resorting massively to replacements. In Sambre-et-Meuse, a department much further away from any British invasion, Prefect Péres was even more cautious than his colleague in Brussels. He certainly applied the orders, carrying out the necessary censuses and convocations. However, he deceitfully explained to his constituents that the organisation of the gardes was a means of countering banditry. In the Saarland, the levy even provoked the beginning of an uprising which was soon suppressed. As Roger Dufraisse – one of the few historians to have taken a real interest in the matter – explained, such disturbances revealed not only the unpopularity of the Garde Nationale, but also the high level of delinquency that affected the Saar region.¹⁶ In a recently annexed territory, these were not a manifestation of patriotic resistance to French domination, but more likely a movement born of circumstances, neither prepared, nor organised, nor directed by agents from home or abroad.

In Paris, the ministers opposed to Fouché did not fail to dramatize in their correspondence the dangerous turn taken by the resurrection of the sedentary Garde Nationale in the capital. Almost all accused the minister of illegality, abuse of power and omnipotence. They also suggested that Fouché was preparing, together with Bernadotte, a political regime change. Reassured about the military situation, Napoleon in turn became worried about these multiple rumours. In fact, he reproached Fouché for having alarmed the Empire with excessive measures and undertook to slow down the movement. In the eyes of the Emperor, the Garde Nationale Parisienne did not bring any serious reinforcement but undoubtedly created a political risk. On 3 September, an imperial decree named *Maréchal* Sérurier, at the time Governor of the Invalides, *Commandant General* of the Garde Nationale Parisienne. Ségur, one of Napoleon's aides-de-camp, was placed at the head of the two chevau-légers squadrons, which were finally dissolved on 18 September. Finally, on 1 October, the Paris Garde Nationale was made dormant. It was the same in the provinces. On 3 October, Fouché sent a circular to the prefects, whom he accused of haste and overzealousness: 'they had anticipated the orders, whereas they should have waited'.¹⁷ On 15 October, Fouché's interim position at the Ministry of the Interior came to an abrupt end. In his defence, the minister tried to persuade the Emperor that the Bonaparte dynasty had benefited from his spectacular initiative. But Napoleon saw in Fouché's excesses only the zeal of a courtier. The minister paid for them with a dazzling disgrace which manifested itself in a violent interview on 27 October 1809. Montalivet, his successor, insisted that no measures be taken to assemble, equip and arm the gardes nationaux. Those who had arrived at their destination in northern France remained there for some time, though their condition was not the best. Ill-equipped, they were more like hordes of beggars than true soldiers, as one officer lamented in early October 1809.¹⁸ After the re-embarkation of the British forces, their actual demobilisation gradually took place between January and April 1810.

Portrait of Fouché, Duc d'Otrante, circa 1815. In 1809, Fouché relied on the Garde Nationale to face British landings on Walcheren. Napoleon approved the measures for the defence of Flanders but disapproved of their extension to the whole Empire. (Musée Carnavalet)

---

16   Roger Dufraisse, 'Une rébellion en pays annexé: Le soulèvement des gardes nationales de la Sarre en 1809', *Bulletin de la Société d'Histoire Moderne*, 10 (1969), p.5.
17   ANF: F/9/345.
18   Carrot, *La Garde nationale*, p.185.

Before sending them home for good, the imperial administration sought to 'give proof of the Emperor's satisfaction to the gardes nationaux of the northern departments'.[19] In reality, it was a question of making the best use of these men. In fact, an imperial decree of 1 January 1810 decreed that a regiment of four battalions would be added to the infantry of the Garde Imperiale, made up of men of good will drawn from the gardes nationaux who had contributed to the defence of the coasts of Flanders and the Channel. Each battalion was to be organised in Lille and treated like the Tirailleurs of the Garde Impériale. Unfortunately, the enthusiasm of the gardes nationaux hardly met the imperial hopes. Only 1,029 men agreed to join at Lille, instead of the 2,200 necessary for the constitution of a regiment with four battalions. In July 1810, the Emperor therefore gave new instructions: the unit – now dependent on the administration of the Chasseurs à Pied de la Garde Imperiale – would be reorganised into two battalions. At the same time, the Emperor ordered that 1,038 men be taken from the reserve companies 'in 57 departments around Paris' to complete the unit's strength.[20] Napoleon wanted the regiment to be able to enter the field as early as 25 August, but it was not until 4 October that it actually set off for Spain. For two and a half years, it was part of the Garde detachment responsible for protecting communications in the provinces of Valladolid and Palencia, and suffered heavy losses there, mostly from disease. In February 1813, the regiment finally returned to France, where it was reorganised and renamed the 7e de Voltigeurs de la Garde Impériale.

'The mobilisation of 1809 had thus ended in a mediocre military recruitment operation', historian Georges Carrot sententiously postulates.[21] In truth, the year 1809 marked a real turning point in the history of the Garde Nationale under the Empire. Until then, Napoleon had limited himself to raising a few thousand gardes nationaux intended to hold fortresses or to contain hypothetical British attacks along the Empire's coasts, manoeuvres he himself had little faith in. These formations were rather painfully set up from 1805 to 1808, and in fact never had to fight until the summer of 1809, when these final reserves were put to the test at the rear of the Grande Armée. The result was disappointing. Gathered in Saint-Omer, the mobilised gardes nationaux had reacted quickly and effectively to the British attempt. On the other hand, nothing was ready to clothe, arm and equip the tens of thousands of guardsmen who were hastily called to serve. Who was responsible for the expenses: the departmental budgets, the war administration or even the individuals themselves? The operation, which cost the princely sum of 3.2 million *francs*, undoubtedly generated a great deal of waste. It was largely financed by a tax levied in departments that did not have to provide a contingent.

---

19 *Annonces et Avis Divers du Département de l'Escaut*, 1292 (1810).
20 Napoléon I, *Correspondance de Napoléon*, vol.XX, p.443.
21 Carrot, *La Garde nationale*, p.186.

The 1812 Cohortes

From 1811 onwards, the confrontation between France and Russia seemed inevitable to astute observers: the French and allied armies were gradually sliding from the Rhine towards the heart of Germany and Poland. So, just as in 1805 and 1809, the coastlines were being depleted. The Walcheren alert in 1809 had revealed the potential danger of an British attack on the coasts, but also the shortcomings of a defensive policy based almost exclusively on the partial raising of gardes nationaux. Numerous projects had been drawn up in 1810 and 1811. On the eve of the Russian campaign, the government chose to reinforce the military personnel in specific defence zones.

Since circumstances required a permanent service, it became necessary to designate those who were to provide it. On 13 March 1812, a sénatus-

A poster announcing the setting up of 88 cohortes of the Garde Nationale's first ban, March 1812. (Musée Carnavalet)

consulte appeared which, apparently taking the form of a reorganisation of the Garde Nationale, divided it into three parts, called bans. The third ban – also known as the 'arrière-ban' – was composed of men from the age of 40 to 60 and the second ban, of men from 26 to 40, as well as those who had paid a substitute. The composition of the first ban is particularly noteworthy. It was made up of men between the ages of 20 and 26 from the classes of 1807 to 1812, in other words, particularly fortunate conscripts who had not been called up for the army when the classes to which they belonged had provided their quota. Indeed, only a part of the contingent was actually called up, as the number of conscripts in a class always exceeded the needs.

In short, the sénatus-consulte of 13 March 1812 inaugurated a 'conscription-bis' and was part of Napoleon's desire to increase his military power without offending public opinion. It allowed the organisation of real 'parallel levies' with retroactive effect on classes that had already paid the 'impôt de sang' (blood tax) in their time and on men who thought they were freed from military obligations. In this context, the Garde Nationale became a pool from which it would be convenient to draw. The sénatus-consulte mentioned the formation of 100 cohortes of the first ban, which an imperial decree of 14 March reduced to only 88. This same text stipulated that each department would be required to provide all or part of a cohorte. Each one of them was to form a battalion with six companies of 140 fusiliers each, an artillery company of 100 men and a depot company of 100 men as well. The gardes nationaux who composed them obtained unusual guarantees. Article 7 of the sénatus-consulte specified in this respect that they were intended for internal police work and were not to leave the territory of the Empire. But it added to their missions the protection of maritime depots, arsenals, fortresses, but also the borders, which allowed for all sorts of interpretations. Similarly, unlike the exceptional levy of 300,000 men decided by the Convention in February 1793, the principle of relief from one class to the next was clearly specified. Thus, Article 5 prescribed that 'the men composing the cohortes of the first ban of the Garde Nationale would be renewed by sixths each year. For this purpose, those of the oldest class would be replaced by the conscripts of the current year. The renewal of the classes of 1807 and 1808 will take place for the first time, in 1814, by the conscription of 1813 and 1814'.[22] Such guarantees would later prove illusory.

---

22 Jean Desenne, *Code Général Français* (Paris: Ménard et Desenne, fils, Libraires, 1819), vol. IX, p.101.

Table 15. The 32 Military Divisions[23] and 88 Cohortes of the Garde Nationale's first ban, March 1812

Military division	Headquarters	Number of cohortes	Strength	Departments of origin
1	Paris	6	5,328	Seine, Aisne, Eure-et-Loir, Loiret, Oise, Seine-et-Marne and Seine-et-Oise
2	Mézières	2	1,776	Ardennes, Marne, Meuse
3	Metz	1	988	Forêts, Moselle
4	Nancy	2	1,776	Meurthe, Vosges
5	Strasbourg	2	1,776	Bas-Rhin, Haut-Rhin
6	Besançon	3	2,664	Ain, Doubs, Jura, Haute-Saône
7	Grenoble	3	2,664	Isère, Hautes-Alpes, Drôme, Léman and Mont-Blanc
8	Marseille	3	2,664	Bouches-du-Rhône, Basses-Alpes, Alpes-Maritimes, Vaucluse, Var
9	Montpellier	4	3,552	Hérault, Aveyron, Ardèche, Lozère, Gard, Tarn
10	Toulouse	4	3,552	Haute-Garonne, Ariège, Hautes-Pyrénées, Gers, Tarn-et-Garonne, Aude, Pyrénées-Orientales
11	Bordeaux	2	1,776	Gironde, Landes, Basses-Pyrénées
12	La Rochelle	3	2,664	Charente-Inférieure, Vendée, Loire-Inférieure, Deux-Sèvres, Vienne
13	Brest	4	3,552	Finistère, Côtes-du-Nord, Ille-et-Vilaine, Morbihan
14	Caen	3	2,664	Calvados, Mance, Orne
15	Rouen	3	2,664	Seine-Inférieure, Eure, Somme
16	Lille	5	4,440	Nord, Lys, Pas-de-Calais
17	Amsterdam	2	1,776	Zuiderzee, Bouches-de-la-Meuse, Yssel Supérieur
18	Dijon	4	3,552	Côte-d'Or, Aube, Haute-Marne, Saône-et-Loire, Yonne
19	Lyon	3	2,664	Rhône, Loire, Cantal, Haute-Loire, Puy-de-Dôme
20	Périgueux	3	2,664	Charente, Dordogne, Corrèze, Lot, Lot-et-Garonne
21	Bourges	3	2,664	Cher, Nièvre, Allier, Creuse, Indre, Haute-Vienne
22	Tours	4	3,552	Indre-et-Loire, Loir-et-Cher, Maine-et-Loire, Mayenne, Sarthe
23	Ajaccio	No cohort provided	–	–
24	Bruxelles	5	4,440	Dyle, Bouches-de-l'Escaut, Escaut, Jemmapes, Deux-Nèthes, arrondissement de Breda
25	Maastricht	3	2,664	Meuse-Inférieure, Bouches-du-Rhin, Lippe, Röer, Ourthe, Sambre-et-Meuse
26	Mayence	3	2,664	Mont-Tonnerre, Rhin-et-Moselle, Sarre
27	Turin	2	1,776	Doire, Pô, Sesia, Marengo, Stura
28	Gênes	2	1,776	Apennins, Taro, Gênes, Montenotte
29	Florence	1	988	Arno, Méditerranée, Ombrone
30	Rome	1	988	Rome, Trasimène
31	Groningue	1	988	Bouches-de-l'Issel, Ems-Occidentale, Ems-Orientales, Frise
32	Hambourg	1	988	Bouches-de-l'Elbe, Bouches-de-l'Heser, Ems-Supérieur

The raising of the first ban cohortes at the end of March 1812 did not seem to cause any particular problems. The correspondence of the 32 senators and dignitaries responsible for organising it shows this. The method of recruitment

---

23 The French *Division Militaire* was introduced in 1791. It was an administrative structure made up of various numbers of departments throughout the Empire. It is not to be confused with an army division that operated and fought in the field. The Divisions Militaires were commanded by an experienced active or non-active general. The Divisions Militaires commanders had the responsibility for all troops and fortresses within their departments, as well as maintaining law and order and of course, raising the local Garde Nationale battalions. At its height, Napoleon's Empire consisted of 32 Divisions Militaires.

was based on the conscription system. All the men had to pass before a recruitment council which met at the prefecture of their department. Composed of the general officer commanding the department, a gendarmerie officer, a sub-inspector of reviews, a war commissioner and the prefect – who chaired it – it had to examine the discharged conscripts from the classes of 1807 to 1812 in order to designate those who could, in spite of everything, be part of the first ban of the Garde Nationale. It also had to decide on requests for exemption, substitution or replacement. In the latter case, it was necessary to be able to present a certificate from the mayor of the commune of residence signed by three fathers of conscripts, as well as the statement of contributions paid by the parents.

Contrary to prior experiences, the gardes nationaux who formed the first ban cohortes not only drilled at regular intervals but were actually incorporated to form permanent units. They were subject, in regard to pay, service and discipline, to the same laws and regulations as the army. Although contemporary reports generally praised the good spirit of the gardes, the officers were neither efficient nor competent. In order not to weaken the active army's command structure, former soldiers, former guardsmen purposely promoted in the moment, and even retired or discharged officers were called upon. In order to avoid as much as possible any drift detrimental to the service, article 50 of the sénatus-consulte of 13 March 1812 reiterated an essential fact: 'Only valid officers and NCOs in a condition to wage war will be admitted'. As for article 44, it set out a precise framework for employment. Fearing 'commanders with their own minds', the Emperor had forbidden grouping the cohortes in the form of legions.[24] So, in groups of six or eight, the cohortes constituted a brigade stationed on the national territory and commanded by a *général de brigade*. They hardly had any cavalry. On the other hand, Napoleon accepted the existence of 88 companies of gunners. Although he was absorbed by preparations for the Russian campaign, the monarch meticulously followed the formation of these cohortes since they were intended to cover the rear of his Grande Armée.

Table 16. Garde Nationale cohortes organisation, 1812

Staff	Fusilier Company	Artillery Company
1 *chef de cohorte*	1 *capitaine*	1 *capitaine*
1 *adjudant-major*	1 *lieutenant*	1 *lieutenant en premier*
1 *lieutenant or sous-lieutenant*	1 *sous-lieutenant*	1 *lieutenant en second*
1 *chirurgien-aide-major*	1 *sergent-major*	1 *sergent-major*
2 *adjudants sous-officiers*	4 *sergents*	4 *sergents*
1 *caporal-tambour*	1 *caporal-fourrier*	1 *caporal-fourrier*
4 *maîtres-ouvriers*	8 *caporaux*	8 *caporaux*
	2 *tambours*	81 *artilleurs*
	121 *gardes nationaux*	
Total: 11	Total: 140	Total: 100

---

24 Napoléon I, *Correspondance de Napoléon*, vol.XXIII, p.384.

They proved to be far from reliable. At dawn on 23 October, *Général de brigade* Malet thus relied on the 1st Battalion of the Garde de Paris and on the 10e Garde Nationale Cohorte stationed at Popincourt barracks – one of the four cohortes making up the Paris garrison – to carry out his *coup de force*. Deceiving *Chef de Bataillon* Soulier by producing fake documents announcing the death of the Emperor in front of Moscow and the setting up of a provisional government, three of the conspirators got the officer to assemble his gardes nationaux straight away. They then took part in the arrest of Savary, the Minister of Police, and Pasquier, the Prefect of Police, before occupying the Hôtel de Ville. On the other hand, *Général de division* Hulin, the military governor of Paris, and his staff officers, Doucet and Laborde, did not let themselves be deceived. This led to the end of the conspiracy. Leading members were arrested before many Parisians had realised anything. Once the conspiracy was foiled, the police and judicial machinery was quickly set into action. Malet and his accomplices were tried by a military commission on 28 October: 15 death sentences were handed down, 13 of which were executed. Soulier, commander of the 10e Cohorte of the Garde Nationale, was shot by a firing squad on 29 October, as were Picquerel, *capitaine adjutant-major*, Steenhouwer and Fessart, *capitaines*, Lefèvre and Régnier, *lieutenants*. Seventeen officers and NCOs of the 10e Cohorte were also arrested. Gendarmerie officers replaced the arrested or executed officers. The repression also affected troops who had compromised themselves by following the conspirators. The gardes nationaux were obliged for a few days to wear their uniforms inside out, with the linings on the outside, so that the Parisian population could see that they had put themselves at the service of the conspiracy. In addition, men of the 1st Battalion of the Garde Municipale and the 10e Cohorte of the Garde Nationale were incorporated into line troops, as the Emperor could not bear to witness the joy expressed by some at the announcement of his death.

From Cohortes to Cohorte Regiments

Following this annoying affair the cohortes were condemned, at least compared to the decree of 14 March 1812. They represented a total of nearly 78,000 men, correctly instructed if not battle-hardened. Did they have a true burning desire to fight? In December 1812, when Napoleon's army was engulfed in the Russian cold, many were more or less pressured to write texts claiming they wanted to serve. These were brought to the sovereign and on the 27th the *Moniteur* distributed them widely. The address of the 87e Cohorte of the Garde Nationale garrisoned in Groningen, that of the 50e, 51e, 52e, 53e and 54e Cohortes garrisoned in Hamburg, but also that of the cohortes organised in the departments beyond the Alps were published. All had a similar request: to be called to the Grande Armée. This desire to defend the Empire was not fruitless. On 5 November 1812, Napoleon had ordered Clarke that the Garde Nationale cohortes employed in the defence of the Pyrenees should not enter Spain, but should be devoted solely to guarding the borders. Once back in France, the Emperor changed his mind: in early

January 1813, when he had to reconstitute a new Grande Armée after the disaster in Russia, the 88 cohortes of the Garde Nationale appeared to be a quality resource that could be used immediately. On 6 January, Napoleon wrote to Clarke that 'the Elbe Observation Corps should be entirely composed of cohortes'.[25] The next day, he announced that 48,000 men from the cohortes were at his disposal to form this corps. On the 9th, prior to any legislative action, he told *Maréchal* Berthier that he had 'converted the 88 cohortes into 22 regiments d'Infanterie de Ligne with four war battalions and one depot battalion. Each regiment gets an artillery company. The other artillery companies of the cohortes form three new artillery regiments of twenty companies each'.[26] As part of measures to make 350,000 men available to the Minister of War, a sénatus-consulte of 11 January 1813 increased the number of cohortes to 100,000 men. In addition, it stipulated that they were no longer part of the Garde Nationale and were transferred to the active army. The following day, a decree of application concretised this decision by absorbing them into 22 regiments d'Infanterie de Ligne numbered from 135 to 156 and specially formed to receive them. Napoleon's various orders immediately directed them to the army corps stationed in Germany and in Italy. As early as 28 January, for example, orders to leave for Mainz were sent to the 136e and 145e Regiments d'Infanterie de Ligne. On 8 February, the 138e Regiment d'Infanterie de Ligne received its departure order from Paris to Mainz, followed three days later by the 139e.

Table 17. The 22 cohorte regiments, 1813–1814

Regiment	*Colonel*	Constituting cohortes	Disbandment	Main battles
135e	Poirson	1, 8, 9, 11	1 May 1814	Halle, Lützen, Leipzig, Hanau, Montereau, Bar-sur-Aube
136e	D'Aubremé	12, 13, 14, 67	1 July 1814	Lützen, Bautzen, Leipzig, Montmirail, Vauchamps, Soissons, Reims, Paris
137e	Gaillard	2, 84, 85, 86	1814	Lützen, Dennewitz, Leipzig, Hanau, Torgau, Genes defence
138e	Maran, then D'Albignac	44, 45, 46, 64	1 August 1814	Lützen, Leipzig, Hanau, La Rothière, Champaubert, Montmirail, Vauchamps, Paris
139e	Bertrand, then Genevay	16, 17, 65, 66	8 June 1814	Lützen, Bautzen, Katzbach, Leipzig, Hanau, Arcis-sur-Aube, Saint-Dizier
140e	Ganivet	40, 41, 42, 43	16 September 1814	Lützen, Bautzen, Leipzig, Hanau, Juliers defence
141e	Pignet	37, 39, 62, 63	12 March 1814	Lützen, Bautzen, Leipzig, Hanau, Paris
142e	Fournier, then Camescasse	5, 36, 38, 61	June 1814	Lützen, Bautzen, Dresde, Hanau, Rosnay, Champaubert, Montmirail
143e	Mouton	28, 29, 30, 31	1814	In Spain: Ribas, Molins del Rey

---

25 Napoléon I, *Correspondance de Napoléon*, vol.XXIV, p.431.
26 Napoléon I, *Correspondance de Napoléon*, vol.XXIV, p.378.

Regiment	*Colonel*	Constituting cohortes	Disbandment	Main battles
144e	Boudin de Roville, then Ruelle	32, 33, 34, 35	1814	Lützen, Bautzen, Katzbach, Leipzig, Hanau, La Rothière, Dienville, Paris
145e	Nicolas, then Dolisie	6, 23, 24, 25	June 1814	Lützen, Katzbach, Dessau, Leipzig, Hanau, La Rothière, Champaubert, Montmirail
146e	Falcon	3, 76, 77, 88	1813	Würschen, Löwenberg, Goldberg. Annihilated near the Bober River on 29 August 1813
147e	Sibuet	15, 71, 78, 87	1813	Bautzen, Plagwitz, Goldberg. Annihilated near the Bober River on 29 August 1813 and transferred to the 154e
148e	Obert	72, 73, 74, 75	November 1813	Löwenberg, Bober, Goldberg
149e	Mandeville, then Druot	47, 48, 49, 79	July 1814	Bautzen, Löwenberg, Goldberg, Drebnitz, Fère-Champenoise
150e	Azemar, then Dereix	68, 69, 80, 81	1814	Goldberg, Katzbach, Wachau, Leipzig, defence of Maastricht
151e	Recouvreur, then Lebron	7, 50, 51, 52	June 1814	Halle, Weissig, Bautzen, Hanau, siege of Glogau, Campaign of France
152e	Raynaud	18, 19, 53, 54	1814	Lunebourg, Katzbach, Leipzig, Strasbourg, Paris
153e	Mathieu, Fremin, Mathieu	55, 56, 57, 58	1814	Wetting, Halle, Weissig, Bautzen, Haynau, Löwenberg, Goldberg, Katzbach, Leipzig, Hanau
154e	Ozilliau, then Chapuzet	4, 20, 21, 22	1814	Weissig, Wurschen, Löwenberg, Katzbach, Leipzig, Campaign of France
155e	Sennegon, then Charlet	10, 59, 60, 70	21 July 814	Weissig, Bautzen, Goldberg, Katzbach, Leipzig, Hanau, Pagny, La Ferté-sous-Jouarre, Orléans
156e	Oudot	26, 27, 82, 83	1814	Bautzen, Luckau, Dennewitz, Leipzig, Dessau, Hoff, Mayence, Voreppe, Paris

On 29 January, Napoleon had told Eugène de Beauharnais that 'the 22 regiments made up of the 88 cohorte battalions are superb. Together with the 11th Corps, they will be sufficient to push the enemy back beyond the Vistula, when Spring arrives and we can have some cavalry'.[27] On 13 February, *Général de division* Lauriston, who had just inspected the 151e Regiment d'Infanterie de Ligne at Magdeburg, sent a laudatory report to Minister Clarke: 'I have just reviewed the 151e Regiment. It amounts to 2,522 men under arms, including officers, and 247 in the local hospital. The men are of the best kind, of the greatest vigour and ready to serve. The NCOs are slightly

---

27   Albert du Casse (ed.), *Mémoires et correspondance politique et militaire du Prince Eugène* (Paris: Michel Lévy Frères Libraires-Editeurs, 1859), vol.VIII, p.287.

young, but they want to do well'.[28] On the other hand, many of the officers proved unable or too old to campaign. So, on 6 February, the Emperor wrote to Lauriston that he had sent 300 to 400 officers from Spain to Magdeburg to replace them. According to Lauriston, such a decision would make 'these new regiments the most beautiful and the best in the army'. If the officers were indeed renewed and their numbers increased, this problem still preoccupied the high command. On 26 March, Lauriston complained that a number of officers were 'old' and 'knew nothing about service'.[29]

From the spring of 1813 onwards, the history of the 22 cohorte regiments merged with that of the units recruited through conscription. All of them had an extremely short existence within the Grande Armée – about 15 months at most – and distinguished themselves in the main battles and combats of the Saxony campaign, but also, as did the 151e Regiment d'Infanterie de Ligne, defending the besieged fortresses in German territory. The remnants of some units also fought in the campaign of France in 1814. After Napoleon's abdication, the restored royal regime showered the *maréchaux* and generals of the Empire with favours hoping to win them over. Yet it endeavoured to disperse units in order to re-form regiments more easily influenced and entrusted to politically secure men, and also to reorganise the army. The decree of 12 May thus reduced the number of Line Infantry regiments to just 105, each made up of battalions or detachments blended from several regiments, in order to break down the *esprit de corps* of Napoleon's soldiers. In July, all was complete and regiments 135 to 156 were disbanded.

The Garde Nationale at the Ministry of War's Disposal

The sénatus-consulte of 3 April 1813 authorised the taking of 80,000 men within the young men of the Garde Nationale first ban, of which 24,000 were intended for the Garde Imperiale. The imperial government thus proceeded to reinforce the army by a retroactive call of five conscription classes. This same legislative text included other important measures. It ordered the anticipated levy of 90,000 men of the class of 1814, organised four regiments of Gardes d'honneur with a theoretical total of 10,000 cavalrymen, and entrusted the defence of the naval yards and maritime places 'to the courage and honour of the gardes nationales' from 49 departments.[30] A long decree of 5 April gave practical application to these principles. New cohortes consisting of two grenadier companies and two chasseur companies of 150 men each were then organised. These were grouped into departmental legions,

Made of a very thin sheet of brass, this plate was displayed by the Regiment de Toulon. This urban unit of the Garde Nationale was created on 5 April 1813 to defend the city's port and was definitively organised on 21 June. Commanded by *Colonel* de Castellane, the regiment was sent to Genoa in November and remained there until 15 March 1814. (Original artwork by Jean-Claude Colrat)

---

28 Jean-François Brun, 'Au crépuscule de l'Empire: L'exemple du 151e régiment d'infanterie de ligne', *Revue Historique des Armées*, 273 (2014), p.74.
29 Brun, 'Au crépuscule de l'Empire', p.74.
30 Duvergier (ed.), *Collection Complète des Lois*, vol.XVIII, p.278.

armed and equipped at the expense of the department and whose officers were chosen locally by the prefect. These legions could also be called upon to provide a temporary active force. The method of appointing such grenadiers and chasseurs was well defined: an itinerant organising council, presided over by the prefect, was to choose from lists drawn up in each commune the most well-off individuals aged between 20 and 40.

Tables 18 and 19. Distribution of the contingents to be provided by the Garde Nationale for active military service

District	Number of 600 men cohortes	Departmental contingent to be provided	Temporarily active contingent
1st Texel shipyards	25	15,000	1,200
2nd Antwerp and Flessingue shipyards	59	35,400	3,600
3rd Cherbourg shipyards	59	35,400	3,000
4th Brest and Lorient shipyards	54	32,400	3,000
5th Rochefort shipyards	41	24,600	2,400
6th Toulon shipyards	53	31,800	3,000
Total	291	174,600	16,200

Department	Main locations	Number of cohortes
Bouches-de-l'Escaut	Flessingue	1
Lys	Ostende	2
Nord	Dunkerque	3
Pas-de-Calais	Calais	1
	Boulogne	2
	Montreuil	1
Somme	Abbeville	2
Seine-Inférieure	Le Havre	3
Manche	Cherbourg	2
	Granville	1
Ille-et-Vilaine	Saint-Malo	2
Finistère	Brest	3
Morbihan	Lorient	2
	Belle-Ile	1
Charente-Inférieure	La Rochelle	2
	Rochefort	2
	Ile-de-Ré	2
	Ile-d'Oléron	2
Var	Toulon	3
		Total: 37

This new legislation relating to the Garde Nationale was broad in scope. In reality, it was initially limited to six maritime districts, those of Rotterdam, Antwerp, Cherbourg, Brest, Rochefort and Toulon. The decree of 5 April envisaged the implementation of 49 legions bringing together 291 cohortes for a total of 174,600 men, that is to say 1,000 to 6,000 grenadiers and chasseurs for each of the concerned departments. A decree of 8 April called only 16,200 of them to duty, that is to say between 100 and 600 men per department, much lower figures than those of the mobilisation of 1809. The wide range of possibilities granted in the search for replacements, as well as a presumed short, local and not very painful service, made the execution of this mobilisation rather easy despite initial reluctance. At the beginning of June, grenadiers and chasseurs designated by lottery had almost all joined their respective units. Placed under the command of six generals-senators, these units took the name of their department or the chief town of the maritime district. A seventh arrondissement, bringing together 10,800 men, was created by decree on 15 May 1813: this was a regularisation of the levies of gardes nationaux carried out since October 1810 on the Pyrenean borders. The decree of 29 August extended the implementation of the provisions of April to all the departments beyond the Alps. Six other eastern French departments were also affected by the decrees of 21 October and 15 November 1813 signed by Marie-Louise, then Empress and Regent.

In addition to the grenadier and chasseur cohortes organised in the departments, the decree of 5 April 1813 also provided for the formation of 37 urban cohortes of 1,000 men each in 19 towns or islands along the Atlantic coast, from Flessingue to Toulon, via Calais and Boulogne, Le Havre and Cherbourg, Lorient and Belle-Ile. They included a voltigeur company, a grenadier company and four fusilier companies of 150 men each, complemented by a gunner company of 100 men. They were raised from the population aged between 20 and 40 in the towns concerned, but also in the nearest communes. Exceptional and urgent needs prompted the imperial government to permanently arm sedentary detachments charged to protect shipyards and important maritime places. On 15 May, four additional cohortes were formed in the Pyrénées-Orientales, then one in Sète on 21 June, prelude to new creations at the end of August. In addition, nine cohortes were formed in the autumn in the border towns of eastern France.

Defeated on 19 October 1813 during the 'Battle of the Nations' at Leipzig, Napoleon promptly crossed the Rhine again to reach the palace of Saint-Cloud. Besides the glaring problems of money that he was facing, he had to rebuild a new army, the third in less than two years. The 1812 and 1813 Campaigns had swallowed up everything: men, horses and equipment. If he was to proceed to new levies of men, the Emperor anticipated having to recourse largely to the Garde Nationale.

Fighting on National Soil: the 1814 Campaign of France

New Cohortes and Reserve Armies
By the end of December, the imperial government effectively called upon the people to defend the now invaded national territory. In order to ensure the defence of the border fortresses, cohortes of fusiliers, grenadiers, as well as mixed cohortes combining fusiliers and grenadiers, and cohortes of

artillerymen were organised, in accordance with a decree of 17 December. In addition, in 184 open towns – meaning those without fortifications – mainly located within the territory of the Empire, grenadier cohorts were formed. They were intended not only to 'maintain calm' in the communes, but also to 'lend a hand to public authorities' by assisting officers responsible for conscription or by facilitating the collection of taxes and duties. Such cohorts were to be composed essentially of 'the most taxed landlords, merchants and all individuals exercising useful professions, as well as the sons of both'.[31] It was certainly a matter of linking the personal destinies of these men to the obviously shaky fate of the French Empire.

The imperial decrees of 30 December 1813 and 6 January 1814 mobilised 101,640 already active gardes nationaux from 18 military divisions. Very carefully divided into 121 battalions of 840 men each, these men were to be organised into 18 brigades intended to form two reserve armies of gardes nationaux covering Paris, Lyon and the fortresses. The imperial decree of 6 January 1814 stipulated that 'such army corps are only intended to prevent the occupation of the territory of the Empire. As soon as the enemy is pushed back beyond the Rhine, the gardes nationaux will no longer have to fight.'[32] A special article of the decree formally states that 'as soon as the enemy will have been driven out of our territory, the reserve armies of the Gardes Nationales will be dismissed'.[33] Such assertions soon proved to be illusory.

The Parisian Garde Nationale's Rebirth

Paris hardly had an urban cohorte and, until the last moment, Napoleon hesitated to recreate the Garde Nationale there. Prompted by necessity, he nevertheless reactivated it on 8 January 1814 and took advantage of the opportunity to reorganise it. The manpower was limited to 30,000 men, divided into 12 legions (one per arrondissement) of four battalions which were themselves made up of five companies, including one of grenadiers. The four companies of grenadiers of the same legion constituted an elite battalion. The Emperor granted himself the command in chief of the Garde Nationale Parisienne, *Maréchal* Moncey becoming its *major-general*. Governor of Paris Pierre-Augustin Hulin, *Grand Chambellan* Montesquiou, *Grand Maréchal du Palais* Bertrand and Comte de Montmorency were named *aides-majors généraux*. The 12 legion chiefs belonged to the high imperial administration, the high aristocracy or the financial sphere. Following the oaths taken between 16 and 22 January, the 900 officers of the various battalions were assembled at the Tuileries Palace on Sunday the 23rd. On the eve of leaving his capital to join his army, the Emperor entrusted the Empress Marie-Louise and the King of Rome to their bravery and loyalty, to which the assembly responded with an apparently enthusiastic 'Long live the Emperor!'[34] The next day Napoleon handed over command of the Paris Garde Nationale to his brother Joseph and left him with detailed instructions, demonstrating both

---

31 Duvergier (ed.), *Collection Complète des Lois*, vol.XVIII, p.395.
32 AN: F/9/357: Levée en masse de 1814, décret du 6 janvier 1814.
33 AN: F/9/357: Levée en masse de 1814, décret du 6 janvier 1814.
34 *Journal de Paris*, 24 (1814).

THE GARDE NATIONALE 1789–1815

Napoleon's goldsmith, Jean-Baptiste Claude Odiot (1763–1850) joined the Garde Nationale Parisienne in 1789. He fought in the 1792 campaign and was a *lieutenant* at the Battle of Jemmapes. In 1809, he led a cohorte of the Paris Garde Nationale. On 30 March 1814, *Chef de Bataillon* Odiot was given provisional command of the 2nd Legion and the detachments defending the Barrière de Clichy and the Chaussée de Saint-Ouen. (Public domain)

his usual attention to detail and his misgivings about the age-old institution. The first priority was to protect the 30 barriers of the capital from the enemy's light troops. This task fell to the 12 newly created artillery companies, whose guns were manned by 700 invalids and as many students from the Ecole Polytechnique and the schools of law, medicine and surgery.

Table 20. Senior officers of the 12 Paris Garde Nationale legions, early 1814

Legion's Number	Legion Chief	Battalion Commanders
1	Comte de Gontaut	Comte Remusat, Baron Labouillerie, Comte de Beauveau, M. Froidefond
2	Comte Regnaud de Saint-Jean-d'Angely	Comte de Laborde, Comte d'Anjusson, Comte Lillers, M. Odiot
3	Baron Hottinger	M. Ternau aîné, Baron Delessert, Comte Perregaux, Chevalier Rouyer,
4	Comte Jaubert	Baron Thibon, Chevalier Fontaine, M. Lemor, M. Marguerite
5	M. Daberjon de Murinais	M. Delafrenay, M. Delon, M.Dallemagne, M. Aubertot
6	M. de Fragnier	M. Titon, M. Aubié, M. Becq, M. Laugier
7	M. Lepileur de Brevannes	M. Guelen, M. Buquet, M. Bellart, M. Chopin Varnsurville
8	M. Richard-Lenoir	M. Nicolaï, M. Saint-Julien des Nœuds, M. Vibert, M. Robillard
9	M. Devins de Graville	M. de Brioudes, M. Chaumer, M. Chanteur, M. Champy
10	Duc de Cadore	Comte Lascarez, Comte d'Hautpouville, M. Philippon, Comte d'Aubusson
11	Comte de Choiseul-Praslin	M. Lebeau, M. Arthus Bertrand, M. Aclocque, Chevalier Roettier du Plessis
12	M. Salleron	M. Bricogne fils, M. Bouvard, M. Lafont, M. Riard

Disappointing Results

Although the Minister of the Interior recalled the usefulness of the urban cohortes for the protection of private property and simultaneously insisted on their strictly municipal vocation, the measure gained only ambiguous support. As the strength to be mustered was relatively modest – 1,200 to 1,300 men in Bordeaux, Toulouse and Marseilles, 600 in Le Havre, 300 in Draguignan – the cohortes were effectively organised during January and February 1814. On the other hand, their members sometimes refused to endorse any pledge of allegiance to the imperial regime. The two Marseilles cohortes thus argued that their adherence could potentially serve as a pretext for sending them to the army. Thibaudeau, prefect of the Bouches-du-Rhône, acknowledged that these units, composed of manufacturers, shopkeepers and tradesmen, were certainly carefully selected and well behaved, but that they should not be trusted: 'In the event of popular unrest, they would have protected people and property. If the enemy had presented himself, it is likely that they would have welcomed him'.[35]

---

35   Antoine Claire Thibaudeau, *Mémoires de A.C. Thibaudeau, 1799–1815* (Paris: Plon, 1913), p.37.

THE GARDE NATIONALE 1789–1815

Grenadier officer of the Garde Nationale. Decorated with the Royal Order of Spain created by Joseph Bonaparte in late October 1808, this *capitaine* pragmatically had the decoration of the Lily, received during the Restoration of King Louis XVIII, added to his portrait. (Osenat, with permission)

The formation of the two reserve armies contemplated by Napoleon also ran into serious obstacles. The events of the campaign of France sometimes went faster than the mobilisation of men. In the departments invaded by the enemy, the imperial prescriptions quickly became obsolete, so that the imperial decrees of 4 and 8 January ordering the creation of corps francs were applied instead. In the interior departments, the prefects tried, one last time, to satisfy the Emperor's wishes; at least, they tried to persuade the Minister of the Interior of their good will. On the field, the reality was quite different. The gardes nationaux appointed for service were often too old or too young, even infirm and disabled. In fact, the last round of recruitments had emptied the country of its vital forces. In addition, resistance to incorporation arose in several departments. Sent to fight ill-equipped and ill-armed, the gardes nationaux therefore represented a burden rather than a support for the military authorities. As a result of their very low morale, their extreme desertion was facilitated by their lack of uniform and was almost desired by commanders. The case of the guardsmen assigned to the defence of the Pyrenees is symptomatic in this respect. On 26 February 1814, *Général de division* Harispe wrote a letter to *Maréchal* Soult in which his bitterness shone through: 'We no longer need ammunition for our gardes nationaux. A panic has seized them. Everyone has withdrawn to their homes, abandoning or taking their weapons. The 3rd Legion was assembled at Artix with orders to make the fords impassable. The defection was complete. The colonel being left alone and no longer seeing any use for his presence, went home'.[36] The same day, the prefect of the Basses-Pyrénées addressed a similar missive to Soult: 'I had managed with much difficulty to gather here a few thousand gardes nationaux. At the first rumour spread, these wretches cowardly fled, in spite of the efforts of General Coutard to retain them. This unfortunate desertion has greatly distressed me'. The next day, *Général de brigade* Coutard, more optimistic, assured Soult that 'the uselessness of the gardes nationaux or their defection made me gather the officers who stayed with me. I urged them to organise themselves into partisans, in order to harass the enemy, to stop his convoys just as the Spanish guerrillas are doing. Several have taken this option. It will be necessary to gather everyone to fall on the enemy,

---

36 Joseph Vidal de la Blache, *L'évacuation de l'Espagne et l'invasion du Midi, juin 1813-avril 1814* (Paris: Berger-Levrault Editeurs, 1913), vol.II, p.135.

Les prisonniers de guerre des puissances alliées passant dans Paris, engraving by Pierre-Michel Alix, 1814. On 17 February 1814, Russian, Austrian, but also Prussian prisoners of war entered Paris through the Porte Saint-Martin. They were escorted by the Garde Nationale. The inhabitants gave them food and water. (Musée Carnavalet)

sometimes together, sometimes alone'.[37] The situation was not much better elsewhere in the country. Between 25 February and 2 March 1814, a cohorte in the Seine-Inférieure recorded 109 desertions out of a total of 334 gardes. During the same period, 112 gardes deserted a Somme cohorte totalling 443 men. A cohorte in the Eure even had more deserters (85) than gardes (53). In contrast, a cohorte of 290 men in the Oise had just 15 deserters.[38] All these cohortes had been organised in departments north-west of Paris. The military operations were taking place east of Paris, so the area from which these units came from was not yet affected by the fighting. Many of the gardes probably felt that they had better things to do than drilling with a pike or a musket while their families, farms or businesses required their attention. Perhaps the gardes in the Oise were more militarily minded.

In Paris, the concrete results of the mobilisation of the Garde Nationale were, on the whole, disappointing. Most of its officers were notables with limited physical abilities. Moreover, they had their service performed by substitutes, and, while the senior officers were fairly reliable, the *capitaines* and NCOs were much less so. Moreover, only about 11,000 gardes were properly equipped at the end of February, barely a third of the total. The Garde was

---

37 Henri de Riancey, *Le général comte de Coutard: Etude historique, la République, l'Empire et la Restauration* (Paris: E. Dentu, Libraire-Editeur, 1857), p.135.
38 SHD: C2 564: Rapport de situation, 2 mars 1814.

performing an honorary service at the Tuileries Palace, but its very existence frightened the Emperor. Napoleon was worried about the quickly acquired popularity of *Maréchal* Moncey. Similarly, unsure of the military value of the Parisian bourgeoisie and even less of its political behaviour, he toyed for a time with the idea of opening the ranks of the Garde to unemployed workers. 'The owners would no longer have to fear the revolt of the proletarians. On the contrary, he would make them contribute to the defence of the city', he wrote on 10 March to his brother Joseph.[39] However, neither the Minister of the Interior nor the Prefect of Police were in favour of this project, which was consequently abandoned.

Gardes Nationaux in Action

All these intertwined measures nevertheless had some effect. From the very first days of January 1814, the gardes nationaux helped line troops defend several fortresses in the northern and eastern parts of France, such as Lille, Maubeuge, Belfort, Thionville, Huningue and Sélestat. The Landau Garde Nationale, which was fairly well equipped and numerous, took part in the defence of its own town walls under the command of *Général de brigade* Verrières. Gardes nationaux from the Moselle and the Vosges also made up the small garrison of 3,400 men who supported a lengthy siege lasting from 2 January to 28 April. In Strasbourg, the gardes nationaux provided active service on the city walls or in the outposts and distinguished themselves on 29 March by repelling an enemy attack at Kehl. In the early days of the Restoration, the mayor of the city paid a heartfelt tribute to the Garde Nationale, which, according to him, deserved 'the highest praise for having shared the defence of the town with the brave garrison and for ensuring tranquillity and good order in the interior'.[40]

Napoleon was aware of the chaotic formation of reserve armies of gardes nationaux. He nevertheless strongly relied on this solution. The mobilised gardes nationaux constituted his ultimate reserve behind his small army of 60,000 men, which was continually at odds with 300,000 coalition soldiers in the Champagne region. The good behaviour of 30,000 gardes nationaux under *Général de division* Pacthod's command at the battle of Montereau convinced the Emperor. However, the latter noted that 'the gardes nationaux are only useful when fully staffed by officers of the line. When there are none, the gardes nationaux are worthless, because without officers and NCOs, there is really nothing good'.[41] From then on, he tried to make the most of this resource, but decisions taken were rarely followed through. On 24 March, 5,000 gardes nationaux commanded by *Généraux de division* Amey and Pacthod were tasked with protecting 100 artillery wagons and 80 supply carriages destined for the Imperial Army. With artillery carriages using the

---

39 Napoléon I, *Correspondance de Napoléon*, vol.XXVII, p.300.
40 Frédéric-Charles Heitz (ed.), *Strasbourg pendant ses deux blocus et les Cent-Jours: Recueil de pièces officielles, accompagné d'une relation succincte des faits, arrives pendant les années 1813, 1814 et 1815, avec le plan du camp du blocus de 1815* (Strasbourg: Frédéric-Charles Heitz Imprimeur-Libraire, 1861), p.82.
41 Napoléon I, *Correspondance de Napoléon*, vol.XXVII, p.264.

OF PURPLE CLOAK AND BATTLEFIELDS

main roads, infantry men progressed towards Fère-Champenoise across soggy fields and were literally worn out. The next day, they were enveloped by Allied cavalry and shelled by artillery. They abandoned the supply convoy which was impeding their march and used the horses to support the artillery carriages. Formed into six strong squares, they bravely defended themselves for seven hours. At dusk, almost 1,000 of them were captured and more than 2,000 others lay dead on the battlefield. Five hundred found refuge in the Saint-Gond swamps. Guardsmen won the adversary's respect, in particular Tsar Alexander's. The battalions of mobilised gardes nationaux of the Mayenne and the Nord were only a few weeks in existence.

Table 21. Order of battle of Pacthod's Division in early March 1814 (The Nafziger Collection of Napoleonic Orders of Battle, after SHD C2/556)

	Officers	Men
1st Brigade: *Général de Brigade* **Rost**		
1er Regiment of Sarthe	25	990
3e Regiment of Indre et Loire	29	662
2nd Brigade: *Général de Brigade* **Bonté**		
2e Regiment of Loire et Cher	44	984
5e Regiment of Seine et Marne	8	263
3rd Brigade: *Général de Brigade* **Kozinsky**		
4e Regiment of Maine et Loire	33	989
Artillery		
6e Artillerie à pied	2	68
Det/2e (bis) Train Battalion	0	22
Det/4e Principal Train Battalion	2	83

On 27 March, coalition troops, having repulsed the weak forces under *Maréchaux* Marmont and Mortier, arrived before Paris, which was hastily fortified. Only modest work had been undertaken to barricade the outskirts, fill in the gaps in the city walls with palisades, and protect the main gates. About 2,400 men were assigned to guard them: 100 men at each of the 12 large ones on the right bank (including the famed Barrière de Clichy) and 60 men at each of the 18 small ones. 3,600 gardes from the 12 legions of the capital could lend assistance to the most threatened barriers. The remainder was to serve inside Paris. However, some of the gardes nationaux took part in the fighting alongside line troops. Moncey had in fact declared to legion chiefs that he did not want to order the Garde Nationale to leave the city walls. He nevertheless added that he did not

Mobilised gardes nationaux, campaign of France, 1814. All of them are dressed in the blue peasant *blouse* worn in both 1814 and 1815. Note the diversity of headgear and the widespread use of black leatherwork. Perhaps they were armed with the n°1 model musket (which was developed during the Revolution), as Napoleon wished to preferentially allocate the 1777 model muskets to the line infantry. (Guillaume Bretegnier)

Strasbourg Garde Nationale during the siege of the city, 1814, gouache by Henri Boisselier. From left to right: drummer, fusilier and grenadier. (Guillaume Bretegnier)

THE GARDE NATIONALE 1789–1815

This print by Girardet vividly illustrates the good behaviour of the Garde Nationale Parisienne when facing Russian squadrons. The scene fits a heroic vision and therefore far from reality. A young officer leads his men into battle. The uniforms are more or less identical: fusiliers and grenadiers are both wearing hats. A guardsman from the district battalions is wearing a top hat and equipped with odds and ends. (Musée Carnavalet)

see any disadvantage in having grenadiers and chasseurs join the soldiers, so that 3,000 to 4,000 volunteers presented themselves and fought on the heights surrounding Paris.

Table 22. The Garde Nationale at the Battle of Paris, 30 March 1814

Legion	Quarter	Strength
1	Roule, Champs-Elysées, Place Vendôme, Tuileries	860
2	Palais Royal, Faubourg-Montmartre, Chaussée d'Antin, Feydeau	1,297
3	Faubourg Poissonnière, Mail, Saint-Eustache,	1,021
4	Saint Honoré, Louvre, Banque de France, Marchés	1,105
5	Porte Saint-Martin, Faubourg Saint-Denis, Bonne Nouvelle, Montorgueuil	919
6	Porte Saint-Denis, Saint-Martin-des-Champs, Temple, Lombards	1,172
7	Saint-Avoye, Mont-de-Piété, Marché Saint-Jean, Arcis	1,046
8	Marais, Quinze-Vingts, Faubourg Saint-Antoine, Popincourt	639
9	Hôtel-de-Ville, Ile Saint-Louis, Arsenal, Cité	611
10	Jardin-des-Plantes, Saint-Jacques, l'Observatoire, Saint-Marcel	721
11	Ecole-de-Médecine, Luxembourg, Sorbonne, Palais-de-Justice	682
12	La Monnaie, Saint-Thomas-d'Aquin, Faubourg Saint-Germain, Invalides	1,063

Total: 11,136 men, including officers and NCOs

The allied attack was launched in the early hours of the 30th. Time was of the essence, for Napoleon could march back to his capital to galvanise the spirit of resistance, mobilise the popular forces of this city of 600,000 inhabitants, and lean on them to launch military operations again. If some Parisian gardes nationaux behaved passively in some sectors, others, on the contrary, participated honourably in their city's defence. They held their own for several hours in a disjointed battle at Charonne, Buttes-Chaumont, Montmartre, but also at the Barrière de Clichy. At the cost of nearly 300 dead and 600 wounded, they held off the enemy's advances. Negotiated on the evening of the 30th and signed at 2:00 a.m. the next day, the capitulation of the capital put an end to the fighting. Although clashes had been sporadic, they had nonetheless lent credence to the image of the Garde Nationale defending the city: Horace Vernet's painting – *La Barrière de Clichy* – further added realism to it.

From Emperor to King

Deposed by the Senate on 3 April, Napoleon resolved to abdicate three days later. In the twilight of the Empire, the action of the Garde Nationale – whether mobilised or sedentary – had proved to be a partial success. As last-chance troops, mobilised gardes had oscillated between massive desertions and undeniable courage. Belatedly organised by Napoleon in the form of urban cohortes, the sedentary Garde Nationale had contributed through the defence of fortresses and open towns to slowing down the enemy, but not to stopping it. The attitude of some urban cohortes, such as those in Marseilles, did help to accelerate the fall of the imperial regime. In the southwest, other cohortes certainly switched to militant royalism. As early as 12 March, the Bordeaux gardes nationaux thus adopted the white cockade and warmly welcomed the Duc d'Angoulême, who was returning to France in the steps of British troops.

Under Talleyrand, the provisional government undertook to put this law and order force at its service. On 5 April 1814, one of its earliest acts was to 'stop the departure of gardes nationaux of all kinds, activated either by imperial decree or by other acts of the former government' and to 'take the necessary measures to recall, if there is still time, those who have been directed to the army'. Meanwhile, the formation 'in each village, town and city, of a sedentary Garde Nationale' was decreed. It was to consist of 'the most honest inhabitants', to be led by 'notable persons renowned for their wisdom and good disposition' and to be 'placed under the orders of the municipal authorities'. It was mainly responsible for 'protecting communes from looting and excesses that isolated detachments might commit and for stopping French fugitives and foreign marauders'. It also had to 'watch over the partisan corps still acting for the former government'.[42]

Although the allies occupied Paris, they had agreed not only to maintain the service of the Garde Nationale, but also to let it keep its weapons. Increased to 40,000 men, the Garde ensured strict and efficient policing within the Paris area. Acting alongside the allied occupation troops, it was

---

42 Anon., *Correspondance administrative du département d'Indre et Loire* (Tours: Mame Imprimeur de la Préfecture, 1814), pp.64–65.

THE GARDE NATIONALE 1789–1815

Le Comte d'Artois, Colonel General of the Gardes Nationales, engraved portrait by Levachez, 1814. (Musée Carnavalet)

On 18 May 1814, Monsieur, Comte d'Artois, was appointed *Colonel General* of all the Gardes Nationales of the Kingdom of France. This most luxurious sabre was made shortly afterwards. (Osenat, with permission)

also the only force that the provisional government could rely on. Yet it did not claim to be openly royalist and continued to wear the tricolour cockade, which the Senate had decided to retain. On 9 April, the Comte d'Artois announced that he was about to enter Paris. In order to win the Garde to the royal cause, to prevent its resistance from slowing down the course of events and to facilitate the political transition, Talleyrand advised Louis XVIII's brother to display the white cockade for this solemn occasion, but to wear the Garde Nationale uniform adopted during the revolutionary decade and retained under the First Empire. Marrying these two a priori antinomic symbols meant to suggest that the new regime was not going to repudiate the last 25 years. The prince looked handsome on horseback and, on 12 April, he charmed his public, in particular the bourgeoisie. In Paris, the allied troops were very discreet. The only other star of the day was the Garde Nationale, which marched along a skilfully laid-out route from the faubourg Saint-Denis to Notre-Dame Cathedral and the Tuileries Palace. It was more at ease on this appeasing and enthusiastic day than two weeks earlier at the city gates. This beautiful spring day could lead the King's brother to believe that the capital's Garde Nationale had been won over and that the Bourbons were now assured of a peaceful restoration without bloodshed.

The Comte d'Artois at the Helm

The Comte d'Artois was pleasantly surprised by what happened on 12 April and immediately sought to exploit this sudden popularity. To do so, he multiplied the reviews and distributed countless decorations, in particular the brand-new decoration of the Lily. In addition, he had General Dessolles, also *commandant en chef* of the Parisian Garde Nationale, join the provisional government. Rejecting the offers that La Fayette indirectly made to him, he managed to convince Louis XVIII to appoint him *Colonel General* of all the Gardes Nationales of the kingdom, which happened on 15 May. Dessolles became his *major general*, whilst retaining command of the Garde Nationale Parisienne. Disgraced until 1808 for hostile remarks towards Napoleon, this general was sent to fight in Spain, then in Russia where he acted as Eugène de Beauharnais' chief of staff. In the spring of 1814, his own chief of staff was Allent, Joseph Bonaparte's former adviser.

Comte d'Artois' appointment was important and went far beyond a simple honorary command. Since 1789, the Garde Nationale had never been centrally organised. It was sedentary and depended on municipal authorities. When mobilised, it was under military command. The very existence of a *colonel general*'s office announced a permanent, uniform and coherent institution. The ordinance of 16 July confirmed this development. All the Gardes Nationales of the kingdom were sedentary. Any movement outside the town, for the urban gardes, or the canton, for the rural gardes, could only take place in exceptional cases determined by a special law. The *Colonel General* was responsible for discipline and training. His general staff prepared the laws and regulations that the Minister of the Interior enforced. Finally, prefects and mayors prepared the lists and supervised the accounting. Two circulars from Dessolles, drawn up on 20 August and then 1 October, specified the doctrine of the institution. They reaffirmed the fact that the Gardes Nationales were, in essence, civil, sedentary, local and selective. Any established and domiciled citizen between the ages of 20 and 60 who paid a contribution and who, 'by virtue of their state, their goods or their industry, had an obvious interest in the maintenance of order and the preservation of property' was enrolled in the Garde Nationale. This reflected the desire to link the most influential part of the population with the government's fate. Those considered dangerous to society,

This engraving shows a chasseur of the Garde Nationale Parisienne. He is wearing a hat, which was replaced shortly afterwards by a bearskin cap. His coat's white cuffs piped with scarlet are unusual for that period of the Garde's history. As a tangible sign of the political transitions underway at the time, this man wears the decoration of the Lily. (Yves Martin)

such as foreigners who had not been naturalised, servants, itinerant workers or those who 'did not pay contributions, as well as all those who, by their public conduct or profession, could compromise the honour of the Garde', were excluded.[43] The youngest individuals were also eliminated, thus leaving middle-aged men with at least elementary military training. A centralised organisation was sought with the creation of an inspector general of the Gardes Nationales post in each department. The creation of departmental legions was not, however, on the agenda, since these corps had been 'suppressed by the government decree of 5 April. If they still existed, they were to be dissolved by virtue of the ordinance of 16 July, as incompatible with the civil, sedentary and local state of the Gardes Nationales'.[44] Implementation of these prescriptions angered the services of the Ministry of the Interior and led to an administrative dispute. As for the prefects, they were worried about having to support in their department an inspector general directly attached to Paris. The Comte d'Artois swept aside all objections. He ordered the prefects to correspond directly with the general staff and to accelerate their set up of the organisation. The service in this new Garde Nationale, which had become socially exclusive and politically conservative, appeared to the population – and to the youth in particular – as bland and boring. Moreover, it was marked by an endless series of royalist festivals and celebrations, such as Louis XVI's death anniversary, the religious service for Marie-Antoinette, the feast of the Duchess of Angouleme, the Mass of the Holy Spirit, or the Feast of the Blessed Sacrament.

The Garde Nationale during the Hundred Days

The Garde Nationale was unpopular with local administrators, faced opposition within the government itself, and was shunned by the population. It suffered from the general discredit that affected the First Restoration. In fact, Louis XVIII had quickly disappointed: the army's manpower was limited and its senior officers and generals had to deal with men emerging from the emigration. Peasants were worried about the possible return of feudal rights, while many workers were reduced to unemployment due to competition from British factories. As for the bourgeoisie, some feared having to return national property acquired during the Revolution. On 1 March, Napoleon, who had been in exile on Elba until then, landed at Golfe-Juan with a small army of barely a thousand men. The 'Eagle's flight' surprised the Garde Nationale in full reorganisation. The royal government's orders of 9 and 10 March to include 'all taxpayers interested in maintaining the government and respecting the *Charte Constitutionnelle*'[45] and to mobilise it against 'the usurper' remained without real effect. When they encountered Napoleon's small army, the gardes nationaux either vanished– as in Lyon

---

43   Anon., *Correspondance administrative du département d'Indre et Loire*, p.252.
44   Vincent Cuvilliers, 'Un département placé sous la protection de sa garde nationale active: Le Pas-de-Calais (1806-1815)', *Revue du Nord*, 350 (2003), p.309.
45   Desenne, *Code Général Français*, vol.IX, p.119.

OF PURPLE CLOAK AND BATTLEFIELDS

– or, as in Châlon, were categorically opposed to any resistance. In Paris, they limited themselves to keeping order in the capital. On the night of 19–20 March, they respectfully greeted the departure of Louis XVIII before coldly welcoming Napoleon on the following day. In the Pas-de-Calais, the prefect had called upon the generosity and patriotism of his department's inhabitants: in order to finance the mobilisation of the Garde, payment of the 1815 contributions was thus anticipated. However, despite the combined efforts of civilian and military authorities, the active Pas-de-Calais Garde Nationale was not ready when Napoleon returned to power on 20 March. Its excessively long mobilisation had been inhibitory. In fact, only a few gardes nationaux battalions, mobilised in the Midi by the Duc d'Angoulême at the beginning of April 1815, found themselves opposed to their counterparts who had joined the Emperor during a brief civil war. In northern France, the Dunkirk Garde Nationale had to be disbanded, as the royalists in its ranks colluded with emigrant emissaries from Ghent to surrender the town. In Douai, it was common knowledge that the Baron de La Grange, commander of the city's Garde Nationale, remained 'entirely devoted to the King'.[46]

On his return to power, Napoleon simply cancelled all of Louis XVIII's ordinances regarding the Garde Nationale, in particular that of 16 July 1814. Following the disappearance of the staff and the departmental inspectors,

The King's departure from the Tuileries palace was scheduled for the night of the 19 to the 20 March 1815. The commentary on this royalist engraving indicates that, when the King appeared, 'all the gardes nationaux on duty fell to their knees and sobs were heard on all sides. Deeply moved himself, the King exclaimed: "I will see you again soon. Return to your families. I am touched by your loyalty"'. (Musée Carnavalet)

---

46   Author's collection: Rapport d'un 'correspondant' envoyé à Bruxelles, 15 avril 1815.

the Ministry of the Interior had full control over the Gardes Nationales. In anticipation of a new military campaign, the Emperor was especially anxious to make the most of this immense reserve of men, both as a sedentary force and the source of a reserve army. The reorganisation – on which Napoleon himself, *Maréchal* Davout but also Carnot, Minister of the Interior, were busy working – began on 23 March. Carnot estimated that more than two million people between the ages of 20 and 60 were available, but only a third could be used as active units. On 10 April, a decree reaffirmed the obligation of service for all Frenchmen aged between 20 and 60, divided into 326 battalions of six companies of 120 men each: four fusiliers, one grenadier and one chasseur. Grenadiers and chasseurs were to be selected from among single men aged 20 to 40 and could, if necessary, be detached from their original battalions to form elite departmental battalions under the command of battalion commanders appointed by the Emperor.

The decree made no fewer than 204 detached battalions available to the Ministry of War, a total of 150,000 men from the 2nd, 3rd, 4th, 5th, 6th, 7th and 16th military divisions. These regions – the north and east of France, as well as the Alpine borders – had been invaded the year before and had retained some painful memories. The levy was relatively easy, especially as the Minister of War had promised that the gardes would be garrisoned in fortresses closest to their homes and that they would not be integrated into the line army.

The imperial government, encouraged by these initial results, decided to generalise their application in order to create a true second-line army. Under the impetus of *Général de division* Mathieu Dumas, who had worked with La Fayette, a series of decrees issued between 19 April and 10 May led to the mobilisation of 150,000 additional men. The results, however, did not live up to expectations. In several departments, protest was at its peak. In those of the west – Brittany and the Vendée – where insurrection was brewing, the prefects' alarmist reports dispensed with further operations. In the northern departments, the protest, due in part to the cessation of trade with Britain, significantly slowed down mobilisation efforts. For example, the Orne provided 107 out of the 2,160 requested gardes and the Pas-de-Calais 437 out of 7,440. In the Midi, especially in Marseilles, public sentiment appeared to be in favour of the King. Even the most favourably disposed departments – such as Moselle, Vosges or Rhône – were unable to provide their entire contingent. These had to muster a greater number of troops than other departments considered to be politically less secure. Nonetheless, the levy gained strength as the opening of the campaign in Belgium approached: 80,000 grenadiers and chasseurs had joined their units by 25 May; by mid-June there were almost 170,000. It was already a tour de force, particularly in financial terms.

Table 23. Organisation of the active Garde Nationale in the 16th Military Division (Northern France), spring 1815

Department	Btns	Strength	Garrison	Notes
Aisne	1e	656	Lille	
	2e	643	Lille	
	3e	54	Lille	
	4e	608	Lille	
	5e	577	Lille	
	6e	607	Lille	
	7e	590	Lille	
Somme	1e	543	Landrecies	
	2e	457	Lille	
	3e	315	Valenciennes	
	4e	531	Maubeuge	
	5e	398	Maubeuge	
	6e	627	Le Quesnoy	Armed
	7e	427	Le Quesnoy	
	8e	291	Lille	
	9e	121	Dunkerque	Not armed
	10e	?	Douai	Did not arrive
Nord	1e	688	Lille	Armed
	2e	258	Lille	Not armed
	3e			Organising
	4e			Organising
	5e	690	Douai	Partly armed
	6e			Armed
	7e	402	Condé	Armed
	8e	461	Cambrai	Armed
	9e	353	Cambrai	Armed
	10e	305	Avesnes	Armed
	11e	206	Avesnes	Armed
	12e			Not formed
	13e			Not formed
	14e			Not formed
Pas-de-Calais	1e	569	Landrecies	
	2e	421	Lille	
	3e	78	Valenciennes	
	4e	370	Maubeuge	300 muskets
	5e	230	Maubeuge	
	6e	429	Le Quesnoy	Armed
	7e	429	Le Quesnoy	427 muskets
	8e	393	Lille	
	9e	576	Dunkerque	Not armed
	10e	604	Douai	Did not arrive

THE GARDE NATIONALE 1789–1815

On 14 May 1815, between 12,000 and 15,000 fédérés from faubourgs Saint-Antoine and Saint-Marcel marched to the Tuileries to parade before the Emperor in the palace courtyard. Preceded by a Garde Nationale band, this demonstration had been regulated in every detail by Réal, the Prefect of Police. Note the banners with the capital district numbers and one of the fédérés playing the *biniou* to the left of the scene. (Musée Carnavalet)

Carnot, newly appointed as Minister of the Interior, made Napoleon aware of the advantages of a more popular recruitment. He was indeed disturbed about the 'eviction of a part of the population of an age to bear arms' and had acutely perceived that in the spring of 1815, the Emperor's supporters were, in addition to his (former) soldiers, those nostalgic for the Revolution.[47] Peasants, as well as the urban poor – workers and craftsmen – were viscerally hostile to the aristocrats. Many were animated by the memory of the revolutionary federations and the enthusiasm of the Volontaires of 1792. Carnot wanted to capitalise on this patriotic upsurge in the face of royalism and the foreign threat. He therefore facilitated the creation of battalions of fédérés despite reluctance by the authorities. The latter were afraid to arm these men, when most of them did not even have the minimum income necessary to be admitted to the Garde Nationale. The Emperor, who had been shunned by the Garde Nationale Parisienne at a military review on 16 April, decided – on the afternoon of 14 May – to review at the Carrousel some 15,000 fédérés from the working-class faubourgs Saint-Antoine and Saint-Marcel. Informed that these men were bitterly disappointed of not receiving any weapons the previous year, Napoleon promised this time to give them some and to provide them with 'officers covered with honourable wounds and accustomed to seeing the enemy flee ahead of them' in order to effectively defend the capital. He also assured them that he would turn them into 'the scouts of the Garde Nationale'.[48] His brief speech, which emphasised the confidence he had in the people and the army, ended with a 'Vive la

---

47   Dupuy, *La Garde nationale*, p.233.
48   Napoléon I, *Correspondance de Napoléon*, vol.XXVIII, p.216.

OF PURPLE CLOAK AND BATTLEFIELDS

Sedentary gardes nationaux, by Henri Boisselier. In 1814 and 1815, Napoleon clearly stated that gardes nationaux should receive a cartridge box and cartridge belt, musket, bayonet and, if available, a shako. Guardsmen would indeed try to give their civilian dress a military appearance. (Yves Martin)

Nation!', to which the fédérés responded by intoning the highly revolutionary song 'Ça ira!' The next day, a decree gave satisfaction to popular demands by ordering the formation of 24 battalions of Parisian tirailleurs-fédérés. Commanded by *Lieutenant-Général* Darricau, they were intended for 'the defence of Paris and the hilltop defences'.[49] Each arrondissement was to raise a regiment with two battalions of 720 men each, making a total of 17,800 men for the entire capital. The actual strength of the tirailleurs-fédérés probably did not exceed 13,000 men. As for the supply of weapons, although the Emperor himself had clearly mentioned this, it was delayed to the great relief of the ministers. Fifteen battalions of tirailleurs-fédérés were also to be set up in Lyon.

The gardes nationaux proved to be of considerable help. Commanded by experienced generals, the detached battalions were integrated into reserve divisions placed in direct support of field armies. They were given the best equipment available as a matter of priority and quickly proved to be suitable for field service. A few days before the outbreak of hostilities, the active Garde Nationale formed a reserve division in the north of the country, another in the Armée de la Moselle and no less than three divisions in the Armée des Alpes. All the fortresses in eastern France saw their sedentary gardes nationaux put into activity, and reinforced by the elite departmental battalions. On 18 May, the prefect of the Pas-de-Calais had called on his department's sedentary gardes nationaux to ensure 'the maintenance of order and public tranquillity through continuous surveillance'.[50] Following a War Minister's instruction, mobile columns, composed of line troops, gendarmes, veterans and, if necessary, sedentary gardes nationaux, were also formed in this border department from the very next day.

Napoléon and the Armée du Nord were defeated at the Battle of Waterloo on 18 June 1815. Three days later, the Emperor was back at the Élysée, his palace since April. After the battle he had just lost a few miles from Brussels, he had another confrontation to fight with the deputies of the Chamber of Representatives. For in the days that immediately followed Waterloo, and even as the Anglo-Prussian troops advanced rapidly towards Paris, the capital became the scene of a fierce political struggle waged against Napoléon's supporters by Fouché, the Minister of Police, and La Fayette, then Vice-President of the Chamber of Representatives. Napoléon hoped to retain power and prolong the war effort against the coalition. Popular acclamations heard in the vicinity of the Elysée encouraged him to do so. But the first proposals to the Chambers were rejected. In truth, the assemblies wanted no less than the Emperor's abdication. Disillusioned, he resolved to do so on 22 June, after having rejected his brother Lucien's proposal to attempt a *coup d'état*, as on 18 Brumaire. He had answered:

> The whole public was then against the Five Hundred and on my side. Today, Lucien, it is the opposite. The dominant idea is that war is being waged because of me, and the Assembly is seen as a brake on my ambition and my despotism. I

---

49   Napoléon I, *Correspondance de Napoléon*, vol.XXVIII, p.216.
50   Cuvilliers, 'Un département placé sous la protection de sa garde nationale active', p.311.

Les Parisiens volontaires, ou qui l'aime [Napoleon] me suit, engraving by Guyot, 25 May 1815. This is one of the few contemporary depictions of the fédérés. The variety of their uniforms and equipment, far removed from the prescriptions of the Ministry of the Interior, is to be noted. (Author's collection)

could, you tell me, throw the representatives into the Seine. But I will meet greater resistance than you believe in the gardes nationaux. The representatives would rush into the provinces to raise them against me.[51]

This letter showed that the Garde Nationale remained an immense force, ill-organised of course, but feared, especially in the confines of the capital. A watchword, an outcry, could make it take up arms and, as a result of contagion, throw the whole of Paris into the streets.

Meanwhile, La Fayette was keen to regain his 1789 command. A representative tabled a proposal to this effect, which was met with murmurs. The Chamber of Representatives finally opted for Masséna as commander of the Paris Garde Nationale. A decree of 28 June placed Paris under siege. The government also decided to send the tirailleurs-fédérés to the entrenchments of Paris in support of line army detachments. They were mainly employed in the northern and eastern parts of the capital. On 2 July they fought at the village of Vertus, as the newspaper *L'Indépendant* reported:

> Yesterday, the village of Vertus was completely occupied by the British. It was attacked by a detachment of tirailleurs-fédérés of the Garde Nationale, to which

---

51 Adolphe Thiers, *Histoire du Consulat et de l'Empire*, vol.XX, p.346.

several guardsmen had joined. They seized some houses and managed to take control of a portion of the village. This is now occupied partly by the French, partly by the British. Each side has crenellated the houses.[52]

The next day, at dawn, the commissioners appointed by the allied armies signed the convention for the surrender of Paris. External fortifications would be given up on 4 July, Montmartre on the 5th and the city gates on the 6th. On the evening of the 4th, some of the city's defenders, both soldiers and tirailleurs-fédérés, showed their anger, a spontaneous reaction that had nothing to do with any attempt at insurrection. Around 11:00 p.m., the Garde Nationale, to whom article 9 of the convention had entrusted the security of the capital, intervened to disperse the demonstrators. The divorce between the faubourgs and the Garde Nationale widened still further. In the end, only the moderates were pleased with this capitulation which ended a war they considered already lost and that should not be revived by any patriotic resurgence, as feared by Carnot and some generals.

The morning of 8 July, 50 gardes nationaux of the 10th Legion forbade the representatives of the Chamber created by Napoleon to enter the Palais-Bourbon. It was, no less, an anti-parliamentary *coup d'état*. That same day, an ordinance signed the day before by Louis XVIII was published: it placed *Général de division* Dessolles at the head of the Garde Nationale Parisienne. In addition, *Le Moniteur* published two daily orders, one from Masséna, the other from Dessolles, ensuring the peaceful handover of power. The King then made his entry into the capital, escorted by 450 gardes nationaux from the 11th and 12th Legions. As for the chiefs of the Garde Nationale, who had claimed that they wanted to 'preserve the national colours forever', they nevertheless complied with Dessolles, who ordered all the battalions to display the white cockade once again.[53] In the following days, the tirailleurs-fédérés were disarmed. During this operation, the 11th Legion, commanded by Acloque, was noted for its relentlessness against them. The Restoration was complete.

In Paris, the Garde Nationale had chosen the losing side. Indeed, in the weeks immediately following the Hundred Days, King Louis XVIII turned toward it to guarantee the restoration of his crown. During this critical period, while efforts were made to disband the so-called 'brigands of the Loire' who remained loyal to the Emperor, the Garde Nationale Parisienne proved to be loyal to the King, resisting siren calls of those still hoping for the return of the Emperor and who

Miniature portrait of a garde national, c. 1814–1815. (Collection of François Vinot-Préfontaine's collection)

---

52   *L'Indépendant*, 64 (1815).
53   Edmé Armand Gaston Duc d'Audiffret-Pasquier (ed.), *Mémoires du Chancelier Pasquier* (Paris: Plon, 1894), vol.III, p.335.

French Garde Impériale and Garde Nationale during the Hundred Days, 1815, original watercolour by Denis Dighton, 1816. As the Bourbons returned to power, two royalist officers of the Parisian Garde Nationale, conspicuously wearing the white cockade on their hats, are attempting to strike up a conversation with a scowling officer of the former Garde Imperiale. (Anne S.K. Brown Military Collection)

had hardly given up ideas of a military *coup de force*. It was charged with symbolically manifesting the continuity of national sovereignty and was de facto responsible for guarding public buildings, but also for protecting and escorting the sovereign's representatives. Furthermore, during the occupation of the capital, the dissolution of the imperial army made the Garde Nationale the only organised armed force allowed by the allied sovereigns. As such, it was responsible for maintaining order. Such simultaneous obligations required the daily mobilisation of some 5,000 Parisian gardes nationaux. They were required to serve one day a week, sometimes even more for certain elite companies noted for their appearance and state of mind.

Elsewhere in France, many gardes nationaux performed well. On 1 July 1815, the 7th Garde Nationale Division commanded by *Lieutenant-Général* Maransin and composed of gardes from the Rhône, Puy-de-Dôme, Loire and Haute-Loire, put up fierce resistance against the Austrian columns at La Faucille and Fort-l'Ecluse, in the department of Isère. In northern France, the gardes nationaux performed extensive service in various fortresses and fortified towns as allied troops advanced. Similarly, the garrisons of Metz and Antibes kept the enemy at bay and preserved for the King fortresses that the Emperor 'had entrusted to their honour'.[54] The defence of the places of

---

54 Carrot, *La Garde nationale*, p.202.

Longwy and Huningue was also to their credit, despite the sporadic acerbic judgements made by some military commanders. 'I would have remained almost alone if the gates had not been continually closed', admitted *Général de division* Barbanègre, who had valiantly defended Huningue.[55]

The gardes nationaux for the most part did not remain in active service for long once the ordinance of 20 July 1815 demobilised them. The 6e Bataillon d'Elite de la Drôme was, however, an exception. It arrived at Fort Barraux, in the Isère, in June 1815, and found itself totally isolated following the capture of Grenoble on 9 July. Although they agreed to the white cockade at the beginning of August, the gardes nationaux categorically refused to surrender the fort to coalition troops. The last of them – barely 200 men – only evacuated the fort in December, without any acknowledgement of their dedication. In the autumn and winter of 1815, Allied troops began the occupation of French territory that was to last three years. In a revelatory manner, the gardes nationaux maintained order in a buffer zone between occupied territories and areas with French royal army units.

The Garde Nationale Beyond the Empire

The Garde Nationale lasted through the consular and imperial regimes, but underwent a radical change. From a simple auxiliary force, it became the real crucible of a territorial reserve army. This change corresponded to the vagaries of Napoleonic politics. Most of the time, Napoleon I turned to this reserve of auxiliaries only after he had established his campaign plan and mobilised appropriate forces. Over time, he drew more and more men from it.

Just as the First, the Second Restoration maintained the Garde. In Paris, however, it did not escape purging. Thus, of the 900 officers in the various battalions, 400 were dismissed and replaced by acknowledged royalists. Denunciation was also encouraged to keep out unrepentant Bonapartists and liberals. From 1816 to 1818, nearly 50 officers and 150 NCOs were thus dismissed in the departments. In 1815, a massively ultra-royalist Chamber was elected and the decisive influence of Comte d'Artois, the King's brother, facilitated in most of the departments the establishment of a reactionary Garde Nationale. It was closely monitored by local aristocrats and carried out police missions at the beginning of the Second Restoration. In Paris, the Comte d'Artois was assisted by *Maréchal* Oudinot, replacing Dessolles. In the departments, inspectors, such as the Prince of Polignac and Comte de Bruges, were responsible for establishing the roles of each unit with the assistance of mayors. They constituted the backbone of the new institution. All of them were of good nobility, and they naturally influenced the appointment of officers, whose nominations by the King were based on the Comte d'Artois' proposals. It was beyond question to return to the principles of officer election. The gardes' and their officers' devotion to the monarchical cause was rewarded by the decoration of the Lily, which was amply awarded to all those

---

55 Paul Leuilliot, *La Première Restauration et les Cent-Jours en Alsace* (Paris: S.E.V.P.E.N, 1958), p.243.

who properly fulfilled their service. In 1818, there were already nearly 23,000 decorated members in Paris alone. Nevertheless, the Garde Nationale set up by the ultra-royalists did not give satisfaction. In 1816, the moderates, distrustful of the institution, gained significant power in the Chamber. They wanted to limit the Garde's strength, as it was more devoted to the Comte d'Artois and his followers than to the actual monarchy.

The ordinance of 21 July 1816 recalled that only the wealthiest individuals, who were able to dress and arm themselves, were to appear on the ordinary control register. Individuals whose modest resources prevented them from equipping themselves appeared on the reserve register and would only be mobilised under exceptional circumstances. In fact, the service weighed quite heavily on the local middle and lower middle classes. Above all, the Garde of 1816 had a fundamentally communal organisation. The Comte d'Artois did not, however, abolish the organisation's hierarchy. A more discreet staff continued to oversee the Parisian offices still managing the gardes' appointments and decorations. The Garde Nationale's daily reality in the departments was thus a sort of permanent negotiation between the prefect's administration, the mayors of the main towns, Comte d'Artois' inspectors and the most influential Garde Nationale commanders. The result was a mosaic of very different situations, depending on the local balance of power and the actual implementation of the law. A new ordinance of 30 September 1818 sought to ensure that the Garde Nationale fit within military institutions being reorganised by the Gouvion Saint-Cyr law. But this is another story...

Guardsman and drummer of Paris Garde Nationale, engraving by Debucourt after a drawing by Vernet, 1816. (Yves Martin)

Uniforms and Equipment

The National Uniform: Persistence and Little Change, 1800–1812

Under the First Empire, the 'national habit' was naturally the Garde's uniform. The decree of 13 July 1791 was silent regarding the cuff flaps. These were of various types. They could, as in the line infantry, be blue, piped with scarlet, but also blue piped with white, blue without piping, or even scarlet piped with white. The decree of 30 September 1805 introduced a novelty in the form of

THE GARDE NATIONALE 1789–1815

Garde Nationale senior officer. He wore a long-tailed coat with silver buttons and bore the Legion of Honour and the decoration of the Lily, a tangible sign of the political transitions underway in 1814–1815. (François Vinot-Préfontaine's collection)

white buttons. These displayed the words 'Garde Nationale' surrounded by a crown of oak and olive leaves. The grenadiers' buttons featured a flaming grenade surrounded by the words 'Garde Nationale'. A hunting horn replaced the grenade for the voltigeurs. Although this same decree did not make this point explicit, silver replaced gold in the rank insignia. This provision concerned the stripes of *sergents* and *sergents-majors*, but also the officers' epaulettes and counter-epaulettes. The gorget was still made of gilded copper and was enhanced by a silver ornament.

Headgear, 1800–1812

The headdress of the gardes nationaux followed the same evolution as that of the army's infantrymen and from 1807, the shako gradually replaced the hat. However, departmental finances coped with replacements even more slowly than line army units.

In Paris, the shako was embellished, for the fusilier companies, with a tin diamond plate embossed with the eagle and the legion number. For the chasseurs, the plate was adorned with a hunting horn. Grenadiers had a dedicated bearskin plate, which was decorated with an eagle. In the provinces, the plates were not numbered when the size of the cohortes hardly allowed the formation of a legion.

The shako was once again regulated in 1810. In Paris, the fusiliers had a tin shako plate with the number either cut out or embossed. In the case of the chasseurs, the legion number was cut out and placed in the centre of an embossed hunting horn. As for the grenadiers, an embossed grenade topped the legion number. The provincial Gardes Nationales, whose strength was insufficient to form a legion, carried a plate without a number. The fusiliers' plate was only stamped with the name of the town or department. The chasseurs' plate bore a hunting horn, while the grenadiers' bore a grenade.

Overseas Adaptations, 1802–1810

According to the decree of 14 October 1802, the Martinique Garde Nationale infantrymen all wore a round hat. Moreover, they had a dark blue cloth coat, red collar and cuffs, blue lapels with white piping. The buttons were cast in yellow metal. Waistcoat and pantaloons were white. European companies wore the long-tailed coat and the companies of Afro-Caribbeans the coatee. Grenadiers were distinguished by their red plume, ganse and epaulettes. Red grenades adorned the turnbacks. Chasseurs had distinctive green plume, ganse and epaulettes. Green hunting horns also adorned their plumes. The other companies wore a white ganse and a tricolour plume on the hat. The dragoons wore a blue frac with white collar, red facings and piping, blue trousers, white waistcoat. They wore a round hat with a two-coloured plume, the lower third black, the upper two thirds white. The *shabraque* was made of blue cloth with red braid.

OF PURPLE CLOAK AND BATTLEFIELDS

Port Nord-Ouest chasseur, 1806, watercolour by Henri Boisselier. (Yves Martin)

Seychelles garde national, circa 1807, ink drawing by Henri Boisselier. (Yves Martin)

In Ile de France, the infantry of the Garde Nationale of the Port Nord-Ouest district was dressed in the national uniform. The grenadiers had their usual distinctive scarlet plume and epaulettes. Two elite companies of chasseurs, created on 18 June 1806, were distinguished by green epaulettes. The chasseurs nationaux were provided with a dark blue coatee, with pointed lapels of the same colour. Collar and cuffs were made of red cloth and the buttons were cast in white metal. The gardes nationaux usually wore a lightweight, tropicalised, locally designed shako made of a wicker frame, reinforced with leather and covered with blue cloth. The two elite companies of chasseurs wore a Polish-style chapska made on the same principle and decorated with a green plume. Waistcoats and breeches were tailored from white nankin. Guardsmen wore either breeches or trousers, or gaiter-trousers that hugged the lower legs. The elite companies of the Port Nord-Ouest Legion, as well as the NCOs, were armed with a sabre-briquet, unlike the colonial chasseurs.

The Seychelles were a dependency of Ile-de-France and did not escape *Général de division* Decaen's attention. On 15 May 1807, he decreed the formation of a company of gardes nationaux on Mahé Island which had two European infantry sections and a section of black chasseurs. The European sections had a dark blue coat, lapels and turnbacks piped red, red collar and cuffs piped white and brass buttons. The black section had a dark blue coatee and lapels piped green, green collar, cuffs and turnbacks and white metal buttons. All gardes wore locally produced shakos, as did nearly all regulars and gardes nationaux on the islands. *Carabines* were specified as the armament of the coloured chasseurs.

Gardes Nationaux of the Garde Imperiale: Special Features of a Little-Known Regiment

On 27 June 1810, *Général de division* Curial decided to define the uniform of the gardes nationaux of the Garde Imperiale. It consisted of a blue short-tailed jacket, with scarlet collar, white lapels piped in scarlet, scarlet cuffs piped in white and white piped scarlet turnbacks. The waistcoat and breeches were white, the half-gaiters black. The regiment was unusual in the Garde Imperiale for its organisation. It originally had four battalions of four companies, but in May 1810 the unit was reduced to two battalions of six companies, including one grenadier, one voltigeur and four fusiliers. The grenadiers were distinguished by scarlet epaulettes, plume, shako cord, pompom and sword knot. The turnbacks bore scarlet flaming grenade devices. The voltigeurs had the same features, but in green, and wore green hunting horns devices on the turnbacks. The fusiliers had blue shoulder straps with scarlet piping, a white shako cord and blue eagles devices on the turnbacks. A tufted lentil disc worn on top of the shako distinguished each company. Finally, unlike the grenadiers and voltigeurs, the fusiliers theoretically were not provided with a sabre-briquet.

Uniforms of the First Ban Cohortes, 1812

Articles 30 to 33 of the decree of 14 March 1812 specified that the uniform of fusiliers and of the 88 cohorte *depot* was that of the line infantry, 'as defined in the decree of 19 January 1812'.[56] It is therefore the new Bardin-type coatee, with white lapels entirely closed and piped in scarlet, white turnbacks, scarlet collar and cuffs piped in white. The buttons were cast in white metal, stamped with an eagle and marked 'Premier Ban de la Garde Nationale'. The shako was decorated with a white metal plate bearing the name of the department. The distinguishing marks of the ranks were in silver. The armament was similar to that of the line infantry. The uniform of the cohorte gunners was the same as that of the foot artillery, 'except for the collar, which shall be blue'.[57] This prescription remains obscure to say the least, as the artillerymen also had blue collars. The white metal buttons were stamped with two crossed cannon. The shako was adorned with a tin plate. It featured two crossed cannon surmounted by the number of the cohorte. At the extremities, two grenades replaced the lion heads.

---

56 Honoré Hugues Berriat, *Législation Militaire, ou Recueil Méthodique et Raisonné des Lois, Décrets, Arrêtés, Règlements et Instructions actuellement en vigueur sur toutes les branches de l'état militaire* (Alexandrie: Louis Capriolo Imprimeur-Libraire, 1812), vol.II, p.859.

57 Berriat, *Législation Militaire*, vol.II, p.860.

This colour plate by Parisian printer Aaron Martinet shows the plausible uniform of the Garde Nationale cohortes. While the shako has a diamond-shaped plate, the uniform is of the Bardin type with stapled lapels. (Yves Martin)

The 135e Regiment d'Infanterie de Ligne was formed on 12 February 1813 from the 1e, 8e, 9e and 11e Cohortes de la Garde Nationale. It was engaged at Lützen, Weissig, Lowenberg, Goldberg and Hanau. In 1814, the unit took part in the battles of Mormant, Montereau and Bar-sur-Aube, before fighting before Paris. This young *fourrier* took part in the defence of the capital. (Yves Martin)

Uniforms of the Cohorte Regiments, 1813–1814

At the beginning of January 1813, the cohortes of the first ban were used to the creation of 22 regiments d'Infanterie de Ligne, numbered 135 to 156. During their short existence, these units presented an undeniable uniformological mismatch. They were all dressed differently, as shown by the clothing records, the written accounts of the protagonists and the few preserved uniforms. Some units were dressed like gardes nationaux. In other regiments, the uniforms conformed from the outset to the recently enacted Bardin regulations. This was the case, for example, with the 141e and 142e Regiments d'Infanterie de Ligne, inspected in early February 1813 by *Général de division* Hulin. According to him, 'the 141e is fully dressed, equipped and armed. The changes to be made according to the new uniform are not yet complete. Approximately 1,200 men still have to receive the new plates on their shakos, chinstraps and buttons'.[58] As for the 135e Regiment d'Infanterie de Ligne, it had made its transition to the

---

58 SHD: C2 138.

Bardin uniform before Napoleon's first abdication. Finally, still other regiments used effects taken directly from the enemy's stocks. The diversity that prevailed for clothing also applied to weaponry. On 8 February 1813, for example, the inspection office of the 19th military division in Lyon wrote to the Minister of War that it had the honour 'to send him herewith the situation of the first three battalions of the 145e Regiment d'Infanterie de Ligne (6e, 23e and 24e Cohortes) at the time of the 6th of this month, the day before its departure for Mainz'. While the clothing and equipment were judged to be 'good', the muskets were described as being 'old and of various models'.[59] Such a situation was probably not an isolated case.

The new regiments d'Infanterie de Ligne had four battalions with six fusilier companies each and therefore theoretically did not have any elite grenadier or voltigeur companies. Yet administrative documents and memorialists' accounts argue in favour of the existence of such companies. Written at the very beginning of February 1813, Hulin's inspection reports and those of the 19th military division inspection office, established in Lyon, mention them in the 141e, 142e and 145e Regiments d'Infanterie de Ligne respectively. As for *Général de division* Puthod, whose division aggregated the 146e, 147e and 148e Regiments d'Infanterie de Ligne, his papers indicate, on several occasions, the existence of voltigeur companies within these units. *Sergent-Major* François Marcq, of the 2nd Battalion of the 153e Regiment d'Infanterie de Ligne, wrote in his *Souvenirs* that on 26 May 1813, at the battle of Haynau, a grenadier from his battalion shot *Oberst* von Dolffs, who commanded the prestigious Prussian Gardes du Corps.

These elite companies were solely distinguished by the size of the men: the tallest were grenadiers and smaller ones were voltigeurs. They had distinctive features, namely an aigrette and epaulettes. In early February 1813, Hulin stated in a report to Napoleon himself that all of the grenadiers and voltigeurs of the 142e Regiment d'Infanterie de Ligne

> have received their aigrettes. In the 3rd and 4th battalions, grenadiers' and voltigeurs' epaulettes are still missing, but all these details are being worked on relentlessly and in a few days everything will be completed. The 142e was organised yesterday. It is quartered at Vaugirard, Issy and surroundings, and it will be able to appear with the 141st at Thursday's parade, if Your Majesty wishes to see these two regiments in their current state. Epaulettes and aigrettes were distributed to the grenadiers and voltigeurs of the 1st and 2nd Battalions of the 142e. The plate, chinstraps and buttons will be distributed in a few days' time.[60]

The Urban Cohortes of 1813

The imperial decree of 17 December 1813 stated that the urban cohorte grenadiers, chasseurs and artillerymen were to dress and equip themselves at their own expense. The fusiliers were not 'required to be dressed in uniform'.[61] In Landau, the urban cohortes' grenadiers and chasseurs wore, at the time of

---

59   SHD: C2 136.
60   SHD: C2 138.
61   Duvergier (ed.), *Collection Complète des Lois*, vol.XVIII, p.395.

the 1814 siege, a lapelless coat which buttoned straight across the chest. The grenadiers wore red plumes on their hats, epaulettes and trousers with a side strip of the same colour. The chasseurs wore a two-tone green and yellow pompom on their hat. They had green epaulettes with yellow crescents. The trousers had a yellow side seam.

Paris Garde Nationale Uniforms and Equipment in 1814

The Paris Garde Nationale was reformed by imperial decree on 8 January 1814, but its recruitment during that month and the following one proved fairly difficult. Several iconographic sources allow us to reconstruct the uniforms, such as Opitz's plates, engravings by imagiers (such as Basset's) and Horace Vernet's painting depicting the fine conduct of the Parisian gardes at the Barrière de Clichy on 30 March.

In January 1814, Emperor Napoleon wore the uniform of a Garde Nationale *colonel* on several occasions. On the 19th of that month, tailor Lejeune had provided him with one of them invoiced at 330 *francs*, as much as for the famous chasseur à cheval uniform. Another set was made during the Hundred Days. While in exile on St Helena, Napoleon still had a Garde Nationale uniform, which he intended for his son in his will. This uniform is of the same cut and colour as the officers': long tails with silver buttons, embroidery and *colonel*'s epaulettes associated with the Garde Nationale. It is nevertheless distinguished by the absence of the regulation white piping on the collar. In Horace Vernet's painting *La Barrière de Clichy*, Moncey can be seen wearing his *maréchal*'s uniform. However, as a *major-general* of the Paris Garde Nationale, he has silver epaulettes and embroidery. The cuffs, as well as the piping on the turnbacks and pockets, are scarlet.

The Garde Nationale Parisienne was concerned with its originality. Perhaps in an attempt to copy the Garde Imperiale, it wore white cuff flaps, just like the Grenadiers à Pied. Similarly, it retained until the Empire's end a hat which, because of its relatively high shape, was similar to the grenadiers' and chasseurs à pied's.

Garde Nationale *aide-major general*'s coat that belonged to *Général de division* Bertrand, circa 1814. It is a Garde officer's coat in accordance with the 1812 regulations. The cuff flaps are of blue cloth, whereas the Garde Nationale Parisienne had them white. The silver buttons have a two-line legend 'Garde Nationale' surrounded by a crown of laurel and oak. (Original artwork by Jean-Claude Colrat)

THE GARDE NATIONALE 1789–1815

Uniforms of Paris sedentary Garde Nationale, coloured engraving, circa 1814–1815. (Collection Yves Martin)

The decree of 8 January 1814 required grenadiers to dress and equip themselves at their own expense. Iconography shows that, depending on the legion, they were dressed either in the Bardin-type jacket – with long tails, though – or in the old-style uniform. A red plume and scarlet epaulettes were a sign of their status. The above-mentioned decree also prescribed that each battalion of the Paris Garde Nationale should have four companies of elite fusiliers. Indeed, they wore green epaulettes and a pompom of similar colour on their hats. On 11 February, Moncey instructed the legion chiefs to create one or more sections of tirailleurs – also known as chasseurs – in each company, by means of guardsmen trained in hunting and equipped with two-shot rifles. They had a straight, lapel-less uniform and green epaulettes with scarlet crescents. Such an arrangement not only differentiated the chasseurs from the fusiliers, but was also an elite company's distinctive feature. A contemporary engraving also reveals that these same chasseurs had short Hungarian-style gaiters and, above all, a blue cloth capote piped in scarlet. This seemingly astonishing provision should not be overlooked in view of the source's quality. However, all the Parisian legions were not so appropriately or uniformly dressed, as Opitz's watercolours testify. Indeed, on 30 March 1814, during the Battle for Paris, many gardes nationaux fought in civilian clothes, with a simple tricolour cockade on their hat.

Just as elsewhere in France, the armament was as heterogeneous as defective. An obvious reminder of the revolutionary decade, a stock of 8,000 pikes produced in 1792 arrived in Paris on 11 February and were distributed to certain fusilier companies. When, on 27 March, a review of 12,000 gardes nationaux was carried out in the Tuileries palace courtyard, entire companies were still armed with pikes decorated with tricolour ribbons, the exact appearance of which remains unknown. As for the muskets, though kept in large numbers in the Paris arsenal, Clarke, Minister of War, had them distributed with the greatest parsimony. At the review of 27 March, muskets seized from Russian, Prussian and Austrian prisoners were therefore mixed in with *mousquetons* and *carabines* and, for lack of anything better, with hunting rifles. Two days later, when the coalition forces were already in the vicinity of Paris, the minister finally agreed to hand over 4,000 muskets to the gardes. By 30 March, more than 20,000 guardsmen were devoid of firearms, obviously reserved for line troops. Iconography shows that fusiliers, grenadiers and chasseurs were given a sabre-briquet. No doubt this was true of some of the best-equipped legions, but certainly not of all.

1814: Doing the Best and Dealing with Shortages

In the context of the 1814 mobilisation, a major concern of the local authorities was to give a somewhat military appearance to the men of the active Gardes Nationales, last-chance troops destined to fight alongside the line army. If mayors and prefects were used to providing conscripts, they now had to provide soldiers, an unusual operation for these civil administrators, and beware of anyone who displeased the military authorities. In January 1814, Rambuteau, prefect of the Loire, was thus sternly admonished by *Maréchal* Augereau, who was then commanding the Armée de Lyon: 'A company of the Garde Nationale Regiment from your department arrived today and was neither equipped nor armed. In its present state, it is more of a burden to me than a help. I do approve of the companies being directed promptly to the army, but on the express condition that they are at least provided with small equipment'.[62]

At the beginning of March 1814, the Minister of the Interior sent to the prefects a flyer listing the effects that were to be provided to the gardes nationaux, as well as their cost. The capote, the shako and the shoes were considered essential because they gave their owners a uniform appearance. Moreover, men lacking a capote and shoes were worthless during a winter campaign. In addition, there were a host of other equipment details. This lengthy list makes it easy to imagine the difficulties the local authorities encountered in meeting government requirements. Following Augereau's bitter reproaches, Rambuteau spared no effort to equip the mobilised men. Thanks to his own efforts and the goodwill of the craftsmen he solicited, he managed to adequately equip the 1st Battalion of Gardes Nationaux Mobilisés who left for Lyon on 8 March. 'This battalion is fully equipped and well behaved', he wrote, with some satisfaction, to the minister. He had taken care, he added, 'of the smallest details'. Thus, the grenadier and voltigeur companies were distinguished by the collar, the epaulettes and the pompoms. Moreover, these 800 men were armed with 'excellent muskets' and officers and NCOs were provided with sabres. In short, all were armed, dressed and equipped 'in such a way as to compete with the finest of the line army'.[63]

A Blouse as a Uniform

Whilst not an exception, this example should not obscure the fact that 1814 was marked by recurrent shortages of uniforms and weapons. In fact, it had become impossible to provide even a coat for all the gardes called up for

---

62   SHD: C426: Correspondance du *Maréchal* Augereau – Armée de Lyon.
63   ANF: F/1/CIII Loire 6: Esprit public, 1813–1814.

duty, and Napoleon was well aware of this. After the battle of Montereau, on 18 February, the Emperor instructed *Général de division* Pacthod to 'collect the muskets and shakos left on the battlefield and to get the shakos, capotes and cartridge boxes of the prisoners in order to properly equip the gardes nationaux'.[64] On the 21st, to *Maréchal* Augereau who complained about the deplorable state of the gardes nationaux under his command, Napoleon answered that he had for his part '4,000 gardes nationaux coming from Angers and Brittany, in round hats, without cartridge boxes, and with clogs. But they have good muskets and I made the best of them'.[65] However, faced with the shortage of clothing and equipment, Napoleon addressed a letter to Clarke, Minister of War, indicating that 'there are 12,000 gardes nationaux in Lyon. It is necessary to make 12,000 *blouses*, which will dress them straight away, give them cartridge boxes and sheepskin bags'.[66] On 5 March, the idea of the *blouse* was taken up again and generalised, as shown by a letter to Montalivet, Minister of the Interior: 'The grenadier and chasseur companies will be dressed in the uniform of the Garde Nationale. All the other companies will be dressed in the Gallic habit, that is to say blue *blouse*. They will have shakos and cartridge boxes. This way, every worker, every bourgeois, puts on his *blouse* and finds himself in uniform. The *blouses* also serve as capotes'.[67] A decree issued the following day effectively prescribed the use of the blue blouse, in order to speed up mobilisation but also to reduce clothing costs. 'This garment, preserved without alteration in the majority of the departments within the Empire, is adopted there in general by the farmers and by all those who lead an active life. Experience proves that it suits the soldier', the Minister of the Interior assured the prefects in a circular dated 8 March.[68] This was certainly a confirmation of the state of affairs. The image of the gardes nationaux wearing the blue *blouse* was popularised by several nineteenth century illustrators, first and foremost Raffet.

Second-Hand and Vintage Muskets and Pikes

It was not an easy task to arm the gardes nationaux. Firearms were scarce. Thousands of muskets had been lost in Russia, abandoned on the battlefields of Saxony, or held in the German fortresses now besieged by the coalition troops. In November 1813, the imperial army needed no less than 435,000 muskets. However, the arsenals had 264,000 muskets of various models at that date, of which nearly 56,000 needed repair. On 14 November, then on 23 November, the Ministries of War and the Interior instructed the prefects to 'search for, collect and pay for all the muskets in private hands'.[69] Such a search was still in progress in January 1814. For lack of anything better, and probably at the instigation of the Emperor himself, the production of more rustic weapons was relaunched in 1814, notably at the Saint-Etienne factory.

---

64 Napoléon I, *Correspondance de Napoléon*, vol.XXVII, p.266.
65 Napoléon I, *Correspondance de Napoléon*, vol.XXVII, p.261.
66 Napoléon I, *Correspondance de Napoléon*, vol.XXVII, p.264.
67 Napoléon I, *Correspondance de Napoléon*, vol.XXVII, p.264.
68 ANF: F/9/357: Lettre du ministre de l'Intérieur aux préfets, 8 mars 1814.
69 Pascal Chambon, *La Loire et l'Aigle: Les Foréziens face à l'Etat napoléonien* (Saint-Etienne: Publications de l'Université de Saint-Etienne, 2005), p.422.

OF PURPLE CLOAK AND BATTLEFIELDS

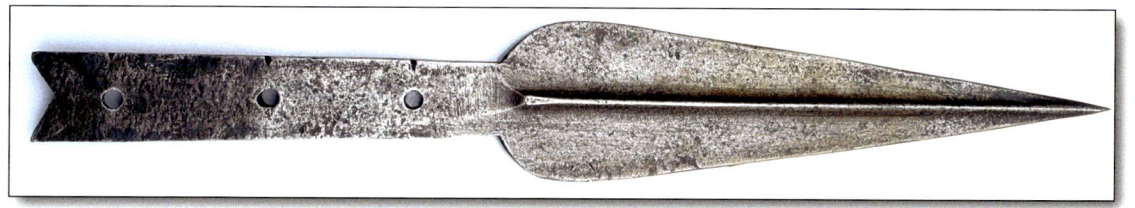

Regnier pike, 1814. In the twilight of the First Empire, the Garde Nationale was issued with pikes for similar reasons to those of 1792: imminent threat, danger to the homeland and shortage of muskets. The Regnier pike, named after its inventor, was produced in a hurry and its very crude appearance is proof of this. (Fabien Pacaud's collection)

This was notably the case for the n°1 model musket: it was a simplified version of the 1777 model musket tested during the Revolution and mentioned in the *Journal Militaire* in 1806. The manufacturing tolerances were wider and parts of earlier models were used, so that the quality of the weapons thus produced proved to be very average. In any case, it was no longer possible to reject weapons because of defects in their aspect. Production, which had been so successful up to that point, seized up because of the deterioration of the military situation. On 1 January 1814, four arms factories, located in territories invaded or threatened by invasion, had already ceased all production. At that date, 12,500 muskets were available, 116,000 needed repair and 60,000 were stored in the prefectures, proving the mobilisation of the administrative apparatus at local level. In this respect, some prefects did not hesitate to offer their department's arms manufacturers substantial sums to repair weapons. For example, Rambuteau, prefect of the Loire, promised 27 *francs* per weapon, even though the cost of a new musket ranged from 25 to 34 *francs*.

Given the context, Napoleon decided to resort to pikes. Stocks dating from the Revolution and existing in the reserves of fortresses were therefore distributed. On 12 January 1814, Minister Clarke indicated that there was 'a large quantity of pikes in Cambrai' and that it was therefore 'necessary to use them'.[70] On 11 February these were distributed to the villages and towns around Paris. That same day, the minister also approved of the sending of 2,000 pikes to Soissons, 2,000 to Montereau and 1,000 to Orléans. At the beginning of January 1814, Edmé Regnier, a curator of the central artillery depot and an inventor in the field of weapons, developed a model of pike whose production was within the reach of any ironworker. The spearhead, about 36 centimetres long, was based on a model dating from the Revolution. It was attached by means of rivets to a 2.3 metres long pole made of beech, hornbeam or ash painted in ebony black. A stamped nail protected the bottom of the pole. Regnier had fixed the unit price of the weapon at six *francs*, but the minister lowered it by one franc. It became possible to obtain five pikes for the price of one musket, but the effectiveness was somewhat limited. Such pikes were to be distributed to the third rank of the Garde Nationale units in order to give them 'a more powerful means of resisting enemy cavalry'.[71] This, at least, was the recommendation of the *Instruction sur l'usage de la pique*, a brochure published on 8 March 1814 in 2,000 copies and distributed shortly afterwards in the communes of the Paris region.

---

70 Michel Pétard, 'La pique de Regnier pour la campagne de France de 1814', *Tradition Magazine*, 105 (1994), p.12.
71 Pascal Chambon, *La Loire et l'Aigle*, p.425.

THE GARDE NATIONALE 1789–1815

Cavalry Units of the Late Empire

In the last years of the Empire, the Garde Nationale of certain towns, and even of certain departments, had cavalry units. In 1814, a small corps was formed in Paris and served as couriers and guides to *Maréchal* Moncey. In 1815, the Landau Garde Nationale cavalrymen wore a colpack with a white plume, as shown in two strictly contemporary gouaches. They also had a Bardin-pattern blue coatee with white lapels piped scarlet. A chamois woollen aiguillette adorned their left shoulder and a trefoil, the right one. Black gloves and breeches with chamois-coloured Hungarian knots and a side stripe of the same colour completed this most attractive uniform. As for the armament, it consisted of a light cavalry sabre. A decree of 22 April 1815 put into activity, in Alsace, two regiments of Garde Nationale lancers under the orders of *Général de brigade* Chouard. They had a Polish-style uniform and wielded the lance. This weapon was easy to produce in large numbers and was therefore in fashion at the end of the Empire, as it was also used by several of the Corps Francs created during the Hundred Days. On 23 May 1815, the mayor of Strasbourg decided to create a cavalry squadron mainly intended to fulfil an ordinance and courier service. The cavalrymen were recruited from among horse-owning citizens, as well as from the former local Gardes d'honneur of the city. The unit, called the Guides du Gouverneur, was disbanded at the end of the Hundred Days. Very similar to that of *Maréchal* Moncey's Guides, the uniform consisted of a colpack with a plume, a blue coat with crimson lapels embellished with white epaulettes and an aiguillette on the right shoulder, as well as grey breeches with a crimson side stripe. The leatherwork was black. In June 1815, a Regiment of Chasseurs-Lanciers was set up in the Moselle department. The patriotic donations of the inhabitants of Metz made it possible to dress and equip some 25 lancers. The other towns in the department also provided a contingent. Commanded by *Colonel* Lapointe, the 400 or so men of the unit proved most useful during the blockade of Metz, as the city had no other cavalry unit available. Finally, a company of mounted gardes nationaux, equipped with the lance, was organised in Lyon during the Hundred Days. In June 1815, however, it had only 22 cavalrymen under the command of *Sous-Lieutenant* Lombard.

Garde Nationale Parisienne Scouts, also known as *Maréchal* Moncey's Guides. Boisselier drew this NCO on the basis of a watercolour by *Général de brigade* Vanson, who had sketched a veteran from this tiny unit during a pilgrimage to the Vendôme Column in 1857. (Guillaume Bretegnier)

OF PURPLE CLOAK AND BATTLEFIELDS

1815: The Blouse is Back

In 1815, as in the previous year, Napoleon recommended that the Garde Nationale be provided with

> a Gallic *blouse* which would only cost 10 to 12 *francs*. There would be embroidery for the officers. The chasseurs and grenadiers who could afford to dress as gardes nationaux and the officers who wanted to wear a coat would be free to decide. However, the *blouse* would be the general uniform and would cost very little.[72]

Articles 23 to 26 of the decree of 10 April stipulated that 'the gardes nationaux must dress at their own expense or, if not, from funds allocated by the departments or communes. The citizens will wear their usual clothing as well as a national cockade on their hat. For the rural cantons' battalions, the clothing usually worn by the inhabitants of the countryside'.[73]

Paris Garde Nationale's Clothing in 1815

In 1815, the Garde Nationale Parisienne consisted of approximately 32,000 clothed guardsmen for a total strength of about 40,000 men. The remainder, about one fifth of the total number, performed their service in civilian clothes. Being part of the Garde was relatively expensive. In addition to the uniform itself, which averaged 150 *francs*, grenadiers had to pay an extra 60 to 80 *francs* for a bearskin cap, depending on the quality of the fur and the ornate metal plate that decorated it. Many gardes nationaux with modest incomes were reluctant to invest in a uniform, or, having done so, the enthusiasm or initial interest having waned, did not replace it once worn out.

The cut of the uniform of the Paris Garde Nationale had hardly changed. However, after a timid appearance in the grenadier companies the previous year, the bearskin was widely adopted this time. It was adorned with a scarlet plume and a white metal plate embossed with a

The general appearance of this grenadier and this chasseur, depicted by Genty in spring 1815, turns out to be very similar to that of their counterparts of the Garde Impériale. It is likely that this resemblance was sought after by the gardes nationaux. (Yves Martin)

---

72 Napoléon I, *Correspondance de Napoléon*, vol.XXVIII, pp.81–82.
73 Duvergier (ed.), *Collection Complète des Lois*, vol.XIX, p.397.

THE GARDE NATIONALE 1789–1815

Top left: On 11 February 1814, *Maréchal* Moncey issued an order authorising the legion chiefs to form a detachment of sappers who would march at the head of each legion. This 1815 engraving by Genty provides the only contemporary representation of these men. (Yves Martin)

Bottom left: Tirailleur-fédéré, Paris, 1815. This representation by Jacques Onfray de Bréville, based on a drawing by Valmont, is incorrect in some respects. The fédéré on the left is dressed in a Bardin-style coatee with white piping on the lapels. Moreover, he is wearing a shako adorned with a crudely made tin plate. This is not impossible, but the Tirailleurs-Fédérés were theoretically supposed to wear a hat. (Yves Martin)

flaming grenade. Genty, a well-known maker of high-quality coloured prints, presented a brass plate. Wishing not to be outdone, the chasseur companies also used the bearskin, but without a plate. The plume was bicoloured, green with a red top.

Tirailleurs Fédérés: The Garde Nationale Light Infantry

If the gardes nationaux dressed and equipped themselves at their own expense, the tirailleurs-fédérés could hardly afford it, so the uniform had to be provided for them. As the fédérés did not perform the usual service of the Garde Nationale Parisienne, they needed a specific uniform defined on 20 May by an order of the Ministry of the Interior. Theoretically, it consisted of 'a blue cloth jacket crossed over the chest and without lapels, yellow collar, blue cuffs, with Garde Nationale buttons. Grey or white cloth trousers, hat with the national cockade topped with a yellow pompom'.[74] Secondary sources – notably a watercolour by Valmont – depict the use of a shako decorated with a white metal plate. There is evidence that such plates were made in 1815. But were they distributed? To cover the costs of clothing and equipment, subscriptions were opened in the town halls and ministries. Thus, the ministers each gave 3,000 *francs*, the Parisian grocers 6,000 *francs*. During the review of 14 May, an anonymous officer handed over 25,000 *francs* to the Emperor, before disappearing. For

---

74 Emile de Labédollière, *Histoire de la Garde Nationale* (Paris: H. Dumineray et F. Pallier Editeurs, 1848), p.355.

all that, the sums collected hardly made it possible to completely dress all 24 battalions. Given the evolution of events, the clothing was in any case hardly worn.

To arm these men proved equally thorny. Of course, Napoleon assured that he would 'give weapons' to the fédérés. But distrusting these men from the 'dangerous classes' and fearing that their hatred of the bourgeoisie and the monarchy would provoke a civil war, he finally did so only sparingly.[75] Moreover, such weapons were to be kept in the arrondissement town halls. On 2 July, when the coalition armies were already at the gates of Paris, Davout, the Minister of War, ordered that 6,350 muskets be finally issued to the tirailleurs-fédérés.

Garde Nationale Flags, 1804–1815

The First Flag Deliveries, 1804–1805

For the ceremony of 5 December 1804 at the Champ de Mars, Napoleon decided that the Garde Nationale would not only be represented, but also that it would receive eagles. In reality, the measure turned out to be improvised, as a letter from Minister Dejean to *Maréchal* Berthier testifies:

> Several delegations of gardes nationaux ask for standards to be issued to them. Your Excellency knows that I have not been charged with having any made for them. It was only on the eve of the Coronation that I was warned that some would be distributed. It was agreed that eagles intended for the Line would be provisionally distributed to them.[76]

On the other hand, 108 delegations – prefects and presidents of electoral colleges at their head – were indeed present at the Champ de Mars on that cold December day. A few eagles were undoubtedly handed over to them on a purely symbolic basis, but definitely not a single flag. As proof, the Garde Nationale of the Dordogne received its eagle on 3 January 1805 and immediately returned the one that had been entrusted to it a month earlier, during the famous ceremony. Two series of shipments appear to have occurred in 1805: first, single eagles, with plinth without number, then eagles with plinth on which the number of the department was inscribed.

The flags, made by the Maison Chaillot, were of a special design. The dimensions of the silk varied from 80 to 84 centimetres wide and 75 to 77 centimetres high. A white lozenge bordered by laurel leaves occupied the centre. The corners were alternately red and blue. The obverse bore the motto 'Force à la Loi, Fidélité à l'Empereur' (Strength to the Law, Fidelity to the Emperor) painted in gold letters. On the reverse, the words 'Garde Nationale' followed by the name of the department and, in the lower part, the number of

---

[75] Kare Dorenfeldt Tonnesson, 'Les fédérés de Paris pendant les Cent-Jours', *Annales Historiques de la Révolution Française*, 249 (1982), pp.405–406.

[76] Pierre Charrié, 'Les drapeaux de la Garde Nationale sous le 1er Empire 1804–1815', *Gardes Nationales 1789–1871*, Carnets de la Sabretache, 50 (1979), p.146.

THE GARDE NATIONALE 1789–1815

the department. Due to lack of space, the words 'Garde Nationale' were placed on a curved line. At each corner of the silk, in the centre of a laurel wreath, were the initials of the department. For these flags, the notions of obverse and reverse remain somewhat imprecise. The flags of the departments of Rhin-et-Moselle and Marne thus have the arrangements indicated above. However, those of the Rhône and Mont-Blanc bear the words 'Garde Nationale' on the obverse and 'Force à la Loy Fidélité à l'Empereur' on the reverse. These flags had gold thread fringes on the three sides opposite the flagstaff. Furthermore, the flag of the Rhône was surmounted by a pike, rather than the regulation eagle, while that of the Rhin-et-Moselle department was embellished with cravats of silver cord and tassels. Finally, the flag of the Ain department was mounted on a flagstaff painted red and its eagle had a plinth without a number. Such flags were carried by an officer of the grenadier company of the 1e Cohorte of the 1e Legion of the department. They were kept in the prefectures and were captured there in 1814 by the coalition troops.

Overseas Flags

In 1803, the Martinique gardes nationaux received from the hands of *Capitaine General* Villaret-Joyeuse, and on behalf of the government, six flags replacing those dating from the British occupation period. Their general appearance remains unknown. In the course of a parade organised on 15 August 1806, Saint-Napoleon's Day, flags were solemnly handed over to the Garde Nationale of Ile de France. In a report sent in September to *Vice-amiral* Decrès, *Capitaine Général* Decaen justified such an initiative. He stated that the old flags dating from the Revolution had to be replaced with new ones of a similar design to those of the Ile de France Regiment. He hoped, he added, that the Emperor would 'deign to send a flag surmounted by an eagle for each of the Gardes Nationales of Ile de France and Reunion'. Two examples of these flags are currently preserved. One in the Musée de l'Armée (that of the Garde Nationale of the Flacq district), the other, in a very degraded state, in Mauritius (that of the Rivière Noire district).

Forming an 84 centimetres square, these two flags differ from the model attributed to the gardes nationaux. They bear the regulation inscriptions in the central lozenge. On the obverse, the words 'L'Empereur des Français / A La Garde Nationale / du Quartier de …' are written in gold and shaded letters. On the reverse, is written 'Valeur et Discipline'. There was nothing in the corner wreaths. The delicacy of their painted decorations suggests that they were made in mainland France and not locally. In 1809–1810, the gardes nationaux of Flacq and Rivière Noire defended the Ile-de-France against British troops. After the surrender, that of Flacq was kept by M. de Jersey, an artillery *capitaine* and district commander. As for that of Rivière Noire, it also fell to the district commander, Jacques Bugeaud Desfayes de la Piconnerie. Both were surmounted by a 20 centimetres high unadorned copper pike.

Garde Nationale Cohorte Flags, 1812–1814

In 1812, the cohortes of the Garde Nationale were given a flag measuring 97 centimetres square, formed of three vertical tricolour stripes, with blue at the staff end. On the obverse, the white part bore the inscription, painted in gold, 'Cohorte / Du 1e Ban / De La Garde / Nationale'. In the upper corner, on the staff end, the number of the cohorte was painted in gold letters. The reverse side of the flag was blank of any inscription. This flag, which had no cravats, was mounted on a black-painted staff topped by an iron spike 25 to 27 centimetres high. A number of flags were captured from depots during and after the campaign of France. Those with numbers above 88 were compulsorily seized from the warehouses. They were in fact made for cohortes that were never formed up in practice.

Eagles and Flags of the Cohorte Regiments, 1813–1814

Of the 22 regiments – numbered from 135 to 156 – which came from the Garde Nationale cohortes, seven received their eagles in Paris, in the courtyard of the Tuileries Palace, on 7 February 1813. These were the 135e, 136e, 138e, 139e, 140e, 141e and 142e Regiments d'Infanterie de Ligne. The 149e and 150e Regiments d'Infanterie de Ligne received their flags in May. As for the 152e and 153e Regiments d'Infanterie de Ligne, they probably received their eagles in July or August 1813. On 29 August 1813, the 146e, 147e and 148e Regiments d'Infanterie de Ligne belonging to Puthod's Division of Lauriston's 5th Corps were isolated on the banks of the rain-swollen Bober. Being unable to cross the river again, they were jointly assaulted by enemy infantry and cavalry and were annihilated. Grenadier Jean Jolly of the 134e Regiment d'Infanterie de Ligne managed to save the eagle of the 147e Regiment d'Infanterie de Ligne by swimming across the flooded river. Eight days later, he handed it to *Maréchal* Berthier. In contrast, the eagles of the 146e and 148e Regiments d'Infanterie de Ligne were captured by *Poruchik* (Lieutenant) Kalinin and *Praporshchik* (Ensign) Bogdanov respectively, both of the 28th Russian Jäger Battalion. The 140e and 145e Regiments d'Infanterie de Ligne lost their flag at the battle of Leipzig, in October 1813. As for the 151e Regiment d'Infanterie de Ligne, it received its flag in May 1813. It was captured on 10 April 1814 at the surrender of the Glogau fortress.

Summer 1814: Lilies return

On 7 September 1814, King Louis XVIII handed the Paris Garde Nationale's 12 legions and cavalry their flags and standards. These white silk colours bore, in their centre, the arms of France and in each corner, the arms of the city. The golden fringed cravats were attached to them by the Duchesse d'Angoulême.

Garde Nationale Flags and Pennants, 1815

On 4 June 1815, during a highly solemn ceremony, Napoleon distributed the 88 eagles of the Garde Nationale to the presidents of the electoral colleges assembled in the great gallery of the Tuileries palace. It was a question of uniting the French people around the Emperor by means of symbols that had worked so well in the army. These tricolour flags were made of a double layer of silk abundantly fringed with silver. They were 80 centimetres square and entirely embroidered in silver following the designs developed in 1812. On the obverse, they bore the inscription 'L'Empereur Napoléon au département

THE GARDE NATIONALE 1789–1815

This part of an engraving depicting the Battle of the Souffel shows a Hessian infantryman taking a French flag, probably belonging to a Garde Nationale unit. However, the depiction is incorrect: a studded sleeve should indeed cover the flagstaff. (Anne S.K. Brown Military Collection)

de …' and on the reverse 'Champ De Mai' written in three lines. These remarkably beautiful flags were priced at 1,400 *francs* each. One wonders why such expensive flags were issued to the Garde Nationale when the line army was given very simple flags. The eagles, made of gilt bronze, were ordered on 28 March 1815 from the bronzesmith Thomire, who charged 85 *francs* each. Their general shape was much less beautiful than the eagles produced in 1804. The flags of the Garde Nationale had no cravats but only a double cord in silver thread. After the Battle of Waterloo, wishing to thank the Duke of Wellington for helping him to regain his throne, Louis XVIII gave him 67 eagles and 68 flags of the Garde Nationale. Packed in boxes, they were shipped to England and are now kept at Aspley House in London.

On 5 June 1815, Davout, Minister of War, proposed to the Emperor that the battalions of gardes nationaux put into activity should receive a tricolour flag surmounted by a pike head and bearing the designation of the department and the number of the battalion. Napoleon approved the measure the very next day. On 17 June, *Général de division* Mathieu Dumas informed the Minister of the Interior that he had given orders to hasten the making of these flags. None were completed, but this did not mean that the battalions were flagless. On 9 May, the 1st Battalion of the Vosges thus received an embroidered flag from the ladies of Epinal. The 2nd Grenadier Battalion of the Loire, raised in Roannais, had a tricolour flag with horizontal stripes. As for the 3rd and 4th Battalions of the Moselle, they received their flag in mid-July 1815, during the siege of Thionville.

10

Conclusion

The Garde Nationale featured in all the major events of the French Revolution and later of the First Empire, but it was variable, changing and its actions proved fundamentally ambivalent.

    The Gardes Nationales, whose genesis dated back to the early months of 1789, appeared as the heirs to the Milices Bourgeoises of the Middle Ages and the Ancien Régime, which they revived. They arose from the failure of the security forces available to the French monarchy to deal with the disorders resulting from the food crisis and the anti-seigneurial protest. They imposed themselves at their expense through a process of arming a mass of citizens who were completed to be directly involved in events that worried them. They found their essential *raison d'être* in maintaining the local order. They were charged with protecting the goods and property of the wealthier sections of the urban population. They had to protect them from possible exactions and looting perpetrated either by the common people exasperated by a brutal increase in their usual misery, or by the King's regiments accustomed to living off the land. In Paris, the organising, as a matter of urgency, of a Milice Bourgeoise was explained by the anxiety of the representatives of the voters of the 60 districts. The latter were faced with Necker's dismissal, the arrival of several regiments in the vicinity of Versailles and the potential reactions of the Parisian population confronted with increasing food difficulties. On 5 and 10 August 1789, the Constituent Assembly effectively recognised the Garde Nationale as the guardian of public order. Martial law of October 1789, the law of 23 February 1790 on the use of the public force and the law of 26 and 27 July 1791, relating to its action, regulated its directive against gatherings and subjected it to a strict regime of requisition. The law of 14 October 1791 confirmed its role. The gardes fulfilled this mission quite poorly, whether in Paris or in the departments. All in all, says Georges Carrot, 'the Garde did not guard well'.[1] Of course, it put down the *jacqueries* in the countryside in 1789, then the Parisian demonstrators at the Champ de Mars in July 1791. In the towns and villages, it intervened in the name of martial law against popular revolts. However, the National Gendarmerie and the army proved to be much less random in their use, so that the Garde Nationale was relegated to missions of secondary importance, particularly from 1795 onwards, when

---

1   Carrot, *La Garde nationale*, p.331.

THE GARDE NATIONALE 1789–1815

Portrait d'un garde national et de sa femme (René Dogereau et Perrine Trouillard), oil on canvas by Remy-Furcy Descarsin, 1791. This exceptionally realistic double portrait reveals a quality portraitist. Descarsin depicted a united couple from Nantes. He also portrayed a social reality: the spouse was probably a housewife and the husband a caretaker, craftsman or small shopkeeper. (Musée de la Révolution Française, Vizille, with permission)

CONCLUSION

the army almost systematically intervened to maintain order. Under the Consulate, the prefects tried to rely on the Garde Nationale, but this was hardly ever done. Two imperial decrees of 3 April and 17 December 1813 conferred on urban cohortes drawn from the urban bourgeoisie the mission of 'maintaining tranquillity and providing assistance to the authorities'. This was more or less a return to the Milices Bourgeoises of the Ancien Régime. The newly restored monarchy of Louis XVIII judged it prudent to maintain, by the ordinance of 16 July 1814, the mission of public order devolved to the Garde Nationale since the Revolution. It nevertheless came up against the resistance of citizens who failed to understand the need for regular service in quiet times. Such duty turned into a real chore.

From the beginning of the Revolution, the Garde Nationale generated a certain mistrust, which was explained by the role that men and events made it play. To write the history of the Garde means to study the attempts of the various political forces to control the institution by relying on the battalions that supported them. Even before July 1789, some Milices Bourgeoises, raised to maintain order, had become involved in political action: such was the case in Rennes and Marseilles. The formation of the Parisian Milice Bourgeoise on 13 July 1789 had a decisive psychological and political effect on the course of events. Driven by their deputies, the provincials followed the movement intensely. In Paris, as in the provinces, the Gardes Nationales were primarily charged to obtain the removal of reluctant municipal authorities, within the framework of the 'municipal revolution'. In short, the Garde Nationale appeared to be a citizen force capable of expressing and acting in defence of its ideas. It was not, therefore, out of sheer boldness that the Gardes Nationales became involved in revolutionary politics, but rather because they believed in it. They claimed a deliberative, revolutionary, almost militant role, including the right to speak out on government policies. It was far from being a mere police force. The vast movement of the federations, which immediately followed the 'municipal revolution', aimed in particular at making the towns that had not yet rallied to the patriots yield. Even prior to the great federative celebration organised in the heart of Paris on 14 July 1790, this process had led to numerous conflicts, including deadly clashes between Catholics and Protestants in the south-west. In several villages in Lozère and the Cévennes, the Garde was in fact a force expressing religious and community concerns. On 6 December 1790, the deputies of the Constituent Assembly passed a law preventing the Garde Nationale from holding deliberations. In condemning the Gardes Nationales to strict obedience, the Constituent Assembly confirmed that they were henceforth forbidden to take any initiative. This prohibition was forcefully confirmed in the text of the law of 14 October 1791, but did not discourage the most active elements of the Garde. From 1789 to 1791, La Fayette had managed to contain the most radical companies in Paris thanks to its most moderate battalions. However, by the winter of 1791–1792, the Garde Nationale was under the control of revolutionary leaders. On 10 August, a second federation, organised by the Girondins, overthrew Louis XVI. The Garde Nationale became the armed force of the Parisian sections and was instrumental in the arrest of the Girondins on 30 May and 2 June 1793, before taking part in the overthrow of the Montagnards on 27 and 28 July 1794. On that day, the activist minority failed to neutralise the moderate battalions and, despite the support of radical companies, did not succeed in saving Robespierre and his supporters. From then on, various measures were taken by successive governments to fully remove the Garde's ability to take action. The *commandant general* was abolished in the days following Robespierre's downfall. Similarly, after the riots of spring 1795, the most popular elements were expelled from the ranks. Under the First Empire, the government reserved the right to appoint officers. Various opposition movements did try to use the Garde Nationale to their advantage. In the summer of 1797, the royalist deputies revived the elite companies for this purpose. In 1809, Minister Fouché summoned it, overriding Napoleon's orders. In the autumn of 1812, Malet, the conspirator, imagined relying on the Garde Nationale Parisienne for his failed *coup d'état*. Finally, in 1814, the ultra-royalists sought to provide the Garde with a centralised and hierarchical organisation. Whether it was bourgeois or popular, urban or rural, the Garde was involved in all the decisive *journées* that punctuated the beginnings of the Revolution: the *Journée des Bricoles*, the Bastille, the King's flight, the invasion of the Tuileries on 20 June 1792, the fall of the monarchy... It thus participated with varying success in all Parisian and provincial affairs. If it did not then vanish as a structured organisation, it no longer took any direct part in the events following the fall of Robespierre and lost all influence on the course of these events, because of the aforementioned precautionary measures. In this respect, the 13 Vendémiaire was a decisive setback.

From 1789 to 1815, the Garde Nationale fulfilled a symbolic role in an almost uninterrupted way. In Paris, its official appearance on 16 July 1789 and its recognition by Louis XVI the following day marked the victory of the Revolution over the Ancien Régime. Its name took the term 'Garde', which until then had generally been reserved for the use of sovereigns, and added it to that of 'Nation', a new form of sovereignty. In short, the term 'Garde Nationale' in itself carried a revolutionary significance. Despite successive modifications, its uniform, combining the three colours on all the pieces of clothing, unambiguously expressed the advent of a new era. The Garde took part in all the great revolutionary civic celebrations and ceremonies, as a plethora of iconography attests. As for the gathering of the Parisian gardes nationaux on 14 July 1790, alongside thousands of others from all the French departments, it marks for history the triumph of patriotic unity. The participation of the Garde gave events, even illegal ones, unquestionable legitimacy. The *journées* of 5 and 6 October 1789, marked by the departure of the royal family from Versailles to Paris, offer a striking example. In the summer of 1790, La Fayette and the Marquis de Bouillé exploited this same logic to have gardes nationaux march at the head of the forces that suppressed the mutinous soldiers in Nancy. On the other hand, the arrest of the royal family by gardes nationaux from Varennes and neighbouring communes on the evening of 21 June 1791 gave encouragement to the supporters of the deposition of the King. The *Constitution* of September 1791 and the law of 14 October 1791 certainly sought to confine the Garde Nationale to the role of a simple civic Milice. However, this hardly prevented part of the Garde Nationale Parisienne from taking part in the fighting of 10 August 1792 at

CONCLUSION

This painting, commissioned from the painter François Schommer in 1886, is entitled *The Defence of Pantin* and illustrates the resistance to the invasion of French territory in 1814. The civilian population participates in the effort to defend the soil of the homeland alongside soldiers from various units. The composition gives the scene a heroic character and makes it a tribute to the defenders. (Musée Carnavalet)

the Tuileries Palace, ending in the fall of the monarchy. On 21 January 1793, a continuous line of gardes nationaux was positioned on the route leading Louis XVI from the Prison du Temple to the Place de la Révolution, where the scaffold had been erected. This was much more than a simple security measure: the massive presence of the Garde Nationale could be understood as the Nation's agreement to the execution of this solemn and dramatic act, definitely breaking with the centuries-old Ancien Régime. After October 1795, the prominence given to the army and its leaders, who were given full powers over the Garde Nationale, prevented citizens from expressing their opinions under arms. As the great stabilising force of the directorial republic, the army took over. It supplanted civil powers and eventually brought one of its own, Bonaparte, to power. Once he became consul, he thought it politically expedient to revive the revolutionary tradition. In fact, the Garde Nationale was associated, on a symbolic level at least, with the success of the Brumaire *coup d'état*. It was later invited to the coronation of the Emperor on 2 December 1804, and then at the end of his reign, to the ceremony at the Champ de Mai on 1 June 1815. When Louis XVIII came back to power in 1814 and 1815, he acted similarly and claimed to be indebted to the Parisian bourgeoisie for his return. A symptomatic example of this was the Comte d'Artois, who marched through Paris on 12 April 1814 wearing the white cockade, but above all the three-coloured uniform. On this occasion he managed to obtain the paradoxical and short-lived rallying of a fairly large part of the capital's Garde Nationale.

In the summer of 1789, the patriots set up a Garde Nationale made up of citizens, not as a replacement for the king's army, but to curb its influence. Nonetheless, the debates of the successive revolutionary assemblies reveal the expectations and contradictions of the deputies. The essential expectation was certainly that the 'people in arms' would prevail over the professional army. Military reformers and the specialists of the Military Committee of

THE GARDE NATIONALE 1789–1815

the Constituent Assembly claimed that every citizen had to be a soldier. But if this 'people in arms' was to constitute the pool of the new army, it could not, according to war professionals, be that army. In other words, soldiering could not be achieved through the civil or civic service of the Garde. The citizen became a soldier only after a more or less long period of amalgamation or specific training. As long as he remained a guardsman, the use of weapons had to be limited to operations directed by the civil power. The fear of an armed conflict in the summer of 1791, followed by the declaration of war in the spring of 1792, led to the creation of battalions of volontaires nationaux drawn from the ranks of the Garde Nationale and intended to intervene alongside the line army. On this occasion, the most motivated and promising guardsmen, as well as the most ambitious, were enlisted. However, this hybrid solution proved unsuited to the real needs of the war and, from July 1792, the Legislative Assembly gradually abandoned the fiction of voluntary service. Even more brutally, in 1793 the Convention ordered the requisition of several classes of young men, prior to accelerating the amalgamation of volontaires nationaux and soldiers of the line army. From then on, there was only one truly national army. Although the Garde had been the antechamber of the army in the context of the volunteer levies of 1791 and 1792, its relevance declined once the army was reinforced. As the army played a growing political role under the Directory, the Garde faded away, as part of a more global reconfiguration of relations between the civilian and military powers. Moreover, this gradual substitution was somewhat of a revenge for the initial phase of 1789–1792, during which the Garde Nationale had seemed to be a potential substitute for the royal army. The conscription law of 1798 established equal military service for all. However, two out of three conscripts remained home. The consular and then imperial government, which pursued an expansionist policy, was tempted to mobilise them within a Garde Nationale conceived as a set of territorial units. This objective was tirelessly followed by Napoleon, in particular through the successive decrees of 30 September 1805, 12 November 1806, 14 March 1812, 3 April and 30 December 1813 and, above all, 10 April 1815, in the form of cohortes and then regiments of the Garde Nationale, and grenadier and chasseur battalions. Napoleon's final defeat of June 1815 put an end to these experiments, despite the interesting results obtained in the course of that spring. In any case, in 1814 and 1815, the Garde took part in the defence of the frontiers and the invaded territory, thanks to a great mobilisation effort similar to that of 1792. With the advent of war, whether in 1792–1793 or in the twilight of the First Empire, the Garde acquired new functions and its role was extended beyond maintaining public order. A large part of its personnel ceased to be purely sedentary and was mixed, in practice as well as in the popular imagination, with the troops of the line army with whom it shared common objectives: to repel the invader and to ensure the essential role of any army, that of defending the homeland. Such an opportunity rarely arose, and certainly in exceptional circumstances.

Between 1789 and 1791, the Garde Nationale undoubtedly embodied the victorious Revolution. However, its institutional existence remained problematic. The deputies of the Constituent Assembly were very cautious

CONCLUSION

about its future and did not agree among themselves about its nature, its composition and its functions. Therefore, the majority of them decreed restrictive, even negative rules. The law of 14 October 1791, which was of fundamental importance, recalled that the Garde was based on an essentially local organisation, identical throughout the national territory. Officers were elected for a limited time and service was compulsory but free. Upon these principles, the Garde remained in existence until 1815 and beyond. All the *Constitutions* – with the exception of that of 1793, which assimilated it to the general force of the Republic – mentioned its existence, either formally or by reference to earlier texts. Similarly, all the legislative and regulatory texts recalled the compulsory but free nature of the service provided by citizens. However, as regimes changed and political transitions occurred, the age limits, the conditions for exemption, reasons for exclusion or replacement facilities were modified. Born in 1789, the Garde Nationale certainly fulfilled the conditions for being defined as a state institution. However, can it be qualified as an institution of the Nation? La Fayette called the Parisian Milice Bourgeoise, whose numbers he increased in passing, the 'Garde Nationale'. Such a name suggested that its recruitment might not be solely bourgeois. In fact, the day after the storming of the Bastille, detachments of armed men, many of them from working-class backgrounds, demanded, as 'Victors of the Bastille', the possibility of being associated with the Garde. Over the following weeks, the new Parisian municipality agreed that citizens who had taken part in the various episodes of this revolutionary *journée* could join the battalions. Right from its birth, the Garde Nationale Parisienne was thus confronted with the problem of opening up to the working classes and La Fayette did not oppose it, insofar as the numbers involved remained modest. In the provinces, the reality of the composition of the Garde varied according to the local balance of power, in a mosaic of situations that was hardly conducive to a homogenous establishment. In June 1790, passive citizens were excluded from the Garde, discriminated against by the limit of three *livres* of direct taxation. Deprived of the right to vote and to bear arms, they were relegated to the rank of second-class citizens. This exclusion of the poorest from 'true' citizenship scandalised part of the public opinion in the populous districts of central Paris. However, according to the advocates of the bourgeoisie, the Garde Nationale was unquestionably an institution of the Nation, since it brought together exclusively active citizens who exercised civic rights. The events of August 1792 lifted the distinction between active and passive citizens for a very brief period. In fact, the Garde of the years 1792–1794 was similar to a people's Garde, its ranks being open to all citizens. However, the events of the spring of 1795 signalled the end of pressure from the working-class districts of the capital and the disarmament of the so-called 'terrorists'. Above all, the Garde, supervised by the '*honnêtes gens*', became for a long time – or even definitively? – a protector of social order. Only the invasion of the national territory at the end of the First Empire allowed, briefly, the entire population to rally behind it. In these moments of national crisis, the Garde was portrayed as the armed people, bringing together voluntary and generous young Frenchmen, ensuring the traditional role imposed on them by the Revolution: that of defenders of the soil of the homeland. On the other hand, once the monarchical Restoration was complete, Louis XVIII placed his trust in the Garde precisely because it represented what the King perceived to be the reliable values of property and social distinction. With its officers from both the nobility and the bourgeoisie, it provided a counterweight to the soldiers of the line army, which the Bourbons viewed with some mistrust.

Other logics, including spatial and temporal ones, were added to these major lines of thought. The towns were most certainly the privileged domain of the Milices Bourgeoises and then the Gardes Nationales. In other words, all towns and cities had a Garde Nationale that succeeded a more or less active Milice. However, archival research shows that the Garde was not only an urban reality, but also a rural one. Although the rural areas were certainly unequally armed, the local authorities frequently complained about the sometimes violent actions of the rural gardes during food riots or anti-seigneurial revolts. Hunger marches aimed at the towns were organised, and the village authorities, in the name of revolutionary legality, placed themselves at the head of the processions. In the same way, the village gardes, who knew how to use solidarity between neighbouring communities when necessary, occasionally opposed the missions that the urban authorities tried to impose on them. Moreover, the history of the Garde went through a period of gestation and structuration, then a period of euphoria culminating in the federative celebrations and the Festival of the Federation in Paris on 14 July 1790, before a period of apparent decline. The latter must be analysed in the light of the Garde's confinement to menial, time-consuming and voluntary tasks, the departure of volontaires from its ranks to the armies, an erosion of patriotic feelings and even a latent distrust of the authorities in the face of a potentially contentious institution.

In sum, the Garde Nationale was multifaceted. It served to maintain order at a local level. It also manifested itself as an insurrectionary force in the service of national sovereignty and human rights. In addition, it performed a military function. The Garde Nationale identified itself with the armed nation that rose up to defend the threatened integrity of the homeland and constituted the elements of an armed force of national nature. Subsequently, it tended to become the supposedly inexhaustible reserve of a conscript army, from which successive governments drew to meet the needs and surges of national defence. It is in this clash of representations and realities, in the contrasting images of revolutionary *journées* and repressive episodes, between these images anchored in the collective memory and the weight of the archives, that the historian can approach the richness and contradictions of the Garde Nationale, which is still so little known, between its genesis in 1789 and the very last days of the First Empire, in the summer of 1815. May these pages help to revive interest in a major player of the 'century of revolutions'.

Bibliography

Archives

Archives Nationales de France, Pierrefitte-sur-Seine (ANF)
AD/VI/50–53 Garde Nationale, armée révolutionnaire 1789–1815
AD/XVIIIC/96–98 Impression des Assemblées – Documents, rapports, discours, sur la Gendarmerie et la Garde nationale An IV–1848
AD/XVIIIC/134 Assemblée des électeurs de Paris juillet 1789
AD/XVIIIC/145–158 Procès-verbaux des séances du Conseil des Anciens An V–An VIII
AF/IV/1093-1099 Extraits de la correspondance du ministre de la Guerre An XII–1814
F/1a/59 Circulaires et instructions ministérielles sur la Garde Nationale 1791–1852
F/7/3616 Garde Nationale, Ain à Lys An IV–1815
F/7/3617 Garde Nationale, Maine-et-Loire à Sambre-et-Meuse An IV–1815
F/7/3618 Garde Nationale, Haute-Saône à Zuiderzee An IV–1815
F/9/1–10 Garde nationale et autres objets militaires 1789–An XI
F/9/339–340 Gardes nationales: Documents antérieurs au Premier Empire 1789–An XI
F/9/343 Gardes nationales : Drapeaux, armement, équipement, subsistances
F/9/348–349 Gardes nationales organisées par décret du 8 Vendémiaire an XIV
F/9/350 Gardes nationales mises en réquisition pour la défense des côtes par le décret du 23 octobre 1806
F/9/351–352 Gardes nationales des arrondissements maritimes
F/9/354–355 Cohortes urbaines
F/9/357 Levée en masse
F/9/359 Gardes nationales Première Restauration 1814–1815
F/9/360–366 Gardes nationales Cent-Jours: Organisation, documents généraux 1815
F/9/424–740 Garde Nationale: Affaires classées par départements 1789–Second Empire.
F/9/742 Volontaires nationaux, piquiers, régiment provincial de Paris 1791–An V
F/9/743 Grenadiers de la Représentation nationale, vétérans nationaux, colonnes mobiles, bataillons auxiliaires départementaux, compagnies franches. An IV–An IX
F/9/745 Colonnes mobiles, légions départementales, garde impériale, armées de réserve An VIII–1832

THE GARDE NATIONALE 1789–1815

Service Historique de la Défense, Vincennes (SHD)
C 10 Correspondance militaire 1804-1815
Xab/23 Gardes nationales devenues le 7e régiment de voltigeurs de la Garde Impériale 1810–1814
Xm/0 Registre matricule de la garde nationale parisienne 1789
Xm/1 Documents généraux, lois, décrets, règlements, rapports, comptes rendus 1790–1840
Xm/2 Mise en activité 1790–1810
Xm/3 Documents généraux – Travail manuscrit sur les Gardes nationales actives 1806–1815
Xm/4–5 Cohortes formées dans les divisions militaires
Xm/6–9 Cohortes
Xm/10–11 Levée en masse de 1814 – Documents généraux 1814
Xm/24–30 Formations diverses 1814–1815
Xm/31 Garde nationale active du Pas-de-Calais 1813
MR 707 Matériaux pour servir à l'histoire des Gardes Nationales 1813–1814

Contemporary Newspapers and Journals

Annales Patriotiques et Littéraires de la France
Journal des Débats et des Décrets
Journal Général de la Cour et de la Ville
L'Ami du peuple
Le Moniteur universel
Les Révolutions de Paris
Mercure de France

Published sources

Contemporary Registers and Regulations

Alletz, Bretelle, *Etrennes Aux Parisiens Patriotes, Ou Almanach Militaire National De Paris* (Paris: Guffier Jeune Libraire, 1790)
Anon., *Règlement pour la formation, organisation, solde, police et administration de l'infanterie nationale parisienne* (Paris: J.-R. Lottin, 1789)
Anon., *Règlement concernant la cavalerie nationale parisienne* (Paris: J.-R. Lottin, 1789)
Anon., *Almanach national pour l'année 1790* (Paris: Cuchet, 1790)
Anon., *Almanach militaire de la Garde nationale parisienne* (Paris: J.-R. Lottin, 1790)
Anon., *Code de la Garde Nationale contenant tous les décrets sanctionnés et acceptés par le Roi* (Paris: Devaux Libraire, 1792)
Dervieu Du Villars, Barthélémi-Régis, *Arrêté du commandant général de la garde nationale de Lyon concernant l'uniforme* (Lyon: Aimé Delaroche Imprimeur, 1790)
Dutemple, Edmond (ed.), *Ordres du jour inédits de Santerre, Commandant des Gardes Nationales Parisiennes en 1792-1793* (Paris: A. Derenne Editeur, 1875)
Tourneux, Maurice (ed.), *Procès-verbaux de la Commune de Paris 10 août 1792-1er juin 1793* (Paris: Société de l'Histoire de la Révolution Française, 1894)

BIBLIOGRAPHY

Nineteenth-Century Studies relating to the Garde Nationale
Alboize du Pujol, Jules-Edouard and Elie, Charles, *Fastes des Gardes nationales de France* (Paris: Ad. Goubaud Editeur, 1849)
Bardin, Etienne-Alexandre, 'Recherches historiques sur la Garde nationale', *Le Spectateur militaire*, 10 (1834), pp.71–79
Cadet-Gassicourt, Charles, *Les quatre âges de la Garde nationale ou précis historique de cette institution militaire et civile depuis son origine jusqu'en 1818, par un électeur du département de la Seine* (Paris: Delaunay, 1818)
Comte, Charles, *Histoire de la Garde nationale de Paris depuis l'époque de sa fondation jusqu'à l'ordonnance du 29 avril 1827* (Paris: A. Sautelet et Cie Libraires, 1827)
Poisson, Charles, *L'armée et la Garde nationale 1789-1795* (Paris: Durand, 1858–1862)

Letters, Memories and Recollections
Bonaparte, Napoléon, *Correspondance générale publiée par la Fondation Napoléon* (Paris: Fayard, 2002–2018)
Calmettes, Fernand (ed.), *Mémoires du général baron Thiébault* (Paris: Plon, 1894)
Carnot, Lazare, *Correspondance inédite du général Carnot avec Napoléon pendant les Cent-Jours* (Paris: Plancher Libraire, 1819)
Echerolles, Alexandrine des, *Une famille noble sous la Terreur* (Paris: Plon, 1907)
France d'Hézecques, François-Félix, *Souvenirs d'un page de la cour de Louis XVI* (Paris: Librairie Académique Didier et Cie Libraires-Editeurs, 1873)
Godechot, Jacques, 'Lettres de conscrits de 1812 et 1813', *Annales Historiques de la Révolution Française*, 210 (1972), pp. 626–652
Marcq, François, *Souvenirs de l'ex-sergent major Marcq* (Paris: Librairie militaire Edmond Dubois, 1901)
Richebé, Ate (ed.), *Journal d'un bourgeois de Lille pendant la Révolution 1787-1793* (Lille: D. Prévost Imprimeur, 1898)
Soulié, Gabriel (ed.), *Mémoires du Colonel Bial ou Souvenirs des Guerres de la Révolution et de l'Empire 1792-1814* (Brive: Lachaise, 1929)
Thibaudeau, Antoine Claire, *Mémoires de A.C. Thibaudeau, 1799-1815* (Paris: Plon, 1913)
Tondeur, Jean-Philippe (ed.), *Walcheren 1809: L'expédition anglaise au jour le jour, Lettres de Napoléon à ses ministres* (Bruxelles: Editions de la Belle-Alliance, 2009)

General History
Ado, Anatoli, *Paysans en Révolution: Terre, pouvoir et jacquerie 1789-1794*, (Paris: Société des Etudes Robespierristes, 1996)
Boulant, Antoine, 'Vincennes au péril de la Révolution', *Revue Historique des Armées*, 250 (2008), pp.94–99
Burstin, Haim, *Une révolution à l'œuvre: Le faubourg Saint-Antoine 1789-1794* (Seyssel: Champ-Vallon, 2005)
Chambon, Pascal, *La Loire et l'Aigle: Les Foréziens face à l'Etat napoléonien* (Saint-Etienne: Publications de l'Université de Saint-Etienne, 2005)
Dupuy, Pascal, *La Fête de la Fédération* (Rouen: Presses Universitaires de Rouen, 2012)
Fournier, Eric, 'Crosse en l'air: L'insaisissable motif d'une histoire effilochée (France, 1789-1871)', *Romantisme*, 4 (2016), pp.121–131
Lefebvre, Georges, *La Grande Peur de 1789* (Paris: Armand Colin, 1932)
Lentz, Thierry, *La conspiration du général Malet* (Paris: Perrin, 2011)

Ligou, Daniel, 'A propos de la révolution municipale', *Revue d'histoire économique et sociale*, 38 (1960), pp.146–177

Liris, Elisabeth, 'Paris pavoisé: Quand Paris apprend la démocratie dans les districts, avril 1789-juillet 1790', in Claude Gauvard and Jean-Louis Robert (eds), *Etre Parisien* (Paris: Editions de la Sorbonne, 2004), pp.293–305

Martin, Jean-Clément, *L'exécution du roi* (Paris: Perrin, 2021)

Sottocasa, Valérie, *Mémoires affrontées: Protestants et catholiques face à la Révolution dans les montagnes du Languedoc* (Rennes: Presses Universitaires de Rennes, 2004)

Tackett, Timothy, *When the King Took Flight* (Cambridge: Harvard University Press, 2004)

Military History

Bertaud, Jean-Paul, *Valmy: La démocratie en armes* (Paris: Gallimard, 2013)

Biard, Michel, *Le siège de Lyon: Entre mythes et réalités* (Clermont-Ferrand: Lemme Edit, 2013)

Crépin, Annie, 'Le 18 Brumaire, une étape dans la constitution d'une armée nouvelle', *Annales Historiques de la Révolution Française*, 318 (1999), pp.663–676

Crépin, Annie, *Vers l'armée nationale: Les débuts de la conscription en Seine-et-Marne, 1798-1815* (Rennes: Presses Universitaires de Rennes, 2011)

Crépin, Annie, 'L'armée de 1789 à 1798: De la régénération à la réforme, de la révolution à la recréation', *Inflexions*, 25 (2014), pp.159–168

Cyr, Pascal, 'La logistique de la campagne de 1814: La France avait-elle les moyens de poursuivre la résistance?', *Napoleonica La Revue*, 35 (2019), pp.20–41

Hippler, Thomas, *Soldats et citoyens: Naissance du service militaire en France et en Prusse* (Paris: Presses Universitaires de France, 2006)

Pedrazzini, Dominic M., 'La défense des Tuileries le 10 août 1792: Légalité et responsabilités', *Revue Militaire Suisse*, 138 (1993), pp.41–46

History of Policing

Andress, David, 'Social Prejudice and political fears in the policing of Paris, January-June 1791', *French History*, 9 (1995), pp.202–226.

Andress, David, *Massacre at the Champ De Mars: Popular Dissent and Political Culture in the French Revolution* (London: *Royal Historical Society* Studies, 2000)

Boulant, Antoine, *La journée révolutionnaire: Le peuple à l'assaut du pouvoir* 1789-1795 (Paris: Passés Composés, 2021)

Clay, Stephen, 'Le brigandage en Provence du Directoire au Consulat (1795-1802)', in Jean-Pierre Jessenne (ed.), *Du Directoire au Consulat: Brumaire dans l'histoire du lien politique et de l'État-nation* (Lille: Publications de l'Institut de recherches historiques du Septentrion, 2001), pp.67–89

Cubells, Monique, 'Marseille au printemps 1789: Une ville en dissidence', *Annales du Midi*, 173 (1986), pp.67–94

Hayakawa, Rio, 'L'assassinat du boulanger Denis François le 21 octobre 1789', *Annales Historiques de la Révolution Française*, 333 (2003), pp.1–19

Markovic, Momsillo, 'La fusillade au village de La Chapelle en janvier 1791: Un drame aux conséquences politiques', *Annales Historiques de la Révolution Française*, 386 (2016), pp.53–76

Neusy, Aurélie, 'Opinions et réflexions sur la loi martiale dans la presse et les pamphlets (1789-1792)', *Annales Historiques de la Révolution Française*, 360 (2010), pp.27–48

Pertué, Michel, 'Le maintien de l'ordre: Questions et réflexions', in Raymonde Monnier (ed.), *A Paris sous la Révolution: Nouvelles approches de la ville* (Paris: Publications de la Sorbonne, 2008), pp.49–66

Poirot, Thibaut, 'L'enceinte sacrée des lois sous les armes: Les mobilisations armées autour des assemblées parlementaires de la Révolution (1792-1795)', *Annales Historiques de la Révolution Française*, 393 (2018), pp.57–76

Vignolles, Henri, 'La dimension répressive de la Grande Peur: L'ambiguïté des mesures défensives contre les brigands', *Cahiers de l'Institut d'histoire de la Révolution française*, 18 (2020), pp.1–17

General Studies Relating to the Garde Nationale

Bianchi, Serge and Dupuy, Roger (eds), *La Garde nationale entre nation et peuple en armes: Mythes et réalités 1789-1871* (Rennes: Presses Universitaires de Rennes, 2006)

Carrot, Georges, 'Garde nationale et recrutement de l'armée à Grasse (1789-1871)', *Annales du Midi*, 89:131 (1977), pp.45–62

Carrot, Georges, *La Garde nationale (1789-1871): Une force publique ambiguë* (Paris: L'Harmattan, 2001)

Devenne, Florence, 'La Garde nationale: Création et évolution, 1789-août 1792', *Annales Historiques de la Révolution Française*, 283 (1990), pp.49–66

Dupuy, Roger, *La Garde Nationale 1789-1872* (Paris: Gallimard, 2010)

Girard, Louis, *La Garde nationale, 1814-1871* (Paris: Plon, 1964)

Before the Garde Nationale (1770–1789)

Achard, Claude, 'Les fastes de la gloire: Milice bourgeoise et garde nationale de Pézenas (1770-1871)', *Etudes Héraultaises*, 2 (1973), pp.29–46

Chagniot, Jean, 'Le Guet et la Garde de Paris à la fin de l'Ancien Régime', *Revue d'Histoire moderne et contemporaine*, 20 (1973), pp.58–71

Déplanche, Nicolas, 'From Young People to Young Citizens: The Emergence of a Revolutionary Youth in France, 1788-1790', *Journal of Social History*, 45 (2011), pp.225–237

Lamarre, Christine, 'Les jeux militaires au XVIIIe siècle', *Histoire urbaine*, 5 (2002), pp. 85–103

Le Lec, Julien, 'Tuez la noblesse et qu'il n'en reste point! Culture de la violence et culture politique lors des journées des Bricoles à Rennes les 26 et 27 janvier 1789', *Société d'Histoire et d'Archéologie de Bretagne* (2017), pp.237–262

Monseigne, Clément, 'Maintien de l'ordre et maintien des ordres: Les logiques spatiales du régiment des Gardes-Françaises à Paris à la veille de la Révolution', *Carnets de géographes*, 15 (2021)

Early Gardes Nationales (1789–1792)

Alpaugh, Micah, 'Les émotions collectives et le mouvement des fédérations (1789-1790)', *Annales Historiques de la Révolution Française*, 372 (2013), pp.49–80

Alpaugh, Micah, 'A Self-Defining Bourgeoisie in the Early French Revolution: The Milice Bourgeoise, the Bastille Days of 1789, and Their Aftermath', *Journal of Social History*, 47:3 (2014), pp.696–720

Arches, Pierre, 'La garde nationale de Saint-Antonin et les Fédérations du Rouergue et du Bas-Quercy (juillet 1789-juillet 1790)', *Annales du Midi*, 68:36 (1956), pp. 375–390

Arches, Pierre, 'Le premier projet de fédération nationale', *Annales Historiques de la Révolution Française, 144* (1956), pp.255–266

Colrat, Jean-Claude, 'La garde nationale d'Orléans et la fête de la Fédération orléanaise du 9 mai 1790', *Le Briquet*, 2 (1989), pp.13–18

THE GARDE NATIONALE 1789–1815

D'Hollander, Paul, 'Les gardes nationales en Limousin (juillet 1789-juillet 1790)', *Annales Historiques de la Révolution Française*, 1992, pp.465–489

Genty, Maurice, 'Controverses sur la Garde nationale parisienne', *Annales Historiques de la Révolution Française*, 291 (1993), pp.61–88

Genty, Maurice, 'Les débuts de la Garde nationale parisienne (1789-1791)', in Serge Bianchi and Roger Dupuy (eds), *La Garde nationale entre nation et peuple en armes: Mythes et réalités 1789-1871* (Rennes: Presses Universitaires de Rennes, 2006), pp.151–163

Jessenne, Jean-Pierre, 'Nationales, communautaires, bourgeoises ? Les gardes communales dans la France du Nord en 1790' in Michel Biard, Annie Crépin and Bernard Gainot (eds), *La plume et le sabre: Hommages offerts à Jean-Paul Bertaud* (Paris: Publications de la Sorbonne, 2002) pp.205–216

Lesaffre-Ramette, Odile, 'Une fête révolutionnaire provinciale et ses aménagements: La Fédération de Lille, le 6 juin 1790', *Revue du Nord*, 254-255 (1982), pp.789–802

Lévy, Jean-Michel, 'La formation de la première armée de la Révolution française: L'effort militaire et les levées d'hommes dans le département de l'Ain en 1791', *Annales de l'Ecole pratique des hautes études* (1972), pp.829–835

Marouche, Mustapha, 'Prosopographie de l'état-major de la garde nationale amiénoise (août 1789)', *Société des antiquaires de Picardie*, 70 (2015), pp.388–403

Shusterman, Noah, 'La seule loi qui soit toujours sûre d'être obéie: Robespierre, les milices et le débat sur l'armée permanente', *Annales Historiques de la Révolution Française*, 398 (2019), pp.25–46

Taillefer, Michel, 'La fête de la Fédération du 4 juillet 1790 à Toulouse', in Michel Taillefer (ed.), *Etudes sur la sociabilité à Toulouse et dans le Midi toulousain de l'Ancien Régime à la Révolution* (Toulouse: Presses Universitaires du Midi, 2014), pp.468–479

Thore, Pierre-Henri, 'Fédération et projets de Fédération dans la région toulousaine', *Annales Historiques de la Révolution Française*, 1949, pp.346–368

The Garde Nationale under the First Republic (1792–1804)

Bertaud, Jean-Paul, 'Notes sur le premier amalgame', *Revue d'Histoire moderne et contemporaine*, 20 (1972), pp.72–83

Bertaud, Jean-Paul, 'Enquête sur les volontaires de 1792', *Annales Historiques de la Révolution Française*, 272 (1988), pp.151–170

Celeri, Angelo, 'Le poids de la nouvelle armée dans la société française en Révolution: L'exemple du département de l'Eure', *Cahiers d'histoire*, 94-95 (2005), pp.183–196

Cobb, Richard, *Les armées révolutionnaires: Instrument de la Terreur dans les départements, Avril 1793-Floréal an II* (Paris: Mouton & Co, 1963)

Cointet, Jean-Paul, 'Le bataillon des filles Saint-Thomas et le 10 août', *Annales Historiques de la Révolution Française*, 182 (1965), pp.450–467

Crépin, Annie, 'Le Nord et le Pas-de-Calais face à la création de l'armée nationale (1791-an II)', *Revue du Nord*, 299 (1993), pp.41–57

Herlaut, Auguste, 'Carnot et les compagnies de canonniers des Sections de Paris au 9 Thermidor', *Annales Historiques de la Révolution Française*, 121 (1953), pp.9–16

Hippler, Thomas, 'Volunteers of the French Revolutionary Wars: Myths and Reinterpretation' in Christine G. Krüger and Sonja Levsen (eds), *War Volunteering in Modern Times from the French Revolution to the Second World War* (Basingstoke: Palgrave Macmillan, 2010), pp.23–39

Monnier, Raymonde, 'La garde citoyenne, élément de la démocratie parisienne' in Michel Vovelle (ed.), *Paris et la Révolution* (Paris: Publications de la Sorbonne, 1989), pp.147–159

Petitfrère, Claude, *Les Bleus d'Anjou 1789-1792* (Paris: Comité des Travaux Historiques et Scientifiques, 1985)

Régent, Frédéric, 'Armement des hommes de couleur et liberté aux Antilles: le cas de la Guadeloupe pendant l'Ancien Régime et la Révolution', *Annales Historiques de la Révolution Française*, 348 (2007), pp.41-56

Rudé, Georges, 'Les sans-culottes et les journées de vendémiaire an IV', *Annales Historiques de la Révolution Française*, 158 (1959), pp.332–346

Slavin, Morris, 'L'épuration de Prairial an III dans la section des Droits de l'Homme', *Annales Historiques de la Révolution Française*, 232 (1978), pp.283–304

Vidalenc, Jean, 'Les volontaires nationaux dans le département de l'Eure (1791-1793)', *Annales Historiques de la Révolution Française*, 114 (1949), pp.116-133

The Garde Nationale under the First Empire (1804–1815)

Alexander, R.S., *Bonapartism and Revolutionary Tradition in France: The Fédérés of 1815* (Cambridge: Cambridge University Press, 2002)

Brun, Jean-François, 'Au crépuscule de l'Empire: L'exemple du 151e régiment d'infanterie de ligne', *Revue Historique des Armées*, 273 (2014), pp.73–82

Cuvilliers, Vincent, 'Un département placé sous la protection de sa garde nationale active: Le Pas-de-Calais (1806-1815)', *Revue du Nord*, 350 (2003), pp.297–312

Darbou, René, 'La Garde nationale de Paris sous le Premier Empire', *Société des Collectionneurs de Figurines Historiques*, 6 (1958), pp.137–139

Declercq, Jacques, *Quand les Belges se battaient pour Napoléon (1813-1814): Le 5e corps d'infanterie dans la tourmente* (Annecy: Historic'One, 2013)

Denys, Catherine, 'Le mot ne fait rien à la chose: Des gardes bourgeoises aux gardes nationales à Bruxelles et Namur, 1706-1814', in Serge Bianchi and Roger Dupuy (eds), *La Garde nationale entre nation et peuple en armes: Mythes et réalités 1789-1871* (Rennes: Presses Universitaires de Rennes, 2006), pp.249–263

Dröber, Axel, 'La Garde nationale lyonnaise sous la Restauration (1814–1830): Les réinterprétations d'une institution révolutionnaire', *Francia*, 44 (2017), pp.165–187

Dufraisse, Roger, 'Une rébellion en pays annexé: Le *soulèvement* des *gardes nationales* de la *Sarre* en 1809', *Bulletin de la Société d'Histoire Moderne*, 10 (1969), pp.2–6

Dunne, John, 'La Garde Nationale sous Napoléon', in Bruno Béthouard (ed.), *Napoléon, Boulogne et l'Europe* (Boulogne: Cahiers du Littoral, 2001), pp.81–87

Hantraye, Jacques, 'Les prises d'armes de 1814-1815, signe et facteur de la politisation des ruraux', *Annales de Bretagne et des pays de l'Ouest*, 118 (2011), pp.47–61

Hudemann-Simon, Calixte, 'Réfractaires et déserteurs de la Grande Armée en Sarre (1802-1813): Comparaison avec les autres départements rhénans annexés et l'ensemble de l'Empire', *Revue Historique*, 561 (1987), pp.11–45

Martin, Yves, 'La Garde nationale de Paris à la Plaine des Vertus', *Tradition Magazine*, 212 (2005), pp.31–35

Mir, Jean-Pierre, *Les gardes nationaux 1813-1814: Les oubliés de l'épopée, Suivi du dictionnaire des gardes nationaux activés victimes des combats* (Paris: Archives & Culture, 2009)

Tonnesson, Kare Dorenfeldt, 'Les fédérés de Paris pendant les Cent-Jours', *Annales Historiques de la Révolution Française*, 249 (1982), pp.393–415

Waquet, Jean, 'La garde nationale active et sa place dans la politique militaire et financière du 1er Empire et des Cent-Jours (an XIV-1815)', *Revue internationale d'histoire militaire*, 37 (1977), pp.31–54

Biographies

Bertaud, Jean-Paul, *Un jour, un homme, la Révolution* (Paris: Robert Laffont, 1988)

Bois, Jean-Pierre, *La Fayette* (Paris: Perrin, 2015)

Bourdin, Philippe (ed.), *La Fayette: Entre deux mondes* (Clermont-Ferrand: Presses Universitaires Baise-Pascal, 2009)

Casselle, Jérôme, *L'anti-Robespierre: Pétion ou la Révolution pacifique* (Paris: Editions Vendémiaire, 2016)

Chatel de Brancion, Laurence and Villiers, Patrick, *La Fayette: Rêver la gloire* (Saint-Remy-en-L'Eau: Editions Monelle Hayot, 2013)

Gouvion Saint-Cyr, Arnaud de, 'Jean-Baptiste Gouvion: Un fidèle de La Fayette', *Traditions*, 22 (2018), pp.55–56

Herlaut, Auguste, *Le général rouge Ronsin, 1751-1794* (Paris: Librairie Historique Clavreuil, 1956)

Le Bozec, Christine, *Barras* (Paris: Perrin, 2016)

Monnier, Raymonde, *Un bourgeois sans-culotte: Le général Santerre* (Paris: Publications de la Sorbonne, 1989)

Petiteau, Natalie, *Napoléon Bonaparte: La Nation incarnée* (Paris: Armand Colin, 2015)

Waresquiel, Emmanuel de, *Fouché: Les silences de la pieuvre* (Paris: Tallandier, 2014)

Iconography

Bianchi, Serge, 'L'image des sans-culottes: Construction et déconstruction', in Christian Amalvi (ed.), *Images militantes, images de propagande: 132e Congrès national des sociétés historiques et scientifiques* (Paris: Editions du CTHS, 2010), pp. 35–48

Bordes, Philippe, *Représenter la Révolution: Les Dix-Août de Jacques Bertaux et de François Gérard* (Lyon: Fage Editions, 2010)

Carbonnières, Philippe de, 'Les gouaches révolutionnaires de Lesueur au musée Carnavalet', *Annales Historiques de la Révolution Française*, 343 (2006), pp.96–122

Carbonnières, Philippe de, *Lesueur: Gouaches révolutionnaires* (Paris: Paris-Musées, 2005)

Carbonnières, Philippe de, *Prieur. Les Tableaux historiques de la Révolution: Catalogue raisonné des dessins originaux* (Paris: Paris-Musées, 2006)

Carbonnières, Philippe de, *Les gravures historiques de Janinet* (Paris: Paris-Musées, 2011)

Hould, Claudette, *La Révolution par le dessin: Les dessins préparatoires aux gravures des Tableaux historiques de la Révolution française 1789-1802* (Paris: Réunion des Musées Nationaux, 2008)

Macé de Lépinay, François, 'Autour de la Fête de la Fédération: Charles Thevenin et la Révolution 1789-1799', *Revue de l'Art*, 83 (1989), pp.51–60

Pacaud, Fabien, 'La médaille de la Fête de la Fédération', *Le Briquet*, 4 (2019), pp.19–24

Uniforms and Equipment

Bordeaux, Paul, *La Garde nationale et les volontaires de Beauvais et de l'Oise au début de la Révolution: Leurs boutons d'uniformes* (Beauvais: Imprimerie de la Société Académique de l'Oise, 1913)

Buttner, François, Charrié, Pierre and Rigondaud, Albert, 'Gardes Nationales 1789-1871', *Carnets de la Sabretache*, 50 (1979)

Celeri, Angelo, 'Habiller, équiper, armer les soldats de la Révolution: L'exemple de l'Eure', *Annales de Normandie*, 59:1 (2009), pp.109–132

Clifford, Dale L., 'Can the Uniform Make the Citizen? Paris, 1789-1791', *Eighteenth-Century Studies*, 34:3 (2001), pp.363–382
Colrat, Jean-Claude, 'Les souvenirs de la garde nationale d'Orléans en 1789 et 1790', *Bulletin de la Société Archéologique et Historique de l'Orléanais*, 88 (1990), pp.15–33
Faget, Renaud, 'L'arme de la liberté: Usage et enjeux de la pique révolutionnaire', *Annales Historiques de la Révolution Française*, 393 (2018), pp.11–33
Fallou, Louis, *Le bouton uniforme français* (Nantes: Editions du Canonnier, 1998)
Guillemot, Pierre-Baptiste, 'Les officiers de la Garde nationale de Paris', *Traditions*, 21 (2018), pp.83–86
Guillemot, Pierre-Baptiste, 'La Fayette à la tête de la Garde nationale parisienne', *Traditions*, 22 (2018), pp.48–53
Lamarre, Christine, 'Le costume rutilant: Les chevaliers des jeux militaires urbains au XVIIIe siècle en Bourgogne', in Christine Aribaud and Sylvie Mouysset (eds), *Vêture et pouvoir XIIIe-XXe siècles* (Toulouse: Presses Universitaires du Midi, 2003), pp.85–99
Malvaux, Bertrand and Pétard, Michel, *Le hausse-col uniforme français* (Nantes: Editions du Canonnier, 2002)
Martin, Jean-Pierre, *Les armes blanches de la Révolution* (La Tour-du-Pin: Editions du Portail, 1985)
Mongellaz, Jacqueline, Pariset, Jean-Daniel and Sabatier, Gérard (eds), *Aux Armes Citoyens! Les sabres à emblèmes de la Révolution* (Vizille: Musée de la Révolution française, 1987)
Pacaud, Fabien, 'Une pique modèle 1792 de la Garde nationale de Moulins', *Gazette des Armes*, 532 (2020), pp.66–73
Pétard, Michel, 'La pique de 1792', *Tradition Magazine*, 69 (1992), pp.31–36
Pétard, Michel, 'La pique de Regnier pour la campagne de France de 1814', *Tradition Magazine*, 105 (1994), pp.11–14
Rigondaud, Albert, 'Les tribulations du costume militaire: Les vrais soldats de l'an II', *Uniformes, 56 (1980)*, pp.16–26

Garde Nationale Flags
Charrié, Pierre, 'Les drapeaux de la Garde Nationale sous le 1er Empire 1804-1815', *Gardes Nationales 1789-1871, Carnets de la Sabretache*, 50 (1979), pp.146–147
Charrié, Pierre, *Drapeaux et étendards de la Révolution et de l'Empire* (Paris: Léopard d'Or, 2012)
Fortunet, Françoise, 'Le drapeau de la Révolution', *Annales Historiques de la Révolution Française*, 247 (1982), pp.129–133
Lachouque, Henri, *Les drapeaux de la Garde nationale de Paris en 1789* (Paris: Editions militaires, 1947)
Liris, Elisabeth, 'De la Liberté à l'Union dans l'iconographie des drapeaux des districts parisiens', *Annales Historiques de la Révolution Française*, 289 (1992), pp.341–353
Regnault, Jean, *Les aigles impériales et le drapeau tricolore 1804-1815* (Paris: J. Peyronnet, 1967)
Reinhard, Marcel, 'Les drapeaux de la Garde nationale parisienne en 1789', in Roland Mousnier (ed.), *Études européennes: Mélanges offerts à Victor-Louis Tapié* (Paris: Publications de la Sorbonne, 1973), pp.525–532